The Great
COUNTRY HOUSES OF
CENTRAL EUROPE

The Great
COUNTRY HOUSES OF CENTRAL EUROPE

Czech Republic, Slovakia, Hungary, Poland

SECOND EDITION

Michael Pratt
Photography by Gerhard Trumler

Abbeville Press · Publishers
New York · London

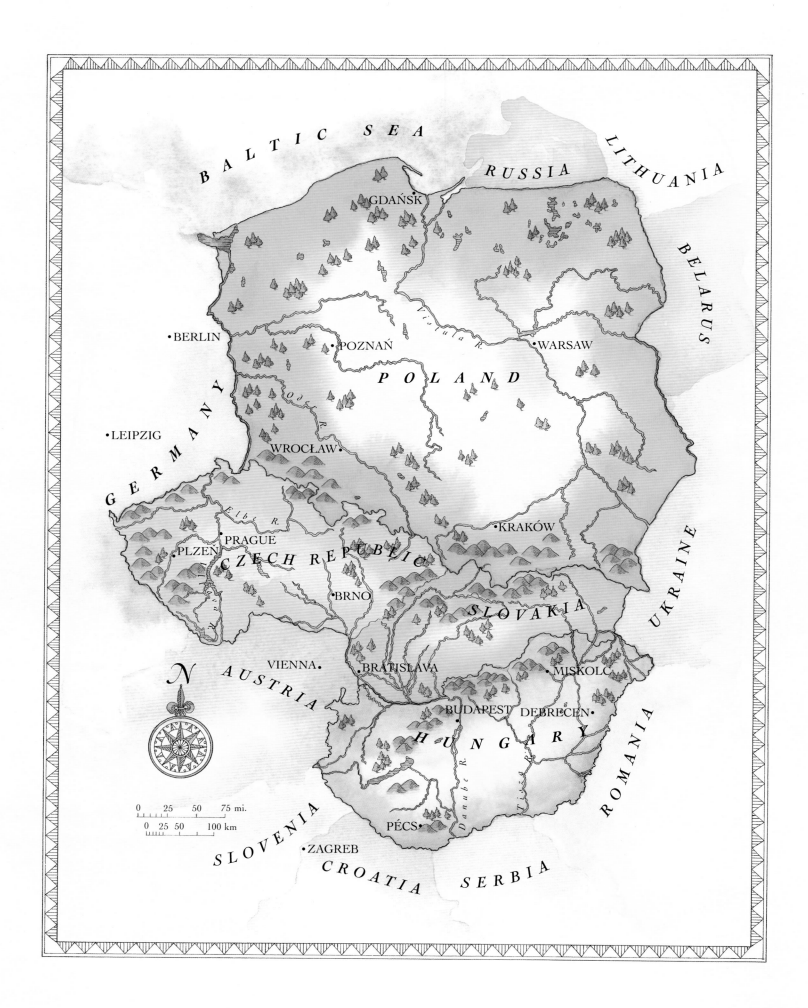

C O N T E N T S

PREFACE
7
ACKNOWLEDGMENTS
10

PREFACE

*F*ourteen years have elapsed since the publication of *The Great Country Houses of Central Europe.* During that time, enormous changes have occurred. Following the downfall of Communism, the Czech Republic, Slovakia, Hungary, and Poland have now joined both NATO and the EU. Although the capitalist and democratic identities of their societies are not yet fully established and the formerly Communist politicians are still sometimes returned to power by the ballot box, the countries are nevertheless making huge strides in the right direction.

The Czech Republic, amicably divorced from its Slovak neighbors in 1992, is enjoying a tourist boom. Prague has become one of Europe's favorite holiday destinations year-round, especially for the young. The country houses may lack the same allure as the capital, but they have benefited from this tourism all the same. Many of them receive large numbers of visitors, both from abroad and increasingly from the native populations. The Czechs have undertaken a widespread campaign of restoration and even returned objects originally belonging to the houses that had long since disappeared into local museums. The atmospheres of the houses now returned to private ownership have begun to resemble the country houses in Western Europe. Attention is also being paid to the recreation of parks and gardens, often for the first time since the Second World War.

Slovakia, admittedly, has retained much of the flavor of the old days. An unreconstructed politician from the Iron Curtain era, Vladimir Meciar, effectively ran the country throughout the 1990s. There were, however, fewer country houses in Slovakia in comparison with Bohemia and Moravia, and most of these had belonged to their hated former masters, the Hungarian nobility. Thus, any attempts to restore private ownership have been slow and faltering, and little has happened to date.

In the Czech Republic itself, always more economically and culturally advanced, the process of restitution has been fairly uneven. It was soon established that families in possession of a valid Czech passport as of February 1948 would be eligible to have their rightful property returned to them. Many noble dynasties of undeniably Czech antecedents, such as the Šternbergs, Lobkowiczes, Kinskýs and Czernins, have indeed won back the bulk of their castles and estates. And others of less obviously Slavic origins, the Colloredo-Mansfelds, for example, have fared equally well.

Many more, however, especially previous estate owners of German extraction have been offered nothing, though they had been settled in the country for centuries. This was justified on the grounds that they had collaborated with the Third Reich by declaring themselves German when the occupying regime demanded it in 1942. In truth, few of them had any realistic alternative at the time. Meanwhile, the two greatest landowning dynasties of all, the senior line of the Princes Schwarzenberg in Bohemia and the Princes Liechtenstein in Moravia, have, to date, both failed to reach agreement with the Czech governments as to how much, if any, of their erstwhile estates should be restored to them. And to the mass of lesser figures who have been offered back their properties, where the houses have been severely damaged or abandoned, the contents have vanished, the farmland has been polluted, or the forestry untended for years, it has sometimes seemed like such a poisoned chalice that they have refused the gift.

Hungary, post-war, by far the smallest of these countries under consideration, presents a somewhat different picture. Surprisingly, since Hungary's inhabitants were the most publicly outspoken anti-Communists during the 1980s, disappointingly little has been done to restore the houses to their rightful owners. The outgoing regime endeavored to ensure as little change as possible occurred by instituting a system of vouchers which, when given to the former proprietors, was supposed to enable them to bid at public auction for their property. Hardly surprisingly, since the vouchers issued were of extremely limited value, the former proprietors frequently found themselves bidding against those on the inside track, members of the old *nomenklatura*, and were thus unsuccessful. Many of those country houses (where war damage had been much worse than in the Czech lands) had once fulfilled the roles of hospitals, schools, mental institutions, or hotels, and still do so today. Even when the original family has managed to return to live in their old homes, like the Károlyis at Fót, they have not been given clear title to the property and must share the residence with the earlier inhabitants, in this case, with a school, since no money is available to rehouse the school in new buildings.

In fact, all the political parties since the so-called Velvet Revolution have done nothing but pay lip service to the principle of restitution of property. Even at Gödöllő, when the Russian army was persuaded to reluctantly move out, the state has merely resumed control and reopened the house as a museum. The voucher system was simply too ungenerous to its supposed beneficiaries—the absolute maximum sum allowed amounted to the equivalent of $50,000. (The Esterházys' administrator in Austria famously remarked that the compensation offered to his employer, once Hungary's biggest landowner, would just buy a middle-range Mercedes sedan). Certainly a few of those who emigrated in 1945 or 1956 have returned to their native land, frequently to settle on some new property, or in Budapest. Only in exceptional cases has the government been prepared to give back the odd country house and then only when any other means of restoring it had already been explored. Of course all those estates now lying in Slovakia, Transylvania, or Croatia, i.e. within pre- but not post-war national boundaries, remain, in practice, nearly as inaccessible as ever.

Poland has paradoxically proved the slowest and most disappointing of all these four countries in effecting a genuine process of restitution. Only in Poland had the aristocracy ever remained in any number. Almost all those aristocrats hardy enough to have stayed on under a Communist government initially eventually left Hungary and the Czech Republic: in Hungary en masse after the crushing of the 1956 uprising, and in the Czech lands after the Prague Spring of 1969 had been suppressed. In Poland many aristocrats had kept a low profile and yet managed to survive as respected members of their local communities, sometimes even retaining some ties to their former properties. It appeared that a more cohesive society had been somehow kept alive, despite all their rulers' attempts to clone everyone as Marxist man.

Sadly, legitimate restitution has not taken place, and empirical rather than ethical considerations have taken on the greatest importance. To return to the pre-1939 landholdings has simply proved too controversial for any government to wish to tackle. In contrast to the other eastern European countries, in Poland state co-operatives had been the norm, and the agricultural land had been divided between umpteen tiny peasant proprietors, each fiercely attached to his own small holding. The Warsaw government has often seemed ready to give back houses in urgent need of repair, provided they are of no public interest and scant historical importance.

Any Polish houses that rank as an integral part of their country's heritage have stayed firmly in the hands of the state. It is deemed right to allow the public interest to override private ones; thus major properties such as Nieborow or Wilanów have not been returned, in defiance of legitimate family claims. The state has pursued a cynical policy of encouraging emigrés to return with their money from America or Western Europe, provided there is no conflict with the state's interest. Naturally no former German estates in Silesia, Pomerania or Polish East Prussia have been offered back, while properties such as the Radziwiłłs at Nieśwież and Ołyka, no longer within the nation's modern frontiers, remain almost as remote as ever.

In all these four countries, therefore, the fate of the country house may best be viewed in shades of gray. If one begins from the premise that it is invariably better for a house to be a living home rather than a dead museum, much, alas, remains to be achieved. Even those proprietors lucky and energetic enough to have regained their former family properties face formidable difficulties. Save perhaps in the Czech Republic, the contents have all too often been dispersed long ago. A period of wanton destruction or indiscriminate looting was followed by an era of mindless and soulless bureaucracy, where, for instance, all eighteenth-century furniture was crowded together in one place, irrespective of its provenance. And when choice pieces have ended up in local or national museums, the curators have usually mounted rigorous resistance before any offers of restitution.

Those who have chosen to give up a comfortable life in the West to return to live in their ancestral homelands face another hazard. In all four countries, the governmental infrastructure has been destroyed by forty years of Communism and is being only slowly and painfully rebuilt. Thus many things regarded in the West as necessities of life are still not available to the returned emigré. Though craftsmanship is often better and cheaper in Eastern Europe, many building materials taken for granted here cannot be found. And if the struggle to lead a carefree and comfortable life is not inconsiderable, it must be combined with a lack of congenial neighbors. It takes a brave former owner to decide to return, especially if the property lies at some distance from the boundaries of Western Europe.

Despite the disgraceful example set by the Kohl government in Germany, which on reunification refused to return properties or provide any compensation to the expropriated estate owners of the defunct DDR, the Poles, Czechs, and Hungarians have made, and continue to make, variable efforts to respect property rights and the rule of law. Any enthusiast for the country houses of Poland, Hungary and the Czech Republic may cautiously take heart at their present situation when compared to that of fourteen years ago, when this book was first published and the Berlin Wall had recently fallen, and when every house described belonged to the state.

On one visit two years ago near Prague, the author and his family stayed with an old friend, scion of one of Bohemia's most illustrious dynasties, who, without a castle of his own to fight for, had elected to buy some derelict farm buildings grouped round a courtyard in open fields and turn the site into an enchanting house and garden—comfortable, elegant, and with enough land for recreation and shooting. He is by far the most important person in the village, being both popular and the biggest source of local employment. So despite the terrible destruction wrought upon the country house heritage of Central Europe during the past sixty-five years, green shoots of a more hopeful future are peeping through.

M.P.

June 2005

In preparing this new Preface, particular thanks are due to: Baroness Elmar von Haxthausen, Count Adam Zamoyski, Prince Friedrich zu Schwarzenberg, Prince George Festetics, Christopher Hudson and Jane Manley

ACKNOWLEDGEMENTS

Such a large number of people have helped with this book in one way or another that I fear shall inadvertently omit some of them from these acknowledgments. To them I offer my apologies, and to everyone listed hereunder my heartfelt thanks, especially to those who have kindly allowed us to reproduce pictures, old photographs, or family memorabilia in their possession.

For their assistance with my work in the Czech Republic and Slovakia, I would like to thank Count Géza Andrássy, Countess Éva Berchtold, László Berényi, Count Georg Clam-Martinic, Prince Honome Colloredo-Mansfeld, Count Karl Desfours, Baroness Marie-Sophie Doblhoff, Count and Countess Josef Kinsky, Dr. Zdeněk Kudelka, the late Count Friedrich Ledebur, Count František Lobkowicz, the late Countess Sophie Nostitz-Rieneck, Paul Prokop, Professor Hugo Rokyta, Prince Franz zu Schwarzenberg, the late Princess Antoinette zu Schwarzenberg, Princess Eleanore zu Schwarzenberg, Ronald Scrivener, Count Zdenko Sternberg, Countess Myna Strachwitz, Countess Eleanore Thun-Hohenstein, and Christopher Wentworth-Stanley.

For their contributions to the Hungarian section, my appreciation goes to Prince Rasso of Bavaria, Dr. Géza Entz, Princess Melinda Esterházy, Prince Alexander Esterházy, Prince György Festetics, Rudi Fischer, Teri Fitzherbert, the late Prince Tassilo von Fürstenberg, Zsuzsanna Gonda, Andrew Hadik, Count John Hadik, Countess Fruzsina Jankovich, Countess Borbála Károlyi, Count László Károlyi, Nicholas Meinertzhagen, Professor Miklós Moyzer, Dr. Endre Nagy, Prince Paul Odescalchi, Marquis Karl Pallavicini, Count Mark Pejacsevich, Professor Georges Rózsa, the late Countess Szapáry, Prince Vincenz Windischgrätz, Princess Natalie Windischgrätz, and Professor Anna Zádor.

For the support I received with my research in Poland, I would like to acknowledge Arthur Baggs, Count Bniński, Anna Branicka Wolska, Count Andrew Ciechanowiecki, Prince Adam Czartoryski, Prince and Princess Paul Czartoryski, Prince Stanisław Czartoryski, Amelie / Dunin, Dr. Wojciech Fijałkowski, Professor Aleksander Gieysztor, Count and Countess Stanisław Krasiński, Dr. Henryk Kondziela, Prince Stanisław Lubomirski, Professor Stanisław Mossakowski, the late Countess Zofia Potocka, Count Andrzej Potocki, Count Edward Raczyński, Princess Izabela Radziwiłł, Princess Mary Radziwiłł, Prince Krzysztof Radziwiłł, Count and Countess Stanisław Rey, Michael Ronikier, Professor Marek Rostworowski, Dr. Andrzej Rottermund, Princess Mary Sapieha, the late Prince Paul Sapieha, Lala Wilbraham, Count Adam Zamoyski, Count Jan Zamoyski, Countess Priscilla Zamoyska, and Krista Żółkowska.

In addition I received much help and advice from the late Franz Josef and Gina Liechtenstein, reigning prince and princess of Liechtenstein; I am also grateful to Hans Adam, the present reigning prince, and to Dr. Reinhold Baumstark, director of the Princely Collections at Vaduz. For encouragement and hospitality, I am indebted to Amia and Billy von Bredow, Elmer and Annina von Haxthausen, Jean Georges and Helga Hoyos, Martin and Ita Hoyos, Norbert Kinsky, Hubi von Perfall, Rüdiger and Sissi von Pezold, Nico and Stefanie Schmidt-Chiari, Kariy and Tese zu Schwarzenberg, and to Cyrille Toumanoff. Last, but hardly least, my heartfelt thanks to Rachel Montagu-Douglas-Scott, whose house has so often provided a refuge for my literary labors.

For all the translation from Czech, Hungarian, or Polish, I must thank Count Josef Czernin, Elżbieta Łubieńska, John Pomian, John Renyi, Katharine Tylko-Hill, and Katya Willig-Frodl.

Over the past four years the staffs of the London Library, the School of Slavonic and Eastern European Studies, the Sikorski Library, all in London, and the Société Historique Polonaise in Paris have provided invaluable assistance. As always, I am indebted to my old history tutors at Balliol College, Oxford, Richard Cobb and Maurice Keen, as well as to Dr. Tim Blanning and Professor Norman Stone. In Vienna, Dr. Brigitta Zessner-Spitzenberg of the Austrian National Library and Christian Beaufort-Spontin of the Kunsthistorisches Museum were most helpful, as was Christian Brandstätter.

Arrangements for my trips to Central Europe were made with assistance from the London staffs of the national tourist organizations—IBUSZ, ORBIS, and ČEDOK—plus my travel agent, Bill Williams of Sotheby's, and organized with the help of the Czech, Hungarian, and Polish embassies in London. Almost all of the directors of the houses we visited and photographed were most cooperative, as were many officials of the culture ministry in each country. Of our numerous guides and interpreters, I should particularly like to mention Robert Morawski in Poland, Romana Továrková in the Czech Republic, and István Varga in Hungary.

Above all, I must thank my publisher, Mark Magowan, my editor, Constance Herndon, and the staff at Abbeville Press, including Molly Shields, Philip Reynolds, and Hope Koturo, for commissioning and then seeing through to completion what has been by any standards a complicated project. Without the skill and patience of Professor Gerhard Trumler, the book's photographer and my companion on these trips, we should never have amassed so many pictures from such a diversity of sources. And without Jane Manley, who has faithfully typed every word I've written, the text would never have been deciphered anyway.

The steps of the Temple of Diana leading down to the lake at Arkadia, Poland.

11

CZECH REPUBLIC & SLOVAKIA

Introduction

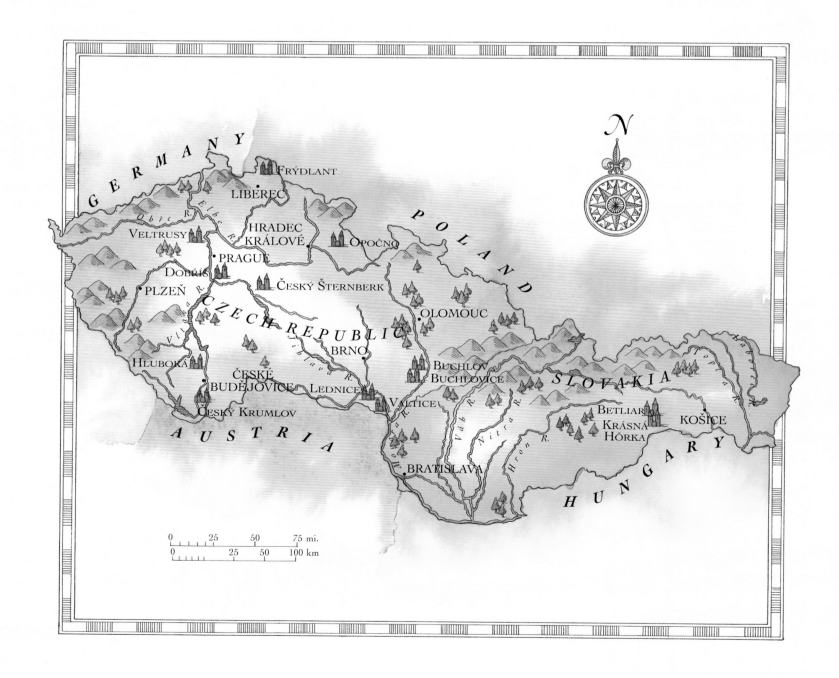

"Though the latitude's rather uncertain
And the longitude also is vague,
The person I pity who knows not the city,
The beautiful city of Prague."

S o wrote the British poet William Jeffrey Prowse in the mid-nineteenth century. His little poem was hardly a serious commentary, of
course, but its underlying sentiment is one shared almost univer-
sally, for Prague in the opinion of many people is a city whose
architecture makes it one of the most beautiful and unspoiled in Europe.
Nor are good buildings confined only to the Czech capital; throughout the
Czech Republic and Slovakia, although admittedly in much greater quanti-
ties in the regions of Bohemia and Moravia than in Slovakia, stand innumerable fine castles, town and country houses, civic buildings, and
churches. Including ruins, over 2,500 monuments have survived in the
Czech Republic and Slovakia, of which more than 150 are open to visitors
today. Comparatively few of the two countries' great houses reflect a stylistic purity, for their history and geographical position have ensured that
they have assimilated cultural trends from all directions. Yet while artistic
development has largely depended on imported styles, sometimes, as with
the late Gothic, Renaissance, and baroque, a cultural style did indeed
emerge. As we can see, the cultural and architectural lives of the Czech
Republic and Slovakia are as complicated as the political history with
which they are inextricably entwined.

Little is known about the earliest histories of those areas that now comprise the modern states. Not until the later sixth century A.D. does evidence reveal the arrival of various Slavonic tribes in the region: during this
time Slovakia was settled by Bulgarian Slavs, and Bohemia and Moravia by
the Czechs, a tribe named after their legendary founder Jech. All were
under the domination of the Avar tribe until Samo, a Frankish adventurer
and the first recorded historical personality, led the natives in several victorious campaigns against their oppressors and loosely united them. After
his death around 660, darkness descended again for 150 years, until the
semi-mythical Princess Libuse, who ruled over much of Bohemia, chose as
her consort Premysl of Stadice, a simple plowman who became a successful co-ruler. Together they founded the only native Czech dynasty.

Meanwhile a powerful early feudal state had arisen in southern Moravia,
the so-called Great Moravian Empire ruled by Mojmír I. As always with
the Czechs, Mojmír began to expand eastward rather than westward, by
this time annexing neighboring Slovakia. On his death in 846 he was succeeded by his Frankish protégé Rastislav. By then Bohemia was paying
tribute to the German emperor, but since Rastislav wished for Moravia to
remain independent he decided to embrace Christianity, asking the
Byzantine emperor for missionaries rather than waiting to be conquered
and forcibly Christianized. Two brothers named Cyril and Methodius
were duly sent from Salonika and within a short time they had converted
Moravia and Silesia. Cyril died, but Methodius was consecrated archbishop of Greater Moravia by the pope. A struggle between priests of the
rival Latin and Slavonic churches ensued, echoing the intrigues between
the local princes.

Soon after 900 A.D. the Great Moravian Empire collapsed under
Magyar attacks and Slovakia was detached from the Czech lands; it would
remain separated until 1918. During this time the political center of grav-
ity moved toward Bohemia. With much of its natural border protected by
forests and mountain ranges, this was a region more favorably sited geographically than Moravia, which was really an open plain whose boundaries were formed for the most part by rivers. In Moravia the largest town
during this period was MikulKice, which consisted of several communities
of earth-floored wooden houses divided into groups for each craft, with

---

*Map of the modern Czech Republic and Slovakia
showing locations of major country houses*

View of Konopiště, central Bohemia.

cemeteries in between. The foundations of a rotunda that must have been the chapel of a magnate and his family have been uncovered; like other churches of the era, it was built under the influence of Byzantine ecclesiastical architecture. Yet the cultural focus increasingly shifted westward toward Saxony and Bavaria. Ecclesiastical structures erected during this time, particularly in the reign of Boleslav II, show the strong influence of Saxon and Bavarian architecture. Of the early descendants of the Přemysls who ruled Bohemia, Václav (Good King Wenceslas) was the most famous. Although he was a genuinely saintly man, his successors showed themselves more capable rulers, even acquiring Silesia and Kraków, albeit temporarily. Bohemia's unregulated succession rights inspired chaos, however, and greatly weakened the country. By the mid-eleventh century Bohemia had become a permanent tributary to the Holy Roman Empire. A hundred years later Emperor Frederick I Barbarossa granted the crown in perpetuity to the Přemyslid dynasty, but the succession problem was finally solved only by the great Přemysl Otakar I. Thanks to skillful politicking, he obtained recognition of the Bohemian kingdom from both pope and emperor, and established the hereditary principle by having his eldest son elected during his lifetime. Furthermore Moravia, which had been divided into several duchies for the dynasty's younger sons, was now raised to the status of an imperial margravate and lastingly united to Bohemia.

Through conquest and dynastic marriage the Bohemian kingdom under his grandson Přemysl Otakar II attained its greatest limits, stretching north from Silesia down to the Adriatic. However Otakar's restless spirit prevented him from stabilizing his dominions, and the jealous German princes thwarted his attempts to be elected emperor, choosing in his stead Rudolf of Habsburg, whom he refused to recognize. Internal unrest accompanied this overexpansion and the king's efforts to play off the native nobility against the mainly German settlers in the royal towns backfired. Unable to field an army, Otakar was forced to watch the conquest of his foreign provinces and to accept Rudolf's moves to make Bohemia and Moravia imperial fiefs. Obsessed with vengeance, he gathered troops and met his enemies on the plain of the Marchfeld in 1278. The Czechs were defeated and the king was killed, effectively ending the Přemyslid dynasty.

The story of the Přemysls had been that of the Czech nation. They left behind a highly organized country with a body of efficient royal officers who had not yet become a hereditary feudal nobility. Having been freed as slaves, peasant farmers now thrived and formed the backbone of the economic system. A special land court with jurisdiction over noble and ecclesiastical estates had been established, although the Church enjoyed substantial independence. In the preceding century towns had been founded in both Bohemia and Moravia, and their settlers issued with royal charters. This in turn had led to the formation of the Diet, in which the three estates—nobles, ecclesiastics, and burghers—were represented, and whose voice was strong enough to be heard by the crown.

As peace, prosperity, and increased links with the rest of Europe had widened the cultural horizons of princes and landowners, the twelfth century had also seen the development of Romanesque art. The network of Premonstratesian and Benedictine monasteries grew thicker and their churches more splendid, although they were subsequently largely obscured by rebuilding. The high point of the style was reached in the early thirteenth century with the construction of several splendid ecclesiastical buildings, especially in the northeast of Bohemia. In Moravia Romanesque architecture developed more slowly, church building beginning again in earnest only during the twelfth century. Of secular architecture from the period there exists only the remains of the bishop's palace at Olomouc, a two-story building with a spacious hall. The twin windows' and arcades' skillfully-designed column capitals show the influence of Rhenish architecture. After 1135 the Hradčany Hill in Prague boasted a stone royal palace plus a bishop's residence, with church, basilica, and convent built in German style; the bishop's country seat at Roudnice, on the other hand, was French-derived. Unfortunately only vestigial remains of other contemporary castles survive, some incorporated in later structures like Buchlov, Nitra, or Spiš.

The Gothic was introduced in Bohemia soon after 1200 by the Cistercians, who had already been building in the same style in Swabia, Franconia, and the Danube basin. For instance, the chapel in the fortress at Cheb, on Bohemia's western border, is in its entirety an early Gothic work. The style did not reach Moravia until around 1230, but in both lands it coincided with important social changes—the growing independence of the higher nobility and of the church, and the foundation of German colonized towns. Traces of northern French high Gothic are also evident somewhat later, particularly in the royal masons' work in the fortress and church of Písek. The French hall church, already familiar in central Germany, now arrived in Bohemia as well. The royal castle of Zvíkov, begun in the 1230s and completed by 1270, was built as a grandiose example of fortress architecture on a spur between two rivers. The pentagonal courtyard has an imposing two-storied vaulted arcade modeled on monastic cloisters, while the chapel has rich ornamentation of the highest quality.

After the Přemyslid dynasty died out in 1306 an interregnum ensued.

View from the lower courtyard at the castle of Pernštejn, central Moravia.

The first choice for the throne, Rudolf of Habsburg's son, died, and war broke out between the German burghers and the Czech nobles. Eventually the latter offered the throne to Heinrich of Luxembourg, recently elected Holy Roman Emperor. His son Jan, married to the Přemyslid princess Alžběta, soon gained control of the kingdom. It proved harder to control the Czech nobility, however, and in 1318 King Jan effectively handed over power to them. "The Knight Errant," as he was called, could not refrain from interfering in foreign wars, first in Italy and then in France, where, having gone to his brother-in-law's aid against the English, the now-blind king was slain at Crécy in 1346. Yet his foreign policy was surprisingly successful: during his reign the kingdom gained Cheb with its surrounding territory, upper Lusatia, and, again, almost all of Silesia from Poland.

Jan's son, who took the title of Charles IV, assumed the throne under far from propitious circumstances but was to prove himself a great ruler. His prestige, like his administrative experience, became immense, especially after he was crowned Holy Roman Emperor. The administration was overhauled, the succession was regulated, and the Czech kingdom's position within the Empire was solidified, the Czechs being given the right to elect a new dynasty should the existing one become extinct. The countryside was cleaned of robber barons, and land tribunals were established to adjudicate impartially between the social classes. The complete absence of wars and the growth of the imperial capital of Prague into a major city advanced national prosperity enormously. Yet perhaps Charles's greatest achievement lay in the foundation of the Charles University or the Carolinum in 1348, a truly universal institution shared equally between Czechs, Poles, Saxons, and Bavarian Germans. Nevertheless this arrangement later created trouble when Czech professors, taking up a nationalist platform, tried to achieve absolute control. Similarly, Charles's well-meant attempts to reform clerical abuses encouraged evangelical preaching, which in turn stirred up nationalist agitation.

The fourteenth century also marked the high point of the Age of Chivalry in Europe and the full flowering of Gothic architecture, as well as the establishment of a new type of fortified residence—the medieval castle. In the south the style was predominantly the Gothic Cistercian, which had filtered in from the Danube basin, and in the north French high Gothic imported from Silesia and Saxony was paramount, while the two styles blended in Slovakia. Cistercian architecture, like the order itself, was simple and ascetic, a gentle transition from the earlier Romanesque style to the Gothic. In contrast, the high Gothic of northern France sometimes verged on the theatrical, its fresh, urgent verticality marked by boldness of conception allied with great delicacy of detail. Characterized by large square habitable towers such as that at Trenčín, the Czech medieval castle was strongly vertical and employed symmetrically enclosed courtyards, as Konopiště, Zvolen, or the reconstructed old Bratislava fortress illustrate. Many powerful noble families used similar ground plans and architectural details for their new castles, among them the Divosivicis' Český Šternberk in central Bohemia, the Rožmberks' Český Krumlov in the south, the Markvarts' Waldstein and Michalovice in the north, as well as Frýdlant, Náchod, and Moravský Šternberk.

Gradually the rich articulation and the vertical composition began to give way to horizontality and a greater unity of the whole, while defence considerations began to lose priority to comfortable living conditions. Together with the region's great nobles, both church and state became major patrons. Bishop Jan IV Dražice of Prague invited in French architects to work on his projects, and in 1333 William of Avignon began to build a stone bridge, fortress, and Augustinian monastery at Roudnice. Charles IV himself summoned Mathias of Arras, who had worked on the papal court of Avignon, to construct Saint Vitus' Cathedral on Prague's

Hradčany Hill in 1344; Mathias was to continue the work until his death eight years later and was probably also responsible for the plans for Karl-štejn castle on the king's commission.

Charles was determined to make Prague into the Rome of Northern Europe and to that end he employed Petr Parléř, perhaps the most important architect of his age. Born around 1330 in Cologne, Parléř had studied French and English building techniques, but his own polymath talents enabled him to vault and shape individual spaces within a conventional plan in a fashion that knew no precedent. Upon arriving in Prague he took over the building works for the cathedral and the castle on the Hradčany Hill and worked on the completion of Karlštejn castle until 1367. The latter, a remarkable edifice indeed, was designed both as a place of rest from the king's labors and as a safe haven for the crown jewels. The tower palace also housed the Chapel of the Holy Rood (Svatý Kříž), which was decorated with semiprecious stones and a cycle of 128 thematically-linked portraits of saints, forceful if mannered in execution. With his nephew Heinrich working in Moravia and numerous master masons following his lead throughout the land, Parléř's fascination with forming interior space through the interplay of walls and vaults became endemic. Inspired by his genius, Czech Gothic reached its apogee, an achievement that raised the country to the highest cultural level in Europe.

This golden age was not destined to last. Charles's death in 1378 removed the strong hand from the nation's helm, and under the weak and irresolute Václav IV, instability was bound to ensue. For ten years a deceptive calm prevailed, but when anti-Jewish pogroms threatened public order, the king's refusal to take action or advice from the nobles led them to imprison him with the encouragement of his own brother, Sigismund (King of Hungary, Margrave of Brandenburg, and later Holy Roman Emperor). Václav managed to alienate the Church and the University as well by permitting wholesale simony and allowing the pope to flood the country with bulls and indulgences. The disreputable state of the Catholic Church, boasting three competing popes at the time, was reflected in its Czech branch, which branded reformers who based their teachings on Wycliffe as heretical. Yet the king responded rather curiously, encouraging the radicals against the archbishop and amending the University's charter to give the increasingly nationalist Czechs a majority vote. Thus emboldened, the reformers led by Professor Jan Hus began to preach more strongly against ecclesiastical abuses. Hus was summoned to appear before the Council of Constance in 1414, and despite a safe conduct issued by Emperor Sigismund he was interned, tried for heresy, and burned at the stake. The incensed Czechs united against this national insult and introduced communion in both kinds despite the directions of the council. When the vacillating king ordered the readmission of loyalist priests to their parishes in 1419, the Hussite incumbents took to celebrating mass in the open air. Václav's death that August was the prelude to anarchy and civil war.

Of course the root cause of the disturbances that followed went deeper than theological differences—the collapse of royal power brought simmering ethnic and social antagonisms to the boil as well. But Hussitism was still an extraordinary phenomenon, one that united an entire nation against external pressures. After Václav's death Sigismund, realizing that his succession to the Bohemian throne was opposed, allowed the pope to proclaim a crusade and to pay for a large army with which he appeared in Prague in 1420 and had himself crowned. The Bohemians rose and, under a soldier of genius named Jan Žižka, expelled the royal troops. When the diet refused to recognize Sigismund, the country came effectively under the control of the military fraternities, in particular the ferocious Orebites and Táborites; monasteries or towns that opposed them were destroyed. Widespread jacqueries followed and whole congregations had ecstatic

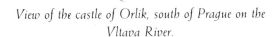

View of the castle of Orlik, south of Prague on the Vltava River.

visions. Only after Žižka's death and the repulse of a papal crusade in 1431 were the Czechs ready to negotiate. A delegation headed by Jan z Rokycan, Archbishop of Prague, attended the Council of Basel in 1433. After a year's deliberations communion in both kinds was conceded, but only to Hussite congregations; otherwise there was a return to the status quo. The fraternities of the radical reformers were opposed to the settlement, but they were crushed at the Battle of Lipany. Having recognized the Compact, as the agreement was known, Sigismund returned in 1436, but died a year later.

Although the infant Ladislaus of Habsburg was finally recognized as his successor, the victorious Utraquists (as the more moderate reformers were called), headed by Jiri z Poděbrad, really ruled the kingdom. Despite the pope's refusal to recognize the Compact, Poděbrad was in full control as regent by 1452, the child-king swearing to respect "Czech privileges." When the young ruler died of the plague five years later, Poděbrad was elected to the vacant throne and recognized by the emperor. The pope remained implacable, however, inciting the Catholic nobility and the king's own son-in-law, Mátyás Corvinus of Hungary, to take up arms. Although he easily defeated them, the brilliant Poděbrad died in 1471 having failed to reunite Catholics and Utraquists. The crown was then offered to Poland's Władisław Jagiełło, but for the next seven years he fought for his rights against Mátyás Corvinus. When the Hungarian ruler died in 1490, Władisław gained Moravia, which Corvinus had occupied, as well as the Hungarian throne. After the long years of isolation dating back to the Hussite wars, the Czechs were again admitted to the community of nations. After claiming the crown, however, Władisław took up residence at Buda and left the nobles to govern the country as they saw fit. His young successor Ludvík only visited his realm once before his death in battle against the Turks at Mohács in 1526. The religious schism worsened, although Catholics and Utraquists found a degree of coexistence in

*View of Jindřichův Hradec,
southern Bohemia.*

uniting against a proscribed group of extreme Protestants called the Unity of the Czech Brethren (Unitas Fratrum). With the advent of the Reformation, the Utraquists split into innumerable factions while the German settlers converted to Lutheranism en masse. Ruled by absentee monarchs the kingdom had grown more and more fragmented, in contrast to the strong nation-states that were developing elsewhere. While the Hussite era came to be seen as a golden age in which the Czechs successfully defended their land against foreign invasion, in reality the cultural and political isolation in which they lived for the next fifty years took decades from which to recover. The university, for instance, four thousand strong in Charles's reign, was reduced to a fraction of its former size a hundred years later.

During this turbulent century-and-a-half, architectural development did not cease. The Hussite wars did end the urban building boom, which had produced fine burghers' houses and magnificent civic buildings—except in areas removed from the fighting such as the Rožmberks' domain in southern Bohemia. The intermittent construction of several great churches continued at Kutná Hora, a Bohemian town grown rich on its silver mines, showing how the prevailing fashion had changed back from the concept of plain and unified space to one that again attached value to the richness of architectural detail, above all to net and star vaulting. In Moravia the high Gothic continued to develop largely undisturbed by the wars. Anton Pilgram's doorway to the Brno town hall is an outstanding example. Another is the transformation of the early Gothic Pernštejn castle. Originally an unassuming mid-thirteenth-century creation built around a keep nicknamed Báborka, Pernštejn became the most spectacular of all Moravian castles. This extraordinary structure was built by Jan z Pernštejna and later his sons Václav I and Vilém II, marshals of the Bohemian court and after the king the foremost men in the land. Following a fire in 1457, they extended the original construction into a grandiose residence—a complicated juxtaposition of buildings with five habitable towers on top of a large rock. The inner keep is surrounded by a courtyard, itself walled in by ramparts falling steeply towards the valley. With its dormers, turrets, balconies, open galleries, and a wooden bridge leading to the detached western tower, the castle makes a worthy stage set for Tannhäuser.

Pernštejn was much influenced by the style of Benedikt Ried, the most innovative architect in the nation, and the most important, during the transitional years between the Gothic and the Renaissance period. Ried, or Rejt, a master builder of uncertain origins, arrived in Prague around 1480 and found employment by the Jagellons on a grand scale. His Vladislav Hall in the Hradčany Palace, if perhaps not wholly satisfying, was one of the most monumental rooms of its age in Europe, and his later Horseman's Staircase nearby is equally impressive. But Ried's activity extended beyond the capital; he also advised on the construction of the large concentric castle at Švihov, much of it subsequently razed, and at Blatná he completed the great moated house begun by the Rožmitáls over a century before. In Prague, however, the first traces of the Renaissance are apparent, introduced by Ried himself. But the Gothic and the Renaissance coexisted until well into the sixteenth century, the latter having first arrived in Moravia under the brief Hungarian occupation. Only with Ried's death in 1534 may it be said that one extended chapter in architecture—the Gothic—came to a close.

The demise of the Gothic more or less coincided with a new era in Czech history. Since the throne was once more vacant, in 1526 the Diet elected Ferdinand of Habsburg, brother-in-law of the late Ludvík and the successor to his Hungarian dominions. Thus after several false starts the Habsburgs had gained the lands of the Bohemian crown, which they were to retain until 1918, as well as Slovakia, which was then considered to form upper Hungary. The need for political stability and prosperity was paramount and the nation was prepared to accept even a foreign ruler if he was strong. Ferdinand certainly proved himself to be that. He skillfully maneuvered the Diet into recognizing that his descendants, by seniority of birth, should have a hereditary right to the throne. He also recreated a proper administrative structure. In addition all provincial diets, which had hitherto enjoyed a substantial measure of independence, were forced to send representatives to the general diet in Prague, while the royal Czech chancellery succeeded in imposing its decrees throughout the entire kingdom.

Although Ferdinand had promised at his coronation to respect both recognized confessions—Catholic and Utraquist—when the latter split and the "neo-Utraquists" became overtly Protestant and evangelical, he adopted a policy of coercion. A new consistorial council was appointed with the new archbishop of Prague as head of both churches. After the victory of his brother, Emperor Charles V, over the German Protestants at Mühlberg in 1547, Ferdinand stepped up the persecution of the unauthorized sects, although strong local opposition thwarted most of his ideas for church reform. Nonetheless in 1556 the Jesuits were brought in. They established a new university, the Clementinum, which attained a high standard, educating and reconverting many sons of the Utraquist nobility. The Jesuits also rapidly discovered a new national saint around whom to galvanize the Catholic population. Saint Jan Nepomucký was an obscure cleric drowned in the Vltava River by Václav IV whose corpse floated down river with a wreath of flowers around its head.

By Ferdinand's death in 1564, order and good government had been re-established. His successor, Maximilian II, was determined to complete his father's work. Unfortunately the problems of his Hungarian kingdom, much of which was now occupied by the Turks, took up most of his time, and his bigoted brother Archduke Ferdinand was left to act as regent. The king, however, was a fundamentally tolerant man who accepted the Bohemian Confession of 1575, which allowed the peaceful coexistence of Catholics with all but the most extreme sects of Protestants. While this only applied to Bohemia and officially non-Catholics had no judicial status in Moravia, in fact religious liberty was widespread in both areas. Yet the tensions remained, just below the surface.

The growth of royal political power during the sixteenth century also produced a flowering of royal patronage. Early in the century the influence of the Italian Renaissance had spread slowly into the Czech lands, but after Ferdinand's accession in 1526, royal patronage encouraged its more rapid growth. The use of stylistic elements of Italian origin such as Serlian doors and window frames reflects the king's interest in the Renaissance aesthetic, as do the shallow reliefs on plinths and spandrels that are to be found in the Letohrádek, or Belvedere, the pavilion he built for his queen on the Hradčany beginning in 1535. The king set the fashion for country-house planning too, beginning the square-turreted mansion at Kostelec nad Černými Lesy in 1549, while his younger son, another Ferdinand, himself designed the star-shaped Hvězda pavilion near Brevnov.

Maximilian's eldest son, Rudolf II, succeeded him in 1577. He too was a keen builder who lived, insulated from the world, in the new north wing of the Hradčany Palace's western courtyard, a wing that was the work of his Italian architect, Gargioli. He had already chosen Prague as his principal residence, so when he was elected emperor eight years later the court was transferred there and Prague again grew into a busy cosmopolitan city. Rudolf was a great patron of the arts, amassing an outstanding collection of curiosities and works of art, and sponsoring projects by many foreign architects. He was also a patron of Czech music, an art with an already well-established tradition, and founded a new royal orchestra, an example emulated by many nobles. His court, with its remarkable cross-section of savants including the Danish astronomer Tycho Brahe and the Irish alchemist Edward Kelly, became the intellectual center of the Empire.

The trailblazers of the Renaissance throughout the country were Italian masons and stuccodores, entire families as well as individuals. A good number came from around Lake Como or the foothills of the Alps (hence the name "Avostalis" given to many of them). Settling in all the larger towns, they often formed their own guilds such as those at Český Krumlov or Jindřichův Hradec. Their skill lay in blending a variety of styles. While emphasizing the horizontality and uniformity of the buildings, they modified the flatness of the facades by decorating plastered surfaces with ornamental and figurative sgraffiti. Instead of an attic story, their

River facade of the castle of Nelahozeves, central Bohemia, decorated with late sixteenth-century sgraffito work.

View of Telč, western Moravia.

houses frequently had gables derived from Italian church architecture. Inside they provided arcaded courtyards, multifarious vaults, and cassette ceilings, usually painted. The Renaissance came as a break in the characteristic national variation of the Gothic style, for it was a conscious revival of the ideas and arts of the ancient world, which properly enough for such a movement began in Italy. Following the lead of the court, the style was quickly adopted by the nobility. The lesser gentry and townsfolk used it less often—indeed many burghers' houses retained Gothic elements for some decades yet—while the Church was only to accept it very gradually.

The Pernštejn lords were among the greatest of Renaissance builders. In Bohemia their Gothic castle of Pardubice was converted into a Renaissance palace so skillfully that the king subsequently employed their craftsmen. Between around 1568 and 1573 a castle at Litomyšl, with its strikingly decorated courtyard, was built for the "splendor-loving" grand chancellor Vratislav z Pernštejna by the architect Jan Avostalis de Sala. The blind walls here are sgraffitoed with false masonry and in the middle of the front entrance a second-story open loggia gives a view onto the courtyard's fantastical frescoes. At Pernštejn, his principle residence, Vratislav also had the gardens and chapel laid out.

Others did not lag far behind. Zachariáš z Hradce of the Rožmberk family, great rivals of the Pernštejns, decided after his travels in Italy to convert his castle at Telč in Renaissance style. Since the silver mines he owned afforded him a bottomless treasure to gratify his every whim, he commissioned Baltasar Maio da Vomio to erect and decorate a new southern wing, onto which a polygonal apse was attached. Below, in a chapel adorned with amazing stucco and gilt by Antonio Melana, Zachariáš and his wife Kateřina lie in effigy.

King Ferdinand's favorite, Florian Gryspeck, began a splendid Serlian castle at Nelahozeves on the Labe or Elbe River in 1553, which was later to pass to the Lobkowicz family. Because of its abnormally long building time—seventy years—the building contains mannerist as well as Renaissance elements. Actually Nelahozeves's greatest claim to fame was to come three centuries later when Anton Dvořák, the foremost Czech composer, was born at the foot of the castle hill to a poor carpenter in the hamlet. In northern Bohemia, on the other hand, the Saxon influence was predominant on new buildings such as Mělník and in such alterations as Frýdlant. But for all its regional variations, by midcentury a national style had certainly developed.

Perhaps the most elegant of all Czech Renaissance monuments is Bučovice, a villa embodying the humanist spirit of Florence in an age when the Moravian nobility was still self-confident and independent. Bučovice was built for the learned Jan Šembera Černohorský z Boskovice, a man rich enough to commission plans from an architect in the imperial service at Vienna named Pietro Ferrabosco di Lagno. Between 1566 and 1582 an impressive perfectly proportioned three-story building surrounded by a moat and ramparts was constructed by a local contractor, Pietro Gabri from Brno. The courtyard had three-storied arcades with Ionic, Corinthian, and composite columns, open balustrades, and carvings on the arch spandrels and plinths. Other members of the remarkable Boskovice family also became noted patrons. One, the nephew of Prothas, the bishop of Olomouc, bought the entire town of Moravská Třebová, rebuilding it and its castle and filling both with a crowd of artists and scholars. His relatives and successors there, the Žerotíns, lived in much the same manner. Jan Žerotín was a tireless builder, beginning a house at Náměšť nad Oslavou in 1573 while simultaneously remodeling his other residences at Rosice and far to the north at Velké Losiny. Náměšť, with its long terraced facade above the Oslava River and its statue-lined bridge, forms a splendid prospect for the passerby, but its arcades seem heavy compared to Bučovice.

The Renaissance stands as an era of great achievement in the Czech lands. Along with country houses, the nobility built magnificent town residences: Giovanni Gialdi's house for the Pernštejns in Brno (1589), for instance, found copies further down the social scale in both public and private commissions. Town gates such as those at Plzeň or Tábor were modeled on the gates of Renaissance castles; town halls as at Olomouc, expressing the self-esteem of the wealthy burghers, were reshaped in the same way. It is no coincidence that where the nobility's building activity was greatest, as at Telč or Litomyšl, the citizens similarly transformed their houses. In Slovakia substantial castles with corner towers were built, such as that at Markusovce, here with Polish influence apparent. Further south in the Danube basin, the Renaissance style prevailed at Krásná Hôrka, Topol'čianky, and elsewhere. By the end of the sixteenth century, however, the classical influence of the High Renaissance began to wane and Italian mannerism was introduced with such constructions as the Matyáš Gate on the Hradčany, attributed to Vincenzo Scamozzi.

Yet the continued flourishing of art and architecture rested on shaky political foundations. Many of the major noble patrons were Protestant, like Jan Žerotín and his son Karel. The latter in his youth maintained a cosmopolitan and intellectual court at Náměšť to which aristocratic youths were sent as pages to complete their education. A great bibliophile, he was also a visionary statesman who steered Moravia through the struggles that would arise between Rudolf II and Archduke Matyáš and through the religious feuds, maintaining peace and envisaging a suprafeudal state in which everyone paid tax. But he was to be overwhelmed by the impending religious and political conflict, like most of his peers; eventually emigrating with his library to Poland, he died in lonely exile.

Although the reign of Rudolf constituted a high point in the nation's cultural development, it also marked the beginning of its political disintegration. Because Rudolf disliked the business of government he let power fall increasingly into the hands of the Czech chancellery, above all

Interior of the chapel at Telč, western Moravia, with the tombs of Zachariáš z Hradce and his wife, Kateřina Waldstein.

Arcaded courtyard at Bucovice, near Brno.

to the grand chancellor. Zdeněk z Lobkowicz occupied this office from 1599 and ensured that his fellow Catholics held all the important posts. In league with the council, he proposed to tax the Czech nobility and their lands, an unprecedented measure. The Diet was deprived of its rights to fix the levels of taxation and to oversee the deployment of troops raised in the kingdom. Many of the nationalistic and xenophobic nobility prepared to resist, along with the Protestant opposition, which found an articulate leader in Václav Budovec z Budova.

When the Unity of the Czech Brethren was again proscribed in 1602, the Protestant opposition proposed an alliance with the German Lutheran princes to force the emperor to negotiate. This in turn alienated the Czech Catholics, although in Moravia they managed to patch up an agreement with the government. Concessions there were granted by Archduke Matyáš who, after successfully rebelling against his brother in 1608, had been given full sovereignty in Moravia, Austria, and Hungary. In Bohemia the nobility remained divided. When the hard-pressed Rudolf issued an edict known as the Letters of Majesty in 1609 permitting religious freedom, the move was welcomed by the moderate Catholics led by Adam z Šternberg, but bitterly condemned by the more intolerant of the government's supporters.

In 1611 the wretched emperor was forced to abdicate (he died shortly afterward), and in May Matyáš was crowned king of Bohemia. The shrewd new ruler was primarily concerned with waging war against the Turks, so he did not interfere with the religious concessions already made. Nevertheless the principle of *cujus regio, ejus religio* often prevailed, and in many places Catholic nobles imposed priests on their Protestant peasantry. Political and religious tensions remained high, especially after it had become clear that the king, concerned with preserving royal power, refused to interfere. This combustible state of internal affairs coincided with the growth of a sharp division throughout Europe between Catholics and Protestants, a situation further exacerbated by the power struggle between Bourbon and Habsburg dynasties. Indeed Europe resembled a tinder box for which the Czechs were to provide the fuse. The resultant explosion changed Czech history as well as that of the continent in a dramatic fashion.

The incident that led to the cataclysm and to the Thirty Years' War occurred in 1618. On May 21 the Czech Protestant nobles assembled at Prague for a general diet. Some merely wanted a forum to debate their grievances but others wished to foment an anti-Habsburg uprising. Two days later a mob invaded the Hradčany and three Catholic officials were seized. Accused of violating the Letters of Majesty that had established religious freedom, they were thrown from the palace windows. Since they landed on a dungheap, however, they remained unharmed. A full-scale rebellion then commenced. The Diet elected thirty directors to administer the kingdom and a professional army was raised, 16,000 strong. The Czech Catholics, however, overwhelmingly refused to join the rebellion; the Moravians too held aloof. Nevertheless the rebels defeated the imperial generals twice and captured the major western Bohemian city of Plzeň. Peace overtures were frustrated by Matyáš's death in March 1619. He was succeeded by the young, vigorous Ferdinand II, whom the Diet, encouraged by belated Moravian and Silesian support, deposed that August. The Elector Palatine, Frederick V, was elected in his place. In November Frederick was crowned and took up residence in Prague. But he had brought no army, and his foreign advisers and English wife, Elizabeth, soon became unpopular.

Frederick's attempts to capture Vienna were bungled, while Ferdinand's diplomatic efforts made him appear the champion of the Catholic cause. Early in 1620 a large Bavarian army joined the Imperial forces and invaded southern Bohemia. On November 8 the two armies met on the White Mountain. The Catholics were well led and trained, but the Czechs were demoralized and commanded by foreigners. Most of the rebels, especially the Hungarians and mercenaries, panicked and fled; only the Moravian contingent stood their ground and died on the field. For his part, Frederick never even arrived until after the battle had been lost, and immediately thereafter left Prague with his family. The Czechs, however, stayed behind to face the emperor's wrath. Prague was occupied and the rebel leaders arrested and tried. No mercy was shown: 27 were publicly executed while many more suffered imprisonment or fines and had their estates confiscated, effectively destroying the Czech nobility. German imperial officials took over the nation's administration and the once-deposed Ferdinand paid off his allies Saxony and Poland, as promised, by handing over Lusatia and Silesia. Thus was Habsburg power reestablished, though at a truly terrible price.

Europe was soon divided into two armed camps. Protestants confronted Catholics, a conflict later complicated by the power struggle between the French and the Habsburgs. Temporarily the emperor was victorious, and he reestablished his power over the Czechs with a ruthlessly autocratic regime. The Catholic Church, seizing its opportunity to recover lost ground and led by Cardinals Dietrichstein of Olomouc and Harrach of Prague, unleashed the full force of the Counter-Reformation on the country. Most Catholic nobles became mere Habsburg followers, and the Protestants were dispossessed or exiled. Many foreign aristocrats of German, Spanish, Italian, French, and even Irish extraction were granted estates by the emperor. Protestant German, Danish, Swedish, and Hungarian troops all periodically laid waste to the Czech lands. In 1631 the Saxons captured Prague under the leadership of the German general Thurn, and many emigrés and pastors reappeared. Albrecht Waldstein's troops retook the city the next year, however, forcing Thurn to surrender with his entire garrison, although he himself was assassinated by his own officers in camp at Cheb a few years later. Ferdinand's son assumed command of the imperial forces and succeeded to the throne in 1637. But the Thirty Years' War dragged on, for the French had joined in too. Swedish armies repeatedly devastated Bohemia and Moravia, although they never recaptured Prague. At last the Peace of Westphalia was signed in 1648, and in 1650 the remaining Swedes finally departed. But the Czech lands had been bled white: 80 towns and 813 villages were destroyed in Bohemia, 22 towns and 333 villages in Moravia, as well as nearly 300 castles. The bases of government along with a quarter of the population had been lost. Over a thousand estates had changed hands and many were not efficiently managed by their new owners, serving mainly as collateral guarantees for debts and mortgages.

The most important consequence for the Czechs was that for the next 270 years they were to be integrated into the Habsburg Empire. Imperial taxation soared: the 3.2 million gulden levied in Bohemia and Moravia was over twice the figure for Upper and Lower Austria, which had been relatively unscathed by the fighting. King Ferdinand also became an absolute ruler with independent rights of succession. As for the Diet, its three estates were reconstituted into four—high and lesser nobility, burghers, and clergy—but because of the rebellion their rights and privileges were forfeited. Ferdinand also rescinded the Letters of Majesty, effectively ending religious toleration and ushering in the Counter-Reformation. Czech Protestants were given the choice of emigration or reconversion, and if they chose the latter were strictly supervised by the Jesuits. Yet the shortage of priests, especially in the countryside, allowed Protestant pastors to minister secretly to their congregations. Most of the peasantry lapsed into indifference or practiced peculiar superstitions. Irrevocably identified with Habsburg centralism and later with Germanizing policies, the Catholic Church by the eighteenth century was nevertheless producing a few leaders of the Czech population, particularly parish priests in remote dis-

Painted plaster ceiling of the Emperor's Hall at Bucovice.

Painted plaster ceiling of the Hares' Hall at Bucovice.

tricts who became their communities' spokesmen. The Jesuits in some towns also provided intellectual leavening.

Leopold I succeeded his father, Ferdinand III, in 1657, but despite having Czech friends like Counts Vratislav Černín and Václav Eusebius z Lobkowicz, his policies towards the region proved no more enlightened. He hardly visited his kingdom, seeing it essentially as a source of revenue—at this point the abjectly compliant Diet was automatically rubber-stamping all taxes. After the Turks had been repulsed from Vienna in 1683, all of Leopold's energies were devoted to reconquering Hungary and to combating French ascendancy, goals he supported partially with Czech soldiers and money. His son Josef I seemed set to reverse these policies but he only reigned from 1705–1711 before succumbing to smallpox, and was succeeded by his unimaginative younger brother Charles VI.

Czech national life had reached its nadir. The seventeenth century had brought tremendous political and social changes, but it had been culturally arid and all the traditional institutions of power had been abolished. As a foreign absentee monarch, the king ceased to embody national sovereignty. The leadership formerly provided by the Czech nobility had been removed and the Church fatally divided from the people. The Charles University was merged with the Clementinum and run by the Jesuits with theology as the principal subject. The depopulated towns were substantially Germanized; indeed only the voiceless peasantry still spoke Czech. The latter's condition was really desperate; forced labor increased ten- or twenty-fold, tax obligations were tremendous, and emigration was blocked. In 1680 jacqueries broke out on 260 estates, although they were mercilessly suppressed and their ringleaders hanged.

Although leading intellectuals like Jan Amos Komenský (Comenius), last bishop of the Unity of the Czech Brethren, lived abroad during these years, a new generation of intellectuals arose, including monks like Šimon Kapihorský and Jesuits like Bohuslav Balbín, both of whom published patriotic histories. Of the artists, Václav Hollar died in London, although the portraitist Karel Škréta did return in 1638. While songs and poems were still composed in Czech, the sole major native composer was Adam Michna.

Under Charles VI, Habsburg neglect of the kingdom reached a peak. As the most highly taxed citizens of all the hereditary lands, the Czechs had to provide recruits to fight in the Emperor's wars in Italy and Hungary. Many of the nobility had also been impoverished in the imperial service—as viceroys of Naples, Counts Martinic and Gallas, and Cardinal Schrattenbach had had to dig deeply into their own pockets—and now they returned home to tend to their economic interests. But at least life was relatively tranquil at home, disturbed only by the renewal of the proscription decrees against the Protestants in 1725. Charles VI's chief concern was to get the Pragmatic Sanction accepted, whereby his daughter Maria Theresa could succeed to the throne. Otherwise the government effectively ignored the kingdom.

A more hopeful sign was the nobility's newfound interest in investing in manufacturing. The Waldsteins established textile factories on their Bohemian estates and the Kaunitzes did the same in Moravia, while others invested in silk, linen, or wool. By 1735 exports stood twice as high as imports. Prosperity began to return, and population surpluses allowed a shift to the new manufacturing centers. But it was to take the rest of the eighteenth century to reverse Czech economic decline and to restore national vitality.

In the history of architecture, the seventeenth and early eighteenth centuries may be seen in the Czech lands, as elsewhere, as the age of the baroque. The first signs of this style were apparent in Prague as early as 1600. During these years it became the fashion among Rudolf's complex court, a fashion that reflected the court's insatiable desire for refinement

View of Námest nad Oslavou, near Brno.

Meeting of the nobels' chamber of the Diet at Prague presided over by Emperor Rudolf, dated 1593. The inscription reads, "These are the King's new judges and elders of the lands of the Bohemian crown." (Opočno collection.)

and exclusivity rather than any ideological program. But with the advent of the Counter-Reformation, the baroque provided an architectural vision to exalt the newly imposed religiosity. Ecclesiastical structures were the most important manifestations of baroque architecture: Jesuit colleges, pilgrimage churches, and, when more settled conditions prevailed, reconstructed parish churches and chapels. Yet secular architecture had close ties to the ecclesiastical, symbolizing the indispensable relationship between Church and nobility in the re-Catholicization of the country. Like pilgrimage sites or monastic complexes such as Broumov or Chomutov, the massive houses of the new landowners who arrived after the Thirty Years' War were sited in prominent positions, the visible signs of their wealth and power.

Whereas originally the baroque arrived in the Czech lands as part of the natural progression of European architecture and art, its later forced imposition ran counter to the political and cultural convictions of the people. With the return of peace and the triumph of Catholicism, the towns particularly underwent a painful transformation. Not only individual houses but entire medieval quarters were demolished to make way for the new buildings, and garden allotments were swept away. All kinds of aesthetic imports from southern Europe were assimilated: brick fortifications following the Italian model sprang up in place of medieval walls, and town halls acquired Italianate decoration. Eventually the design of farmhouses changed as well. The ruling classes consciously promoted these changes to secure their own position and legitimacy in the country and to create strong centers for Catholic worship. The confiscation of Protestant property as the spoils of war and the arbitrary policies of government were contributory means to this end.

During the Thirty Years' War the most important lay builders were the Imperial generalissimo Albrecht Waldstein and the regent of Bohemia, Karl von Liechtenstein. The Jesuits, who were formally established in Bohemia in 1623, were preeminent among the religious orders. But the fortunes of war decreed that their projects should either remain unfinished or be ceaselessly interrupted by enemy invasions and occupations. Only after the return of peace in 1648, when the shattered country started to regain its breath, can the development of architecture be traced.

By the later seventeenth century a new generation of patrons had matured who were prepared to invest their wealth in high-quality building projects. Frequently well travelled and with broad cultural exposure, they were attentive to Italian and later to French developments. The result was a Czech variant of high Baroque. The first master of this style of architecture was Francesco Caratti, who by 1652 had redesigned the castle at Roudnice for Wenzel Eusebius z Lobkowicz. Its grandiose style befitted the family who had now become the dukes of Roudnice. However Lobkowicz, Leopold's closest adviser and president of the imperial war council, fell suddenly from favor in 1674, a fate not unique among those who served the Habsburgs. He retired to Roudnice to compose bitter prose and verse tirades in diverse languages against his foes at court and to enjoy the wonderful library collected by his kinsman Bohuslav Lobkowicz z Hassenstejn. "The Bohemian Ulysses," as the latter was known, was Protestant and had long since emigrated.

Caratti's project at Roudnice was completed by his pupil Antonio della Porta. The latter used most of the same stylistic elements including pilasters in the fine house he built nearby at Libochovice for the Dietrichsteins, which makes a far more pleasing architectural ensemble. In its grand hall stands a monumental mantelpiece depicting Saturn, one of the gems of baroque sculpture. For Jan Humprecht Černín, who returned from being ambassador to Venice in 1664 with a vast art collection, Caratti also planned an enormous palace on the Hradčany. Although the plans were much amended later so that they lacked proportion, they are still the first example of the colossal order in Bohemia, contemporary with the Liechtensteins' buildings in Moravia.

The influence of the Roman baroque of Gianlorenzo Bernini and Carlo Fontana was felt before the turn of the century, and Jean-Baptiste Mathey, a Frenchman, was the major local interpreter of these trends. At Troja, a house on the outskirts of Prague that he completed around 1685 for the Sternbergs, he raised the building's middle section and emphasized its corners with towers. He further expanded on the principle of a dominant central hall at Duchcov, which he constructed for the Waldsteins in northern Bohemia. A building's silhouette was of vital importance to Mathey, who derived his steeply pitched roofs from Roman villas. The same may be said of Giovanni Battista Alliprandi, whose buildings, mostly in Prague, have a uniformly joyful character and excellent proportions. Another Bohemian contemporary who followed a more Viennese style was Pavel Ignác Bayer, who worked mainly for the Schwarzenbergs and whose chef d'oeuvre is Ohrada, the hunting lodge built for them.

The greatest of Bohemian baroque architects were Jan Santini-Aichel, born in Prague in 1677 of naturalized Italian origins, and the Bavarians Christoph Dientzenhofer and his son Kilian Ignác. The latter were primarily ecclesiastical builders, whereas Santini could build anything. But they all followed the path blazed by Francesco Borromini and Guarino Guarini, which imparted unity and movement to spaces by spherical vaulting and curvilinear walls. These elements, undulating in the interplay of concave and convex lines, gave a heightened plasticity to the architecture. While the effect was quite emotional, in fact the concept underlying it, in contemporary architecture as well as painting and sculpture, was based on complicated mathematical calculations.

Santini, all of whose independent works were concentrated in the last twenty years of his life (he died with a dozen major projects under way), found his most lavish patrons in the monasteries. For them he revived the use of the Gothic, not as a reconstruction of medieval forms but with an original and often a flamboyantly eccentric twist known as "baroque Gothic." His talent was extraordinary. Whereas the Dientzenhofers would rely on compact, closed forms and never lacked a decorative solution if invention failed, Santini was forever creating new spaces and experimenting with strange and novel shapes. For the Kinskýs, a famous Bohemian

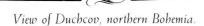

View of Duchcov, northern Bohemia.

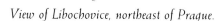

family and notorious rebels in the Thirty Years' War, Santini in 1721 transformed the hunting lodge of Karlova Koruna to commemorate a visit by Charles VI. Two concentric circular halls form the middle of his show-piece and six pillars support a flat ceiling above which rises a galleried ballroom. The house also had three star-shaped wings with guest rooms, a grand entrance staircase, and, crammed down over it all, above gables and projections, a steeply pitched roof, which assumes the shape of a crown. At Rychnov nad Kněžnou, Santini gave a new front to the church at the Kolovrats' castle, ingeniously turning it slightly to avoid its being blocked by the house, for it stood directly behind it and on its main axis. He may also have completed the castle. His collaborator, František Maximilián Kaňka, a talented architect in his own right, laid out the gardens and de-signed the houses at Veltrusy and Jemniště, both baroque masterpieces. Another quieter influence may also be detected here, that of Vienna and of one of its artistic geniuses, Johann Bernhard Fischer von Erlach.

Moravia, although politically united with Bohemia in 1628, was of course far closer geographically to Vienna and the Danube basin and therefore more strongly affected by developments there. Furthermore the lack of a true provincial capital and the competition between Brno and Olomouc increased that dependence. During the Thirty Years' War the sole important lay patrons of the arts in Moravia were the Liechtensteins and Cardinal Franz Dietrichstein. The latter commissioned Giovanni Giacomo Tencala to build him a town palace in Brno. The architect, whose work was influenced by Italian mannerism, worked extensively for the Liechtensteins as well. In 1625 he also built a church for Cardinal Die-trichstein at Mikulov. In the castle at Mikulov, which Maximilian II had given his father and where he normally resided, the cardinal signed the peace treaty with Bethlen on the Emperor's behalf in 1621.

When building activity picked up with the return of peace, most commissions were still clerically linked. In 1664 when the energetic Karl von Lichtenstein-Kastelkorn became bishop of Olomouc, he immediately commissioned a new episcopal palace from Filiberto Lucchese, architect of the Leopoldine wing at the Hofburg in Vienna. He then set about the reconstruction of his summer residence at Kroměříž, which had been ruined in the wars, employing first Lucchese and then Giovanni Pietro Tencala, a cousin of Giovanni Giacomo, to finish the job. The result, a gigantic four-winged edifice whose cornice stood seventy feet above the ground, retained only the medieval lantern tower and corner bastions of the earlier building. Although it was begun in 1679, work continued into the next century to house the splendid library, archive, and picture collection, much of the latter bought from the English Commonwealth's sale of the deposed Charles I's paintings. After being gutted by fire in 1752, the interior was redone in rococo style with giant frescoes by Franz Anton Maulbertsch. Meanwhile Bishop Lichtenstein-Kastelkorn was simultaneously laying out a model baroque garden on the other side of the town. "The Garden of Flora," as it was called, is a delight: paths radiate like a star from the cupola-crowned rotunda and the grounds are filled with fountains, grottoes, groups of statuary, pavilions, and miles of clipped hedges. The north side is closed by a 250-yard-long Doric colonnade displaying forty-six busts of Roman emperors.

Even before 1700 the Moravian connection with Vienna began to grow stronger. Fischer von Erlach had been summoned to build the riding school and stables at Lednice for the Liechtensteins, and in 1688 to reconstruct the medieval castle of Vranov nad Dyjí for the von Althan family. The castle stood in a peerless position approached over an arched stone bridge. Flouting all convention, von Erlach added a high pale oval building with an emphatic entablature, which he situated dramatically on the edge of a rocky outcrop. Called the Ahnensaal, or Ancestors' Hall, the building is reminiscent of ancient Roman baths. Its silhouette must have looked even more imposing before 1740 when the balustraded attic story, crowned by heavy urns, was replaced by a mansard roof. The interior is a light-filled pantheon of the von Althan family; ten statues of the builder's most celebrated forefathers stand in the niches, while the dome is filled by Johann Michael Rottmayr's depiction of the family's apotheosis, a magnificent conceit. Von Erlach's final work for the von Althans on this site was a little round castle chapel consecrated in 1700. The ceremonial staircase is flanked by two grandiloquent sculpture groups, a present to the builder's widow, née Maria Anna Pignatelli, from Charles VI.

Although he worked primarily in Austria, von Erlach's great rival, Johann Lukas von Hildebrandt, was also active in Moravia. Between 1700 and 1737 Count Johann Adam von Questenberg employed him to remodel Jaroměřice nad Rokyntou. A projected view of the never finished palace shows one long block crossed by two shorter ones, but the design was never completed. On the garden front the building sits on irregular Renaissance foundations. Only the chapel, an oval with eight piers from which a dome on a tall drum rises, is really satisfactory. At Slavkov, the Italian architect Domenico Martinelli designed a Roman baroque building for the Kaunitzes between 1698 and 1705, and at Buchlovice a delightful chateau was built for the Petrvald family, probably also by Martinelli. Moravia had no lack of noble patrons, and their number was to grow with the spread of eighteenth-century prosperity.

However, national recovery was delayed after Maria Theresa's accession in 1740 by the Prussian attack on Silesia and the two decades of war-

Overleaf, the sala terrena *at Libochovice.*

fare that ensued. Bohemia was invaded in 1741 and a Franco-Bavarian army captured Prague until forced to withdraw by the Imperialists. Eventually almost all of Silesia became Prussian territory until its incorporation into Poland in 1945. Although the loss of this rich province left the Germans in a permanent numerical minority, paradoxically it was to prove beneficial to the rest of the country, for it encouraged its industrialization.

Under Maria Theresa a number of administrative and political reforms were instituted that contributed to the centralization of the state. Bohemia and Moravia were again divided into two provinces and directly ruled from Vienna, where a Czech chamber of imperial civil servants was based. Only the governor of Bohemia had to be drawn from the ranks of the Czech nobility; all other historical institutions except the hapless Diet were abolished. This modernization evoked a national outcry, although the nobility, now shorn of the remnants of their political power, did little to take the lead. Instead they concentrated ever harder on their economic activities: glass, coal, and iron production supplemented the textile manufactories. In 1779 the Bohemian Society of Sciences was founded and a Bohemian Economic Society was set up to coordinate investment. When the empress was succeeded by Josef II, he expelled the Jesuits and set up a state education system, which provided a new elite of bureaucrats and technicians needed for these programs. By 1780 the population of Bohemia had reached around four million, almost a fourfold increase over a century; the same story unfolded in Moravia. With many peasants flooding into the towns after the robot (or forced labor) had been drastically reduced, the economy was further stimulated by this growing mobility of the work force.

Josef's autocratic decree that the Diet might only meet to deal with his demands eventually enraged even the Czech nobility, however, and some began to sponsor the numerous national organizations that sprang up in consequence. But the emperor's abolition of the last vestiges of serfdom and his grant of religious toleration actually facilitated Czech entry into the professions. The official policy of Germanization was also reversed and pupils began to be admitted to the state schools on a far more democratic basis than the Church had ever done. From 1790, circumstances favored the national revival. Improvements in the postal and transport systems facilitated the spread of ideas and German nationalist intellectuals actively encouraged their Czech counterparts. Josef's establishment of university chairs in Czech and Polish was intended to make his officials more efficient, but it too further fueled nationalism. The spread of literacy also created a reading public and a mass market for books and journals in Czech. Under the patronage of Count F. J. Kinský, an ex-Jesuit named Father Josef Dobrovský compiled the first comprehensive Czech grammar in 1809. Sermons and poetry started to appear as well, and the Royal Czech Society of Sciences (as it had become) began to publish its proceedings in the vernacular. With historical and literary research flourishing, studies, often by Germanized Czechs or Bohemian German scholars, were published simultaneously in both languages.

Unlike the Hungarians, the Czechs were cultural rather than political nationalists; thanks to this revival of culture and learning, Czech nationalists proved largely hostile to the French Revolution and loyal to the Habsburgs, who were shrewd enough to appeal to their cultural pride. Increased communication with other Slavic peoples within the empire was gradually maturing into a pan-Slavic movement. Many soldiers fought bravely for the emperor, and Field Marshal Karl von Schwarzenberg was intensely proud of his Bohemian background.

During the decades following Waterloo the wily imperial chancellor, Prince Clemens Metternich, managed to contain the nationalist agitation within the Habsburg dominions with remarkable success. He himself sprang from a family that originated in the Rhineland and that had ac-

37

*The remarkable mantelpiece in the Hall of Saturn
at Libochovice depicting the god surrounded by putti.*

Dietrichstein coat of arms at Libochovice.

quired the estate of Kynžvart in western Bohemia in the seventeenth century. He also bought another at Plasy, near Plzeň, which allowed him to claim some understanding of the country. Politically he ensured that his fellow aristocrats remained impotent, a situation that encouraged them to continue to pursue entrepreneurial activities. The textile and wool industries suffered from foreign competition but iron, coal, and glass prospered. When Count Karel Chotek became governor of Bohemia in 1826 he proceeded over the next twenty years to transform it into an industrialized economy. Agricultural and trade fairs were organized, more roads were built, and shipping was established on the Vltava and Elbe Rivers. Admittedly agriculture did not enjoy quite the same rate of progress. Likewise the robot was not finally abolished until 1848, although the peasants could buy their freedom from it. A financial crash in 1811 followed by a sharp price rise caused a slump and periodic agrarian disorders.

Because no political reforms seemed possible, nationalism was directed into cultural channels. Literary Czech was now taught in the schools and by the 1830s two journals had achieved stable circulation. Several good poets found an enthusiastic public, as did dramatists like J. K. Tyl and V. K. Klicpera, who benefited from the presence of local theaters, which performed their plays. Under the guidance of František Palacký, a Moravian Protestant and an outstanding historian, the Czech Museum became a cultural powerhouse. The Museum, funded by the nobility, produced a stream of literary and scientific publications. As the political temperature rose in the 1840s, it was Palacký who tried to persuade the nobles to take up the leadership of the nationalist cause before it was too late.

The second half of the eighteenth century brought a change of direction to the development of architecture in the Czech lands. After the death of Kilian Ignac Dientzenhofer, who in his last years turned increasingly towards neoclassicism, no outstanding designer emerged; though technically skilled, architects were more concerned with carrying out their patrons' wishes than with artistic experimentation. The impoverishment of the Church brought about by the secularization of its property that Josef's reforms entailed meant far less Church patronage. The nobility, on the other hand, following the lead given by the imperial court, largely withdrew from commissioning huge building projects. There were, of course, a few exceptions like the elegant neoclassical Dobříš, built in the French style by Jules Robert de Cotte and his collaborator, Giovanni Nicolo Servandoni. But the majority of these projects were minor schemes such as the garden pavilion at Český Krumlov, a baroque structure shorn of pilasters and plaster ornamentation.

With the stabilization of economic conditions, the newly rich bourgeoisie became the chief late-eighteenth-century builders. The baroque gables, doorways, and window frames on their town houses show the heavy influence of Viennese urban architecture. Streets and squares became not just thoroughfares but complex architectural ensembles and the well-laid-out gardens of these middle-class patrons stretched to the vineyards on the towns' edges. Yet they lacked the confidence to develop a distinct culture of their own, preferring to emulate that of the aristocracy.

Several important houses were built in Moravia nevertheless. Rájec nad Svítavou was constructed between 1763 and 1769 by Isidor Canevale for the Salm family. This three-winged, two-storied house, which is centered on a square cour d'honneur, is pure Louis XVI. Hugo Franz Salm was one of the pioneers of Moravian industrialization and cofounder of the Provincial Museum in Brno. He was also the friend of international scientists as well as of Dobrovský and the Viennese poet Ferdinand von Saar. Vizovice, a comfortable, pretty house of the 1750s, was built by the Brno architect Franz Anton Grimm for the future bishop of Hradec Králové. Although of no great originality, its protruding oval painted hall on the garden facade is an attractive feature that derives from French Regency examples. At Mikulov, following the disastrous fire of 1719, the rebuilding of the castle continued, possibly according to Hildebrandt's plans, but the Dietrichsteins' monstrous memorial church remained unfinished. And at Slavkov, Maria Theresa's distinguished chancellor Prince W. A. Kaunitz, had the house redesigned on property his family had owned since 1531. Its present horseshoe shape with a deep cour d'honneur was designed by Fischer von Erlach's son Josef Emanuel. Sadly it does not succeed, the effect being too heavy and lacking in proportion. In Slovakia, too, the high and late baroque found their echoes in Diviaky, Veľky Biel, and the alterations to Markusovce.

By the 1780s pure neoclassicism had arrived in Bohemia, spearheaded by the military architecture commissioned by Josef II. But the ensuing building activity produced unpretentious houses, designed either as single-family residences or rental accommodation, for which the architects needed to adapt their plans to the immediate environment rather than produce innovative ideas. Nevertheless some of the results are of undeniably high quality. In the Czech lands many of the buildings from this period are to be found in the spa towns: Teplice, Mariánské Lázně, and Karlovy Vary. Prague, on the other hand, was not to receive grandiose monuments like Paris or Berlin, for the aristocracy preferred to spend its recently augmented wealth on town palaces in Vienna.

One especially enchanting country house was erected for the Černíns by Václav Haberditz from 1784 to 1789. The rooms of Kozel, as it is called, have retained their original rococo furnishings and frescoes. Its ensemble of low, neoclassical buildings blends perfectly into its wooded landscape, foreshadowing the mania for natural settings that was all-pervasive by 1800 and that led the nobility to lay out their parks and gardens in the English style. Thence spread the roots of the romantic movement, which would soon replace the cult of the ancient with that of the medieval world. An early enthusiast of this movement was Count Jan Rudolf Chotek, who was busy redesigning his park at Veltrusy and who shortly was to embark on the building of Kačina, the purest expression of neoclassicism in the country. In Moravia the Liechtensteins were also about to begin the ambitious creation of an entire landscape between their houses at Lednice and Valtice. At the bishop's summer residence at Kroměříž the lower castle garden leading from the baroque parterres was redesigned in the new style. As a unified ensemble of art and nature, a neoclassical villa was built between 1833 and 1839 by Peter von Nobile for Chancellor Metternich at Kynžvart on the site of the baroque chateau. A decade earlier the same architect had redesigned Boskovice for the Dietrichsteins, a pattern of manicured Empire elegance on the foundations of the dissolved monastery.

Life in the great houses had become steadily more civilized and music played a major part in this. Even in the early eighteenth century Count Questenberg had arranged a string of festivities with the talented Giuseppe Galli Bibiena as his impresario and the composer František Václav Mica as his music director. He seems to have judged even his servants more for their choral or orchestral than their domestic abilities. Indeed so devoted was the count to this art that when he chose to be painted it was as a happy musician. Christoph Willibald Gluck's father was in the Lobkowicz family service and Carl von Dittersdorf was for twenty-five years music director at the castle of Jánský Vrch in northern Moravia. Not far away Ludwig van Beethoven was entertained by the Lichnowskýs, who

View of Karlova Korůna, central Bohemia.

also played host to Niccolo Paganini and Franz Liszt. In Prague Wolfgang Amadeus Mozart gave the first performances of *Don Giovanni* (1786) and *La Clemenza di Tito* (1791). Admittedly many leading Czech composers, including J. Benda, J. V. Stamic, and J. Mysliveček, worked abroad. But music and theatricals remained a vibrant tradition, as shown by the construction of private theatres at Litomyšl and Český Krumlov. The latter also had suites of rooms frescoed with the figures of the Commedia dell'Arte, so beloved by exponents of gallantry in the Ancien Régime.

Eccentricity was nurtured too. For twelve years until his death in 1798, Giovanni Giacomo Casanova was the librarian at Duchcov, where he wrote his scandalous memoirs. Travelers to the nearby castle of Teplice, if its owners the Clarys were entertaining there, might see the old man striding along the road dressed in a red silk, gold-embroidered coat with a feathered tricorne hat on his bare head. Alongside him would run a barefoot boy carrying a box containing his wig, for Casanova was worried lest the wind ruffle it. Although he long remained vain, the object of his passions changed. "As he no longer wishes to be a god in the gardens, or a satyr in the woods," the Prince de Ligne remarked in his memoirs, "he has become a wolf at table." At Kynžvart Metternich, with his magpie-like fondness for collecting, created a cabinet of curiosities including the first chronometer, Napoleon's washbasin, and Queen Hortense's cap. "The area is rich in artistic settings," he wrote. "Enormous woods, high mountains, broad valleys, tumbling streams surround a well-furnished chateau . . . with many old family portraits, including my own at the age of five. I must have been a really ugly little boy, or else the painter was bad." The nobility's way of life then had something of a fairy-tale quality about it, secluded from tumult and revolution. Yet revolution was fast approaching.

Early in 1848, "The Year of Revolutions," the Diet, hastily convoked by the governor, entirely failed to satisfy the radicals' grievances regarding Czech autonomy, and an impromptu meeting in the Prague public baths elected the National Committee in its stead. A list of reasonable demands was drawn up, and on March 20 a delegation visited Vienna to present them to the emperor. They were met by the new prime minister, Count F. z Kolovrat, himself a shrewd Bohemian politician who promised them linguistic equality with the Germans in the schools as well as in the provincial administration but refused requests to reestablish the historical Czech kingdom. Another separatist petition was referred to an impending meeting of the pan-imperial Reichsrat, which was planned to discuss all the empire's problems. Meanwhile that June in Prague a Slavonic congress was organized to coordinate pressure on the government. On the first day rioting occurred. Chaos reigned for a week in the city until imperial troops bombarded Prague, which, after a few hours, surrendered unconditionally. The congress was disbanded and the Diet forbidden to meet.

Czech delegates duly attended the Reichsrat. However in October they, like the emperor, had to flee the mobs in Vienna; the former reconvened at Kroměříž. There František Palacký laid before them a conservative reform program, which the liberal majority duly rejected, voting instead for the abolition of the noble and ecclesiastical privileges. In March 1849 the Reichsrat was dissolved and the weak Ferdinand was succeeded by his determined nephew Francis Joseph. At first the non-Hungarian provinces were offered their own constitution, but once Russian troops had crushed the Hungarian revolt the offer was canceled and a return to the status quo ordained. Surprisingly little trouble ensued in the Czech lands; a few radicals were deported or imprisoned while the other nationalists resumed their customary cultural activities. Indeed they had emerged from the maelstrom with renewed confidence. After centuries of separation the Czechs recognized potential allies in their fellow Slavs, especially the Slovaks, with whom they had rediscovered an identity of common interests despite the growth of a linguistic divide. Naturally this precluded any alliance with the Magyar oppressors of the Slovaks against German domination. They also faced a political dilemma. Because it was the German bourgeoisie who advocated modernization and political reform, these became unacceptable to the nationalists. Instead they advocated the re-creation of the historic Czech kingdom and sought rightwing alliances with other aristocratic and clerical factions.

Although politically barren, these years saw much economic and social progress. The population exploded, more than doubling during the nineteenth century and exceeding ten million by 1920; Prague quintupled and Brno quadrupled in size. Distilleries, breweries, and sugar-beet factories sprang up throughout the country, four heavy engineering works were founded in Prague, and the Waldsteins' factory at Plzeň grew into the giant Škoda armaments and heavy engineering works. By 1900 the Czech provinces were the most industrially developed in the Habsburg Empire. Agriculture also began to expand and, although half the population now lived on the land, yields per hectare doubled. Notable cultural developments included the enactment of a language law in 1849 whereby Czech could be taught officially in the schools; indeed by 1880 the nationalists had taken over the educational system. A new generation of poets, novelists, and artists emerged and a national theatre was founded. Five mass-circulation daily newspapers informed a large intelligentsia. In Anton Dvořák and Bedřich Smetana the country possessed two composers of international fame; likewise Alphonse Mucha earned worldwide attention as one of the founders of art nouveau in Paris. The Czechs were in a strong position; economically they were the most important and numerically they were the largest group in the non-Hungarian parts of the empire.

Yet the political situation remained dismal. When political and financial difficulties forced Francis Joseph I to offer his subjects constitutional government again, the Czechs proved reluctant. A tiny minority, they withdrew from the Reichsrat within two years. Unlike the Hungarians, they failed to exploit Austria's defeat by Prussia in 1866. Palacký's successor and son-in-law, František L. Rieger, led the so-called Old Czechs, who in 1879 were persuaded to return to the Reichsrat. The government, recognizing the necessity of making more concessions to its Slavic subjects, arranged for the Czechs to gain an overall majority in the Diet. And once again the University of Prague was redivided into German and Czech branches. In return the Old Czechs agreed to keep the right-wing coalition in power.

Sadly little was achieved. German tactics obstructed all legislation and paralyzed the Diet, but the Czechs merely formed an unimportant minority in the Reichsrat. Attempts to make Czech the second language in provincial courts and administration led to widespread German demonstrations. In the general election of 1891 the party's progressive wing, known as the Young Czechs, came to power. At first they scored a string of victories, bringing down the ministry and being courted by successive premiers. Yet they could not ally with the German liberals, who refused to meet their linguistic demands. Finding their aims unattainable, the Young Czech party fell apart, some members opting for cooperation with the government and others, like the young Tomáš G. Masaryk, seceding to form new parties. An impasse had been reached, although by 1900 the Czechs occupied many influential positions within the empire in the judiciary, civil service, and universities, as well as such professions as architecture, engineering, and banking. But the system was paralyzed by rival nationalisms, which readily resorted to spontaneous rioting. The introduction of universal suffrage provided no panacea because in the Czech lands both the Agrarians and Social Democrats soon proved themselves thorough nationalists. No solution to the problems was in sight, for no one believed in the practicality of independence, and pan-Slavism, if superficially attractive, meant subjection to Russia, a prospect scarcely more alluring than absorption into the German hegemony. Not until World War I was the mold broken.

Well before the convulsions of 1848 the Gothic revival style had arrived in the Czech lands. From the 1830s, fired by the spirit of romantic historicism, owners began rebuilding their castles in the new style, aiming for both grandiose layouts and every modern comfort. In Bohemia the Schwarzenbergs reconstructed Hluboká in a manner reminiscent of Windsor Castle in 1839; over the next fifteen years the vaguely Tudor edifice of Hrádek u. Nechanice was built for the Harrachs according to the plans of an Englishman, Edward Lamb. At Sychrov in the north, the small baroque chateau bought from the Waldsteins in 1820 was remodeled between 1848–63 in Gothic revival taste for Camille Rohan, a scion of the distinguished French family. Special attention was paid to the garden, where a magnificent allée of pyramid oaks stretched a mile from the house. The library's botanical collection was of particular merit, while a picture collection over 240 strong covered the walls.

In Moravia the Liechtensteins were, as always, in the vanguard of patronage. Their reconstruction of Lednice, begun in 1845 by Georg Wingelmüller, was a monument to the Gothic revival. Indeed the style persisted longer in the province than elsewhere. In the late nineteenth century the head of the German Order, successors to the crusading Teutonic Knights, remodeled his residence, the enormous castle of Bouzov, in Gothic-revival style. The Order, expelled from its native land by Napoleon, had taken fresh root in the Habsburg dominions after being given extensive estates in Austrian Silesia. In Slovakia, where taste was still dictated from Budapest, it was less in evidence, although there were a few reconstructions such as that at Bojnice (Bajmoc in Hungarian), or new buildings in an historicizing style like Budměřice.

By the 1860s, however, the Gothic revival had fallen out of fashion. Mid-nineteenth-century sentimentalism was replaced by a new realism that, combined with the industrial boom and the growth of national consciousness, demanded new styles and new approaches. The neo-Renaissance, evoking the proto-capitalist culture of sixteenth-century Italy, seemed to suit the nouveau-riche status-minded bourgeoisie. The Church, on the other hand, was chiefly preoccupied with preserving and restoring its Romanesque and Gothic monuments. Indeed restoration during these years became more scholarly and stylistically pure, as the careful work at Karlštejn by Josef Mocker shows (1887–97). Some of this architect's other efforts, such as in Saint Vitus's Cathedral on the Hradčany, were

View from the river below of Vranov nad Dyji, western Moravia.

Overleaf, view of Jaromerice nad Rokyntou, western Movaria.

less fortunate, however. Not many country houses were still being re-modeled, although the alterations at Konopiště, (also by Mocker, 1889–95), and the remodeling of Betliar in Slovakia for the Andrássy family must not be forgotten. But many chateau parks were altered by combining the classic French or Italian garden with new arboretums or beds of exotic trees and shrubs, a result of the scientific interest in botany; Sychrov and Konopiště were outstanding examples of this trend, as was the redesigned Buchlovice.

Historicism had played itself out by the end of the century, its archi-tectural and decorative possibilities exhausted. In this climate a short-lived Secession movement based on the Viennese model flourished and a fresh generation of architects led by Jan Kotěra and Josef Gočár liberated their art from its historical ballast. They developed a naturalistic orna-mentation instead and obtained original effects by employing new materi-als such as ceramics, glass, and metal. The flat surface they deliberately produced was only slightly modified by reliefs or murals, designs placed asymmetrically, and the embellishment of the intentionally stark architec-ture by sculpture. Although the style permeated the cities, sometimes taking on a local flavor, it did not last, and by the 1900s Kotěra and his colleagues came under the influence of Otto Wagner's more functional aesthetic. In any case, this style had little to do with country-house build-ing, for the overwhelming majority of the nobility were not interested in these modern trends and regarded Prague and Brno, in comparison with Vienna, as depressingly provincial.

This did not mean, however, that they had ceased taking a lively inter-est in other social activities. Taking the cure at the spas had been a favor-ite aristocratic pastime throughout the nineteenth century. Karlovy Vary (the former Karlsbad) had long enjoyed the foremost reputation, its foun-dation dating from Charles IV's reign. Under the Clarys' able management, Teplice, the oldest Bohemian thermal bath, became quite fashionable dur-ing the Napoleonic Wars, as did Mariánské Lázně (Marienbad). By 1900 they constituted some of the most fashionable watering places in Europe, the haunts of the Prince of Wales and a horde of foreign royalty and aristocrats.

Hunting and racing were favored pastimes too. Count Octavian Josef Kinský, known as Taffy, founded a celebrated steeplechase near Pardubice in 1846, easily winning the first race himself despite riding without a bridle. The owner of Karlova Koruna, he was famed throughout the empire for his carriage driving, equestrian skills, and wild antics. Guests were ad-vised to make their wills before arriving to stay. One recorded, "In the evening we were splendidly entertained; finally Count Taffy drove his four-in-hand up to the second floor of the chateau, did a turn around the ballroom and drove out again." A few decades later his family traditions were maintained by another Kinský, Karl, also a brilliant horseman, who won the English Grand National and became the lover of Lady Randolph Churchill.

Life on the nobility's estates retained plenty of vitality and style. The late-nineteenth-century's appetite for enormous house parties and colossal shoots, at which the day's bag habitually ran into thousands, was amply indulged in the Czech lands. One of its foremost exponents was Arch-duke Francis Ferdinand, the heir to the Habsburg throne who had pur-chased the castle of Konopiště, largely rebuilt it in an eclectic style, filled it with the collections inherited from his Este cousins, and laid out an extensive rose garden. It became his favorite residence. There, a crack shot, he presided over endless battues at which the German kaiser was a frequent guest, and there he loved to relax with his family. Francis Fer-dinand is supposed to have told the mayor of nearby Benešov that on becoming emperor he would turn this small provincial town into the im-perial administrative capital. Reputedly he and the kaiser planned the war

against Serbia within Konopiště's gloomy walls; it is unquestioned fact, however, that he set out almost straight from here for Sarajevo for the curtain raiser to the armageddon of 1914.

World War I took most Czechs by surprise and many were unenthusiastic about fighting with Germany against their fellow Slavs, the Serbs and Russians. No one could conceive of what defeat might mean, but the initial reverses induced widespread depression, for the Habsburg armies went into battle ill-prepared and lacking their adversary's inexhaustible manpower. At its outset few had seen the war as a pretext for destroying the Austro-Hungarian state, but as morale deteriorated at home, abroad, exiled nationalist leaders like Masaryk supported an Allied victory.

General collapse seemed imminent in 1916 as widespread mutinies occurred and internal repression grew. Yet Francis Joseph's death that year caused important changes; his great-nephew Charles reversed his predecessor's policies, releasing political prisoners and returning to parliamentary rule. As he announced, "Austria is no longer either a German or a Slavic state; true, the Germans were the founders of the monarchy . . . but they can only remain as leaders of younger cultures if they themselves set an example of the highest cultural standards, and offer the newly-emancipated peoples love, respect and magnanimity."

The nationalists refused to be conciliated, however. Masaryk's skill in forming a legion of Czech P.O.W.s in Russia led to its recognition as an Allied force, and for the first time in 1917 the Czech independence movement received recognition at an international level. The Peace of Brest Litovsk in March 1918 afforded the monarchy a breathing space. The Emperor encouraged federalist ideas, appointing two Bohemians, Counts O. Černín and J. Clam-Martinic, as foreign and prime ministers respectively. Yet their proposed reforms aroused fury from the Germans and Hungarians and by October the monarchy had collapsed. The Allies then recognized Eduard Beneš and Masaryk as Czech representatives. On October 28 the national committee proclaimed independence from Austria, which the Allies welcomed immediately, and three days later the Slovaks proclaimed their independence from Hungary, opting to join Bohemia and Moravia in one state. A government was recognised with Masaryk as president and Beneš and Milan Štefánik as ministers of foreign affairs and war. After the Ruthenes had joined the new republic, it contained around 8.8 million Czechs and over 3.1 million Germans, of 13.6 million inhabitants (the Slovaks insisted on being counted separately). Two German districts, Deutschböhmen and the Sudetenland, declared independence too, demanding to join Austria, but they were forcibly reannexed. In Slovakia, a Hungarian invasion by Béla Kun's revolutionaries was repulsed. Only by 1920 were the frontiers of the Czechoslovak state secured and finally recognized.

Undeniably the artistocracy's position in the new country was anomalous. Most families had become Germanized to a greater or lesser extent over the preceding centuries and had long served the Habsburg dynasty, yet while few had participated in the nineteenth-century nationalist movement, most also had a real affection for the country of their birth. Although many were of foreign origins, after centuries of residence in the Czech lands they could only be regarded as natives. The Liechtensteins had held land in Moravia since the mid-thirteenth century, for instance, and the Schwarzenbergs, Colloredos, and Clarys had been there for three hundred years. It is true that branches of some of the noble families like the Kinskýs and the Schwarzenbergs identified themselves more strongly as Czechs than their cousins, but quite a few of them—the Lobkowiczs, Kinskýs, Sternbergs, Černíns, and Waldsteins—were ethnic Czechs anyway. Their problem lay not with foreign allegiances but with their alienation from the new government, as a consequence of which almost all eschewed politics.

View from the park of Slavkov, near Brno.

The new government's policies included a certain amount of land redistribution, which obviously threatened the wealth and the way of life of the nobility. During the previous century their holdings had remained extensive and in some instances had even increased. In 1918 no fewer than 56 estates of over 10,000 hectares, including those belonging to the Catholic church, were listed in Bohemia, Moravia, and Austrian Silesia. These estates comprised 18 percent of the land mass in Bohemia and 13 percent in Moravia. The largest single proprietor in the empire was Prince Esterházy with 243,500 hectares, but the Schwarzenbergs with 207,000 hectares and the Liechtensteins with 192,000 were not far behind—each holding over three times as much as any other estate in either Bohemia or Moravia.

Overall the government's land distribution policy was carried out reasonably. Theoretically the reform they introduced allowed every proprietor to retain 500 hectares, 250 of which could be agricultural land, but this was never enforced. Individual cases of petty spite occurred, especially against the former Habsburg ministers Clam-Martinic and Černín. But most big estates lost a third of their land at worst, generally in the case of those aristocrats deemed Germanophile. The Schwarzenbergs, for instance, lost barely a tenth of their holdings.

With a long entrepreneurial tradition in the Czech lands, the big estates ran 475 breweries in addition to other industrial interests, as compared to under 100 in Austria. And only a few of these were nationalized by the new government. Indeed the Czechoslovak republic confounded sceptics by becoming surprisingly stable. As president, Masaryk wielded great power and largely used it well. During the interwar years the country remained an industrial giant, maintaining the highest living standards of any Central European nation and establishing an advanced social security system.

The racial minorities posed the most intractable problems, however. The Slovaks proved particularly obdurate, persistently proclaiming their different national identity and agitating for more autonomy even when internal self-government had been granted. Many Germans, too, were never reconciled to Czech rule. Yet in fairness the Sudeten cause was not unreasonable, for while the German minority was economically and numerically significant, it had justifiable fears that its interest and identity

The reception hall at Kozel, western Bohemia.

Detail of a mural at Kozel.

were in danger of being disregarded in the post–World War era; the difficulty lay in reconciling the Sudeten cause with the territorial integrity of the state.

Czechoslovakia's position internationally was bolstered by signing an alliance with France in 1924 followed by the formation of the Little Entente with Yugoslavia and Romania. Its weakness lay in these allies' geographical separation from each other, which made them incapable of mounting a serious challenge to the revived might of either Soviet Russian or Nazi Germany. After Hitler's rise to power in 1933, he quickly espoused the Sudeten cause for his own ends. President Beneš, who succeeded Masaryk in 1934, tried on several occasions to negotiate with him, to no avail. A treaty with the Russians proved purely formal, for the Soviets felt they had no vital interests at stake in Central Europe. In March 1938 came the Anschluss with Austria, after which Hitler publicly promised the Sudeten Germans his help. The response was hysterical enthusiasm, although the alarmed Czech government hastily prepared an amended nationality law to pacify them. All summer long the crisis mounted, finally involving the Western powers. That September, Hitler invited the British and French prime ministers to Munich where an agreement was reached. The Sudeten districts were detached from Czechoslovakia and in return the frontiers of the truncated Czechoslovak republic were guaranteed. However, the Poles and Hungarians then promptly annexed the districts they were claiming. The Czech government resigned forthwith and Beneš went into exile. The rump of the Czech parliament elected Dr. Emil Hácha as president. The farcical pretense of Czech independence lasted until March 1939 when the aged Hácha was summoned to Berlin and forced to agree to all the Nazis' demands. German troops occupied the Hradčany and it was announced that the Czech provinces had now joined the Third Reich as the "Protektorat of Bohemia and Moravia."

During these two interwar decades little new construction took place, either in the towns or in the country. The aristocracy continued to maintain their houses and manage their estates, although a well-run forestry business became more profitable than farming. Much of the land was rented out in two- to three-hundred-hectare holdings, which helped to allay envy, and ménages were reduced but country-house life continued, especially in the summer and autumn when the shoots began. Occasionally large balls were still given in Prague, but although some German industrialists were invited there was little intermingling of the classes, for the haute bourgeoisie was mainly Czech or Jewish, and few aristocrats spoke good Czech.

In Slovakia a curious art-nouveau house called Kunerad was constructed in 1916, the only grand country villa undertaken since the turn of the century apart from one more traditional residence for the Lobkowicz family and two hunting lodges for the Clam-Gallas family. Nevertheless, the republic produced some fine architects such as Bohuslav Fuchs and Adolf Loos. The latter designed several modernist villas of variable quality for the rich in the suburbs of Prague and Plzeň, the best of which, the Villa Miler, is still filled with Loos's furniture as well. More significant was the villa Mies van der Rohe constructed for the Tugendhat family in 1930 on the outskirts of Brno. One of the great masterpieces of early modernist architecture, it brilliantly illustrates his open-plan concept and his fascination with the continuity of space. But its Jewish proprietors emigrated in 1938, never to return, and today, stripped of its furniture and fittings, it is a rather forlorn monument to a vanished age.

World War II was a particular nightmare for the Czechs. As national resistance to the Germans mounted, the brutal Reinhard Heydrich took over as Reichsprotektor in 1941. Martial law was declared and wholesale executions and deportations of the Jews began. Heydrich's assassination by a special commando merely unleashed a fresh wave of terror. Beneš's government-in-exile in London had been recognized by the Allies and he signed another treaty with Russia. In 1944 Soviet forces entered Slovakia, which then rose against the Germans, but Stalin's ambitions were already apparent when he annexed Ruthenia over Czech protests. He readily agreed that all ethnic Germans could be deported to the defeated Reich and Beneš had to consent to the postwar banning of all right-wing political parties. In May 1945 the Czech government returned to a Prague that had been liberated by the Russians. In October Beneš was once more elected President. The government having endorsed a transition from capitalism to socialism, all foreign-owned banks and enterprises were nationalized and 60 percent of all industry became state property.

In the elections of 1946 the Communists, led by the ruthless Klement Gottwald, emerged as the largest single party, controlling the new national assembly and the key ministries. A coup d'état in Slovakia in 1947 led to a Communist takeover there; by February of 1948 Gottwald had forced the resignation of the coalition ministers, and by June he had replaced Beneš as president. The Soviet grip on Czechoslovakia tightened. The historical provinces of Bohemia and Moravia were abolished, the judiciary and civil service purged, and a series of show trials accompanied persecution of the Catholic Church. By 1949 the country was thoroughly totalitarian. Gottwald died in 1953, replaced by the colorless Zápotocký, who in turn endured until the Prague Spring of 1968 when Aleksander Dubček's reform regime briefly promised a return to democracy before it was crushed by Russian intervention.

Deportation of the German minority, over four million strong, had been systematically commenced in 1946 and two years later hardly any ethnic Germans were left. Many of the landowners were also expelled, often on the flimsiest grounds, to gratify social or racial prejudice; others, seeing the writing on the wall, had fled before the Russian advance in 1945. Almost three million hectares of what was called "enemy land" were expropriated, along with that belonging to "Czecho Slovak traitors," a term capable of elastic application. In almost every case houses were left

An early nineteenth-century baby carriage at Kozel.

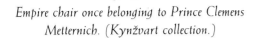

Empire chair once belonging to Prince Clemens Metternich. (Kynžvart collection.)

behind virtually intact with all the contents, and luckily, by comparison with neighboring countries, there was relatively little looting. Some proprietors chose to stay, preferring an uncertain life in their native land. But eventually they too were compelled to leave, most during 1948 when, in the aftermath of the Communist takeover, they were declared a parasite class and their property was nationalized without compensation. By a bitter irony of history, after suffering under the Nazi occupation they were to see their property confiscated and their ties to their native country severed by the government installed by their supposed liberators. The omnipotent state suddenly found itself in possession of numerous fine houses and castles, completely furnished, monuments from every period and style of architecture, which it lacked both the interest and the resources to maintain. The resulting years of neglect have only relatively recently been compensated for by belated restoration growing from the realization that these buildings form part of the nation's cultural heritage as well as a sizeable portion of its tourist appeal.

The wheel of destiny may now have nearly turned full circle. Those who were stripped of their possessions and nationality are still in the process of regaining them. The futures of the Czech Republic and Slovakia look infinitely brighter than they did just a few years ago.

KRÁSNÁ HŎRKA
& BETLIAR

E astern Slovakia is beautiful, wild, and remote. Surrounded by high mountains, it is closer geographically to Budapest or Kraków than to Prague, and its connection with the rich and civilized countryside of Bohemia or Moravia is at best tenuous. For a thousand years Slovakia served as Hungary's backyard, only being re-united with its western Slav neighbors after World War I. It is therefore hardly surprising that most of the great houses situated in modern Slova-kia were built and owned by families whose origins were Hungarian. One of the most illustrious of these aristocratic dynasties was that of the An-drássys, whose two seats, Betliar and Krásná Hŏrka, lie only a few miles apart, separated by the small town of Rožňava. While they are com-pletely different in appearance, both are of unusual interest.

The name Krásná Hŏrka, literally "beautiful mountain," first appears in 1243 when the Hungarian king Béla IV gave large estates in the district of Gömör, including one by that name, to members of the Akos clan. He had sought refuge near here after being defeated by the Mongols at the Slaná River two years before, possibly in an old fort above the village of Drnava. The patriarch of the clan, Benedikt Akos, have five sons who decided to divide the property among themselves in 1318 after his death. Dominik, whose nickname, Bebek, was applied to all his descendants, re-ceived the part including Krásná Hŏrka and Betliar. However, for some thirty years he remained in dispute over ownership with the Mariassy family, who had been granted a royal patent for mining precious metals in the area. After legal and illegal means had been employed, the dispute was only settled in Bebek's favor in 1352 by brute force.

Standing on a sugarloaf-shaped hill in the center of an oval valley ringed by mountains, where it dominated the route west from Košice into the ore mining regions of central Slovakia, Krásná Hŏrka was evidently a site of strategic importance. The nucleus of a fort was built early in the thirteenth century, a tall square tower surrounded by walls and con-structed on the highest slope of the hill facing east. Once the Bebeks had gained possession they hastened to improve its fortifications, constructing a two-story building attached to the tower. Of uneven rectangular shape to adjust to its rocky base, most of the structure's ground floor was used for storing food and arms, although the middle section contained one large raised hall lit by four southern windows; an adjacent room on the same level had an enormous fireplace. From here a narrow corridor led to the tower where there were residential quarters, an unusual feature for castles of this date. The inner courtyard with its water cistern was guarded by a vaulted gate tower and entirely enclosed. So strong was the fortress deemed to be that there were few alterations made to it for the next two hundred years. During this period the Bebeks remained firmly in control—except for the two decades following 1441, when Krásná Hŏrka

Distant view of the castle of Krásná Hŏrka, eastern Slovakia.

Old view of Krásná Hŏrka by D. Kunicke.
(Austrian National Library, Vienna.)

Entrance to the courtyard at Krásná Hŏrka.

View of the Countess Francesca Andrássy's
bedroom at Krásná Hŏrka.

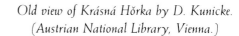

was occupied by a Moravian robber baron named Jiskra. Thereafter István Bebek built a further wing as barracks to accommodate a larger garrison.

The Bebek family remained for a long time one of the most influential in Hungary. Serious trouble struck in 1526, however, when the head of the family, János, perished fighting the Turks at Mohács. His heirs then began a bitter struggle over the enormous estates. Ultimately a cousin named Ferenc, a treacherous and malevolent man, prevailed, blatantly exploiting the confused political situation by playing off the rival claimants to the Hungarian throne, Ferdinand of Habsburg and Jan Zápolya, while frequently switching sides. His lawless soldiers controlled several local trade routes, exacting exorbitant tolls from passing commerce and terrorizing the local population. At last he overreached himself by attacking neighboring landowners and by establishing a secret mint at Krásná Hŏrka where counterfeit coins were struck. The National Assembly then proscribed the Bebeks as outlaws and an armed force was sent against them. Ferenc appealed for help to the Turks, whose troops proceeded to attack the royal soldiers in September 1556, forcing them to retreat to Rožňava. Nevertheless the Bebeks' position was now untenable, for the emperor was determined to oust them. Ferenc fled to Transylvania with his son György and was murdered shortly afterwards. György sought pardon from the Emperor, however, promising to raise men for the Turkish war, and was given back his properties. But the rapprochement was short-lived and he soon recommenced plotting. Imperial troops retaliated, capturing his castles by steady degrees after 1565, and finally György died in penurious exile in Transylvania, bringing his family's line to an end.

The castle of Krásná Hŏrka had been greatly expanded by then. In 1544 Ferenc Bebek had commissioned plans for new fortifications to surround the old castle precincts, for with the growing sophistication of siege artillery Krásná Hŏrka was no longer impregnable. The approach road remained the same, but the castle entrance was guarded from the southeast by a massive new bastion connected with another to the southwest by thick retaining walls, and with a third to the north. A broad terrace was also laid out, on which stood heavy guns. The interiors of all the buildings were simultaneously reconstructed.

Despite all this work, Krásná Hŏrka was in a dismal state of repair by the century's end. With the extinction of the Bebeks their huge estates

reverted to the crown, and their administration was entrusted to captains appointed by the war council in Vienna. The remuneration of the captains as well as funds for the upkeep of the fortifications derived from the income yielded by the properties, but the turnover of captains was so fast that any incentive to spend the money wisely was lacking. At last one was appointed who fulfilled his duties conscientiously. Peter Andrássy from Szent-Kiraly in Transylvania was a faithful servant of the Habsburgs whose family sprang from Sekler stock, a warrior tribe traditionally charged with defending the borders of the realm. After opposing Zápolya's rule in Transylvania, Andrássy had been forced to flee and join the Emperor's service. In 1578 he was appointed to the vacant captaincy of Krásná Hŏrka, the income for which was meant to come from twenty villages on the estate.

Finding everything dilapidated, Andrássy, with characteristic energy, started on restoration forthwith. By 1585 he had expended 85,000 forints of his own money, and the war council, unable to repay him in cash, mortgaged the castle and estate to him for ten years. Indeed Andrássy spent his entire fortune on the task and died a disillusioned man, followed soon afterward by both his sons. Finally, in recognition of his services,

Nascendo Saxo. Tacendo Hampo.
Silendo Vivo Nemini Noceo.

the imperial government allowed his redoubtable widow, Zsofia, to succeed as acting captain of Krásná Hŏrka, and she managed to preserve the
inheritance for her infant grandson Mátyás. He came of age, married,
and in 1642 the Emperor granted his family the property in perpetuity.

*Portrait of a former drummer in Ferenc Rákóczi's
army, Andras Dobos, painted at
Krásná Hŏrka, 1747.*

The Andrássys' position in Slovakia was finally secured by Mátyás's son
Miklós, who became Foïspan or lord-lieutenant of Gömör County, a member of the magnates' chamber, and a baron. A Lutheran by birth, he nevertheless converted to Catholicism, leaving his seven sons on both sides of
the religious divide. When the great Protestant leader Ferenc Rákóczi's
revolt against the Habsburgs took place in 1703, three of them joined the
rebels, although on capitulation they contrived to have their persons and
property spared.

*Portrait of Krásná Hŏrka's village fool holding a
dove, 1744.*

Much more was done by the Andrássys during the seventeenth and eighteenth centuries to improve the castle, which now exhibited a mixture of
baroque and Renaissance styles. A lower castle was constructed, linked
internally with the old medieval nucleus, and a bakery plus a kitchen was
added against the western walls of the fortress. In the 1730s a baroque main
gate was built and later the southeast bastion was made into a fine chapel
focusing on the Andrássy *Madonna* (a painting of the Virgin and Child,
which became an object of local pilgrimage). Krásná Hŏrka was now transformed into a comfortable and attractive residence. During the lifetime of
István Andrássy, author of *Triplex Philosophia*, family members were also
created counts and allowed to place the crown of Saint Stephen above the
lions rampant on the coat of arms. Several generations had proved themselves successful generals, and a room at Betliar displayed portraits of the
officers of the Nádasdy Hussars, one of the regiments they commanded.

During all the renovations at Krásná Hŏrka, Betliar remained a modest
turreted castle, and there, after making limited renovations in 1712, István
Andrássy settled with his family on retirement. His great-nephew Leopold,
who succeeded there at the end of the century, had it remodeled in the
neoclassical style common to Gömör County between 1780 and 1795. The
dark passage leading from the front door through to the cour d'honneur on

the north side was refashioned as an artificial cave to compensate for the absence of a *sala terrena*. Heinrich Nebbien, a landscape gardener, was instructed to transform the park in the Romantic style.

Count Leopold was the most remarkable among his generation of the Andrássys; a former cavalry officer who had travelled much and lived abroad, he was an ardent Freemason and a passionate bibliophile who established the once-famous Betliar library, initially in a rotunda in the park specially designed for the purpose. He cohabited with an aristocratic mistress who produced five daughters, all of whom were married off with generous dowries. Fascinated by dwarfs, he kept a colony of them, erecting houses of suitable sizes for them in the park—all, alas, have vanished. A theatre was also maintained, and on Sundays the castle park was thrown open for the enjoyment of the local populace. Yet perhaps Leopold's greatest contribution grew from his interest in mining. Under his stewardship the family's hitherto rather poorly-run mines were developed by a team of experts into a highly profitable operation, the precursor of the Andrássys' great foundries and steelworks.

Leopold's eldest brother and nephews, who lived at Krásná Hŏrka, proved less talented, and progressively the house was abandoned during the early nineteenth century. In 1817 the upper castle was struck by lightning and burned to the bare walls; only the brave efforts of the resident staff

*Portrait of Count György Andrássy as a young
man in uniform, early nineteenth century.*

The mausoleum at Krásná Hőrka.

Lion handle on the mausoleum door at Krásná Hőrka.

Dome of the mausoleum at Krásná Hőrka with mosaic by Franz Tholl depicting the twelve saints bearing devices.

prevented the entire complex from being destroyed in the conflagration. At a family council the Betliar branch of the Andrássys declined to take on the expense of restoration, so for the next hundred years the estate became the property of more enterprising cousins. The first of them to live at Krásná Hőrka was György Andrássy, an austere, hard-working figure who inherited a large fortune from his Festetics mother. He established a family museum in the castle in 1857 and subsequently opened it to the public. An assiduous observer named John Paget noted in his *Travels in Hungary and Transylvania* (1839), "We passed an old fort belonging to Count Andrássy. Although the fort is somewhat spoiled by new repairs, the village under it is so clean, its houses so pretty, and its people so happy that the man responsible for it can surely say with pride this happiness is my work. And that sums up well enough the Andrássy family's attitude to their retainers."

Further trouble, however, soon struck the family. While working at the foreign ministry in Vienna, György's son Denes met and fell in love with Franciska Hablawetz, the daughter of a composer and conductor. Despite the family's outraged opposition to what they regarded as a misalliance, they married, but Denes was disinherited by his father and went to live in Munich under the name of Monsieur de Szent-Kiraly. Thanks to his maternal inheritance he remained comfortably off and became a knowledgeable collector of contemporary art. Despite his earlier disinheritance, on his father's death in 1872 he received all the property including Krásná Hőrka; he then resumed his name and title, although he continued to shun all contact with his Andrássy relations. A large proportion of Denes's considerable income was devoted to good works and charity—he even pioneered the establishment of a pension fund for his agricultural employees. Childless when his beloved wife died in 1902, Andrássy had an art-nouveau mausoleum designed for her remains. Created primarily by the German architect Richard Berndl with a team of architects and artists imported from Munich, the resulting structure stands in its own fifteen-

acre garden. The front entrance to the cupola is guarded by life-sized angels and its lantern is supported by eight pillars. Inside the walls are faced with Venetian mosaic and twelve angels fill the spaces between the windows. In 1913 Denes died and he too was interred in the mausoleum, extinguishing his branch of the family.

Meanwhile the Andrássys at Betliar continued to flourish. During the latter half of the nineteenth century the house was owned by Leopold's great-nephew Emanuel, nicknamed Mano, who proceeded to remodel it in a primarily French historicizing style. His architect, a man called Müller, unfortunately did not have a clear view of what was wanted, and the resulting work from 1880–86 produced something far from beautiful in a heterogeneous style resembling a luxurious shooting lodge. The Renaissance hall was replaced by a bigger entrance hall and grand staircase; the library, music, dining, and drawing rooms were all remodeled and filled with a catholic mix of contents. The pictures, mainly by German, Czech, or Hungarian masters, were of high quality overall, as was the library, which had grown to over twenty thousand volumes. Big game trophies covered the walls in accordance with the taste of the age. Luckily the park with its rotunda, grotto, and romantic landscape remained untouched, although some questionable statuary was added and in the garden a terrace bordered by a balustrade was created. Further

The park façade of Betliar.

Portrait of Countess Katěrina Károlyi (née Andrássy) by John Quincy Adams, early twentieth century. (Private collection.)

work on Betliar between 1907 and 1912 led to the portico on the south façade being lowered to first-floor level. All the fronts of the house now had an eclectic, rather ugly appearance.

The senior branch of the Andrássys produced an array of distinguished statesmen. Mano himself was a privy councillor and member of the Academy of Sciences. His younger brother, Gyula—who was proscribed as a rebel and hanged in effigy after taking part in the Revolution of 1848—rose to be Hungary's prime minister and the principal architect of the Compromise of 1867 between his country and Austria, which established the Dual Monarchy. He also played an important role in European diplomacy as did his son, another Gyula, who in turn became imperial foreign minister. Mano's own son and then his grandson succeeded him at Betliar and at Krásná Hŏrka, the latter of which had reverted to them on Denes's death in 1913. Conditions became more difficult, however, when Slovakia was partitioned from Hungary and assigned to the new Czechoslovakian state in 1919. Although some of their property was taken by land reform, the Andrássys nevertheless managed to hang on to much of their land and industrial enterprises, as well as estates within the new borders of Hungary and property in Budapest. World War II and the ensuing Communist revolution changed all that; the family lost everything in both countries and was forced into exile in the West.

Both Betliar and Krásná Hŏrka survive today in good conditions as museums. They have undergone many vicissitudes of fortune, and their connection with the family that owned them for over three centuries has been severed. However on both architectural and historical grounds both rank among the finest monuments of this remote and beautiful region of Slovakia.

ČESKÝ ŠTERNBERK

Distant view of the castle of Český Šternberk, southeast of Prague.

Central tower of the castle.

S pectacularly perched on a rocky ridge some fifty miles southeast of Prague stands the castle of Český Šternberk, seat of "the heroes with the stars," as the family was once called. Today this area of central Bohemia is a pastoral landscape of steep, thickly wooded valleys and rolling meadows. Indeed during the Middle Ages it was covered by impenetrably thick forests, and human settlements resembled islands in a sea of green, penetrated only by a few ancient trade routes. In such romantic surroundings the history of one of the greatest Czech medieval fortresses has unfolded.

The site of Český Šternberk above the valley of the Sázava River had always been of strategic importance, in earlier centuries guarded by two fortified encampments belonging to the Zlíčané and to the Doudleby tribes. In the mid-eleventh century a Benedictine monastery was founded nearby, although all traces of its buildings have long since disappeared. The discovery of new silver deposits during the twelfth century brought an influx of miners, and small villages grew up. One of the larger local landowners was the Divisovici family, descendants of a man named Diviš who was mentioned in 1130 as an adviser and friend of the king's. (The suffix "ovici" referred to the settlement of Divisov, which they had founded further along the Sázava.)

In 1242 Zdislav, the great-great grandson of Diviš, began to build a castle above the river. That same year he seems to have adopted the name Šternberg in accordance with the heraldic symbol on his coat of arms, an eight-pointed gold star (*stern* in German) on a blue field. Zdislav was a confidante of the last Přemyslid king, Otakar II, who appointed him high steward for defending the city of Olomouc against the Hungarians in 1253. Further military exploits brought him extensive lands in Moravia, where he proceeded to build another castle known as Moravský Šternberk. The branch of his family who inherited this property were to survive for another three centuries, while the castle itself eventually fell into the hands of the Liechtensteins, where it remained until 1945. For his part, Zdislav continued to enjoy a distinguished career until he died alongside the king fighting the Austrians on the Marchfeld in 1278.

The castle above the Sázava River was one of a number of fortresses built throughout the land in the wake of the Tatar invasion of 1241 to protect against future such attacks. Built on a narrow promontory where the Blanice Stream joins the main river, its foundations lay on a high pointed ridge, which gradually changed into an elongated hillside. Each flank was guarded by a formidable tower, the northern and southern of which rose above deep moats. Along the eastern side were situated the living quarters and a chapel, matched on the west only by a containing wall connecting the towers. Bearing contemporary siegecraft in mind and recognizing that the only possible position for catapults was above the Blanice Stream, the builders constructed an edge wall capable of deflecting the trajectory of

Old view of Český Šternberk, eighteenth century.
(Austrian National Library, Vienna.)

The Šternberg family emblem, the gold star.

The castle chapel.

any missile fired from that direction. An archers' gallery enabling the defenders to shoot from various angles was added to the western containing wall, which was also equipped with timbered stairs and passages, while turrets facilitated cross fire.

Rising so steeply from the river, the eastern side of the fortress was virtually unassailable. To the north a three-story prism-shaped tower was added low and directly above the river as an external bastion connected to the castle by a high rampart. The original entrance was probably at this end, the difference in height between the outer bailey and the main courtyard solved by stairs or a driveway guarded by a drawbridge and postern gate. The southern and weakest flank was protected by fortified masonry, bits of which can still be seen embedded in the outer walls; otherwise nearly all traces of the thirteenth-century castle's internal buildings and residential quarters have been obliterated. Below the complex lay the town, which, following ancient Czech custom, bore the name of the family that founded it. While many family names during this period, and thus town names, were of Germanic origins, the consistent use of Slavic Christian names by family members shows that they had no connection with similarly named families in Germany.

In 1315 the Šternbergs inherited the nearby estate of Konopiště from their cousins, the lords of Benešov. The castle there was of the French type, in contrast to Český Šternberk, which was based on German models. The family's central Bohemian domain was thus extensive and influential, so it was hardly surprising that King Charles IV, wary of over-mighty subjects, divided it into two parts in 1377 and declared one half a direct fief of the crown. For over a century Český Šternberk remained unaltered, although in 1420 its very existence was imperiled. Peter Šternberg, then-owner of the castle, a strong Catholic, and an outspoken opponent of the Hussites, was killed that year together with three of his close cousins, all of whom had remained faithful to the Emperor Sigismund, in the last of several battles he fought against the Hussites. Only his widow Perchta's declaration that she, her two sons, and all her vassals would recognize the four Prague Articles averted the confiscation of all the family's estates by the victorious Hussites.

A cousin named Aleš Holický Šternberg was made guardian of Peter Šternberg's young sons, and when they came of age the family estates

were divided between them, one receiving Český Šternberk, the other Konopiště. When the elder died unmarried at an early age, he left the castle in gratitude to his guardian. The younger, Zdeněk, became a close friend and adviser of King Jiří z Poděbrad, and by the 1460s had in his turn become the guardian to Aleš Holický's orphaned grandson, Peter. Unfortunately he chose to break with the king. In company with other disaffected nobles they united in the League of Grünberg and rose in open rebellion in 1466. Since his men were occupying Český Šternberk along with his other residences, the castle was besieged by royal troops. Suffering from a lack of water and under intensive bombardment, they rapidly surrendered and the soldiers proceeded to destroy the fortifications. With its youthful owner in hiding in Moravia, the royal commander, Burian Trčka z Lípa, was given the property.

Thirteen years later, however, in 1479, the estates were restored to the family. That year Peter Holický married Kateřina z Rožmberk, a member of a powerful South Bohemian dynasty. In favor with the Jagellon kings, he was appointed grand justiciar and chamberlain, and was one of the main authors of the new constitution, designed to curb Czech aspirations for social change. Not surprisingly he wished to restore his ruined castle, so large-scale work began at Česky Šternberk. Two new bastions were built, nicknamed the "Hunger" and "Post" towers. One, a freestanding oval some two hundred yards from the main fortifications, was protected by a deep moat and its own bulwarks. A bottle-shaped vault designed as a storeroom occupied its ground story and was accessible through an aperture in the central chamber's floor, thus enabling the tower's garrison to

The Yellow Salon, with portrait of Frantiska Šternberg by George Romney, mid- to late eighteenth century.

Portrait of Adam Vratislav Šternberg, late seventeenth century.

Watercolor of Český Šternberk, c. 1800.

hold out independently for some days. The new main entrance was now reached from the less steep western side via a path guarded by two gates and connected by a wall, while the upper entrance was protected by a semicircular bastion that led up a roofed-in staircase to the main doors. Light guns were placed to cover the fortifications and the main walls were topped by battlements as well as pierced by loopholes.

Although the thirteenth-century living quarters had sufficed for their age, in the more civilized Jagellon era more was required. Because of the castle's layout on steep slopes, further structures could only be added between the existing ones. So the courtyard shrank to a small court surrounded by new rooms, while the balcony above it was suspended on stone consoles. A residential building replaced the west wall and other structures were erected on the promontory's northern and southern ends. The present kitchen with its Gothic window and stone benches dates from this era; other details such as door jambs and portals have also survived. A few Renaissance elements from later centuries can be found too: an oriel on the west front, an Italianate chimney in the northeastern corner, and the remnants of sgraffiti in the lower courtyard.

Český Šternberk's extensive reconstruction during the late fifteenth and early sixteenth centuries marked the last important chapter in its architectural history. By then the structure we see now was substantially put in place, although many of the turrets, gables, and little roofs so characteristic of the Gothic silhouette have since disappeared. Until his death in 1514 Peter Holický carried on work, which was continued by his son Jan for the ensuing three decades. Extensive debts were incurred in the process yet Jan left behind an even stronger estate, which now included a brewery, two mills, three farms, two small towns, and all or part of eighteen villages. Lucrative bridge tolls from the roads across the Sázava River also helped fund the estate as did a number of fish ponds, a feature of many Bohemian properties.

68

When Jan Holický died in 1548, the family's assets were divided once more and Václav Holický, one of his sons, inherited Český Šternberk. A typical product of Renaissance taste, having made a lengthy tour of Italy, he found the castle's lack of spacious arcaded courtyards and lofty halls a drawback, so he left it to house the estate offices with a handful of guards and resided mainly in Prague. The Šternbergs were firmly established among the principal Czech aristocratic houses by this time. One cousin, Adam, became the high constable of Bohemia at the age of only 37. An oustandingly good and learned man like his friend Karel Žerotín, he served Emperors Rudolf and Matyáš loyally. At the Prague Defenestration, his dignified bearing and universal popularity ensured that he did not share the fate of Martinic and Slavata, although he warned the rebellious nobles of their folly. The consequent disasters of the Thirty Years' War deeply grieved him and he died a few years later.

Adam Holický's relations were scarcely more fortunate. Český Šternberk, effectively abandoned by its owners, fell easy prey to the peasant uprising of 1627 and was thoroughly plundered. Government troops soon regained control, and the castle was turned into a military stronghold with a permanent garrison. Indeed it was the only fortress in Imperialist hands between Prague and České Budějovice to defy the victorious Swedes as they laid siege to the capital in 1648. Decades of warfare were to take a dreadful toll. In the 1650s it was recorded that four townships and thirty villages in the area only counted 342 families between them; 51 deserted farmsteads and 322 deserted cottages stood on the estate. As in much of Bohemia, only one-fifth of the prewar population remained. One anonymous local chronicler wrote, "In those years they found sustenance from sundry herbs and foliage, dying in numbers . . . others roamed the country begging for a piece of bread, having not even a miserable rag to cover their nakedness with, wandering about with their unclad womenfolk and children, causing grief to the onlooker's heart."

Václav Jiří Holický, who had inherited Český Šternberk as a minor forty years before, was nevertheless determined to restore it again. Created a count, he enjoyed a favorable position at court and filled several lucrative offices. To begin his work on the castle he employed a Milanese

stuccodor named Carlo Brentano to refashion the interiors. A wide stair-case was built giving access to the second floor of the west wing, where Václav Jiří combined a number of old rooms into the Knights' Hall with a chapel to Saint Sebastian situated on an extended axis. The plasterwork here and in the adjoining Yellow Chamber and boudoir still preserves Brentano's decoration. All is notably plastic in conception: the white stucco work stands out in relief against a colored background while scrolls, fruit baskets, festoons of leaves, tendrils, and flowers jostle with figures of putti and caryatids. In the Knights' Hall a broad band of stucco deco-ration forms a festive wreath below the cornice, and white-framed car-touches carry painted coats of arms. Every element was intended to stress the past glory of the Šternbergs, a theme on which the highly intelligent Václav Jiří, a shrewd man of business who had made an advantageous mar-riage, was very keen. Externally the towers were demolished but there was no attempt made to rebuild the whole edifice in baroque style, thanks perhaps to its owner's historicizing tastes.

For all his family piety and love of splendour, Václav Jiří's line was not destined to last much longer. At his death he left only one son who in turn died in 1712 leaving one daughter, Anna Maria Amabilia. The Ho-lický branch was now extinct but the Šternberg name was carried on by their cousins. One of them, Adolf Vratislav, became a confidante of Em-peror Leopold I, who repeatedly sent him on diplomatic missions and made him both a count and high constable of Bohemia. The builder of town palaces in Prague and Vienna, Adolf Vratislav bought the eastern Bohemian estate of Častalovice in 1694; his descendants would one day repurchase Český Šternberk.

Anna Maria Amabilia and her husband, Count Johann Maximilian von Götzen, now took over the estate and continued to embellish their resi-dence, constructing a "new castle," as it was called, against the wall of the lower courtyard to provide extra rooms for staff. A broad terrace was built covering the debris of the medieval fortifications and on the far side of the river a garden was laid out complete with an elaborate summer house. The castle then passed to the von Götzens' only daughter, who married Franz Anton von Roggendorf, but the pair proved so extravagant that the estate was reduced to bankruptcy. In 1753 an inventory of all their prop-erty was drawn up comprising ten farmyards, five sheep pens, fifty-two fish ponds, a brewery, a glassworks, and two distilleries, with forests and agricultural land housing a total population of around three thousand people. Despite enforced economies, Český Šternberk was put up for auction in 1760. The castle was then described as having one large hall, two dining halls, twenty-five chambers, eight smaller rooms and vaults, a kitchen, two cellars, and a drying room for fruit. The "new castle" con-tained seven rooms with a kitchen on the upper floor along with a coach shed and stabling for eight horses on the lower level. The gardens con-tained numerous walnut and trained fruit trees, a summer house, and an orangery.

During the next eight years Český Šternberk passed through several hands. In 1795 it was bought by a newly ennobled lawyer, Ferdinand Hirsch, who began to call himself von Šternfeld after the estate. He did little to change the castle except for constructing a broad driveway with an arched stone bridge spanning the deep moat on the southern side. Hirsch's grandson sold it in 1841 to Zdeněk Šternberg of the Častalovice line, a rich man thanks to the coal mines he possessed near Plzeň. Having thus reestablished his family's ownership, Zdeněk made little effort to move into the largely unfurnished castle, which was therefore spared the neo-medieval alterations inflicted on so many of its peers. Instead he chose to buy and reside at the nearby chateau of Jemniště, an elegant ba-roque edifice with a magnificent chapel, built for the Trautmannsdorf family in the 1720s following František Maximilián Kaňka's designs. Not

Portrait of Count Caspar Maria Šternberg by F. Hirschmann, early nineteenth century.

Entrance front of the Šternbergs' chateau of Jemniště.

Portraits of three of the Šternbergs, from left to right: Philipp, Georg, and the young Zdenko, early twentieth century. (Count Zdenko Šternberg.)

until early in the twentieth century was much done to the castle beyond strengthening the foundations, refurbishing the facade of the eastern wing, and renovating some of the baroque state rooms.

When Zdeněk's nephew Jiří, or George, succeeded to Český Šternberk in 1907 he decided to turn it back into a habitable home. The round tower on the upper level was converted into a chapel dedicated to Saint George and an early Gothic tympanum depicting the Madonna amid branches was placed above its Gothic revival portal. Having installed water mains and electric wiring, George moved into the castle after his marriage in 1922, selling the Vienna town palace and using Jemniště only occasionally. Furniture and pictures once more filled the rooms: two interesting collections were installed, one relating to the family's history and the other to the Thirty Years' War, the latter including some 400 prints and drawings. Before the land reforms of the 1920s the estate was still large with over seven thousand acres and as much again near Plzeň. Family members, including no less than nine children, felt themselves truly Czech and enjoyed reasonably good relations with the Masaryk government. Therefore when the Nazis occupied Czechoslovakia, Český Šternberk was soon requisitioned and the family was left to live in just a few of the rooms. Although the property was restored to the Šternbergs after 1945, the Beneš government had nationalized the coal mines, the chief source of their wealth. A few months after the Communist takeover in 1948, total expropriation followed. Old Count George gallantly stayed on in the castle as the state curator, conducting tourists around his former home until shortly before his death in the mid-1960s. Despite the change in their circumstances, many of his children elected to remain in their native land, demonstrating the strength of the Šternbergs' Czech roots.

In the seven-and-a-half centuries of its existence, Český Šternberk has stood as one of the grandest and most important of all Bohemian castles, while the family who has owned it for most of that time has produced a succession of warriors, statesmen, and diplomats.

FRÝDLANT

The great border fortress of Frýdlant lies in the far north of the Czech Republic, near modern Poland and Germany and adjacent to the historic frontiers of Bohemia, which have scarcely altered for many centuries. The castle lies in a pretty rolling landscape with extensive views and the Giant Mountains (the Krkonose, in Czech) forming a dramatic backdrop to the east. Frýdlant is "simultaneously fortified by nature and by art," observed the seventeenth-century Jesuit historian Bohuslav Balbín. Like any border castle, however, it has seen its share of struggle and conflict. Yet while during the seven centuries of its existence the castle has had many different owners, it has continued to play a part in the history of its native land.

Frýdlant's origins are lost, but legend tells of its foundation on a high basalt rock early in the twelfth century by a knight from the powerful Czech clan of Ronovici, ancestors of the illustrious Berka z Dube family. It may have been built as part of a countrywide chain of fortresses in the wake of the Tatar invasion of 1241; what is clearly recorded, however, is that in 1278 Přemysl Otakar II sold it to a Saxon nobleman named Rulko or Rudolf von Biberstein and his heirs in perpetuity for the sum of 800 silver marks. Rulko's descendents were to continue to live there until the mid-sixteenth century. A vigorous and powerful family consistently loyal to both church and crown, they fought on the side of Emperor Sigismund against the Hussites, who burned down the nearby towns of Liberec and Frýdlant but never managed to capture the castle of Frýdlant. They also took part in the Catholic League of Grünberg's revolt against King Jiří z Poděbrad from 1467 to 1469. After the last male Biberstein heir, Kryštof, died there unmarried in 1551, the property reverted to the crown.

Little remains of the original castle except for its principle feature, the huge, round Indica Tower. This structure is fifty yards high and over ten yards in diameter with seventeen-foot-thick lower walls. Presumably once castellated, the tower still displays a dome-shaped roof and two lantern-shaped turrets. With no stairs between floors and the two large vaulted spaces at ground level designed to serve as prisons or storerooms, the main entrance was located on the second floor. Another tower located in the northeastern corner of the castle complex is separated from the main edifice by a basalt outcrop picturesquely if not obscurely named the Devil's Music Box. The entrance gate is located on the south front and between it and the irregular ellipse of the walls a narrow courtyard stood.

The residential buildings at Frýdlant were sited between the main tower and the northwestern curve of the castle walls. The original small oblong block was extended with a similar structure in the fifteenth century; the cellars of both with their barrel vaulting survive, although the upper floors were swept away during the Renaissance alterations. More fortifications were added at the time of the Hussite Wars, including a rectangular tower on the south front surrounded by a freestanding circular stone wall as well as by reinforced semicircular bastions that acted as gun emplacements. During Křystof von Biberstein's lifetime, another two-story building was constructed in Renaissance style across the southern end of the

Distant view of the castle of Frýdlant, northern Bohemia.

outer bailey. In the year of his death he had two tablets with a Latin inscription put up to record this: *"Magnificus et generosus Dominus Christophorus Baro de Biberstein Dominus Soraviae, Friedlandiae, Boskoviae, Fieri Jussit Anno 1551"* ("The magnificent and generous Christopher, Baron of Biberstein, Lord of Frýdlant . . . was proud to commission this in the year 1551").

Short of money as usual, Emperor Ferdinand I soon sold the property to a suitable purchaser, Friedrich von Redern, president of the Silesian estates. Although his family was to own Frýdlant for less than seventy years, it was to have a major influence on its architectural evolution. The greatest impact was at the hands of Melchior von Redern, a general in the imperial service who distinguished himself in the Turkish wars and in 1582 had married Kateřina, Countess Schlick, a lady of taste and energy. When they succeeded, a period of intense building activity commenced. Several towns on the estate were largely reconstructed and a chapel was added to the Frýdlant parish church containing a magnificent marble epitaph commemorating the von Rederns, the work of the Dutch sculptor Christoph Gerhard Heinrich of Amsterdam.

The castle itself, ill-suited to the luxurious tastes of the Renaissance nobility, was extensively rebuilt. The main fortifications were destroyed to make way for a more spacious upper castle on the crown of the hill, which followed the line of the outer walls and at one point even exceeded it. Four gables designed in the Silesian style decorated the roof, while the Indica Tower was covered by an Italianate helmet containing three galleries, the appearance it has retained to this day. A splendid new chapel was constructed opposite the entrance to the upper castle and connected to it by a covered viaduct-like passage. Here there was an upper bailey connected to its lower counterpart by a steep track, while steps led through

Corner view of the castle of Frýdlant.

Old view of the town of Frýdlant with the castle above on the hill. (Austrian National Library, Vienna.)

a gate to the upper castle, which surrounded the narrow, high, and irregularly-shaped courtyard. The new lower chateau was enlarged, its lower rooms being used for stables and administrative offices and the upper ones housing an oratory. The facades were adorned with oeils de boeuf windows and covered with magnificent black and white figurative as well as botanical sgraffiti, only discovered during recent restoration. The chateau had a ridge roof with a broken Renaissance gable over the entrance portal and four more gables with elaborate finials. From the lower bailey a long sloping corridor descended through the gate of the former entrance tower of the whole complex to the main entrance.

Melchior von Redern died in 1600 in the midst of all this work, but the project continued under his indefatigable widow, who survived him by another eleven years. Their principal architect had been the Italian Marco Spazzio di Lancio, a man of considerable inventiveness. It was he who softened the monotony of the roofline with turrets, gables, and windows; and on the north side of the castle he added a loggia, subsequently destroyed. The interior of his chapel was especially ingenious given the constraints of available space—a short nave and three apses with star vaulting. Here the Lutheran von Rederns worshipped and gained many local converts by their piety, although they were all buried in their grandiose mausoleum in the parish church. Melchior's only son, Christoph, succeeded in 1611 but he was not to enjoy his inheritance for long. Having joined the Czech estates in their anti-Habsburg rebellion, he was forced to flee abroad precipitately after they were crushed at the Battle of the White Mountain. In 1620 he was condemned to death in absentia and his property declared forfeit. Although he lived on for some years and made several ineffective attempts to regain Frýdlant, the von Rederns were destined never to return.

The new owner, who purchased the property from the crown in June 1622, was a man of a very different caliber. Albrecht Eusebius Waldstein ("Wallenstein" to posterity) was then barely forty years old and at the height of his remarkable career as one of the age's most powerful politicians, financiers, and generals. He was born of an old northern Bohemian aristocratic family originally called Markvart, who like so many others had taken their names from their castles built by German mastermasons. Orphaned at an early age, he was raised by his sister, who was married to Karel Žerotín, the Unity leader, and who had him educated as

View of the lower Renaissance chateau.

Detail of the sgraffiti in the chapel courtyard.

Portrait of Albrecht Eusebius Waldstein by Christian Kaulfersch, early seventeenth century.

a Protestant. Nonetheless Waldstein converted to Catholicism early on, started life as a soldier, and soon married a wealthy widow whose estates he inherited. Having served as Archduke Matyáš's chamberlain and joining the initially neutral Moravian forces, he had openly allied himself with the imperial army, and after the battle of the White Mountain became one of the main figures to benefit from the reestablishment of Habsburg rule. In return for lending the emperor badly needed money he received as collateral the Smiřickýs' estate of Jičín, where he acted as guardian to its owner, his simpleton cousin.

Waldstein had long coveted the Redern estates, so when the opportunity to buy them came up he promptly did so, acquiring the domains of Frýdlant and Liberec for the modest sum of 150,000 gulden (a new coinage derived from a debased version of the mark). Soon afterwards he bought the Smiřický allodial estates for 500,000 gulden, and his aim became to unite the two properties, separated by some thirty miles. A whirligig of purchases, exchanges, and resales ensued, and by 1624 Waldstein had created a domain of over 100 square miles in northern Bohemia, stretching from its frontiers nearly to Prague. He was also remarried, this time to Isabella Harrach, daughter of one of the closest of Ferdinand's advisers and sister to the cardinal archbishop of Prague.

A grateful emperor created Waldstein duke of Frýdlant, and he began the creation of a state within a state. His capital and residence were actually at Jičín, a town that he more than doubled in size. Nonetheless his grandiose plans with a team of Italian architects were never completed; only the palace, Jesuit college, and church on the main square were finished along with the avenue of lime trees running to the Carthusian monastery and the stables with pleasure gardens nearby. Here he maintained a quasi-royal court, keeping sixty pages, fifty gentlemen-at-arms, traveling with a retinue of sixty carriages, and seldom sitting down less than a hundred to meals. Yet as his ever-active brain needed quiet, no noise of wheels was permitted near his quarters and the streets of Jičín were often barred with chains. In Prague he began to build an enormous palace along the lines of the Palazzo Farnese, at the foot of the Hradčany Hill. And his duchy was impeccably administered—"*Bohemia felix,*" according to Habsburg officials, in comparison with the rest of the country, which was "*Bohemia deserta.*" The twenty-four estates were each run by their own bailiff and the duchy had its own independent courts as well as the right to mint money and to mine silver, tin, and copper. While Waldstein could bestow fiefs on friends and relatives, he remained the liege lord. Small wonder that all this produced 700,000 gulden per annum for the almost-autonomous potentate.

Curiously, in the eleven years he possessed it Waldstein only visited Frýdlant castle four times, never for longer than a few days (although he wrote from there to Ferdinand in 1628 about the Danish peace overtures, begging his master "to exclude nothing which might assist the peace and unity of Christendom"). His hectic life at the center of great events left him scant time for repose. Twice appointed imperial generalissimo and twice dismissed, accumulating the duchies of Sagan in Silesia and Mecklenburg in north Germany, the only strategist capable of matching the all-conquering Gustavus Adolphus of Sweden, whom he defeated and killed

Marble statuary of the von Redern family in the parish church by Cristoph Gerhard Heinrich of Amsterdam, late sixteenth century.

at Lützen, he was for the emperor the indispensable but impossibly over-mighty subject. His end was inevitable: hopelessly compromised in visionary conspiracies to refashion the map of Europe, he was murdered by his own treacherous officers in 1634, an event immortalized by Friedrich von Schiller's play, *Wallenstein's Lager (Camp)*. His beloved duchy, which he had protected so long from the horrors of the Thirty Years' War, was rapidly dismembered, the spoils divided with Vienna's blessing among his faithless generals; soon it was reduced to as miserable a state as the rest of the country.

Frýdlant's next proprietor was one of the soldiers of fortune who had risen to fame and riches under Waldstein. Count Matyáš Gallas, born in the northern Italian area of the Trentino, served first in the Bavarian and then in the imperial military. Although he had once been involved in his patron's schemes, he had hastened to abandon Waldstein once his star was waning and had profited greatly from his downfall, buying Frýdlant, Liberec, and the Prague palace for a mere 500,000 devalued gulden. A mediocre commander, Gallas was given early retirement in 1639 but was reinstated and soundly trounced by the Swedes. His dipsomania and increasing corpulence made him the butt of many jokes. As he was dying in 1647 he suffered terrible remorse over his involvement in Waldstein's assassination, publicly burning letters compromising him in the event after the emperor had refused him an audience.

Gallas never actually lived in the Frýdlant castle but left it in the charge of the veteran castellan Heinrich Griessel, who survived from the Redern days. Soon after his death it fell into Swedish hands and was temporarily recaptured, but lost once again. Both sides ransacked the buildings of their medieval and Renaissance contents and in 1646 the Swedes installed a permanent garrison. Its captain, Benjamin Nortmann, embarked on a major refortification, building a massive new wall around the north, east, and west sides plus a barbican protected by five square bastions. In the courtyard he erected a tablet bearing the inscription, "Peace is stronger than war. I follow my preordained destiny." Nevertheless even after the Peace of Westphalia had been signed in 1648, the Swedes took another year to evacuate the castle.

Frýdlant then fell to Matyáš Gallas's son and daughter-in-law, Franz Ferdinand and Johanna Emerentia, who undertook its restoration. A major fire in the 1670s had gutted the interiors and a serious jacquerie on the estate in 1680, led by the blacksmith Ondřej Stelzig, had caused further devastation. The internal redecoration was entrusted to Marcantonio Canevale and the facades were resurfaced where necessary, while a polygonal tower with baroque helmet was added to the front of the new chateau. Unfortunately since the next two Gallas proprietors seldom visited the castle, this good work was followed by sixty years of neglect. Happier times returned only when the widow of the last male Gallas died in 1759 and the castle was left to the nephews she had adopted from the old Austrian family of Clam. The only nephew who survived, Christian Philipp, took over the property in 1770, although after the havoc of the Seven Years' War it was once more dilapidated. A man with a highly developed historical consciousness, he painstakingly restored the chapel and both the lower chateau and the upper castle. The latter was opened to the public in 1801 as a museum mainly dedicated to Waldstein's memory, one of the first in Bohemia. Since Christian Philipp supported the Josephine educational reforms, he also encouraged the industrial development of Liberec's linen and textile manufactories, which brought prosperity back to the area.

The Clam-Gallases' sense of duty persisted. Christian Philipp's son and grandson were art connoisseurs and dedicated preservers of the castle's past. Count Eduard Clam-Gallas with his wife Clothilde, née Dietrichstein, extensively remodeled the new chateau in neo-Renaissance style,

Portrait of Count Matyáš Gallas by Franz Leux, mid-seventeenth century.

The Knights' Hall, decorated with painted plaster coats of arms of the Gallas and Rosenfeldt families, c. 1680.

Portrait of Eduard Clam-Gallas by F. Schrotzberg, 1852.

helped by the Viennese architect Wilhelm Heckel, who also remodeled the adjacent wing erected by Christian Philipp in the eighteenth century. The living quarters now resembled a home as well as the headquarters of a large estate. Here Count Eduard mainly resided until his death in 1891, especially during the winters, after his early retirement from the army. A distinguished military career, mainly in the Italian campaigns, had led to his promotion to cavalry general in the Austrian army, but he had the misfortune to command a corps in the disastrous war against Prussia in 1866; although subsequently exonerated of all blame for the defeat, he preferred to retreat into private life.

The property that his son, Count Franz Clam-Gallas, inherited was indeed a flourishing concern. Each of the four estates—Frýdlant, Liberec, Lemberk, and Grabstejn—had its own castle, although the last three were not principal family residences. At Frýdlant a delightful Biedermeier spa, Lázně Libverda, had been founded near a wooden shooting lodge up in the forest. From there the road led downhill to the village of Hejnice, with its imposing church containing a magnificent Gothic altar and the Clam-Gallases' burial vault. Admittedly not all visitors were impressed by the state of the buildings. In his diary Franz Kafka described Frýdlant in 1911 as having "ivy everywhere; a grand view from a steeply sloping square; one staircase to the ramparts ceases halfway up, the chains of the

The Moorish Room, decorated in the late nineteenth century.

Head forester's livery from the mid-nineteenth century.

Seventieth birthday party of County Franz Clam-Gallas (seated in the middle) with family members including daughter Clothilde, who inherited the estate (second from left at back), 1920s. (Baroness Marie-Sophie Doblhoff.)

drawbridge hang neglected from their hooks."

Before the land reform of the 1920s the family owned some 66,000 acres of forest and over 10,000 acres of farmland, although by the time of the count's death in 1930 this had been reduced to some 27,000 acres. In addition, his possessions included the small spa, two brick foundries, one sawmill, and three breweries, plus his four castles, town palaces in Vienna and Prague, and several apartment houses. All this was divided between his five daughters, for Franz Clam-Gallas, widely respected as a decent and generous man, was the last male representative of his line. His widow continued to live at Frýdlant in considerable style: in the 1930s there were estimated to be four staff members in the museum, five in the stables and garages, half-a-dozen or so in the gardens, and anywhere between twenty and twenty-five inside servants including four in the kitchen and three in the nursery. A retired English governess and an archivist, who with the count's enthusiastic help had sorted out and cataloged the enormous castle archives, completed the ménage. After her mother's death the youngest daughter, Clothilde Clam-Gallas, succeeded to Frýdlant, where she resided unmarried in reduced but quite comfortable circumstances. She was fortunate to have been in Vienna in 1945 when, after the horrors of Nazi occupation, the castle was garrisoned by Russian troops and subsequently expropriated by the Communist government.

Today, perched on its spectacular site, Frýdlant is a much-visited historic landmark kept in excellent condition. It has endured many vicissitudes during its long existence: captured, plundered, burned, yet always eventually restored once more. Although the Gallases and their Clam successors have owned it for the last three centuries and more, its most famous associations will always be with the proprietor who probably spent the least time there—Albrecht Eusebius Waldstein, whose brooding, violent, enigmatic presence seems to hover over the castle. Perhaps it is his restless spirit that makes the castle one of the most romantic if melancholy sites in the Czech Republic.

ČESKÝ KRUMLOV & HLUBOKÁ

Of the many and varied landscapes of the Czech Republic, that of South Bohemia stands out by itself. Divided from neighboring Austria and Bavaria by the Bohemian Forest, it is surrounded and traversed by steep hills and thick woodland. Rivers, the Vltava in particular, meander along its narrow valleys and through its gorges, affording magnificent sites for the region's numerous ruined castles. In comparison with the fertile farmland further north, South Bohemia seems sparsely cultivated. In fact, the wealth of the countryside lies more in its abundant water, for in many places this is a fen landscape. This shut-in region, half-hidden by steep hills, was a virtually independent realm in the Middle Ages, the property of the richest of all the Czech noble families.

This is the land of the Rožmberk lords, whose device was the five-petalled wild rose on a silver ground. A branch of the mighty Vítkovici clan who dominated South Bohemia, they claimed descent from the semi-legendary Vítek (or Witiko), who had helped King Vladislav II win his throne in the twelfth century and had accordingly been rewarded with large estates. One of his descendents, Vok, the trusted councillor of Přemysl Otokar II and a military hero, founded the castle of Rožmberk around 1250 and brought Cistercian monks from Wilhering on the Danube to the monastery he founded nearby at Vyšší Brod. At about the same time his cousin Vítkovec Záviš built a small fortress further up the Vltava, but his line died out by 1302. Thus Záviš z Rožmberk of the line of the red rose became an enormous landowner when he inherited this with many other properties. Married to Kunigunde, the widow of Přemysl Otokar II, Záviš was an ambitious subject who dreamed of reestablishing the Bohemian empire—news that was most unwelcome to his rival, Rudolf of Habsburg. The latter so skillfully blackened Záviš's name with Václav II that the young king arrested his stepfather, confiscated his property, and had him publicly executed in front of his horrified relatives on the meadow next to Záviš's castle of Hluboká. Zàviš, nicknamed "Falkenstein" ("Falcon Stone"), had been the most brilliant scion of his family but fortunately his brother Vítek rose to the occasion and succeeded in getting the decree of confiscation largely revoked.

Throughout the Middle Ages the Rožmberks continued to flourish. Oldřich z Rožmberk was the pillar of the party supporting Emperor Sigismund and implacably opposed the Hussites. So powerful was he that he managed to exclude their forces from South Bohemia, which remained loyal to the Catholic Church and the Empire. His daughter Perchta, unhappily married and rejected by her father, was the famous beauty whose

View of Český Krumlov, southern Bohemia.

82

ghost "The White Lady," reputedly haunted the Rožmberk castles. Her apparition was supposed to presage great events—for happy ones like a birth or wedding she wore white gloves but for illness, death, or strife she wore black.

Krumlov, as the small fortress on the Vltava was called, had long since become the family's main seat. After the Rožmberks had inherited it in 1302 they enlarged the turret into a mighty tower around which a nucleus of residential quarters grew up. In the mid-fourteenth century they constructed the upper castle, which was approached via a drawbridge at the end of a steep path up from the lower castle's broad courtyard. An enormous rectangular stone edifice, eventually over three hundred feet long with two small internal courtyards, it sat on a rocky outcrop the south face of which rises sheer above town and river. The Rožmberks also promoted the growth of what was effectively their own town, located below in a maze of crowded alleys dotted with fine churches and merchants' houses, in direct competition with the nearby royal city of České Budějovice.

During the fifteenth century Oldřich z Rožmberk refurbished parts of Český Krumlov in late Gothic style—especially the Chapel of Saint George, the little sacristy of which received an ingenious rib vault with emblems of the rose on its bosses. He also extended the upper castle with a three-winged building that stretched to the edge of the rock and formed a second courtyard. A more fundamental remodeling was undertaken from 1506 to 1513 under the supervision of the Bavarian court architect Ulrich Pesnitzer, who designed the mullioned, crisply carved windows around the courtyard. For the next several decades work continued intermittently under Antonio the Italian, who laid out a now-vanished Renaissance garden. In 1575, however, Baltasar Maio da Vomio commenced twenty years of improvements including adorning the massive tower of the lower castle with an open-arched gallery, adding a niched clock story, and constructing an elegant dormered lead roof in the shape of a tent rising to an open lantern. In the lower courtyard a three-story structure was added, its foundations sited on the filled-in moat that had formerly separated the upper from the lower castle and its walls painted by Bartoloměj Beránek to simulate masonry. The courtyards in the upper castle were also redecorated in Renaissance taste with frescoes by Gabriel de Blonde depicting the planets, the seven virtues, and scenes from Ovid's *Metamorphoses*. The interiors were treated in the same style although few

Portrait of Petr Vok z Rožmberk as a young man, late sixteenth century.

Old view of Český Krumlov, nineteenth century. (Austrian National Library, Vienna.)

Frescoed courtyard at Český Krumlov by Gabriel de Blonde, early sixteenth century.

have survived (the best example being the suite of Rožmberk rooms with cassette ceilings and de Blonde's Old Testament frescoes).

By now the vitality of the Rožmberks was failing. Although Vilém z Rožmberk was chancellor of Bohemia he preferred the tranquility of country life over the affairs of state and soon retired to his estates. There he commissioned Maio da Vomio to build another pleasure house, Kratochvíle, before dying childless in 1592. Vilém's brother Petr Vok succeeded to all the property and at first proved energetic, beginning an archive, library, and picture gallery at Krumlov. Yet with his health undermined by debauches and dabblings in alchemy, he soon sank into a torpor. Vilém had left behind considerable debts so to clear them his brother sold Krumlov to Emperor Rudolf II in 1601. He then retreated to his home at Třeboň, another ancestral property, where he died in 1611. Since he left no issue the Rožmberks were now extinct, although their memory lingered. Adalbert Stifter, the nineteenth-century Austrian writer, was fascinated by the family and in his last book, *Witiko*, described their rise to power in an era when, for all its instability, the dream of a Bohemian fatherland uniting both Czechs and Germans appeared possible—as was the case in his day too.

Krumlov was given by the emperor to his bastard son Don Julius, who was not destined to keep it for long. His dissipated life and the orgies he held in the castle became so notorious that the town council addressed a

View of the Mantle Bridge at Český Krumlov,
completed in 1764.

The Schwarzenberg coat of arms at Třeboň.

Main facade of the chateau of Třeboň.

protest to the court in 1606. Undeterred, he fathered a child by the
daughter of the town barber and then in a drunken fury pushed her out a
window into the river below. At last the emperor acted; Don Julius was
deprived of his property and died a lunatic one year later. In 1622 the
castle once more became a royal gift, this time to Emperor Ferdinand II's
loyal friend and adviser Johann Ulrich von Eggenberg. The new owner, a
pure Austrian from the Styrian city of Graz, had no Czech affiliations
whatsoever but, keen to become a prince of the Holy Roman Empire, he
persuaded his imperial master to elevate Krumlov to a dukedom. Neither
he nor his son spent much time on their South Bohemian estates, which in
fact constituted a large portion of the former Rožmberk property but
which suffered considerable damage in the Thirty Years' War.

The von Eggenbergs' grandson Johann Christian decided to change
that when, having inherited and married young, he chose to restore and
live at Krumlov. The neglected castle interiors were redecorated in baroque taste during the 1670s, a wooden theatre was specially built, and
the library was given a valuable book collection. The heights of the buildings were unified by either increasing or reducing them as appropriate,
while the medieval corner towers were demolished. The castle garden
were laid out as a formal parterre with statuary, avenues, and terraces by
Giacomo de Maggi, who also designed the garden's Bellaria pavilion from
1706 to 1708, a delightful square building with a mansard roof and a
divided external staircase. Krumlov had again become a home and an aristocratic residence. But Johann Christian, disliking his surviving Eggenberg relations and divining correctly that his own line would soon be
extinct, determined before his death in 1710 to bequeath his Bohemian
estates to his wife's nephew, Adam Franz zu Schwarzenberg. The latter
duly succeeded following his aunt's death after nine years of widowhood.

Descended from the ancient Franconian family of Seinsheim, the
Schwarzenbergs appeared quite late in the history of Krumlov but their

The Chinese room at Český Krumlov, decorated by
František Jakub Prokys, 1755.

Doorknob at Hluboká with the Schwarzenbergs'
heraldic device of a raven pecking out a Turk's eye.

connections with Bohemia were quite old. Their seat was situated near
Nürnberg in northern Bavaria, and since the early fifteenth century they
had served the Habsburgs with distinction, being granted fiefs in Bohemia
in return for their military services in the Hussite wars. One of the numerous soldiers they produced, known as "Türkenadolf," was murdered by
his own mutinous troops in 1598 after defeating the Turks at Raab (Györ
in Hungary)—hence the picturesque heraldic device the family adopted
of a raven pecking out a Turk's eye. Johann Adolf, more of a statesman
than a warrior, had been appointed president of the imperial council in
1670 and simultaneously raised to princely rank. He had already been rewarded with the old Rožmberk estate of Třeboň in 1660. The next year,
nearly sixty years before Český Krumlov fell into the Schwarzenbergs'
possession, he bought the nearby castle of Hluboká from the Maradas,
Spanish followers of the Habsburgs who had acquired it during the Thirty
Years' War.

The history of Hluboká had been somewhat different from Krumlov's.
A long rectangular building dominated by a round tower, it too had been
constructed by the Vitkovicis in the mid-thirteenth century and remained
in the hands of the Rožmberk's until Václav II executed its owner, Záviš z
Rožmberk. While Krumlov was returned to the family, the king kept
Hluboká. Several times it was granted to various noble families, then regained by the crown. In the late fifteenth century the Pernštejns restored
the damaged castle, improved its fortifications, and dug numerous fish
ponds in the locality. Finally in 1561 it had been bought by another
branch of the Rožmberks, the Hradces, who soon commissioned Baltasar
Maio da Vomio to convert it into a Renaissance castle. The buildings were
grouped around two courtyards, a ground plan preserved in its essentials
today. Little more was done by successive owners during the next century
or so until Adam Franz zu Schwarzenberg inherited Hluboká at the age of
only 23 in 1703.

Portrait of Princess Pauline zu Schwarzenberg by
Franz Sales, early nineteenth century.

Portrait of Field Marshal Karl Philipp zu
Schwarzenberg by François Gérard, early
nineteenth century. (Orlik collection.)

The young man was immensely rich, for by inheritance and shrewd
management both his grandfather and his father had turned the Schwarzenberg estates into a major property with land in Austria, Bavaria, and
Bohemia. Almost Adam Franz's first act was to form a guard of grenadiers
at Hluboká consisting of a lieutenant, two corporals, a drummer, and
twenty-four men. He commissioned pictures from the famous animal
painter Johann Georg Hamilton and had the family architect, Pavel Ignác
Bayer, build him a hunting lodge barely a mile from the castle (although
unkind gossip suggested it was really meant for his mistress). Anyway, the
result was a symmetrical baroque chateau completed from 1708 to 1713
with a pleasing facade slightly overornamented by stucco and a magnificent central hall rising through two stories. Bayer also undertook work in
Hluboká itself, transforming many of the interiors and gradually disman-
tling the fortifications. Adam Franz had plenty of other projects as well:
the Fischer von Erlachs, father and son, were commissioned to build him
a town palace in Vienna while outside the city walls he bought a half-
finished design by Luca von Hildebrandt which today is the Schwarzenberg Palace.

Despite so much activity Adam Franz was not to enjoy his aunt's legacy
for very long. In 1732, while shooting with the Emperor Charles VI at
Brandýs, he was struck by a stray bullet of his host's and died the next day.
His son Josef I Adam, a small boy at the time, grew up to succeed his
father in the imperial court post of Master of the Horse and to continue
his enthusiasm for architecture. Now it was Krumlov's turn for attention:
first a riding school was built in the park, then a splendid cascade fountain
with superb statuary. After the Bellaria pavilion was remodeled in rococo
style, an extra story was added by Andreas Hohenberg, a Viennese architect who Italianized his name to Altomonte. He also designed a ballroom
in the upper castle known as the Maškarní Sál, which featured trompe-
l'oeil frescoes on all its walls derived from Venetian Carnival scenes, the
work of the Viennese painter Josef Lederer. Equally charming was a Chinoiserie room decorated by František Jakub Prokyš, containing superb
Chinese porcelain. Saint George's Chapel was also redesigned and given a
rococo interior, all gilt, stucco, and colored marble. Finally, in 1764 a
covered roadway was constructed connecting the upper castle to the garden behind. The Mantle Bridge, as it was known, was lined with statues
and stood between parapets and rows of arches. Resembling a Roman aqueduct, it carried three floors of galleries across the gap in the rocky ridge
to a new stone theatre, perhaps the crowning achievement of all the eighteenth-century improvements. Its blue and gold galleries looked on to a
big stage with twelve full sets of standard scene changes painted by the
theatre designers Johann Wetschel and Leo Merkel, a masterpiece with
few rivals in Europe.

Josef Adam with his beautiful Liechtenstein wife seemed the model of a
grand seigneur and at his request Empress Maria Theresa created an entail
of the family estates, thus assuring his descendants of the title of duke of
Krumlov. Although the prince was much respected personally, some of
his officials were less popular: the bailiff Grandjean was accused in a pam-
phlet entitled "Patriotic Thoughts on the Present State of Schwarzenberg"
of having "an insatiable thirst for money" and of being a man "who does
not possess the least competence, and has neither the birth nor the taste
befitting his position." Josef Adam died in 1782 and his middle-aged son
followed him a mere seven years later, his main achievement having been
to produce thirteen children. Thus came to a close the great age of the
Schwarzenbergs at Krumlov, where family members had escaped as often
as possible from their duties at court. A new age was dawning, one whose
leading figures looked askance at some of the frivolities of the Ancien Régime and aspired to a very different sort of life. Of these new leaders, two
of Josef Adam's thirteen grandchildren, the eldest, Josef II, and his brother

Karl Philipp, were to attain real distinction.

Both young brothers were employed in the imperial service. Josef married the talented and artistic Princess Pauline Arenberg and continued to increase the family estates, buying adjoining land in South Bohemia and near Vienna. Since his troops from the principality of Schwarzenberg fought in the Austrian armies, after Napoleon's victory the property was sequestrated by the French. Despite this Josef was made the Habsburgs' ambassador to Paris in 1810, where he attended the marriage of Archduchess Marie Louise to Napoleon. On July 1 of that year he was giving a dance in the embassy when a fire broke out. Pauline, who ran back to look for her daughter in the burning ballroom, was incinerated, and legend records that the nurse of Pauline's youngest child, who was sleeping back at Krumlov, saw the ghost of the mother appear at the very moment of her death. Fortunately she left behind numerous offspring and her husband survived her by over twenty years.

Josef's younger brother Karl Philipp was also an ambassador to Paris and Saint Petersburg, but he was a brilliant soldier as well who rose to be field marshal and commander-in-chief of the allied armies that crushed Napoleon at the Battle of Leipzig in 1813. Since in gratitude the emperor created him a prince in his own right, henceforward there were two lines of the Schwarzenberg family. Karl Philipp had already inherited a medieval castle located north along the Vltava called Orlik, which had come as part of the Eggenberg legacy. This he was to refurbish after the interiors were destroyed by a fire in 1802. His heirs then reconstructed the castle in the fashionable Gothic revival style in the 1850s and held the property until it was expropriated by the Communists in 1948. The Orlik line, whose land lay entirely in Czech-speaking areas, came gradually to regard themselves as more Czech than their cousins, although distinguished public servants were still to come from both branches.

Josef's three sons were all to distinguish themselves in very different ways. The remarkable Felix was a diplomat, soldier, and statesman, the celebrated lover of Lady Jane Digby while posted in London. In the after-

Portrait of Johann Adolf zu Schwarzenberg by J. K. Stieler.

Old view of Hluboká surrounded by images of other Schwarzenberg properties, 1854. (Austrian National Library, Vienna.)

View of Hluboká from the park.

*House party in the courtyard at Hluboká,
late nineteenth century.
(Austrian National Library, Vienna.)*

*Wooden stags' heads on the walls of the courtyard
at Hluboká.*

*Entrance porch on the southwest facade
of Hluboká.*

math of the Revolution of 1848 Emperor Francis Joseph I appointed him chief minister and he quickly succeeded in reestablishing Habsburg authority. Yet he was not a well man. Nearly blind and suffering from typhoid, he succumbed at an early age in 1852. The family's youngest brother, Friedrich, went into the church, becoming a cardinal at 33, the archbishop of Prague at only 40, and living on to a ripe old age as a respected Catholic elder statesman, at once scholarly, spiritual, and worldly. The eldest brother, Johann Adolf II, on the other hand, was a shrewd businessman and a good agronomist but personally bucolic and unexciting. Indeed his clever, vivacious, and witty wife, Eleonore, née Liechtenstein and nicknamed "Go," cruelly remarked, "*Cardinal, général, mais moi, je suis mariée à l'animal.*"

The epithet was hardly just and Johann Adolf was certainly an indulgent husband. Supported by his extraordinary holdings, he was perfectly happy to allow "Go" to rebuild Hluboká along the romantic lines she envisaged from her travels in Scotland and her reading of Sir Walter Scott. Beginning in 1841 and for three decades the castle was transformed into a style loosely described as "English Tudor Gothic" under the supervision of the prolific architect Franz Beer. The new Hluboká has been called a pastiche of Windsor Castle, and although elements of the earlier buildings were retained, certainly the vast, white, turreted, castellated, and machicolated edifice is not to everyone's tastes. The illusion of a medieval knight's abode was created with wooden floors, stained glass, and wall hangings, all supposedly of the period, although the rows of wooden stags' heads around the courtyard were all too typical of high Victorian taste. More incongruous still was the huge cast-iron and glass winter garden constructed to the left of the main entrance. A menagerie was founded and a succession of expert head gardeners changed the grounds into a romantic mid-nineteenth-century landscape. A certain amount of work along the same lines was undertaken at Krumlov but by degrees the Schwarzenbergs ceased to live in it, preferring the romantic historicism of

93

Library at Hluboká.

*Birthday party at Hluboká for Prince Adolf zu
Schwarzenberg, c. 1930.
(Prince Karl zu Schwarzenberg.)*

Hluboká, to which the best furniture, pictures, and tapestries were transferred.

Succeeding generations eschewed politics, concentrating on the good management of their estates. Before the emancipation of the peasants in the 1840s, Johann Adolf's vast estates had totaled over 1,500,000 acres (around 2,400 square miles) and 230,000 people had lived on his lands. Even after emancipation, when the state bought the land peasants had cultivated and endowed them with it, he was left with 440,000 acres and the compensation paid by the government. In later years a canal was dug to enable the family to ship their timber north or south of the nearby watershed. Breweries, stone quarries, brick kilns, and malthouses, as well as farms and forestry, kept some 35,000 men employed in the late nineteenth century. Prince Johannes zu Schwarzenberg took the breakup of the Habsburg Empire badly, and during the land reform of the 1920s the Czech government reduced his estates to 135,000 acres. Minor properties were sold off but the core of the inheritance—Krumlov, Hluboká, and Třeboň—remained intact. The prince's death in 1938 occasioned a grand funeral where all the insignia of the duke of Krumlov were displayed and the Schwarzenberg grenadier guard made its last appearance. In World War II, the Germans requisitioned both castles but after their defeat the then-owner, Adolf zu Schwarzenberg, did not return. The state then confiscated his property, passing a special law for this purpose. Yet since the family still possessed lands in Germany and Austria as well as the town palace in Vienna they remained far from destitute.

Any visitor to the Czech Republic today will find Hluboká and Krumlov two of the most impressive though not perhaps the most beautiful of the country's castles. Sadly the Maškarní Sál ballroom and the theatre at the latter seem to be under indefinite reconstruction and a hideous revolving concrete stage has been built in the garden. The feeling that these estates form the legacy of one of Bohemia's greatest families persists nonetheless. As the early-twentieth-century author Karel Čapek wrote in Obrázky z domova (Pictures from Home), "I don't know how often the Vltava twists at Krumlov . . . cross it and wonder each time how golden-brown and fast it flows . . . you can see nothing but the picturesque, the venerable and historic glory. The castle dominates it all, especially the tower . . . such a tower of towers I have never seen."

OPOČNO & DOBŘÍŠ

East of Prague the fertile central Bohemian plain stretches for some eighty miles past the city of Hradec Králové, until the ground begins to rise into rolling hills, which in turn merge into the chains of mountains flanking the border with Polish Silesia. This has always been a prosperous countryside, the heart of old Czech-speaking Bohemia, and it is scattered with fine houses. Just where the hills begin there is a clutch of them: Ratibořice, Nové Město nad Metují, Častalovice, Rychnov nad Kněžnou, and Opočno. Both internally and externally the latter is as impressive as any. Its tall three-sided courtyard stands in a peerless position on a bluff, facing out over the deep valley of the Zlaty Potok or Golden Brook toward the little town of Opočno and the Orlické Hory or Eagle Mountains beyond.

The settlement at Opočno originated along a medieval trade route leading from Bohemia into Silesia and on to Poland; its name derives from a calcareous marlstone called opuka, which can be found in the region. The existence of a border stronghold there is mentioned by a chronicler as early as 1068. During the fifteenth-century Hussite Wars its owner, Jan Méstecký, first sided with the rebels, then fiercely opposed them. In 1425 the castle was destroyed in the ensuing fighting and all that remains of it today is the vestigial east bastion on the front overlooking the park. In 1495 the ruined fortress and estate were bought by the Trčka z Lípas, a Bohemian knightly family. Especially exploiting their fishpond, a sure source of profit at the time, the Trčkas rapidly rose from their modest origins until they ranked among the country's richest nobles.

Not until midway through the next century did the estate receive much attention from the family. In the 1550s the proprietor, Vilém Trčka z Lípa, travelled to Italy. There he much admired the Renaissance mansions, which stood in marked contrast to the drafty uncomfortable castles of his homeland, and thus encouraged he determined to rebuild Opočno in this style. Vilém engaged Italian craftsmen with an architect whose name has unfortunately gone unrecorded and work lasted from 1560 to 1569. Not surprisingly the result had strong overtones of the architecture of Northern Italy. On a rectangular ground plan a simple symmetrical building was constructed. The chateau's high three-sided courtyard opened out over the valley of the Golden Brook, affording magnificent views of the Eagle Mountains. On each side the courtyard was surrounded by three tiers of arcaded galleries, the lower two of which rose to arched vaults. The top was capped with a flat ceiling and crowned by an architrave directly under the sloping tiled roof. The courtyard was originally closed by a low galleried wing on its fourth side, but in 1820 this was demolished and replaced by a balustrade with steps leading down to the terraced garden. A moat with a drawbridge and outer bailey protected the entrance but the open space in front of it gradually filled up with farm

View from across the park of Opočno, eastern Bohemia.

96

buildings, stables, and domestic offices—even with a mint for a brief spell, and in the eighteenth century the moat was filled in.

The uniformity of the stonework around doors and windows emphasized a purity of style that stood in marked contrast to the interior, where suites of richly decorated rooms led off one another or the galleries. Virtually nothing of the interiors from the Trčkas' period has survived—the Italianate lunette vaults have been preserved in the ground-floor hall but the Renaissance sgraffiti that covered the external wall surfaces have vanished under the colored baroque facades. A hall church, one end of which was attached to the chateau, was built with a grandiose family vault, and in 1602 a games hall and a summer pavilion were added to the castle.

Vilém's successor Jan Rudolf Trčka z Lípa was one of the richest men in Bohemia by the early seventeenth century. His estates were efficiently exploited and after the Battle of the White Mountain his wife, Maria Magdalena, increased their fortune by busily buying and selling property confiscated by the crown. She was an exacting taskmaster, which, together with the unpopular re-Catholicization of the countryside, caused a serious peasant uprising in 1628 in the area around Opočno. Disorder spread, and the rebels' advance was only crushed by Albrecht Eusebius Waldstein's troops. A grateful Emperor Ferdinand II ennobled Trčka for his part in restoring order but the family's fall from grace was not long in coming. Feeling excluded from the new Habsburg order, they began to intrigue with Waldstein and others who wanted a greater degree of independence from Vienna. Jan Rudolf's son Adam Erdman Trčka z Lípa became one of Waldstein's most trusted lieutenants and was murdered with his master at Cheb in 1634. Jan Rudolf died just before his estates were confiscated and so escaped the executioner's axe.

Opočno then passed to one of the beneficiaries of the Trčkas' demise, the imperial general Rudolf Colloredo. His family sprang from Friuli, the northeastern area of Italy around Udine, and as a soldier of fortune he had risen high in the Habsburgs' service. Grand prior of the Order of Malta, he was an able if ruthless general who remained at the top of his profession and commanded the imperial armies defending Prague against the Swedes in 1648. However, he seldom visited the chateau before his death in 1657 and scarcely altered its appearance at all.

Change was forced on the Colloredos nevertheless, for a severe fire at the end of the seventeenth century gutted Opočno. Reconstruction in baroque style began in 1709, supervised by the Italian architect Giovanni Battista Alliprandi. The Renaissance gables and the high tower above the central block were removed and blue geometrical panels were installed on the walls facing the outer courtyard. The elegant Tuscan arcades of the inner courtyard were luckily left untouched, but the two end blocks plus the park facades were painted a dull terra-cotta with the baroque fenestration and panels picked out in white. Internally, Alliprandi installed the chapel of Saint Anne in the south wing with a dome depicting a fine Annunciation, and was responsible for the lovely stucco work in the main reception rooms of the north and west wings. In 1716 two towers were added to the west front of the church adjoining the chateau and the church too was redecorated in baroque style. Thereafter little more was done for another hundred years.

In the meantime the Colloredos were significantly increasing their property and had established themselves as an aristocratic dynasty—one cousin, Hieronymus, became prince-archbishop of Salzburg and the young Wolfgang Amadeus Mozart's patron. In 1711 they were made counts of the Holy Roman Empire and in 1763 elevated to the rank of princes. In 1771 Franz Gundakar Colloredo, heir to the property and a career diplomat, married Maria Isabella Mansfeld, the sole heiress to the splendid chateau and estate of Dobříš. From now until the Communists' expropriation, both houses were to be inseparably linked by the ownership of one

family, so to understand subsequent history it is necessary to look at the development of Dobříš as well as Opočno. Situated some way from Opočno in central Bohemia, only about twenty miles south of Prague in a charming valley between the Vltava and Berounka rivers, it had been a royal hunting preserve since the early thirteenth century, although the crown had pawned it repeatedly over the centuries and the small castle on the site had been destroyed several times. Finally in 1630 Emperor Ferdinand II, in chronic need of money, had sold the property outright to one of his counselors, the master of the royal hunt Bruno Mansfeld.

In contrast to the Colloredos, the Mansfelds were a purely German family of Saxon origins. One of their ancestors, Peter Ernst, had been a leading Protestant general in the Thirty Years' War but the remainder were Catholics. Yet imperial favor availed Bruno Mansfeld little in the enjoyment of his new estate. It was incessantly plundered and burned by passing soldiers—Swedish, Bavarian or Habsburg—and he died in 1648 having had no chance to rebuild. His son Franz Maximilian established an ironworks nearby and slowly converted the remains of the Renaissance manor house into a baroque chateau, probably with the help of a provincial architect from Příbram named Aegidius Cesaroni. The elongated new structure had four wings enclosing a courtyard, and a chapel in its southern wing that led out into the conventionally laid out gardens. There a terrace was constructed over the cellars of the estate brewery. Dobříš's main entrance through its northern wing faced the church that Franz Maximilian had built. At his death in 1693 he left an economically viable domain, although a severe plague epidemic, a forest fire of 1720 that sub-

stantially destroyed the chateau, and the premature death of his elder son, which left only a minor as heir, provided serious drawbacks.

When young Heinrich Paul Mansfeld came of age he decided to restore Dobříš further and commissioned the French royal architect and director of the Gobelins tapestry workshop, Jules Robert de Cotte, to draw up plans. The Florentine Giovanni Nicolo Servandoni, a longtime resident of Paris, collaborated by designing the interior decoration. The plans involved replacing the badly damaged western wing with a cour d'honneur. Adding to the transverse eastern wing would establish the house's symmetry, while the northern block would be extended to match its southern counterpart. The elevated pilastered central pavilion would include a *sala terrena* at ground level with a main hall on the second floor. Similar elongated blocks would flank the central pavilion, although monotony would be averted by having three independent mansard roofs. The overall appearance of the exterior was markedly horizontal and the effect sober, the balcony above the *sala terrena* and the pediment in front of an urn-surmounted balustrade being the only ornament.

Because of cost not all of de Cotte's designs were executed, but the western wing was torn down and the discarded materials used to construct the top garden terrace and the orangery. After work commenced in 1745 construction on the house progressed so rapidly that internal decoration started within a year, although thereafter it slowed and wasn't completed until 1765. Some of the internal workmanship was of variable quality, especially the stucco decoration in the main hall. There Jan Peter Molitor

General view of Dobříš.

Portrait of Maria Isabella Mansfeld, early twentieth-century copy of lost eighteenth-century original.

Portrait of Franz I Colloredo, husband of Maria Isabella Mansfeld, in the robes of the Order of the Golden Fleece, early twentieth-century copy of lost eighteenth-century original.

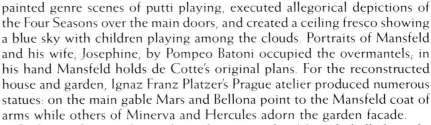

painted genre scenes of putti playing, executed allegorical depictions of the Four Seasons over the main doors, and created a ceiling fresco showing a blue sky with children playing among the clouds. Portraits of Mansfeld and his wife, Josephine, by Pompeo Batoni occupied the overmantels; in his hand Mansfeld holds de Cotte's original plans. For the reconstructed house and garden, Ignaz Franz Platzer's Prague atelier produced numerous statues: on the main gable Mars and Bellona point to the Mansfeld coat of arms while others of Minerva and Hercules adorn the garden facade.

Such was the superb neoclassical mansion that Maria Isabella brought with her to her marriage in 1771. In 1775 her descendants to come, the future proprietors of both Dobříš and Opočno, were permitted to adopt the combined names of Colloredo-Mansfeld. When her father died five years later, her husband, newly retired from his diplomatic career, took over the running of the two estates. From 1792 to 1797, Franz Gundakar employed a local builder, František Moravec, to construct a new chapel on the site of the earlier church following Josef Jöndl's designs. His son Rudolf Josef continued the improvements after he had inherited the properties in 1807. Within a decade he had turned the old pheasantry bordering Dobříš's formal gardens into a landscape park some seventy acres in extent. At Opočno he similarly refashioned the valley of the Golden Brook below the castle into a large garden in the Romantic taste, steeply terraced and falling away to several small lakes he created by damming the stream, with follies behind dotting the opposite slope. A balcony was placed in the middle of the southern wing from which to contemplate these new delights.

Rudolf Josef, who had himself enjoyed an exciting military career in the Napoleonic Wars, maintained close connections with the Viennese court and in 1813 he had his chance to play a part in high politics. That June, Opočno for a week served as the meeting place of the leading statesmen in the allied coalition confronting Napoleon: Austria's Metternich and Gentz, the Prussian chief minister Hardenberg, Nesselrode, who conducted Russian foreign policy, the czar's brother, and Czar Alexander I himself. The result of their deliberations was the declaration of all-out war against France and the resounding allied victory at the Battle of Leipzig that October.

Throughout the nineteenth century the Colloredo-Mansfelds made no major alterations to either of their chateaux. In 1876 they bought yet another estate thirty-five miles due west of Prague called Zbirov, formerly the property of the Lobkowicz and then the Kolovrat families. The castle there, large and forbidding, was let for a long period at the turn of the century to the artist Alphonse Mucha. In 1879 the ridge-tile roofs at Dobříš were replaced by slate ones, and some internal redecoration was carried out. Josef Franz, then the proprietor, moved the brewery, mill, and other farm buildings near the chateau's eastern end so that he could enlarge the landscape park. At Opočno a riding school with coach house had been added earlier in the nineteenth century and the summer pavilion refurbished in Empire style.

As the second-largest private landowners in Bohemia, with almost 140,000 acres just before World War I, the family could not, however, refrain from the mania for remodeling houses and gardens current in the early twentieth century. At Dobříš the garden was partially redesigned in 1911 by a Frenchman named Touret. His work modified the unified eighteenth-century conception by reducing its symmetry, removing the central steps between the first and second terraces, and closing the vista through the middle door of the orangery. At Opočno, French craftsmen were at work on the interiors from 1903 to 1912. The result was ostentatious but not particularly attractive, for the plaster work was heavy and much of the period furniture then installed frankly ugly. But the armory installed to display the magnificent family collections of guns and armor

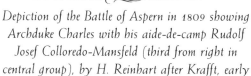

Depiction of the Battle of Aspern in 1809 showing Archduke Charles with his aide-de-camp Rudolf Josef Colloredo-Mansfeld (third from right in central group), by H. Reinhart after Krafft, early nineteenth century.

The armory at Opočno with sixteenth-century Milanese suits of armor.

The ballroom ceiling at Dobříš.

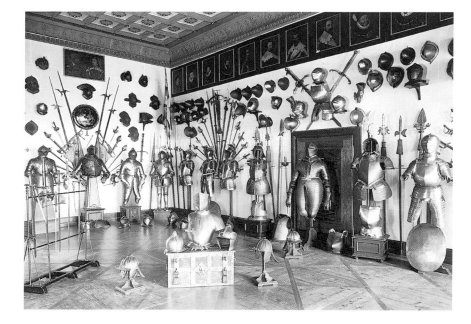

was most impressive. The picture collection, mainly focusing on Italian works from the sixteenth to the eighteenth centuries, was moved from Döbling near Vienna and briefly exhibited in the family's town palace in Prague before being brought to Opočno in 1895. The ethnographic collection amassed by Josef II Colloredo-Mansfeld included big game trophies and important native art, which he brought back from Africa in 1902, along with a variety of Native American exhibits bought on his trips there in 1904–5.

Childless himself, Josef II adopted his nephews as his heirs. Between the wars the family adapted to changed circumstances, all becoming Czech citizens. They also lost three-quarters of their agricultural property and half their forests to land reform. In the winter months they lived at Dobříš, which was easier to heat, and from April to October at Opočno. The latter was also opened to the public three times a week, then quite an unusual occurrence. During World War II the family was expelled from Dobříš, which became the country residence of the German Reichsprotektor. The

house was much changed internally and almost all the contents disappeared. The more fortunate Opočno, where the Colloredo-Mansfelds were allowed to retain a few rooms, remained virtually intact except for a few small items stolen. In 1945, undeterred by questions of legality, the Beneš government took over Dobříš as enemy property and it became the conference center for the Writers' Union, a purpose it still fulfills today. Opočno was seized in the general expropriation of the nobility and the Colloredo-Mansfelds retreated to Austria.

Neither of these splendid houses is among the best-known in the Czech Republic, yet they deserve a wider fame. Dobříš, with its wonderfully proportioned chateau and garden, terraced on five different levels and rising through pond and fountain to the elegant orangery, is still a feast for the eye. And Opočno, which has seen some of the tragedy and drama of Czech history, today stands as a monument to the best of Renaissance taste.

BUCHLOV &
BUCHLOVICE

Westward from Brno toward Slovakia lie a number of the Czech Republic's most interesting places, notably the battlefield of Austerlitz where Napoleon crushed the allied Russian and Austrian armies in 1805 and, a few miles farther on, the splendid Renaissance chateau of Buňovice. Continuing across the gentle hills of the Moravian countryside through the thickly wooded Chřiby Hills, we descend again to the valley of the Morava River with the Slovak frontier beyond. The highest of these hills is nearly 1,600 feet. It and its nearest neighbor are crowned by buildings that are just discernible from the east as a fortress and a small church complex. But there is little apart from its dramatic position to indicate that Buchlov, "the castle of the philanthropists," and its baroque sibling Buchlovice, sited hundreds of feet below on the plain, encapsulate such an interesting cross section of Czech cultural and political history.

No one knows precisely when Buchlov was built, but it was probably during the earlier part of the thirteenth century, since late Romanesque elements may still be found such as the arched portal of the present castle kitchen and the claw shapes in the entrance frame of the main gates. The house was probably constructed as a royal foundation on the orders of Vladislav Jindřich, margrave of Moravia and brother to King Přemysl Otakar I. Under his auspices the neighboring Cistercian monastery of Velehrad was completed, and both structures have features in common. The castle's first mention in official records, however, only comes in 1300 in connection with its administrator, a royal official called Protiva of Buchlov. Indeed it remained in the possession of the crown until the late fifteenth century as an important link in the chain of fortifications designed to prevent invasion from Hungary, which included the new towns of Uherské Hradistě and Uherský Brod.

The offspring of this marriage was a daughter, Kunhuta, who married Bernard Diviš Petrvald. Succeeding to Buchlov on her parents' death, they became the first of four generations of the family who were to live there—almost a record for Buchlov. In 1662 the original castle gate was reopened and the defenses strengthened by a new bastion. Giovanni Pieroni, an engineer in imperial service who was redesigning the fortifications of nearby Uherské Hradistě, may have lent a hand with this project as well as with the arcaded passage connecting it with the northern wing. These functional changes were concluded in 1691 with a covered pathway linking the castle's upper and lower courtyards. The Ptrevalds' main architectural achievement, however, was a baroque chapel and mausoleum, which they built in 1672–73 on a hilltop linked by a promontory to the castle. Consecrated to Saint Barbara (and hence christened "Baborka" in the locality), it was constructed on a stellar groundplan and covered by a cupola carried on a polygonal tambour. The interior especially

View of the gardens of Buchlovice, west of Brno.

suggests the influence of late-Italian mannerism and perhaps of Giovanni Pietro Tencala.

Only a few more improvements were made at Buchlov, although some of the first-floor rooms were to be refurbished in baroque taste by Zikmund Karel Petrvald in 1737. But its owners found what was essentially a medieval castle an increasingly uncomfortable residence. By the turn of the century matters had come to a head. The young Jan Detrich Petrvald had married Agnes Eleonora Colonna-Fels, a still younger wife of Italian extraction who, not unnaturally, complained of the discomforts of Buchlov. To please her, he was to commission one of the jewels of baroque architecture.

A suitable site existed down in the plain below Buchlov to the east of the Chřiby Hills, and here, on the slope of the so-called Mars Hill, the foundations of a new residence were laid during the 1690s. The architect's name is not formally recorded, but most sources have ascribed it to Domenico Martinelli, who was certainly known to have been working nearby in Moravia at about this time. The building must have been largely completed by 1701, for this is the date given for the painting work in the oval hall. The main block of the chateau faces northward down the hill, so that what is the piano nobile from the garden side is on ground level with the cour d'honneur at the front entrance. The concave, pilastered, semicircular facade of Buchlovice, as it was known, boasted a cupola-crowned upper story in the center flanked by two one-story wings. This faced one-story stables and domestic offices; these were constructed later, between 1710 and 1738, across the courtyard and behind an ample balustrade standing a few steps higher up the hillside. The cour d'honneur thus formed was entered from the right by a drive through imposing wrought-iron gates.

The garden or park facade was probably not completed until around 1720 and is less satisfactory. Large pilasters rise through the first floor of the two-story building to a balustrade underneath a sloping roof. From this side the central cupola looks like the roof of an octagonal tower. An iron-railed balcony frames the second floor's central window while a flight of shallow steps leads down from the *sala terrena* into the garden. Only finished in the mid-eighteenth century, this was designed as a formal baroque parterre in the Italian style, with statue-lined allées lead-

Petrvaldsky-Schrattenbach family tree in the shape of a peacock, mid-eighteenth century.

Old view of Buchlov with pilgrimage church on the hill behind. (Countess Eva Berchtold.)

The Petrvald and Colonna family crests at Buchlov.

ing in various directions from a large circular fountain along beds edged by clipped box, laurel, and stone urns. The interiors—in particular the oval hall with its impressive ceiling fresco by an unknown artist—displayed high-quality stucco work typical of Baldassare Fontana. The panels represented allegories of justice, virtue, bravery, and love of art, while around the inside of the cupola ran a balcony underneath which were circular medallions depicting the four elements and the four seasons.

Although the Petrvalds now divided their time between the two residences, they did not abandon Buchlov. However, the limited redecoration undertaken there in the 1730s was the last effort of the proprietor, Zikmund Karel, who died in 1751. His son briefly succeeded before dying young himself, thus extinguishing the family in the male line. Since the elder sister remained unmarried, the sole heirs were the children of his second sister, Maria Theresa, and her husband, Prosper Antonín Berchtold. Although the Berchtolds were of German origin, they had long been settled in Moravia. Owners of the castle of Uherčice since 1628, which they had beautified with splendid, almost three-dimensional stucco work, they had been created barons and then counts by the Habsburgs. First by his Petrvald wife and then after her death by a later marriage, Prosper Antonín produced numerous daughters and two sons, the half-brothers Leopold and Friedrich.

They were to prove a remarkable pair. Leopold was a physician by training, a scholarly doctor who travelled continuously for twenty years around Europe, Asia, and Africa. Possessed of an omnivorous curiosity, he conducted an international correspondence with savants and philosophers. In 1800 he at last became the absolute owner of Buchlov and Buchlovice (for the estates had reverted to his maiden aunt on his mother's death), and there he settled. Leopold promoted reforms of every kind—in the school curricula, in the local agrarian economy, and in health

*Old view of Buchlovice with Buchlov
on the hill on the left.
(Austrian National Library, Vienna.)*

*View of the stables at Buchlovice from across
the courtyard.*

care—liberally founding and endowing hospitals and almshouses. His petitions to the court at Vienna on these matters were innumerable; small wonder that he was so widely loved in the neighborhood. During the Napoleonic Wars he put up notices on the borders of his property announcing in both Czech and German that any invalid would receive free medical attention. Buchlovice was turned into a seventy-bed hospital, the wards divided according to the sex and ailments of the patients and detailed case histories being recorded. Sadly, while visiting the makeshift hospital in the Cistercian monastery of Velehrad, Leopold himself contracted typhoid fever and died in 1809, aged only fifty.

In a very different way Friedrich was equally distinguished. Another intrepid traveler, to the New World as well, his main interests were cultural and he became a major figure in the Czech national revival. For fifteen years he published and coedited with H. S. Prasl the periodical *Rostlinář* (*The Herbarium*), and was the joint author of *Flora Czech* (*Czech Botany*) along with a mass of other scientific monographs. As one of the founders of the Royal Bohemian Museum, he too earned a claim to his country's gratitude. Principally thanks to Friedrich's impetus, Buchlov became a museum with a variety of herbal, geological, and exotic collections representing the diverse interests of this botanist and ethnologist. By the mid-nineteenth century—when Friedrich, who survived to the age of ninety-five, was still alive—Buchlov's galleries were regularly opened to the public along with its outstanding library; the latter had partly come down from the Zástřižlys, one of whom had studied with and bought all the books of Theodore Beza, the Protestant theologian who was John Calvin's successor in Geneva.

The Berchtolds now resided in Buchlovice even though regular visits were paid up the hill to the castle. Leopold's son Sigismund, a political activist, took part in the 1848 revolt in Hungary and was condemned to death for his role in it, but was pardoned by the emperor on the condition that he retire permanently to his estates. With his uncle's encouragement he created new collections for the family museum, one relating to Hungary, another to Egyptology, a third to a magnificent selection of Renaissance glass; he also added books in diverse languages and on a variety of subjects, especially magic and demonology. The interiors of the chateau, largely untouched since its construction, were modified in the prevailing

Chamber leading off Leopold Berchtold's drawing room; here, the Russian and Austrian foreign ministers held a secret meeting in 1908 that helped pave the way to World War I.

Lavatory with Delft tiles, built at Buchlovice in the early twentieth century.

Smoking room at Buchlovice, early twentieth century. (Austrian National Library, Vienna.)

neoclassical taste and changed again in the late nineteenth century in an eclectic style best described as neorococo. Under the supervision of the architect Dominik Fey, the works were finished around the turn of the century. An entrance porch dated 1905 was added to the chateau along with a balustrade on the garden front. The Silver Drawing Room, the paneling of which was decorated with silver, was his creation as was most of the rest of the internal paneling. Fay also had further ideas, as two proposed models of the buildings prove. But so skillful was the workmanship of his additions that they were virtually indistinguishable from the original and the impression made on any visitor was that of an eighteenth-century house.

The most celebrated of all the Berchtold owners was also destined to be the last. Sigismund's grandson, another Leopold, was born in 1863 and succeeded his father in 1900, having already made a brilliant marriage to Nandine Károlyi of the great Hungarian family. Clever and ambitious, he was also vain, devious, and indecisive. Having decided on a diplomatic career, he rose rapidly through the ranks and was appointed Austrian ambassador to Saint Petersburg in 1907. The next year he was to give a house party at Buchlovice that was to have fateful consequences. Both the Russian and Austrian foreign ministers were his guests and in a small cabinet off their host's drawing room the two men agreed secretly that if Russia would raise no objections to Austria's annexation of Bosnia and Herzegovina (in modern Yugoslavia), Vienna would not oppose the reopening of the Dardanelles for the Black Sea fleet. In fact the Austrians simply proclaimed the annexation a month later, thus gaining a sly diplomatic triumph without granting any concessions—another milestone on the gradual march to World War I. But Berchtold's reputation did not suffer;

House altar in the dining room at Buchlovice; the central picture dates from the seventeenth century while the side panels are late Gothic.

Nandine Berchtold (née Karolyi) with her mother, Sophia, at Emperor Charles's coronation in Budapest, December 1916.

Leopold Berchtold in Hungarian magnate's uniform, early twentieth century.

Members of the Berchtold family seated before
the gates of Buchlovice, 1914.
(Countess Eva Berchtold.)

far from it. He himself was appointed Austria's foreign minister in 1912. From that position he supported the party advocating war with Serbia— indeed, it was his drafting of the inflexible ultimatum to the Serbs in July 1914 that ensured its rejection and sparked the chain of events that led inexorably to the war.

For all his political shortcomings, Berchtold loved his home, turning the park at Buchlovice into a pretty English-style landscape full of fine trees, many of them interesting botanical specimens. When the roofs at Buchlov were destroyed by fire in 1931, he quickly renovated them. Some 20,000 acres in extent, the property was of a good size if not among the largest, and it was well managed. After his retirement from the political scene before the end of the war, Berchtold lived on his estates. Land reform did involve the loss of some of the property but Berchtold was largely untroubled by the Masaryk government. He died in the middle of World War II, leaving his two surviving sons little time to enjoy their inheritance before the Communists expropriated the estates. Today both are dead and, having left no children, the Berchtold family is extinct.

Yet even though the former owners are no more, their legacy still flourishes. Buchlov is a fine example of medieval fortress architecture, containing one of the most diverse aristocratic museum collections in the Czech Republic. As a baroque masterpiece, Buchlovice presents a complete contrast; a monument to elegance and good taste, its charm has been little spoiled by later generations. These two fascinating houses bear witness to some of the most dramatic moments in Czech history, even as they have sheltered many of those families that have determined its path.

V E L T R U S Y

The main road to Dresden runs northwest from Prague through suburbs that today are a great deal less beautiful than the city center. Fairly soon, however, the traveler reaches open countryside—a rather flat pastoral landscape well watered by two great rivers, the Labe or Elbe and the Vltava. At a distance of about ten miles from the capital the road passes by a nondescript small village called Veltrusy. The boundaries of a thickly wooded park running along its main street are clearly visible, but there is nothing to indicate that this little town contains one of the earliest and finest exercises in late-eighteenth-century Bohemian landscape in the romantic style, or a chateau that can best be described as a pure delight.

The first records of a settlement at Veltrusy date from 1226 when King Přemysl Otakar I presented the property to the abbey of Doksany. During the next four and a half centuries it passed through the hands of a number of proprietors, among them members of such great families as the Smiřickýs, the Lobkowiczs, and the Waldsteins; it was the latter who sold it in 1676 to Ferdinand Christoph von Scheidler. A lawyer who had risen to the rank of chief state prosecutor, Scheidler was one of the numerous German civil servants who ran Bohemia for the absentee Habsburg monarch. At his request his substantial estates were divided among his four daughters, one of whom, Maria Theresa, received Veltrusy before she married Václav Antonín Chotek in 1698.

The Choteks were an old Bohemian knightly family who had never risen beyond the ranks of the minor nobility and whose property had been confiscated after the Battle of the White Mountain. Václav Antonín, then aged 24, had been born after his father's death in modest circumstances but, well-educated, capable, and ambitious, was determined to restore his family fortunes. Helped by his father-in-law's connections and by his wife's substantial dowry, he embarked on a career in government service, holding a string of public offices that culminated in his appointment as governor of Bohemia in 1731 with a seat on the royal council at Vienna. Having been long since created a count, in 1745 he was raised to the dignity of count of the empire (Reichsgraf). Václav Antonín lived on until over eighty, although he had already had the rare foresight to hand over his estates to his two equally energetic sons.

As a young man in his twenties, his son Rudolf had been entrusted by his father with the completion of the chateau he had begun building at Veltrusy. A grand house had never been built on the property, perhaps because its geographical situation was so exposed to flooding. Rudolf's new villa was located in a park created from the woodland bordering two tributaries of the Vltava, which meet to form an open islet originally known as the "Ostrov" or "island". The precise date on which Václav Antonín started work on his new house in unknown but it was certainly early in the second decade of the eighteenth century. Nor can it be definitely stated who the architect was for the project. It has been attributed to František Maximilián Kaňka, an able-enough practitioner, but many fea-

View through the front gates of Veltrusy, northwest of Prague.

Watercolor of Veltrusy, early nineteenth century.
(Austrian National Library, Vienna.)

Portrait of Count Rudolf Chotek by L. Farenschön,
mid-eighteenth century.

The Delft Room with its collection of
Dutch porcelain.

tures of the ingenious ground plan point to a far more considerable fig-ure—perhaps Jan Santini-Aichel, the predominant exponent of Czech baroque.

The chateau had a central cylindrical core containing at ground floor level an open *sala terrena* and on the first floor a circular main hall rising through two stories. Emanating radially from the core on a rectangular plan were four one-story blocks. Between the two north-facing additions a divided external staircase was constructed, ceremonial in character and lined with stone vases; on each side at the bottom appeared statues at-tributed to František Antonín Kuen (1716–19), one of a rearing horse being held by a groom and another of a gamekeeper restraining his dog. Two further rectangular blocks of varying heights were linked to the main building on an east-west axis by small enclosed courtyards, the parapets of which were formerly lined by statuary. The eastern building was de-signed for stables, while the western one was occupied by administrative offices. The cour d'honneur thus formed by these structures was closed by a statue-surmounted wall. Another wall set back a further two hundred yards divided the garden from the park, and on this wall stood twelve allegorical statues representing the months; in a semicircle in the middle stood four more figures representing the seasons of the year. These flanked statues of Venus and Cupid by an unknown hand, which stood on the twin pillars of the main gates. Beyond this a long tree-lined avenue ran north from the chateau to the edge of the woods, around the south-ern, eastern, and western perimeters of which stretched a formal French baroque garden several acres in extent. Although not laid out on the gran-diose scale of many of its French counterparts, it displayed certain im-pressive features beyond the geometrical plan of trees and flower beds. In the eastern part, for example, stood a fountain between twin rectangular pavilions and facing it a group of ten stone statues and vases along with six more set on pillars marked the external wall.

Large reception rooms, including drawing rooms, a library, and a din-ing room, led off the main hall, from which a vestibule opened onto the ceremonial staircase. The family's bedrooms, on the other hand, were lo-cated in the wings. Much stucco decoration was used, particularly on the ceilings, which matched Veltrusy's richly finished interiors. On ground level the vaults and walls of the *sala terrena* were covered by trompe-l'oeil painting—today much faded—which in some places was reinforced by stucco to form three-dimensional reliefs. Much of the subject matter was

taken from the engravings of the seventeenth-century artist Jacques Callot, while the pillars were covered with rococo figures based on the Commedia dell'Arte.

Rudolf Chotek had taken over the direction of the works at Veltrusy from his father around 1730, and with his wife, Aloysia, née Kinský, moved into the house not long afterward (records show that the building was finished about 1744). Like Václav Antonín, Rudolf rose high in the state's service: appointed a privy counselor to the empress in 1745, he became director of the chamber of commerce four years later, with particular responsibilities for foreign trade, and was appointed chancellor of the Empire in 1760. As a trained economist, he was of course well-versed in the good management of his estates as well. Thus in 1754 he organized in the courtyard at Veltrusy a two-day fair of "goods manufactured in the Kingdom of Bohemia," the first of its kind in the world. Potential buyers could not purchase what they wanted on the spot, but could order from the numerous items and catalogs on display.

Until his death in 1779, Rudolf continued to busy himself with improving Veltrusy. He formed the property into an entail of *Fideikomiss*, which could not be divided and could only be inherited by the elder son; childless himself, however, he nominated his nephew Jan Rudolf as his heir. Wishing to enlarge his residence, he extended the four wings of the main block around 1764, thus nearly doubling the living space. In the process some of the side walls between the central building and its wings were destroyed, and the double cylindrical roof of the central hall was replaced by the copper-covered cupola that can still be seen today. Simultaneously

Rococo gilt console displaying a rare vase.

Portrait of Count Jan Rudolf Chotek, late eighteenth century.

he transformed the interiors of the chateau, replacing the original baroque stucco work in most of the principal rooms with rococo decoration. In 1765 Josef Pichler was commissioned to paint an allegory of the Four Seasons on the inside of the cupola over the main hall, and at about this time the Chinese Salon and the Maria Theresa room were decorated.

As a keen landscape gardener, Rudolf Chotek had already planted what was called the Turkish Garden on the southwestern tip of the Ostrov. So when the Vltava River burst its banks in 1764, effectively destroying the French garden, he seized the opportunity to enlarge it to nearly thirty acres, extending the park across the right bank of the river. He also cut vistas through the surrounding woodland to give fine views from the chateau. Although the garden was substantially re-created in the style of the French baroque, some traces of a freer and less formal approach to nature were apparent, traces that were to bear fruit in the years to come.

Jan Rudolf succeeded to Veltrusy at a moment when nature was being recognized as a source of aesthetic value and as a model of harmony for human society. His opportunity to refashion the landscape as a reflection of these trends was expedited by large-scale flooding in 1784–85, which destroyed the Ostrov itself, in the middle of which the chateau had been built. Henceforth water levels were controlled by a dry bed, flooded when necessary from several sluices, and the channel thus created was used by the family for boating expeditions. Cultivated farmland was treated as an integral part of the park in a Louis XVI–style *ferme ornée* where agricultural workers and farm animals became the living components of the decorative background. From 1785 the park was relandscaped in the natural English style, mainly in accordance with the ideas of Richard van der Schott, the director of the Imperial Gardens at Vienna.

A stream of ornamental buildings also went up, including a grotto with ruins, a hermitage, a Doric bridge, a Chinese pheasantry, and the Dutch-style blue pavilion, later converted into a hunting lodge; all these have now substantially vanished. Many such projects were designed for the Choteks by the Prague architect Matyáš Hummel. It was he who built the colonnaded Maria Theresa pavilion from 1811–13, as well as a Doric pavilion in the park's southeastern corner at the same time and a bridge topped by a sphinx, nicknamed the Egyptian Cabinet, a few years later. Already before the turn of the century he had constructed, from models seen on his travels in England, the charming Ionic Temple of the Friends of the Countryside and of Horticulture (1794) and three years afterward the Laudon pavilion, copied from the one at Prior Park in Bath, England, and containing one of the main sluices. The Gothic revival Red Mill was also completed in the 1790s along with a variety of follies no longer extant—a chalet, a shepherd's hut, and an elaborate porch. Although not all of Jan Rudolf's energies were so favorably directed—he also destroyed the chateau's enclosed inner courtyard and replaced a delightful glass orangery dating from the 1740s with a stone one—with justice it could be said that Veltrusy was one of the finest landscape parks created in Bohemia.

His architectural ambitions did not end with Veltrusy, however. On another property he owned east of Prague, Jan Rudolf began work in 1802 on a large neoclassical chateau named Kačina, built according to legend in imitation of the palace near Saint Petersburg. A professor at the Academy named Georg Fischer was the architect, although the initial plans were drawn up by Christian Schuricht. Here in an extended semicircle, closed by two end pavilions, Chotek constructed a large chateau nineteen bays long, probably the purest neoclassical monument ever erected in Bohemia. Over the Ionic front portico he placed the inscription in 1822, as the project was nearing completion after twenty years, "Jan Rudolf Chotek, for himself, his friends and descendants."

By the time of his death in 1824 Jan Rudolf had, like his forebears, enjoyed a distinguished career. He had been granted the honorific title of grand burgrave of Bohemia and had served for over two decades as the president of the Royal Czech Society of Sciences. Unfortunately so much building activity had seriously depleted the family coffers and during the next forty years under his grandson Jindřich, who succeeded to the Chotek estates, little more was done to Veltrusy. A classical statue of Mars was erected around 1831 and Empire-style entrance gates leading to the park from the village street were installed in 1845–46, but the family lived mainly at Kačina, where work continued intermittently. There, a ballroom and a library in the shape of a two-story pilastered rotunda were completed by 1850. The properties were still considerable, however—at Veltrusy they included twenty villages and parts of nine others by midcentury.

The fact that the chateau was little lived in for most of the nineteenth century proved to be quite an advantage, for during these years the fine interiors were not altered. But after an incompetent thirty-year stewardship by Jindřich's eldest son, Rudolf, the family was deeply in debt. After his death in 1894 his brother Emerich took on Veltrusy, while Kačina was sold to their Thun-Hohenstein brother-in-law. Although the park had been systematically planted with interesting botanical specimens in accordance with the fashion of the age, from the 1880s it, like the chateau, had been increasingly neglected. Just as the diversion of the Vltava River deprived the water-channel of its sources, so too did the Choteks' vitality seem exhausted. Emerich was succeeded by his younger brother, Arnošt, at whose death without issue in 1927 the main line of the family came to an end. Veltrusy passed to a second cousin, Karel, who was destined to be the last proprietor, for the house was expropriated by the Communist government after World War II. Karel had only one sister, the saintly Ada, who had founded her own order of nuns called the Sisters of the Holy Eucharist, so at his passing the Choteks became extinct in the main line.

Veltrusy is not one of the best known or most architecturally remarkable of the great houses of Bohemia. Yet it is still in excellent condition nowadays, and both externally and internally it has a charm that few others can match. Its park, one of the first of its kind in the country, stands as a pale shadow of what it must have been in its heyday around 1800, but it retains some charming monuments. The family who created all this, although now vanished, provided a remarkable succession of able public servants and discriminating patrons of the arts. Yet except for a distant cousin, Sophie, who happened to be the morganatic wife of Austria's ill-

View of the neoclassical chateau of Kačina, central Bohemia.

View of the park at Veltrusy from the house.

The Maria Theresa pavilion in the park.

fated Archduke Francis Ferdinand, the Choteks are not well known to posterity. Nevertheless they were a remarkable family who created one of the most beguiling of all Czech chateaux. As the late-nineteenth-century German poet Rainer Maria Rilke wrote about Veltrusy, "How many wonderful interpretations of its experience and self knowledge the human spirit has created—how discreetly and yet how revealingly it has entered the very nature of such a design, extended and glorified itself within it as the world has extended and glorified itself in the starry heavens."

LEDNICE & VALTICE

The region southeast of Brno, near the borders of Austria, Hungary, and Slovakia is quintessential border country; until recently Slav, Teuton, and Hungarian have all intermingled here. It is thus only fitting that what could be regarded as two of the major country houses in Moravia were created by a family of German origins whose strongest links were always to Vienna, a city scarcely further from the area than is Brno. Between these two former Liechtenstein family chateaux, now so utterly different in appearance, stretches one of the finest park landscapes in all Europe, crowded with follies and monuments.

The Liechtensteins (the name means literally "stone of light") first appeared in history in the mid-twelfth century and took their name from the large castle they built around then at Maria Enzersdorf near Vienna. In 1249 Heinrich von Liechtenstein was recorded as being granted fiefs in Moravia by King Václav I, and in 1322 the family gained control of the small Gothic fortress at Lednice. About seventy years later they took possession of another neighboring castle called Valtice, formerly the property of the bishops of Passau. Although situated in lower Austria (as indeed it was to be until the frontier was changed in 1919), it was only five miles or so distant. No trace of either medieval edifice remains. Until the union of Austria and Moravia under Habsburg rule after 1526 the Liechtensteins had to maintain a frequently difficult balancing act, but their links with Austria were always of paramount importance. They loyally served the Babenberg dynasty and their successors the Habsburgs, and in 1386 Johann I was appointed Obersthofmeister (High Steward), then the effective head of the administration.

During the Middle Ages several branches of the Liechtensteins emerged and eventually a system of seniority was introduced to prevent a breakup of the estates (although this never really functioned properly). Hartmann II von Liechtenstein, who married and succeeded to the properties around 1570, was a noted bibliophile who demolished the moated castle at Lednice and replaced it with a Renaissance house. He may be regarded as the direct ancestor of later generations, for he left three sons: Karl, Maximilian, and Gundakar. Maximilian was to die childless and Karl's line died out after four generations, but Gundakar's descendants flourish to this day. The three brothers, all men of outstanding ability, inherited their father's numerous estates at his death in 1597. Karl, then aged 28, had been educated by the Moravian Brethren but had converted to Catholicism and was rising in the Habsburgs' service, as marshal of the court, first to Archduke Matyás and later to Emperor Rudolf. Of the three, Karl was the politician, Maximilian the soldier, and Gundakar the diplomat, and the careers of all of them continued to flourish. Karl and Maximilian

The forecourt of the chateau of Valtice, southeast of Brno.

were married to the two daughters of Jan Šembera Černohorský z Boskovice and therefore enjoyed future prospects from that great inheritance. In 1606 the brothers met and agreed to entail the family's estates with rights of succession to the first-born male descendant, an arrangement that was of major significance in preserving the Liechtensteins' enormous wealth and that was to last until 1938, when family ownership was replaced by that of a foundation.

The role of the Liechtensteins in reimposing Habsburg authority on the Czech lands in 1620 was decisive: Karl urged the hesitant Catholic commanders into battle at White Mountain while Maximilian led the vital cavalry charge. Appointed viceroy of Bohemia in 1622, Karl appealed for clemency for the rebels, although the emperor insisted on merciless retribution. After the rebellion the Liechtensteins were in an extremely favorable position to acquire confiscated properties; indeed by various means they contrived to quintuple the original size of their estates until Karl became the country's largest landowner. For their unstinting loyalty to the Habsburgs, all three were created hereditary princes, Karl being given the duchies of Troppau and Jägerndorf to underline his status. He was keen to improve his new residences, Valtice particularly. At that time it was an irregular mass of buildings grouped around the old keep, scarcely habitable and lacking in any ornamentation. He commissioned Giovanni Battista Carlone, the imperial architect, and expended large sums of money from 1613 to 1617. The castle's great hall was roofed in, but the project for a ceiling fresco remained unfulfilled at his death. Similarly at Lednice, Karl labored with Carlone for four years although to no great effect, and he started to lay out the large park.

His only son, Karl Eusebius, inherited his mantle in 1627. A very different sort of character with a cosmopolitan education but scant interest in public affairs, his passion lay in art and architecture. The "Treatise on Architecture" that he composed primarily as a pedagogical work for his son defined architectural patronage as an ongoing tradition that enhanced the family's reputation and preserved it for posterity. Partly devoted to the patrons' artistic and aesthetic considerations, it also contained a section of practical advice on actual construction. "The sole use of money," as he saw it, "is for the bequeathing of beautiful monuments"—for "there is nothing more splendid and distinguished to be created and left behind than excellent buildings."

Certainly Karl Eusebius attempted to put these theories into practice. His first big project was the rebuilding of the huge Valtice parish church, for which he summoned the architect Giovanni Giacomo Tencala. Their collaboration was to run a troubled course as work started, stopped, and then recommenced. The church's foundations were laid in 1629 but after the dome collapsed nine years later Tencala was sacked and his Brno colleague Andrea Erna took his place (although in 1643 Tencala, unabashed, returned). Work was then interrupted by war, so the church, a cold baroque echo of the mannerism of Vignola, was only consecrated in 1671. In the castle the interior painting was finished but no major reconstruction was undertaken. A contemporary view shows it as a polygonal tower flanked by two Renaissance buildings with enclosed courtyards, the whole surrounded by a moat. The front elevation projected parallel wings, built by Erna with Tencala's stucco decoration, which ended in corner towers flanking the gate. Karl Eusebius ultimately found Lednice too small for his court but before that point he spent much money on extending the grounds. Reports told of an orangery with three thousand trees and glass houses full of the rarest orchids, although it was hard on such flat land to get sufficient pressure for the waterworks. He also employed stuccodores and frescoers to enrich the interiors. The greatest legacy he left, however, was his collection of sculpture and pictures, although because he believed that tapestries rather than paintings should adorn the walls of his

Distant view of the Liechtensteins' chateau at Plumlov.

Portrait of Prince Karl I von Liechtenstein in Austrian field marshal's uniform, c. 1625. (Collections of the Prince of Liechtenstein.)

Watercolor of Lednice before rebuilding, by Ferdinand Runk, c. 1820. (Collections of the Prince of Liechtenstein.)

residences, the latter were exhibited only in specially designed galleries.

Karl Eusebius's theorizing about architecture had not been wasted on his heir, Johann Adam Andreas. He had already built the chateau at Plumlov under his father's epistolary tutelage, a tour de force echoing Karl Eusebius's ideal of a long expansive building. Standing on a steep rock above a pond, Plumlov's one finished block had tier upon tier of free-standing columns rising above the courtyard—Doric, Ionic, and Corinthian, fifty-four in all. Backed by pilasters, they carried broken entablatures and were coupled in pairs to mark the ends and center. On the other facade a massive pilastered order projected above the sheer rock face.

Johann Adam Andreas's fiscal circumstances were not encouraging, for he inherited an 800,000 gulden debt in 1684. Nevertheless he immediately began reviving the estates and founded a splendid court. He also bought a city palace in Vienna from the Kaunitz family, which he completed, and then built a large summer palace on his Rossau estate following Domenico Martinelli's plans, with a model housing development nearby in the suburb of Lichtental. At Valtice little was constructed except for a *sala terrena,* which Johann Bernard Fischer von Erlach added to the east wing.

But it was a different story at Lednice. There Fischer von Erlach was instructed to design "a palace for the horse." The monumental stables, a square self-contained building located near the main house and in direct juxtaposition to it, sheltered up to 180 horses and overshadowed the other relatively modest buildings. The inner courtyard's arrangement was consistent and unified, the exterior less so, but both displayed the rich columnation reminiscent of Plumlov that harked back to Karl Eusebius's ideas.

125

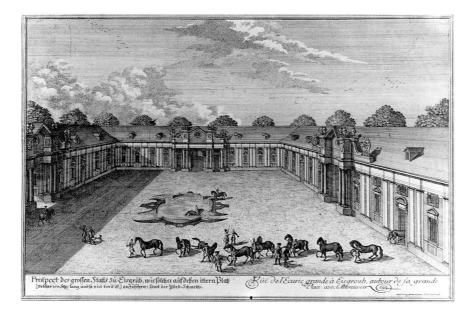

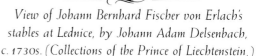

Work began in 1688 and the south wing was nearly completed two years later. Then for reasons unknown Fischer von Erlach left the prince's service to be replaced by Domenico Martinelli, and a decade later three of the envisaged four wings had been built and adorned with statuary by the sculptor Giovanni Giuliani. The small mannerist chateau was refashioned as a single-story, three-winged structure with a mezzanine floor under the attic; an orangery and summer pavilion were also created in the park.

"The Croesus of Austria," as Johann Adam Andreas was known, left no surviving male posterity at his death in 1712, so his second cousin, Anton Florian, the grandson of Gundakar, succeeded to the entail. Having already enjoyed a distinguished career as ambassador to the Vatican and minister to Emperor Charles VI, he survived to enjoy his splendid inheritance only another twelve years. Nevertheless during that brief period a great deal of further work at Valtice was completed. Martinelli's grandiose plans involved building a riding school and a wine press, remodeling the mid-seventeenth-century stables, and constructing gate towers above Erna's parallel wings. Two coach houses were erected as well with a ramp up to the gate from the town square, while the low wall connecting the towers was demolished. At Lednice the facade was restored and the idea of adding another story was discussed. A contemporary engraving by Johann Adam Delsenbach (who depicted all the family residences) provides the sole clue to the chateau's appearance in the eighteenth century: the side wings were articulated in the same manner as the garden front, the northeastern facade had a central gable that looked out on to a formal Italianate parterre, glades were cut through the forest, and an avenue of trees was planted between the two properties.

During the first half of the eighteenth century the artistic activity of the Liechtensteins was unwontedly muted, partly because Johann Adam Andreas, disliking his successor, had left everything except the entail to his wife, her only daughter, and her nephews. Thus the reigning prince, Anton Florian, did not possess the main part of the picture collection again for some years. Neither his son nor his young grandson made much impact on the property, although the finishing touches were put on the south wing of Valtice in 1729 by the architect Anton Johann Ospel. The chapel, however, was the outstanding achievement, a fine example of baroque art rising through two stories, its walls lined with marble and its chambers containing superlative statuary by Giuliani.

In 1748 Josef Wenzel succeeded his cousin, Anton Florian's grandson,

Winter landscape in the park with the minaret in the background.

Portrait of Prince Josef Wenzel von Liechtenstein by Antoine Pesne, 1735. (Collections of the Prince of Liechtenstein.)

The Lake Castle in the park between Valtice and Lednice.

as head of the family. Perhaps the most distinguished figure the Liechtensteins ever produced, he was an accomplished diplomat and an outstanding soldier. Trained under Prince Eugene, he rose to the rank of field marshal and director of the Austrian artillery, the improvement of which was his life's achievement. Of reserved temperament, he was never a mere place-seeking courtier but represented the empress on the greatest occasions. A magnificent golden carriage, one of many from the era but almost the only such to survive the French Revolution (and still in the family's possession), was one of five he commissioned for his formal entrance into Paris as ambassador in 1738. Drawn by the piebald horses from the Lednice stud—six or eight of them pulling each carriage, the matched pairs perfectly synchronized in build and movement—it must have provided an unforgettable spectacle, although the ceremony was planned in imitation of Anton Florian's entry into Rome nearly fifty years before. In an age dedicated to ceremonial splendor, Josef Wenzel's gesture was of major importance. Yet so public a man had scant time to spare for architecture, so little was done at Valtice or Lednice in his twenty-four years of ownership. Nevertheless the prince did add extensively to the picture collection with purchases in France and Italy, and his library was deemed among the finest in Central Europe.

The lull in the Liechtensteins' long architectural tradition was not destined to last. Josef Wenzel's nephew and two great-nephews between them directed the family's affairs from 1772 to 1836, a period that saw a positive frenzy of building activity. Improvements at both Valtice and Lednice were immediately contemplated, plans for that purpose being commissioned from Isidor Canevale. Little was done at first, but in 1790 major work began when a collaboration was established between Prince Alois Josef I and his court architect, Joseph Hardtmuth, whose other claim to fame lies in the invention of the lead pencil. Once changes had been made to prevent the Dyje River from regularly flooding the countryside, the new efforts were concentrated in the four miles or so of wooded

swampy land straddling the Austro-Moravian border that separated the Liechtensteins' two residences.

First the Swan Pond was dug in 1790, at the end of which Hardtmuth erected a Turkish-inspired minaret, rising from a square galleried base topped by a golden sickle, which could be seen from various points in the park. A Chinese pavilion, bathing house, and sun temple—all vanished today—were also built, while Hardtmuth produced plans for a pyramid of strict classical proportions. When Prince Johannes I, a field marshal of great genius, succeeded his childless brother in 1805, the transformation of the landscape was accelerated. More large ponds were excavated from the marshy ground and little islets made in them with the displaced earth. A system of transplanting large trees was developed, which, along with the other projects, frequently engaged six hundred men between spring and autumn.

Johannes I employed Hardtmuth as his court architect and from the period of his reign dates the Roman aqueduct as well as the picturesque Hansenburg, a mock medieval ruined fortress. But relations between the two men had cooled by 1812 after two of Hardtmuth's constructions, a Hussar temple and a copy of Trajan's Column, had collapsed; by mutual agreement the latter left the Liechtensteins' service to be replaced by Josef Kornhäusel. Two important projects were now completed: the colonnade on the Reistenberg Hill, which overlooks the modern frontier, and the

Temple of Diana, a great triumphal arch sited in a forest clearing with an entire upper floor occupied by one large room designed for hunting breakfasts. Kornhäusel built the elegant Lake Castle, as it was known, a compact two-story pavilion planned around a semicircular stairwell and located above a gently sloping meadow. He also began the Apollo Temple, which featured a large ellipse in the middle and a relief of the god in his sun chariot around the entire frieze. But by 1818 Kornhäusel too had fallen foul of his patron, and Franz Engel took his place. He produced the Temple of the Three Graces (so-called because of Johann Martin Fischer's statuary group in its center), and the Frontier Castle. The latter was precisely that, for half the building stood in Moravia and half in Austria, the border marked by a stream that flowed under the hall and emptied into a fish pond. Engel's career was cut short, however, for he went mad in 1825 and died soon afterward.

Plenty of architectural activity continued nevertheless. The chateau at Lednice was thoroughly remodeled by Kornhäusel from 1812 to 1818, leaving only the first floor interiors untouched. An entire new wing comprised of four big reception rooms was constructed connecting the main building to the orangery. The architect was also commissioned to enlarge the Liechtensteins' family vault at the pilgrimage church of Vranov just north of Brno, for which he suggested a pyramidal freestanding mausoleum that was never built. Engel did construct a new Empire-style vault on a level below the church in 1821, with numerous coffins, statues by the Viennese sculptor Josef Klieber, and rosewood benches bearing silvered symbols of mortality.

The family's picture collection, totalling more than a thousand works, had passed to Johannes I's brother Alois Josef I, a noted art connoisseur who proceeded to have the works cataloged and reorganized. Many of the lesser paintings were sold at auction in order for superior works to be purchased. Music and theatre were also loves of his and he had a theatre built at Valtice along with an open-air stage in the park at Lednice. Although he maintained a permanent troupe of actors, their heavy costs were defrayed by letting them give public performances. Alois Josef's tastes also extended to botany and mineralogy, while Johannes I's main passion was agriculture. With the best sheep and cattle in the Habsburg Empire, in 1809 he had Hardtmuth design an extraordinary beehive-shaped barn with colonnades and balustrades in which his famous Swiss cows were kept.

Portrait of Prince Johannes I von Liechtenstein, by Johann Baptiste Lampi, c. 1855. (Collections of the Prince of Liechtenstein.)

Watercolor of the Temple of Diana or the Rendez-Vous at Lednice, by Ferdinand Runk, c. 1820. (Collections of the Prince of Liechtenstein.)

Watercolor of the library at Lednice, by Rudolf von Alt, 1852. (Collections of the Prince of Liechtenstein.)

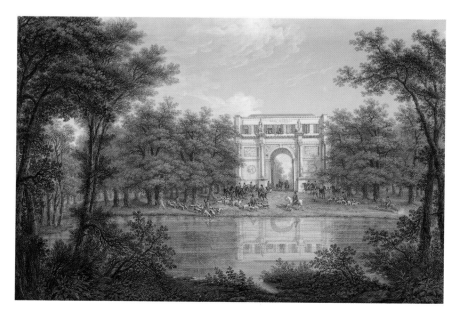

Building activity did not cease with Johannes I's death in 1836, for his eldest son Alois Josef II had as great a passion for architecture if a lesser interest in the fine arts. He refashioned the family's Vienna town palace in late Biedermeier style but showed very different tastes at Lednice. There he accepted the architect Georg Wingelmüller's plans to rebuild the entire chateau in English Gothic style in 1845, and the next year sent him on a tour through Western Europe to gather ideas. Work began immediately, but unfortunately Wingelmüller died in 1848 and his deputy Johann Heidrich saw the project through, which took a further ten years to completion. The original walls and windows were retained along with the earlier ground plan, although steps, terraces, and two visually dominating towers were added. The facades were adorned with balconies, crenellations, and ornamental gables, while the window frames were enlarged and decorated with elaborate mock-medieval carving. To simulate sandstone the paint was even mixed with sand.

Adjoining Lednice's main building an enormous iron palmhouse designed by the Englishman Peter Hubert Desvignes was erected in place of the orangery and theatre. The suite of reception rooms, finished a mere thirty years before, were panelled and given carved cassette ceilings. The chapel and kitchen block were similarly remodeled, the gap

created between them and the main block filled by a monumental, unsupported staircase. In the library Wingelmüller's winding oak steps decorated with plant and animal motifs led up to the princess's workroom. Corridors, stairs, and many rooms had net or cross vaulting to sustain the illusion of a medieval castle, which, in contrast to the carved stone exteriors, were made from marble and limestone. Two of the immense chandeliers were of Nuremberg workmanship from around 1690 while sixteen others had been carved in Hollenstein's metal foundry in Vienna. Otherwise the Gothic reigned supreme, except for the baroque stables, which survived unscathed.

Alois Josef II died at Lednice a few weeks after the work was finished in 1858. His son, Johannes II, was to live for another seventy-one years, becoming a generous patron of museums and of botanical science. Yet although the interiors of the castles of Moravský Šternberk and Vaduz in the principality of Liechtenstein were refurbished, he undertook no major architectural projects. The picture collection, which his grandfather had increased to around 1,650 paintings by somewhat indiscriminate buying, was again refined to little more than half that number. A bachelor himself, the prince had no great appetite for society, although up to eighty guests at a time were entertained during the shooting season. The estates were well-managed and their revenues formed an ever-larger part of the total income—from 30 percent in the 1820s up to 70 percent by midcentury. The forestry business was modernized, a number of industrial enterprises were fostered, and farming on a huge scale was still undertaken. Indeed the Liechtensteins remained one of the two or three largest landowning families in the Habsburg Empire: in 1914 their holdings amounted to some 460,000 acres, the vast bulk in Bohemia and Moravia.

The advent of the independent former Czechoslovakia and the land reform it instituted after World War I deprived the Liechtensteins of more than half

View of Lednice, refashioned in neo-Gothic style in the mid-nineteenth century.

Detail of neo-Gothic gargoyles at Lednice.

The palm house at Lednice by Peter Hubert Desvignes.

Watercolor of the armory at Lednice by Rudolf von Alt, 1845. (Collections of the Prince of Liechtenstein.)

their estates. Likewise, the adjustment of the Austro-Czech border did them no service, bringing Valtice and its surrounding land within the frontiers of Moravia. Yet the family's numerous castles and superlative art collection remained untouched and they continued to exert considerable influence within the new republic. Johannes died in 1929 and his brother succeeded him for nine years, until in 1938 the succession of his great-nephew Franz Josef II heralded a new generation. A young and vigorous hand was sorely needed, for the situation was extremely dangerous. Hitler's annexation of the former Czechoslovakia and the world war that soon followed endangered the future of the Liechtensteins' heritage and indeed that of all Europe. Fortunately the principality of Liechtenstein, now joined with Switzerland in a customs union, remained neutral and was never invaded by the Germans. At great risk the bulk of the art collection was moved to Vaduz in the closing months of the war and thus saved for the family. But the subsequent Communist regime in Prague expropriated all the Liechtensteins' estates and residences without compensation, thereby removing over 85 percent of their landholdings. Still, with the Vienna palaces, the Austrian properties, and their position in the principality of Liechtenstein, they could survive comfortably.

The recent changes in the Czech Republic and Slovakia give rise to the hope that some arrangement may eventually be made between the family and the state. Although depleted by postwar sales, the still-splendid art collection rightfully seems to belong at Valtice and Lednice, as do the Liechtensteins themselves. Their two magnificent, albeit quite different, chateaux with a magical park landscape connecting them were described by the early twentieth-century philosopher Rudolf Kassner in his book Second Journey as "a place of the utmost delight and highest happiness . . . with canals, sluices, little bridges and paths slippery with the damp, hedged in by the wine and wheat growing hills."

H U N G A R Y

Introduction

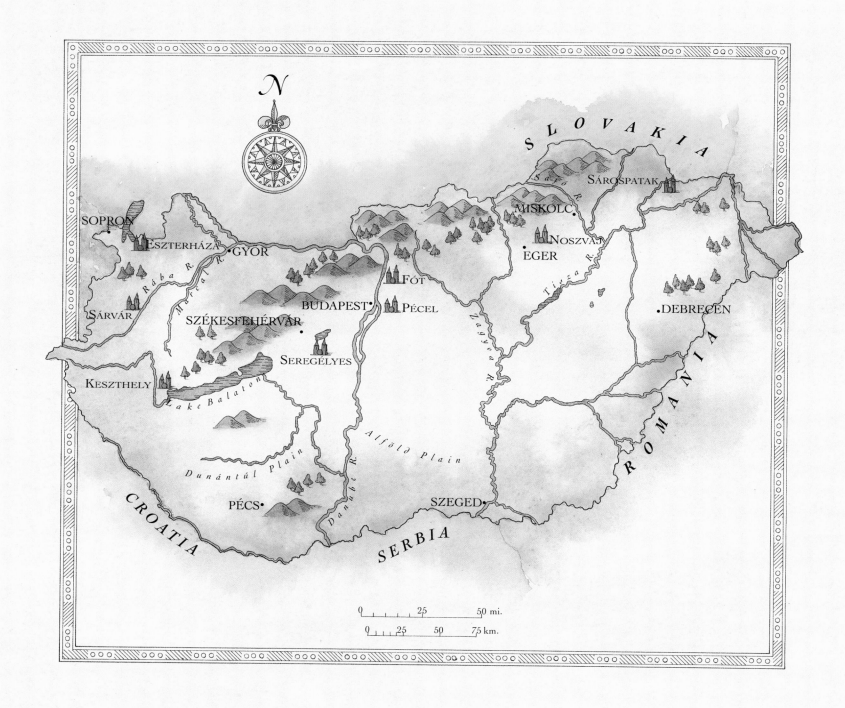

*I*n 1632 an English traveler named William Lithgow wrote, in his book *Rare Adventures and Painefull Peregrinations*, "Now as for the soil of Hungary and kingdom itself and for the goodness of it, it may be termed the granary of Ceres, the garden of Bacchus, the pasturage of Pan and the richest beauty of Sylvan." Hungary has long been noted as a rich and beautiful land, and one of great diversity. North and west of the Danube River, which flows through the country in a great arc, first east then south, lies the undulating landscape of the Dunántúl. On the other side of the river the endless plain called the Alföld stretches to the Carpathian foothills.

The extraordinary variety of the Hungarian countryside is matched only by the rich diversity of political and cultural influences that have molded its history. During Roman times the western part of Hungary, known as Pannonia, became part of the Empire; there the Romans built significant stone structures, which were copied by the Slavic tribes that succeeded them. The eastern area remained beyond the Empire's borders and was overrun by successive waves of nomadic horsemen. This division was repeated later in the sixteenth century when the east of Hungary fell under the Ottoman sway and the west was ruled by the Habsburgs. Still another sort of geopolitical distinction must be observed today, for after two world wars and numerous revolutions the modern national frontiers within which the great houses described hereafter are confined comprise less than a third of the area that in the nineteenth-century days of the Dual Monarchy constituted historic Hungary.

The Roman presence in Pannonia only lasted until the fourth century, to be followed by a series of conquests and occupations that culminated in the arrival from the east of the Magyars around A.D. 900. The Magyars were basically a Finno-Ugric people who spoke a language related to Finnish, Estonian, and other tongues for whom the clan functioned as the basic social unit. Tradition has it that the seven great chiefs elected Árpád, the most powerful of their number, to lead them. Within a decade they controlled all of the area that would become Hungary, and for the ensuing half-century they were the scourge of half of Europe. It was Árpád's great-great-grandson, the newly-converted Vajk, rechristened István (and later canonized as Saint Stephen), who applied to the pope in A.D. 1000 to be recognized as a Christian king. This was duly granted; regalia and a piece of the True Cross were sent from Rome, so the legend goes, and on Christmas Day István was crowned. Thus was the Hungarian nation born.

The efforts of István to unify the country and to establish order were undermined by struggles over the succession after his death, but by degrees the foundations of a nation-state were created. Unlike the Czechs and Poles, its monarchs had no ties of fealty to the Holy Roman emperor and enjoyed untrammeled sovereignty. It was only partially feudal, for the descendants of the early Magyars were still "freemen" owing no allegiance to an overlord. Yet they did form an oligarchy that owned most of the land itself and ruled over a large unfree population. In 1241, however, the country suffered a terrible setback when a Mongol invasion destroyed half the population and devastated the region in less than twelve months. After their withdrawal a year later, King Béla IV vigorously set about the task of rebuilding, founding new towns and encouraging foreign colonists while employing Italian and German masons to restore the royal fortresses. But after his premature death a further period of dynastic chaos intervened culminating in the death of the last male member of the House of Árpád in 1301. Charles Robert of Anjou then seized the crown, restored the disintegrating royal estates, and began to promote the growth of the towns, including one in the unpopulated vicinity of the fort of Buda. The Italo-Dalmation influence that had characterized medieval Hungarian architecture until around 1200 gave way to the French Gothic, a style that was fostered by the arrival of the Angevin rulers. With indi-

Map of modern Hungary showing locations of major country houses.

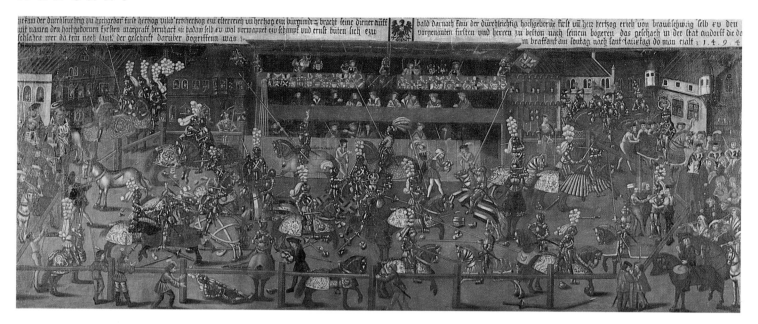

viduals beginning to build more elaborately, the country's growing wealth was reflected in a grander and increasingly sophisticated architecture.

Under the Angevins, especially Lajos the Great, Hungary became a European power and enjoyed a period of peace and growth. Largely freed from external threats, the country prospered greatly—thanks principally to the production of its gold mines, which also enhanced the splendors of the court. A new social structure more akin to western feudalism was fostered, with the king at its apex. Land was granted to an emergent magnate class whose members were richer and more powerful than most members of the old oligarchy. Thus by about 1380 some fifty of these families owned a third of the country. The power of the magnates was to an extent counterbalanced by that of the gentry, descendants of the original Magyars who were encouraged by the crown to exercise power on a local level through their own elected representatives.

In 1351 Lajos confirmed the nobility's privileges, originally granted 130 years before by the Golden Bull. Land tenure was also stabilized by entailing estates in the owner's male line and only allowing them to revert to the crown on the extinction of all heirs; daughters were jointly entitled to a quarter of the estate's assessed value in cash. Under such conditions the landowning classes, especially the magnates, flourished and major building projects such as the castle of Sárvár in western Hungary were commenced.

Lajos's death in 1382, however, heralded an era of renewed instability. His son-in-law Zsigmond, whose reign was to last fifty years, was resented as a foreign intruder, especially after gaining the German and Bohemian thrones as well. While he promoted economic, military, and administrative reforms, he spent much time abroad, a situation that led to the creation of the office of palatine, which represented the king in his absence. His extravagant foreign policy also forced him to sell so many of his lands to the magnates that at his death the crown owned only 5 percent of the land whereas once it had owned a third. And Zsigmond's request to the Diet for new taxation increased the burdens suffered by the peasants during an era in which Hungary began the transition to a money economy.

Even before the end of Zsigmond's reign, a renewed threat from the Ottoman Turks was evident. The king's death in 1437 was followed almost immediately by that of his son-in-law, Albrecht of Habsburg, so that at this critical juncture the country was leaderless. Only the genius of János

Painting of a medieval Hungarian tournament dated 1492, now hanging at Sárvár, western Hungary.

Castle of Frakno or Forchtenstein, now in modern Austria.

Hunyadi saved the situation. A minor noble who had begun life as a condottiere, Hunyadi in 1456 decisively routed the Turkish army that was besieging Belgrade. When Albrecht's son died unmarried the nobles elected Hunyadi's son, Mátyás Corvinus, in his stead.

A golden age returned to Hungary under the rule of this great monarch. A true Renaissance prince, he encouraged the arts and architecture, while scholars of international repute flocked to his court. A man of boundless energy, after a demanding day of governance he would dispute for hours with visiting intellectuals and read learned books half the night. It was he who transformed Buda into one of Europe's cultural centers. By 1480 the Renaissance style had taken root there, several decades earlier than anywhere else north of the Alps. The transition was helped by the close ties between Hungary and Italy promoted by the king's marriage to Beatrice, a Neapolitan princess. Florentine craftsmen and architects came to Buda, enlarging a workshop extant since the fourteenth century and creating an ornamental style that was distinctly *all'antica*, in contrast to France or Germany. This repetitive modular architecture, developed by Filippo Brunelleschi and adapted to Vitruvius's theories by Leon Battista Alberti, could easily be employed in a country where straightforward masonry techniques were more common than elaborate stone dressing. The red marble quarried near Esztergom, for instance, which had hitherto been used only for tombs, was ideally suited to this kind of decoration.

Mátyás Corvinus's palace at Buda was the most important example of Renaissance architecture in Hungary and became a model for secular buildings in Bohemia and Poland as well, although sadly it has now almost entirely disappeared. Terraced into a hillside, the fountains and gardens of his summer palace at Visegrád were also the first notable examples of landscape design in the country. The archbishop of Esztergom, Miklós Oláh, described it as "indeed worthy of a king in its splendid position, while there are more than 350 rooms in it. . . . [It has] a court planted

with lime trees, which give off a sweet smell in spring. In the middle of it a fountain plays, an artfully sculpted work in red marble, which is decorated with reliefs of the Muses."

After Mátyás's death, his successors from the Polish Jagellon dynasty continued to commission projects in the same style, including their residences in Prague and Kraków. Thus the Bakócz Chapel in the Esztergom Cathedral has close similarities with the Zsigmond Chapel in the Wawel palace at Kraków—perhaps both were by the same architect, Bartolomeo Berrecci. Renaissance loggias were added to some of the nobility's castles (the earliest at Simontornya dates from 1508), as well as major new additions such as the Red Tower at Sárospatak in eastern Hungary.

During this period military architecture too became more sophisticated as well as more decorative, a development that the improvement of firearms and the political circumstances in Hungary made imperative. Under Mátyás's weak successors, government declined, revenues dwindled, and the peasantry's condition deteriorated dramatically. A savage jacquerie broke out in 1514, which was brutally suppressed; the Diet, much alarmed, condemned the entire peasant class to "real and perpetual servitude," irrevocably binding them to the land and raising the corvée to fifty-two days per annum. When the succession to the throne became uncertain the Diet passed a resolution in 1505 never again to accept a foreign king and proposed Ján Zápolya, a former palatine and the country's largest landowner. Despite their strident nationalism, however, the nobility failed to look to the nation's defences, which were in ruins for lack of money. In 1520 the Turkish sultan, Süleyman the Magnificent, demanded tribute, and when this was refused, marched on and captured Belgrade. A belated recognition that a new army was needed failed to produce the necessary funds, however, and the Turks invaded in earnest in 1526. The tiny Hungarian army, only 25,000 strong, met Ottoman forces of about 100,000 at Mohács. After an ill-advised attack they were virtually annihilated, the king himself killed in the rout.

This disaster heralded two centuries of partition and warfare. Although the Turks temporarily withdrew, a lengthy civil war ensued between Ferdinand of Habsburg, who had proclaimed himself king, and Zápolya, who was crowned by some of the Hungarian nobles. The latter's death in 1540 gave the sultan another excuse to intervene and resulted in the Turks occupying the central part of the country. Habsburg attempts to control Transylvania proved unsuccessful; thus Ferdinand's dominions were confined to the western areas of Hungary, known as "Royal" Hungary. When the ambitious Báthorys, a family of Hungarian nobles, succeeded the Zápolyas in Transylvania, the trisection of the country was complete.

The Turkish zone of occupation fared worst of all. The peasants were brutally exploited and those nobles who had not fled were reduced to servile status. All land was confiscated by the state, which managed a fifth and let out the rest in small fiefs. Since none of these were inheritable, their holders' sole interest lay in squeezing the maximum profit out of the land. Farming was primitive and, with life so insecure, people abandoned villages and congregated in the towns. The Ottomans were satisfied to adapt existing buildings to their requirements and constructed little apart from a few mosques, minarets, and baths. Such characteristics of Eastern architecture as were introduced struck no deep roots.

If the Renaissance style withered away in central Hungary, it lived on in the Royal or Transdanubian provinces and in Transylvania—although its traditions were continued in a more functional way, with less Italian and greater local influence. At Sárospatak the Perényi family used a Lombard architect and masons from Kraków who were later supplemented by local serfs trained as stonemasons. In contrast, developments in western Hungary remained closer to those prevailing in Austria, Bohemia, or southern Germany, although many Italian craftsmen worked there; in-

Renaissance-era portal in the Red Tower at Sárospatak, northeastern Hungary.

deed the imperial war council placed them in charge of rebuilding the obsolete fortifications along the frontier in 1556. These castles typically featured bastions at each corner enclosing rectangular, arcaded central courtyards, as exemplified by Tamás Nádasdy's reconstruction of Sárvár.

Throughout the later sixteenth century, however, sporadic border warfare continued; the Habsburg frontiers lacked an unbroken line of defence, a situation that did little to create an environment in which the arts of peace could flourish. Furthermore Ferdinand of Habsburg and his successors Maximilian II and Rudolph showed scant interest in Hungarian problems and subordinated national defence to the far wider needs of the Habsburg dominions. A spirit of discontented nationalism was fostered by the coming of the Reformation, which produced a vigorous strain of Hungarian Protestantism.

During the early seventeenth century, Transylvania and eastern Hungary provided the impetus for cultural development. Under the independent princes Gábor Bethlen and later György Rákóczi I, whose fierce Calvinism made them natural enemies of the Habsburgs, a revival of architecture and the arts took place. The Renaissance style dating from Corvinus's early models now spread back from Bohemia and Poland. Floral motifs and vernacular patterns appeared on village and country church architecture as a local development of the style, while small towns began

to construct civil buildings. The nobility, too, began to build houses again such as those at Bethlenszentmiklós or Bonchida in Transylvania. Sadly, however, the region's princes overreached themselves—after conquering much of Royal Hungary and protecting the Protestant communities from their Habsburg overlords during the Thirty Years' War, they fell foul of their ultimate protector, the Ottoman government. Turkish troops invaded in 1660, stifling most of this cultural revival.

By then, however, things had at last begun to stir within the Habsburg dominions. As the Ottomans' power grew less aggressive and expansionist and the Treaty of Westphalia restored peace to Central Europe in 1648, life in Hungary became somewhat more stable. The Counter-Reformation had made some progress in Hungary in regaining Catholic converts, and a party of magnates, largely recatholicised and loyal to the Habsburgs, came into being, who with the higher prelates formed a separate upper house in the Diet. Resented by the lesser nobility, still mainly Protestant, they were also distrusted by the bureaucrats in Vienna as potential separatists. As for the emperors, they still had to submit themselves for election and swear to respect the Diet's privileges.

Some members of the magnate class like the Esterházy family were busy amassing vast wealth during this era and were keen to spend some of it on visible display. Hence Pál Esterházy commissioned Carlo Martino Carlone in the 1660s to remodel the original family seat, Kismarton (better known today as Eisenstadt), in the fashionable baroque style. The form of baroque that was introduced into Hungary via Austria originated with the French and Northern Italian schools. The style had already been well established in Western Europe, but with Hungary partitioned and racked by continual fighting, cultural development had lagged decades behind. Moreover the baroque had been identified with the Catholic and absolutist tendencies of the great Habsburg and Bourbon monarchies, and therefore received a mixed reception from many Hungarians. Nevertheless baroque architecture did take root in the seventeenth century. Seen at its best in aristocratic residences or ecclesiastical buildings, it also influenced many new houses constructed in towns outside the sphere of war.

Despite the cultural and artistic flowering that occurred during this era, many Hungarians chafed under the harsh and repressive rule of the Habsburgs. Ironically, however, just as opposition to and hatred of the Austrians reached its height, they began to liberate the country from its Turkish occupiers. In 1686 Buda was recovered from Turkish control, and within several years all of Hungary and Transylvania except for a southeasterly pocket had been reconquered. With the Treaty of Karlowitz in 1699 the sultan relinquished almost all of his claims and the Ottoman occupation came to an end. But the cost of reunification was terrible. The exactions of both armies destroyed agriculture, and towns were left in a ruined state by the Turks. Under the Austrian government, political and religious persecution was instituted and, although the emperor swore to observe Hungary's traditional privileges, the Diet was not convened. Discontent mounted until in 1703 Ferenc Rákóczi II, heir of the former princes of Transylvania, raised the standard of open revolt—albeit reluctantly, for this gentle character knew that he faced overwhelming odds. The rebellion continued for eight long years until peace was concluded with the Habsburgs in 1711.

While the Hungarian revolt had indeed failed, the new emperor, Charles VI, was friendlier to his subjects and respected their rights more faithfully. In 1723 the Diet therefore voted to accept the succession in the female line of his daughter, Maria Theresa, conceding also that Hungary had lost the right to elect its own monarch in favor of the inseparable connection with the Habsburgs. Simultaneously a standing army was created, two-thirds foreign, and a new council, under the palatine's presidency and sitting at Pozsony or Pressburg (now Bratislava in Slovakia), be

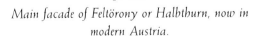

Main facade of Feltörony or Halbthurn, now in modern Austria.

came the chief administrative body. Its independence from Vienna together with that of the court chancellery was formally confirmed.

The eighteenth century, then, was an age of recuperation for Hungary, one providing a long era of peace, at last. The population increased enormously, probably tripling during the century, villages were resettled again, and land was cleared for cultivation. The taxable land surface, i.e., that consisting of urbarial peasant holdings, multiplied fivefold, a development that produced huge increases in the rent rolls for the great landowners. Those families loyal to the dynasty—Forgách, Esterházy, Pálffy, Rudnyányski or Grassalkovich—were well rewarded with office and government contracts, thus becoming enormously rich. One obvious way to spend this money was on grand new residences both in the city and in the countryside.

It is against this background that the cultural and architectural history of Hungary must be viewed. Fittingly the first major commission for a chateau after the Turks were expelled came from the foremost military hero of the reconquest, Prince Eugene of Savoy. In 1698 he bought an estate called Ráckeve on the Danube just south of Buda and commissioned the Viennese architect Johann Lukas von Hildebrandt to build a castle on an island in the river. Hildebrandt was nearly thirty years old, an unknown military engineer who had taken part in two of the prince's campaigns, while his patron was only thirty-four. This was to be the start of a collaboration that was to produce the Belvedere Palace in Vienna and would last for three decades. The Italian-trained Hildebrandt, a natural genius influenced by Andrea Palladio and Francesco Borromini, took the floor plans of Vaux-le-Vicomte as a partial model. Although not finished until the mid-eighteenth century and never really lived in by its busy owner, Ráckeve epitomizes the ideal baroque chateau. Elegant and well-proportioned, with a domed central pavilion flanked by protruding wings, this distinguished castle was to be widely copied by local architects later in the century. In 1711, nine years after finishing his work at Ráckeve, Hildebrandt began work on another house, this one for the Harrach family in the far west of the country. For Feltörony (now called Halbturn and located in contemporary Austria), he evolved plans based on François Mansart's Maisons Lafitte, designing a huge central hall surrounded by a double corridor on each side, which led to smaller adjoining rooms.

Taking Hildebrandt as his chief mentor, one architect, András Mayerhoffer from Pest, carried out some important commissions. The houses he designed—Pécel, Hatvan, and especially Gödöllő, for the Grassalkovich family—have a basic U-shaped plan with wings extended either to form a cour d'honneur before the main entrance or inverted to enclose a terrace at the back leading onto the gardens. Mayerhoffer's proportions were exceptionally good. The height of the central section was sometimes raised to house the main hall and surmounted by a cupola, while suites of well-proportioned reception rooms led off on both sides from this main axis. The bedrooms on the upper floors were reached by wide staircases and broad, light corridors. On a basement floor were found the kitchen areas and the servants' quarters. The flexibility of the U-shaped plan allowed Mayerhoffer to endow these houses with highly individual details; indeed some display novel ideas of picturesque and even theatrical conception. State rooms, staircases, and small rooms, too, were decorated with friezes and cornices, rich in their plastic effect, and sculptural ornamentation. The overall impression created was one of great spaciousness, an effect carried over into the design of the large formal gardens. Not all buildings were as skillfully planned as Mayerhoffer's, however. At Edelény near Eger, for example, an unknown architect designed a house with the wings too short and the disproportionately thick end towers only the same height as the main block.

As the century advanced, both the magnate class and the prelates be-

Main facade of Ráckeve, on the Danube south of Budapest.

Prince Eugene of Savoy's coat of arms on the facade of Ráckeve.

came richer. The primate, the archbishop of Esztergom, for example, lived on a 350,000-forint income. In their prosperity he and other churchmen began to commission buildings: the small episcopal residence at Sümeg was constructed by the art-loving bishop of Veszprém, Márton Biró, in 1757. The parish church there, decorated with frescoes by Franz Anton Maulbertsch and dating from the same period, is a particular delight. A grander edifice is the bishop's palace at Veszprém built from 1765 to 1766 by the tireless Jakab Fellner, who designed churches, colleges, and castles at Mór and Tata as well. The main effect of Veszprém lies in its dramatic site along the ridge of the hill opposite the cathedral. The curving carriage drive under the wide balcony betokens worldly as much as ecclesiastical pomp. Prelates like the bishop, however, did not enjoy the

same immunity from taxation as the nobility; indeed they regularly contributed to the state-controlled church foundations and made loans to the crown, which were seldom repaid.

Free of this burden, the incomes of the magnates soared during this period. Prince Esterházy was estimated to receive 750,000 forints a year, Count Batthyány, 450,000; two other magnates' annual incomes were estimated at 350,000, while a further four got over 150,000. In contrast, a skilled workman during this era would receive about 1½ forints per day. Despite their dazzling incomes, most of these magnates were relatively new to the ranks of the Hungarian aristocracy. The old nobility had been so badly decimated at Mohács that not more than ten of its families still survived by 1700, and so a new aristocracy grew up, mainly created by and usually loyal to the Habsburgs. Their residences provided a substitute for the court of their absentee king, and they, rather than the king, were often the chief patrons of aspiring artists or architects. Yet during the eighteenth century this powerful class became less and less Hungarian in language, custom, and sentiment. All too many were first-generation foreigners anyway who had been awarded citizenship at the behest of the government. Moreover, titles were now awarded without regard to ownership of or a grant to landed property, and consequently they proliferated. By 1778 there were 20 princes (all of the Holy Roman Empire), 151 counts, and 184 barons. And although the volume of houses built increased, around two hundred altogether during Maria Theresa's reign, no distinctive national style developed.

Emperor Francis Joseph and Empress Elizabeth with family at Gödöllő, c. 1870. (Hungarian National Museum, Budapest.)

Detail of the Grassalkovich coat of arms on the pediment at Gödöllő.

While constitutionally the Hungarian nobility remained a homogeneous group, actually it was now highly stratified, with great aristocrats at the top and poor gentry who had lost their immunity from taxation at the bottom. In between came the main body of the gentry, the so-called *bene possessionati*. Now mostly lawyers and agriculturalists rather than soldiers, they controlled the county administrations. This class of the gentry was also numerous, estimated at around 390,000 men and women in 1788, or nearly 5 percent of the population. With increased prosperity they too began to build more dignified residences both in the towns and in the country, where their houses had formerly been of clay with reed roofs. Unlike the gentry, the great nobles began to be lured to Vienna by Maria Theresa, a move that strengthened their connection with the throne at the expense of that with the rest of the nation. With the cost of life at court leading to massive debts and an indecorous scramble for office, the gentry increasingly came to be seen as the embodiment of Hungarian culture and nationhood, the precursors of the nationalist revival that was to come with the nineteenth century.

Before that, however, there were several setbacks. Maria Theresa died in 1780, to be succeeded by her son Joseph, an enlightened autocrat who wanted efficient, centralized government. He immediately introduced far-reaching reforms to counteract the stagnation in Hungary's economy and society that had set in, and to promote the centralizing absolutism in which he believed. The Patent of Tolerations in 1781 allowed complete freedom of worship and equality for the Protestant and Eastern Orthodox communities; the Livings Patent dissolved some of the religious orders and applied their property to founding new parishes with elementary schools attached; and the Peasant Patent granted the peasantry freedom to leave their holdings on paying their dues, to marry, and to put their children into any trade. The storm of noble and Roman Catholic protests grew when the emperor tried economic pressure to force the nobility to

Interior of the chapel at Gödöllő.

*Portrait of Count Antal Grassalkovich, mid- to
late eighteenth century, now in the church at
Gödöllő.*

renounce its fiscal exemption. Furthermore a general land tax was announced, the entire country was declared united, and German became the compulsory language of administration. When an unsuccessful war with Turkey was started in 1787, revolt nearly broke out, intrigues with Austria's enemies began, and the counties, unauthorized, resumed their old powers. A crisis was narrowly averted in 1790 when Joseph, mortally ill, revoked most of his controversial measures and shortly thereafter died.

His successor, Leopold, compromised by acknowledging Hungary's status as an independent kingdom and permitting the teaching of Magyar in the schools. The incipient feudal revolt was aborted, yet it proved impossible to return to the status quo ante, for the French Revolution had broken out and its ideals were being disseminated throughout Europe. Many of the younger nobles whose cultural horizons had been broadened by their travels desired a degree of change—albeit not the radical challenge to the ruling classes posed by the French revolutionaries. They were supported by the few Protestant aristocrats, who shared with the reformers a decided anticlericalism and an advocacy of religious toleration.

In this intellectual climate the baroque style and its derivative, the rococo—whose richly ornamented, often fantastic designs had appeared in Hungary too late to have widespread appeal—gave way gradually to a neoclassical architecture of simple composed lines. Frequently the baroque facade was retained, giving rise to the term "braid architecture," a term that derived from the fashionable braided wigs and was propagated especially by the indefatigable Jakab Fellner. Landscape design had not changed either from the formal gardens modeled on the seventeenth century style of André Le Nôtre. Even in the 1780s at Eszterháza, the grandest aristocratic residence and setting in Hungary, the complex of buildings in the park and monuments such as the great waterfall were still designed in this manner. The preoccupation with proportion remained so that the house fitted in harmoniously with its surroundings and all features, both internal and external, stemmed from the central axis.

With the dawning of the nineteenth century the predominance of neo-classicism was assured. Italian in inspiration, the buildings remained symmetrical, while the revival of ancient Greek and Roman aesthetics involved the use of columns as principal elements of design and decoration in a well-proportioned whole. The projecting sections of the facade grew less pronounced, the curvature of the baroque was eliminated, and lines became less emphatic as if to stress the harmony of the entire facade rather than its details. Neoclassicism advocated nothing novel in its theory of construction or in its use of space, aiming only for more refined and harmonious buildings. But many of the neoclassical architects, a number of them French or German, were extremely competent. Mihály Pollack, the prime mover in the Town Improvement Commission of Pest, was an able and prolific Hungarian who designed municipal buildings (his masterpiece being the National Museum), city palaces like those for the Zichy and Festetics families, and such country houses as Gyömrő, Fót, Alcsút, and Dég. His compatriots Mihály Péchy and Jozsef Hild were equally noteworthy, the latter like Pollack founding an architectural dynasty that lasted for two generations.

After 1800 academic learning introduced from abroad supplemented the training provided by Hungary's traditional guilds. Master builders still received their initial training by working on local projects, but now many had some experience working abroad, experience usually supplemented by academic studies. Nevertheless there was seldom a clearly defined theoretical foundation for their designs; most of the native-born architects like Pollack relied more on personal experience and on academic exemplars.

Although most building activity was still carried out under the aegis of the guilds, foreign architects were frequently brought in by their clients. Thus, for example, the French architect Charles de Moreau was commis-

Coburg family coat of arms at Edelény.

Wrought-iron gates at Edelény, northeastern Hungary.

General view of Edelény.

sioned by the Esterházys to remodel Kismarton, while those of German origin like Heinrich Koch, Sr., Alois Pichl, and Anton Riegl all designed buildings without needing special government endorsement. (The office of architecture under imperial supervision nevertheless remained a powerful force.) Guild participation was arranged by appointing a guild master to a supervisory position—hence the Károlyis employed Koch to draw up the plans for their new mansion in Budapest but hired Pollack and József Hofrichter to supervise the construction.

The alterations made to Kismarton illustrate the point. The French architect Charles de Moreau drew up grandiose plans, which involved building two new wings joined up to the main house by colonnades. A double row of Corinthian columns rising through the building's three storeys were added to the garden facade. Moreau planned for the main block to be set on a podium ground floor with an approach on both sides via a carriage ramp. He also intended that the library and picture gallery at either end of his new wings should be surmounted by towers. This scheme was never realized because of the Napoleonic Wars, but limited alterations were carried out by Johann Ehmann, the Esterházy family architect. The building's external appearance changed considerably: the four towers received identical low tent-shaped roofs, while the front facade was given a balcony supported by fourteen Tuscan columns framing a portico over the main entrance. The moat was filled in and a park *à l'Anglaise* was laid out. Moreau was again consulted about the colonnaded

General view of the Bishop's Palace at Veszprém, near Lake Balaton.

Sculptural ornament over the facade of the Bishop's Palace at Veszprém.

rotunda, completed in 1819 and named the Leopoldinen Temple in honor of the prince's Liechtenstein wife, whose statue by Antonio Canova stood within it.

Country houses were not the only feature of this building boom. Theaters, concert halls, and public libraries such as Pollack's grandiose reading room in the Calvinist College at Sárospatak were now erected to meet the cultural needs of society, while the proliferating county and town halls attested to growing urbanization. Most of these new structures were characterized by modest ornamentation. Neoclassicism favored carved capitals, masks, and bosses, with stone reliefs placed in recessed panels under windows. Entrance halls, with their pilasters, wall recesses, and statues, were the most distinctive feature, although internal courtyards were models of simplicity. With such straightforward tenets, the new style carried considerable popular appeal—in the towns the bourgeoisie adapted it for their houses and even apartment buildings, while in rural areas it came to influence the design of simpler dwellings too. With its rational and modular simplicity solving as it does a range of architectural problems, neoclassicism has also been commonly used in the post–World War II era by the Communist regime.

The cultural rebirth of Hungary, of which the neoclassical building boom formed a significant part, was not paralleled by developments on the political front. The Diet, like the emperor, did not want the revolutionary upheavals that convulsed France. Leopold died suddenly in 1792, to be succeeded by his timid son, Francis, and for the next twenty-five years a stalemate ensued between the Habsburg government and the Diet. The emperor refused to call the Diet except to request funding, which the Diet resented and which it refused to provide at one point—a move that resulted in the body not being reconvened again for thirteen years. When Francis was finally forced to summon the Diet and beg them for subsidies they demanded in return the restoration of the country's ancient liberties and the wider use of the Magyar language.

This development formed one of the cornerstones in the growth of Hungary's national consciousness. Lexicographers having revived Magyar as a literary language, poets, novelists, and playwrights now began to write in it. Their effusions may have been of mixed quality but their enthusiasm for costumes, dances, or anything else authentically Magyar was genuine. Here the nobility took the lead. The diminished appeal of a life spent at court and the increased profitability of the agrarian economy combined to encourage landowners to spend more time on their estates. Interest in the Magyar heritage was just one facet of their renewed identification with national life. The number of new country houses continued to grow while many existing buildings had one or two additional stories erected over the original ground floor of the traditional Hungarian manor house, known as a curia. Imposing facades overlooked both parks and forecourts and were often surrounded by beautifully manicured landscapes. Yet the interiors frequently remained architecturally unpretentious, chapels being the most ambitious features along with the colonnaded porticoes, ranging from dignified peristyles to rustic verandas, which every neoclassical mansion boasted. The similarity of style and the lack of display made it hard to draw a clear line between the great noble seats and the smaller manor houses of the gentry.

The identification of common political interests between the nobles and the gentry had also grown more marked. Most of the educated classes fretted under the stifling conservatism of Vienna. The Diet of 1830 was quiescent, agreeing to support Austria's chief minister Klemens Fürst von Metternich in containing the revolutions of that year, but its successor of 1832 was very different. One of its most vocal leaders was István Széchényi, scion of one of Hungary's most illustrious families and son of Ferenc, founder of the National Széchényi Library. His forebears, huge

Main facade of Kismarton or Eisenstadt, now in modern Austria.

landowners in western Hungary, were already known for their cultivated tastes. A pleasant mid-eighteenth-century house at the family's seat, Nagycenk, had already been extensively remodeled around 1800 by József Ringer of the nearby town of Sopron, who worked for the Esterházys as well. He had also designed the charming funerary chapel in which the rusticated stone crypt supports a dignified entrance framed by two Doric columns and crowned by a frieze of triglyphs and a pediment. Now Széchényi turned his attention to literature. In his book *Hitel* (*Credit*), he exhorted his peers to renounce some of their privileges and permit the needed modernization from which they too would ultimately benefit. In 1828 he divided part of his estate among the landless poor, writing, "We must give the example that not only can every man have enough but can also grow rich. We must strive for the common good." Unheard-of words from a member of the nobility, then 400,000 strong. Loyal to the dynasty, he recognized nevertheless how sadly backward and undeveloped his country was in comparison with Western Europe.

At last the floodgates had opened. The Diet did not rise until 1836, but by that time far more radical demands for reform than Széchényi's had been voiced. An anti-Habsburg party emerged under the leadership of Lajos Kossuth which, even if partially aristocratic in composition, sought far-reaching innovations: universal taxation, abolition of the "robot" or forced labor, emancipation of the peasants, an extended franchise, and reform of the press. In the Diet the unassuming Ferenc Deák led the reformers, and even conservatives like József Eötvös argued for an efficient central government responsible to the electorate and not to Vienna. In 1840 Magyar finally became the official language, which enraged all the non-Magyar minorities, and a moderate reform ministry under György Apponyi took office promoting mainly economic changes. The reformers were not appeased however, and demanded a genuinely national ministry along with universal taxation. The Diet of 1847 met with both parties of reformers, the moderates and the radicals, which were roughly equal in strength. The probability of far-reaching change was in the air.

The fall of France's king Louis Philippe in February 1848 ignited the spark of revolution throughout Europe. Metternich and Apponyi soon resigned office. A deputation from both houses of the Diet went to Vienna with an address to the crown that, inspired by Kossuth, embodied Hungarian demands for a responsible national government. This was immediately conceded; a constitutional monarchy was set up, universal taxation introduced, and the peasants became freehold proprietors of their holdings. A union with Transylvania was also enacted and independent ministries of defence and finance were established.

Although the emperor had approved these changes, opposition from Vienna continued, if covertly. And the non-Magyar minorities—Slovaks, Saxons, Romanians, Croatians, and Ruthenes—expressed misgivings. Soon enough the new dawn proved false. Croatian forces rebelled and in March 1849 an Austrian army occupied Buda, proclaiming the partition of the country into five parts. The Diet responded by declaring that the

Main façade of Dég, central Hungary.

Habsburgs had forfeited the throne, and appointed Kossuth provisional head of state. In June, however, Czar Nicholas sent two armies to the new Austrian emperor Francis Joseph's aid, and the rebels were outnumbered by over two to one. Kossuth resigned in August and fled the country, while two days later the Hungarian forces surrendered. In the ensuing reign of terror, many were executed and an absolutist bureaucratic government was installed. The country was redivided into five crown lands, the counties' and municipalities' autonomy was abolished, German was reinstated as the official language, and taxation increased more than tenfold during the next decade. Many nobles were exiled or imprisoned, while the peasants, 625,000 of whom remained in possession of their freeholds, for once suffered least.

Austria's defeat in 1859 at the hands of France and Italy convinced Francis Joseph that some settlement was necessary, although negotiations lasted six years. Only after the catastrophe of the Austro-Prussian War was Vienna at last prepared to agree to terms. Under the *Ausgleich* or Compromise of 1867, Hungary remained tied to Austria—the emperor continued as head of state and Hungary did not gain the right to act autonomously in foreign affairs—but internally the nation regained total independence. Joint Hungarian and Austrian ministers for finance, defence, and foreign affairs were appointed, answerable to both legislatures; Transylvania's reincorporation into Hungary was sanctioned, and a responsible ministry under Deák's lieutenant, Gyula Andrássy, was formed. A Croat-Hungarian deal was also struck giving some scope to the former's claims, and various minority languages were accorded a protected status, although Magyar was the official tongue. In March the Diet accepted the Compromise, and in June, Francis Joseph, accompanied by the empress, was crowned amid much pomp in Budapest. Thus began the Dual Monarchy.

Austro-Hungarian relations were improved by the popular success the Empress Elizabeth enjoyed with her Hungarian subjects. In 1867 thanks to the personal intervention of Andrássy, the imperial couple were presented with the former Grassalkovich estate of Gödöllő. This was the

Front door and portico of the episcopal palace at Sümeg, western Hungary.

Main facade of Nagycenk, northwestern Hungary.

fulfillment of a dream for Elizabeth, who had long coveted it, although Francis Joseph had refused to buy the property, claiming that he did not have the money. Recently modernized by Miklós Ybl, it contained 100 rooms, including a magnificent ballroom with white and gold plasterwork and a huge chapel, which now serves as the parish church. The residence was set on a 10,000 hectare estate on which the empress could indulge her passion for hunting, a passion that ran so deep that she graded her guests according to their equestrian abilities. Elizabeth's frequent visits to Gödöllő received wide publicity and helped to foster the goodwill engendered by the Compromise.

During these eventful years much changed on the cultural and architectural as well as on the political scene. Neoclassicism retained its dominant role until the 1840s when it began to be displaced by the Gothic revival style, which employed features borrowed from medieval prototypes. For thirty years or so this style remained dominant until it in turn was eclipsed by the new idiom of eclecticism.

If sobriety and proportion were the keynotes of Hungarian neoclassicism, the Gothic revival architects, unconcerned with serenity or symmetry, delimited opposite values. Anxious to revive a neglected medievalism as expressed in the teachings of Eugène Viollet-le-Duc, they nevertheless made scant efforts to copy all its details, especially in Hungary where styles usually arrived late and developed haphazardly. Although their work leaned toward the Romanesque and Gothic, an additional interest in Byzantine and Islamic design, not inappropriate in a Balkan country, also developed. In this period French and Italian influences, formerly paramount, were replaced by others from Britain and Germany.

Perhaps the most important architect of the age was Miklós Ybl. After studying at Munich and Vienna, he became a pupil of Mihály Pollack, with whose son Ágoston he collaborated on an early Gothic revival house

for the Batthyánys at Ikervár. His career took off in the 1850s when he completed the church at Fót for the Károlyis and the Vigadó, an apartment block in Budapest—arguably the two most important buildings in their style in Hungary. But a host of lesser architects, families like the Zitterbarths, Breins and Kasseliks, developed flourishing local practices in this era. Foreigners like Alois Pichl and Franz Beer also continued to receive many commissions. All deliberately sought to incorporate national features in their architecture. Forged iron, for instance, was replaced by cast iron and glass. And informal landscape gardens *à l'Anglaise* replaced the French and Italian parterres, a trend already apparent in neoclassical design. Indeed a "parkomania" (to use Prince Hermann Pückler-Muskau's terminology) developed with some landowners, who borrowed from their farmland for the grounds surrounding their houses. A number of landscape designers like Ignác Erményi who worked at Fót found a ready market for their services.

Most earlier Gothic revival houses in Hungary, such as Orosvár, built by Franz Beer for the Zichys, were distinctively castellated and harked back to English medieval architecture. Gradually an asymmetrical tower, the sole purpose of which was symbolic, became commonplace. The layout of the rooms, culminating in a grand hall of ancestors, often resembled a museum's. This was in marked contrast to the predictable neoclassical layout in which the ballroom, salon, library, and dining room were located on the ground floor with guest and family bedrooms above. Frequently a neoclassical house was remodeled in the Gothic revival style so that it contained a mix of these features. A picturesque example of this is the Brunszwick family mansion at Martonvásár, where at the turn of the century Beethoven had stayed and composed. Not only was the great musician a friend of Count Franz Brunszwick, he was also an admirer of his middle daughter, Josephine. Her eldest sister, Therese, lamented in her diaries that the two never married. Later, over a twenty-year span from 1855 to 1875, Martonvásár was redesigned by an unknown architect as a two-story house with a crenellated attic, one displaying the pure line of the English Gothic. The arrangement of tall and short windows and projecting facades achieves a degree of symmetry. The entrance section survives from the older neoclassical building, where clustered columns bound by broken arches form a covered entrance that supports a tracery stonework balcony onto which the reception hall's triple windows open. The deeply notched and crenellated gables and turrets enhance the picturesque effect.

Opportunities were not lacking for others who wished to indulge their architectural fantasies, for these were, on the whole, years of economic boom. The Compromise of 1867 placed Hungary in a more stable position than at any time since the pre-Mohács era. The country was unified under one government whose wide powers were answerable to a new parliament, and the crown enjoyed rights not much exceeding those of a constitutional monarchy. Hungary's joint voice in the conduct of finance, foreign affairs, and defence was far from insignificant, for the country was by far the largest unit in the Empire. Even the 30 percent of the common expenditure payable by Hungary was not inequitable. In Parliament, Deák's followers were opposed by Kossuth's disciples, who still yearned for independence, while the left centrists, who accepted the Compromise, still repudiated any institutions not compatible with the nation's autonomy. Many laws were introduced to modernize the country, and in an era of growing prosperity and good harvests agriculture flourished and foreign capital poured into Hungary. The financial crash of 1873 created some shock waves, but Deák's followers joined with Kalman Tisza's left centrist faction to form the new Liberal party, which held power for the next thirty years. It retained the support of the magnates and small nobles, even if many farmers and bourgeois still believed in Kossuth's policy, but its majority was essentially maintained by gerrymandering and by imposing strict educational qualifications on non-Magyar voters.

Agriculture, which engaged 65 percent of the work force, was the foundation of the nation's wealth. Hungary had always been a fertile country and this still held true—indeed the volume of produce had doubled between 1870 and 1890. The great estates had not begun to decline: in 1895 nearly one-third of the land surface, 17.5 million acres, was owned by under 4,000 proprietors (some of whom, like the Church, were not private individuals). Almost 9 million acres were held by only 128 proprietors, a statistic not so different from a century earlier when 108 families were reckoned to own a third of the land. The larger farms tended to swallow up the smaller landholdings, the owners of which, if they were members of the gentry, involved themselves with political life and provided the chief revolutionaries in 1848, or sank to the ranks of the peasantry. Yet problems were looming. By the turn of the century competition from overseas wheat had reduced returns dramatically and many of the more extravagant nobles were mortgaged to the hilt. Some of the gentry who had never really recovered from the post-1848 disasters were ruined by the depression of the 1880s, or barely escaped it by entering government service in large numbers. Among the peasants, the repeated subdivision of the land meant that three-quarters of the 2.8 million peasant

Porch over the front door of Martonvásár, central Hungary.

holdings were under ten *"hölds,"* a *höld* being 1.46 acres (75 percent of these were actually around five, although eight was regarded as the minimum on which to support a family). Moreover half of the agrarian population was now entirely landless.

In other spheres the pre-1900 outlook in Hungary appeared more positive. Financial order had been restored—budgets were balanced and the national debt was better funded. The railways network had been completed, the main rivers made navigable, and the roads improved. Industry and trade had expanded enormously, putting new fortunes into new sorts of pockets. And the big cities were growing. Budapest now numbered 800,000 inhabitants, and six bridges spanned the Danube. A huge new royal palace crowned Buda Hill matched by an imposing array of public buildings, in particular a neo-Gothic parliament building modeled on Westminster. Hungary's contribution to European culture had by now earned the world's respect, and its artists, musicians, and authors had achieved well-merited fame. The nation's millennium celebration in 1896 produced a flood of self-congratulation, obscuring the fact that many endemic problems nevertheless remained unsolved.

A new type of country-house builder emerged in this changing society. The rich bourgeoisie and the industrialists were now interested in establishing their position in society by commissioning residences worthy of their status. In 1883 a wholesaler named Zsigmond Schlossberger had a castle built at Tura by Miklós Ybl, a structure strongly reminiscent of the Loire chateaux to which the architect had just paid a visit but with an enormous conservatory attached. French examples returned to fashion although the Nádasdy castle at Nádasdladány, constructed from 1873 to 1884 with a massive porch, pointed towers, and gables with Tudor-style windows, harked back to earlier Gothic revival models. Drawing its inspiration from a variety of styles, the Eclectic movement and its chief propo-

nent Antal Gottlieb became increasingly important. Some older architects like Jozsef Hild preferred to work with earlier styles but others like
Ybl adapted to the new fashions. Under the impetus of Gottfried Semper
certain of their younger colleagues even fostered a neo-Renaissance
movement.

The emphasis was increasingly on size; larger houses inevitably meant
larger staffs, provided the owners could pay for them. The vastly rich
Festetics family enlarged their castle at Keszthely during the 1880s, but at
least their additions constituted a coherent whole. By the 1890s architectural style was in danger of losing its way. Facades lacked balance, and a
highly idiosyncratic individualism, often designed to draw attention to
the owner's wealth, could result in the abandonment of normal architectural standards. Count János Pálffy had a fantastic mock-medieval dream
castle built at Bajmoc in this decade. In 1900 eclecticism can be said to
have reached its apogee at Budafok, a house near Budapest built for the
champagne king József Törley, which contained a Byzantine smoking
room, a Japanese study, a classical marble ballroom, a winter garden, and
an enormous English-style hall with a hammerbeam roof. Yet if taste frequently became questionable, this and other buildings of the period were
often placed on magnificent sites and their technical layout was usually
good. A great one-story central hall, for instance, which contained the
main staircase and off which the other rooms led, was a pronounced feature of turn-of-the-century design.

After 1900 economic and political prospects in Hungary became
markedly less favorable. Dissatisfaction grew with some economic and military aspects of the Compromise, industrial unrest spread, and the threat of
universal suffrage worried ministers, as did the uneasy balance between the
Germans and the Slavs who between them constituted the rest of the Dual
Monarchy. In Hungary the Magyarization of the state and the educational
system had alienated the racial minorities and irredentist feeling was growing, especially among the Croats. The Jews, however, began to play a major
role in Hungarian life; nearly a million strong by 1900 and recently fully
emancipated, they controlled banking and finance, much of trade and
industry, and owned a fifth of all estates over 1,000 *bölds.*

Hungary's long-serving premier István Tisza saw the best hope of
national salvation in maintaining a close connection with Austria and the
Dual Monarchy's alliance with Germany, and so Hungary was dragged
reluctantly into World War I on the side of the Central Powers. With all
the country's potential enemies—Serbia, Romania, and a nascent
Czechoslovakia—ranged on the side of the Entente, Hungary stood to be
dismembered if the war was lost. As the military situation deteriorated
one prominent politician, Mihály Károlyi, proposed that the Austrian
connection should be severed and the Hungarians should sign a separate
peace while simultaneously introducing reforms and concessions to the
minorities. In October 1918 he became prime minister, but by then most
of the country was occupied by foreign armies and near chaos and starva-
tion prevailed in Budapest. In March 1919 renewed Allied exactions led
to Károlyi's resignation, and a Communist regime under Béla Kun seized
power. Kun, however, was no better able to solve the nation's problems.
In August he fled and the Allies dictated peace terms to a prostrate
Hungary.

The terms of the Treaty of Trianon were harsh indeed. All areas inhabited
by non-Magyars were taken away from Hungary, often illogically—the
Ruthene populations in the northeast, for example, were attached to the former Czechoslovakia and the German communities in the south to Serbia.
Even Austria's claims to the fringe of territory across the Leitha River were
recognized. Of around 325,000 square kilometers that once comprised
historic Hungary, only about 92,000 remained, and of a population of
20.8 million, only 7.6 million. Over three million Magyars had been allo-

General view of Martonvásár.

cated to other states. Hungary was required to disarm totally and to pay unspecified reparations. The new frontiers cut off long-established markets and supply sources, while a huge influx of refugees strained existing resources. The national reserves stood at one twenty-fifth of the prewar figures. Social tensions were acute as the rising expectations of the working classes collided with the bitterness of the formerly wealthy.

Responsible government was restored by Parliament in 1920. All measures of the Károlyi and Kun regimes were annulled, as were the provisions of the Compromise of 1867, and Hungary became nominally an independent monarchy, although the crown's powers were exercised by a regent, Admiral Miklós Horthy, ex-commander of the imperial navy. A new ministry under Pál Teleki tried to enact a modest land reform, but the owners, who could choose which land to surrender, picked the least fertile areas, and promises of a second installment were never fulfilled. Nevertheless economic stability returned in the 1920s. Reparations were fixed, a League of Nations loan negotiated, and the budgets balanced. Foreign capital returned, inflation fell, and industrialization proceeded apace, even though agriculture remained the backbone of the economy.

Unfortunately the crash of 1929 undermined the high price of wheat and the maintenance of international credit, the twin pillars of Hungary's political stability. When the Depression hit Hungary in 1931, a government representing the radical right rose to power, essentially anticapitalist, anti-Semitic, and anti-monarchist, but constrained by the realities of the situation. Nervous of too close a link with Nazi Germany, Horthy appointed ministers like Teleki with links to the Western democracies. Yet many believed that Hungary's only chance of reversing the

Hungarian noblemen in magnate dress, including a member of the Széchényi family on the left and Lajos Károlyi on the right, early twentieth century. (Private collection.)

Trianon settlement lay in a German alliance. And indeed in 1939, after Germany dismembered Czechoslovakia, the region of Ruthenia was recovered, followed in 1940 by much of the land lost to Romania, and in 1941 by some of the territory incorporated in Yugoslavia. Teleki's efforts to keep Hungary a non-belligerent lasted eighteen months; then, under intolerable pressure, he committed suicide. As his successors joined Hitler's attack on Russia, war was declared on Hungary by the western powers and the die was cast. Yet Horthy, convinced of an ultimate Allied victory, managed a tight-rope act until 1944 when, with the gradual collapse of the eastern front, he was forced into full cooperation with the Germans. An overtly Nazi government was formed, the Jews were deported en masse, and finally Horthy was deposed. The inexorable Russian advance led to the collapse of all resistance by April 1945. A provisional government under Soviet auspices signed an armistice renouncing all Hungary's territorial gains since 1938 and formally reinstating the Trianon frontiers. The country was physically devastated even more severely than in 1918, and although the Communists moved cautiously, taking power by degrees, within five years they had gained complete control of a one-party state with a Sovietized economy. The old Hungary was gone, never to return.

During the interwar years, even after stability was restored, it was evident that the time in which large new country houses could be built was past. Most families had lost some of their land and a few had lost most or even all of it in the partitions of 1919. In the case of the Esterházys at Eszterháza and Kismarton, which were now on opposite sides of the new frontier, they managed to maintain their way of life on both estates, but this was the exception rather than the rule. Although homes continued normally to be well-maintained and servants were still cheap and plentiful, the volatile economic situation meant that few followed the example of Horthy, who extended and embellished his family home at Kenderes. Moreover artistic fashions had moved away from this sort of architecture. Hungarian activism, a literary and aesthetic movement with connections to constructivism and later to the Bauhaus school, allied itself with the theoretical tenets of modern architecture. Although banned by the Horthy regime, it disseminated its views from Vienna and one distinguished exponent—Farkas Molnár, a close associate of Walter Gropius—published woodcuts of his house designs including his utopian Red Cube House of 1921. Gradually the new prophets mellowed and were allowed back into Hungary, where, like Molnár, they designed villas for the rich bourgeoisie. Usually located in city suburbs or holiday resorts such as Lake Balaton, these projects embodied the principle that the residents should enjoy as much sunlight, open space, trees, and lawn as possible insofar as the existing population density would allow. But apart from this development the interwar years added little new to Hungarian architecture, which, like every other branch of cultural life, was to feel the stultifying influence of the postwar regime.

All was not lost, however, for Hungary is a nation proud of its history and heritage. Now, after more than forty years of one-party Communist rule, the country has returned to a free and democratic system. Individual liberty and the revival of the economy offer the hope of national regeneration. It is this rebirth that has encouraged the restoration of many neglected parts of the Hungarian national heritage, including the country's castles and country houses, which in today's very different political environment are again becoming sources of pride to local and foreign visitors alike.

SÁRVÁR

The rolling landscape west and north of Lake Balaton known as the Dunántúl largely escaped the Ottoman occupation and remained a part of Royal Hungary, that portion of the Habsburg kingdom that they managed to hold onto continuously and that therefore has perhaps the closest ties to Austria. Near the intersection of two of the major roads running across the plain, one down from Vienna to Lake Balaton, the other leading from Graz to Budapest, lies the small town of Sárvár. A pleasant place with a fine church and a quite newly developed thermal bath, it also contains one national landmark: the great castle that for several centuries played a momentous role in Hungarian history.

There are few traces of an earlier settlement of Sárvár, but by the later thirteenth century the town was recorded as being royal property and shortly thereafter it was granted to the Németújvári family. In 1327 the local judge, Sándor Köcski, took possession of it in the name of the crown, and in 1390 King Sigismund granted Sárvár again, this time to the Kanizsai family. By now a one-story wooden fortress had been constructed with a square tower and a fortified stone wall. Köcski had enlarged the structure considerably, joining up the two southern and western facing wings of the pentagonal fortress, which was protected by earthworks reinforced by boards. However, while it remained in the possession of the Kanizsais during the following century and a half, little more was done to the castle.

The turning point of Sárvár's history came in 1534 when Orsolya Kanizsai, heiress to the property, married Tamás Nádasdy. In the debacle that had ensued after the battle of Mohács, he had become one of the leading Hungarian nobles, although his family, which can be traced back to the thirteenth century, had up to then made little national impact. A highly-educated man in the humanist tradition, Tamás soon attained political office; appointed governor of Croatia by the Habsburgs, he became palatine of Hungary in 1554. Sárvár under his auspices grew into a cultural and scholastic center. The printing press he founded there produced a Hungarian-Latin dictionary in 1539, János Sylvester's *Grammatica Hungaro-latina*. Two years later the press produced the first book to be printed in Hungarian, a translation of the New Testament. Regular visitors to the castle included Sebestyen Tinodi, the most accurate chronicler of the Turkish wars, Mátyás Biró von Deva, a famous protagonist in the struggle for religious toleration within the Empire, and Benedek Abádi, an outstanding Protestant pastor.

Nádasdy initiated important architectural changes at Sárvár. Between 1550 and 1560 the western wing of the fortress acquired its final form and was made into living quarters with a loggia, the arcade of which featured arches cut in the shape of stone arrows. The gate tower was also modified by being given a pointed tile roof surmounted by a domed lantern; the magnificent Renaissance entrance portal, probably of Italian workmanship, is from the same date. The earthen ramparts were transformed into stone walls in some sections. Surrounding the castle a ditch and moat

View of the castle gate-tower, completed between 1550 and 1560.

Aerial view of the castle and village of Sárvár, northwest Hungary. (Prince Rasso of Bavaria.)

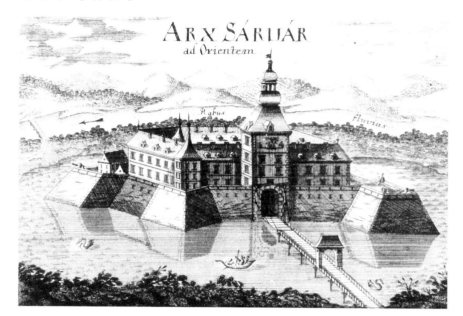

Old view of Sárvár by Mátyás Greischer, early sixteenth century. (Hungarian National Museum, Budapest.)

Nádasdy coat of arms in the courtyard at Sárvár.

were dug, across which a bridge was built. Much of the nearby river bank and woodland were cleared and fruit gardens were planted.

The interiors were richly furnished and decorated and adorned with fine decorative details such as the stone Renaissance door surrounds and lintels. Ferenc Nádasdy II and his son Pál continued with the improvements at Sárvár, rebuilding in stone the five corner bastions of the fortress, previously constructed of wood, between 1588 and 1615. An outer machicolated rampart spared the buildings from the need to be fortified, so that they came increasingly to resemble an Italian palazzo.

By the time Ferenc Nádasdy III inherited the castle in the mid-seventeenth century, it was a splendid piece of predominantly Renaissance architecture, which had survived a century of warfare unscathed. He too had risen to judicial and political eminence and, eager to create a residence worthy of his status, decided on further changes. The gate tower was joined onto the other buildings, and a vaulted entrance area was made at the ground-floor level. All five facades were given a uniform finish by reducing the height of the earlier wings from three to two stories, as a contemporary view by Mátyás Greischner shows. Outer ramparts now entirely surrounded the buildings. A huge dining hall and several adjoining rooms were decorated in baroque style. Keen to perpetuate the memories of the Turkish wars and of his ancestor Scanderbeg, the hero of the Albanian resistance to the Turks, Ferenc commissioned frescoes for the dining hall's enormous coved ceiling. These were executed in 1653 in square plaster-faced panels by an unknown artist whose initials, H.R.M., suggest that he may have been the minor baroque painter Hans Rudolf Müller. The first work of their kind to be seen in Hungary, they all depict battle scenes, with extravagantly moustached and turbaned figures, cavorting horses, and flashing scimitars.

This martial theme proved appropriate to Nádasdy's subsequent career. Disgusted by the Habsburgs' craven appeasement of the Porte by signing the unnecessarily favorable Peace of Vasvár in 1664, he began to plot against the government. Soon the conspiracy was joined by Ferenc Wesselényi, the Palatine of Hungary; by Péter Zrínyi, brother of the national hero whose rising against the Turks had not been supported by the imperial troops; by his son-in-law Ferenc Rákóczi; and by Count Ferenc Frangipani. Although the palatine's death deprived them of their most experienced leader, the conspirators planned a nationwide revolt against the Habsburgs to take place in 1670. The plot was betrayed, probably by the

Portrait of Tamás Nádasdy, 1560. (Hungarian National Museum, Budapest.)

Portrait of Ferenc Nádasdy, mid-seventeenth century. (Hungarian National Museum, Budapest.)

Turks, who had no more wish than the emperor to foster Hungarian independence, and most of the ringleaders were seized by the government before they could muster their forces. The magnates—especially Nádasdy, who still held the post of chief justice—could expect little mercy from Vienna. They were duly tried and executed in 1671. As the property of a convicted rebel, Sárvár was sequestered by the crown.

Perhaps the saddest result of this disaster was the dispersal of the Nádasdy collections of books, pictures, and furniture. Tamás had been enthusiastic, but Ferenc had proved to be the most important, indeed compulsive, collector of them all. Inventories of his numerous chattels, all of which passed to the government at his execution, reveal more that 200 paintings, 140 carpets including 39 Gobelins tapestries, many silver and gold objects spread through 32 cupboards in 18 different rooms, some marvellous armor, etchings, furniture, and a library of several thousand books.

In 1677 Count Miklós Draskovich, husband of Ferenc's daughter Krisztina, bought the estate back from the government for the enormous sum

Detail of the gate-tower room frescoed by István Dorfmeister, mid-eighteenth century.

Detail of frescoes in gate-tower room.

of 326,520 forints. He did not keep it for long, however, and it passed through a string of proprietors in the eighteenth century. The most notable of these was Ádam Szily, who in 1769 commissioned István Dorfmeister, the fashionable painter of the period, to execute nine more murals in the dining hall representing scenes from the Old Testament. He was also asked to paint murals in rooms on the middle or second-floor level of the gate tower, based on designs from François Fénelon's *Telemachus*, a novel in which the adventures of Ulysses' son were made into a political tale. Probably the paintings of flowers, foliage, and tendrils in the adjoining room are of a contemporary date.

In 1803 Sárvár, having most recently been the property of a branch of the Pallavicini family from Genoa, was sold to the duke of Modena. The son of Duke Francis IV of the house of Este and the last ruler before the Risorgimento, Francis V was married to Adelgunde, daughter of King Ludwig I of Bavaria and the sister of Luitpold, who was to become the prince regent. When they died without issue, Sárvár was inherited by his younger brother, Ferdinand, the husband of Archduchess Elizabeth of Habsburg. Their daughter Maria Theresa in turn married a Wittelsbach, King Ludwig III, so despite the quirks of genealogy the estate stayed in the family. Ludwig, the last king of Bavaria, retired to the castle in 1919 following his abdication and died there two years later. His second son Franz, the younger brother of Crown Prince Rupprecht, had already inherited the estate in 1875 at only three months of age directly from the Modenas, although his mother enjoyed the rights of a life tenant. Since she lived on into old age he came into his inheritance fairly late. He was to be the last private owner of Sárvár.

A thoroughbred stud had been founded at Sárvár by the Modenas around 1820 and one Bischl, a Bavarian cavalry officer, put in charge of it.

Dining hall with frescoes possibly by Hans Rudolf Müller, mid-seventeenth century.

Corridor at Sárvár with trophy heads, early twentieth century view. (Prince Rasso of Bavaria.)

Thanks to his good management it became one of the best studs in Hungary. Indeed before World War II the Hungarian government, which had a right to first pick of the yearlings, had bought more horses from Sárvár than from any other stud in the country. The Wittelsbachs also made some changes to the castle after it came into their possession in 1875. The arcade carved with stone arrows for arches was incorporated into the main wall, the moats were emptied and turned into a landscaped park surrounding the fortress, and the bridge was given the wide-spaced arches it still has today. The demolition of the inner ramparts made it possible to walk round the perimeter of all the outlying buildings of the castle.

Sárvár underwent little change in the first half of the twentieth century. The Wittelsbach proprietors, a family with two boys and two girls, became quite Hungarian in their way of life during the 1930s, and committed to their family roots. Yet with another home at Leutstetten in Bavaria, they only lived at Sárvár for part of the year and seldom mixed socially with their neighbors. From the beginning of 1939, however, after Crown Prince Rupprecht had rebuffed Hitler, the family based itself in Hungary, while their cousins in Germany were effectively placed under house arrest. Thanks to the personal intervention of Miklós Horthy they were allowed to leave the country in 1944, taking their most treasured possessions with them. They still owned some 8,000 hectares of land, although a further 3,000 had been lost in the land reforms of the 1920s. About half was farmland and half woodland, of which a small part still exists today in the Burgenland, now a part of Austria, in the ownership of their descendants. Most of the horses were moved to Germany in 1945, but in the mid-1980s fifty animals were returned to Hungary and a new stud was set up.

Much has been altered at Sárvár during the past hundred years. The Wittelsbachs destroyed some of the eighteenth-century frescoes in the tower by reducing the height of the rooms by a third to make them easier to heat. Outside, ramparts within the outer perimeter were demolished so that in no way does the building now resemble a fortified enceinte. The powder storage vault built at the foot of the tower was filled in to make it possible for carriages, or indeed cars, to drive straight across the front bridge into the inner courtyard. Additionally an entrance was created at the back of the fortress where none had existed before. Fortunately, despite a brief Russo-German battle over the town in 1945, World War II caused no damage to Sárvár beyond the loss of the castle's contents, which were looted. More recently several new houses have been constructed around the edge of the moat.

Since 1945 the house has been made into a major national museum. Chattels from other properties were put into the house and in 1951 the Ferenc Nádasdy Museum was opened. An excellent perspective is offered to visitors on the life of Sárvár, a market town that has enjoyed a distinguished past from its earliest origins. Documents and artifacts from the past are on show, a social facility for the local population in the form of a youth club is located in the cellars, and one hall is used as a forum for debates and theatrical performances. In the basement is a museum concerned with the town's development as a spa and with the history of mineral water and thermal baths in Hungary. Upstairs the castle contains a suite of fine baroque rooms and others decorated in the style of the eighteenth and early nineteenth centuries. The existence there of one of the great centers of Hungarian intellectual life in the sixteenth and seventeenth centuries does, it must be admitted, require the exercise of historical imagination. Nevertheless any visitor to Sárvár today can see that it is a major monument, both to the Renaissance in Hungary with all that it implied and to the saga of one of its more remarkable families.

SÁROSPATAK

The name Sárospatak should be familiar to any educated and patriotic Hungarian. Not only was it the stronghold of the Rákóczis, the champions of national independence in the seventeenth century, but it was also the seat of the Calvinist College for over four centuries, both factors making it one of the cultural and intellectual centers of the country. Thus this little town, situated about 250 kilometers northeast of Budapest in the foothills of the range whence come the world-famous wines of Tokaj, is of an importance disproportionate to its size. Near modern Hungary's border with Slovakia and the Ukraine, its history evokes memories of a more gracious and glorious past.

The word "Patak" appears early in history. Prince Árpád granted the land there to one Ketel in 896 A.D., although it was royal property again by the mid-eleventh century. A Mongol invasion ravaged the settlement in 1295 but it gradually recovered under Angevin rule. Walloon "hospites," or free foreign settlers, established themselves in this area, with privileges conferred by the king, and a monastery was built in the town. So was a stone castle, one of a string of royal strongholds, but this did not stand on the site of the present-day buildings. According to tradition, Saint Elizabeth, daughter of the Árpád king András II and the margravine of Thuringia, was born here, and over her grave at Marburg the cathedral was later built. King Sigismund declared Patak a royal town in 1429 and donated it to the three Pálóczi brothers, one of whom, György, was archbishop of Esztergom. They were to hold it until 1526, the fateful year of the battle of Mohács when Hungarian power was overthrown by the Turks.

Although the precise date at which the present castle was begun is unknown, it was probably before 1500, for a contemporary document speaks of a "lower castle" of the Pálóczis standing near to a bridge over the Bodrog River. This is supported by the close resemblance of the Red Tower, central keep of the castle, to the numerous square plan keeps built at that time in Central Europe, and by the late Gothic door frames visible on its lowest level. A Renaissance door frame bearing the date of 1506 and fragments of red marble carvings discovered in the parish church testify to the family's continued building activity and their cosmopolitan tastes.

Antal Pálóczi, the last of this line, fell at Mohács and the estates were arbitrarily seized by Péter Perényi, keeper of the royal crown and supporter of both Ferdinand of Habsburg and János Zápolya. He then lent it to both of them for their coronation ceremonies. After a brief spell of Turkish captivity he returned to Patak, eager to establish a secure family seat there. In the 1530s he began an extensive building campaign that was to last for fifteen years. Walls were erected around the medieval nucleus of the town and at the southeastern corner of the fortification system, which was linked to the keep. Perényi designed a castle with a moat in front and curtain walls running parallel with the outer ramparts. The keep was then one level lower than it is today, with nothing but loopholes on its four sides and its interior divided into stories by wooden ceilings. He transformed it into vaulted halls embellished with Renaissance carv-

View of the Red Tower, central keep of the castle of Sárospatak, northeastern Hungary.

172

173

ings and installed an external staircase resting on a huge pillar rising right beside the gate, the pediment of which was decorated with an angel holding the family coat of arms.

In order to enlarge his residence, in 1540 Perényi began a palace wing on the eastern side of the castle yard, the most striking part of which, still visible today, is the triple arcade transformed into a window. Peter Kmyta, palatine of Kraków, informed him in a letter dated on Palm Sunday of that year that in response to his request the master mason Laurentius, with twelve assistants, had been dispatched to help with the works. These, however, proceeded intermittently. Thanks to his continual changes of allegiance and the accusation that he collaborated with the Turks, Perényi was jailed by the Habsburgs. Released from captivity in 1548, he died soon afterwards. He had already become a Protestant, founding in the town a Reformed school, which from modest origins was to become the predecessor of the famous college.

Gábor, his son, was allowed to inherit the estates, and in the 1560s completed the palace wing, placing there the inscription "Regia fundavit quae tecta Perenius heros Iam Gabriel decorat, parce Christe precor: 1563" ("The royal house, which the hero Perényi built, Gábor now decorates, spare me Christ I pray: 1563"). The decoration of finely carved architraves, medallions, and stunted capitals illustrates the influence of Italian motifs on distant Hungary. Gábor also had laid out the Gombos Garden, celebrated for "abounding in all kinds of beauties," on the riverbank south of the keep. The works were supervised by the Lombard mason Alessandro da Vedano, who had been employed on the project since the 1530s. In recognition of his exemplary services he was rewarded with a vineyard. Patak was flourishing when Perényi fell ill in 1567 and died at only age thirty-five. As he was childless, the property reverted to the crown. Interestingly, the oldest known plan of the castle from this period, now at the Karlsruhe Archives, probably came from the general staff maps of "Türkenlouis," the margrave Louis of Baden, and dates from 1573 when it was drawn up for the Imperial War Council.

Under royal ownership, the Patak estates were negligently managed, although the fortifications were further reinforced. Old Alessandro da Vedano was again involved in the work—as he claimed in a petition to the king, "everything that is nice and strong at Patak was created by the help of God and by my own two hands and skill." Recognizing that under bureaucratic control the castle was bound to decay, it was granted to the Dobó family, loyal Habsburg supporters who were bound by contract to keep up the buildings. They also lived there and at Christmas 1584 one of them, Krisztina, was secretly married to Bálint Balassa. The outstanding Hungarian lyric poet of the sixteenth century, Balassa was described as a bold warrior and an adventurous scandalmonger; he also happened to be her uncle. Under the Dobós' patronage both the town and the Calvinist school prospered, but the last of the family died in 1602 and during the next years the castle passed through various hands. Both Imperial and Transylvanian troops looted it before it passed into the possession of the Dobós' distant relations, the Lorántffys.

It was the marriage of one daughter, Zsuzsanna, to György Rákóczi that brought Sárospatak, as it now became known, on to the national stage. Rákóczi's father had established the fortunes of this hitherto unimportant family thanks to a brilliant military career. As Protestant nobles they supported Gábor Bethlen, the new prince of Transylvania, and when the castle became György's property on his marriage in 1616 it soon developed as a center of anti-Habsburg resistance. In 1619 Bethlen entered the Thirty Years' War and was immediately joined by Rákóczi. The prince paid two visits to the castle, at which time the upper floors of the Red Tower were embellished with draperies, a throne, and a special gallery for musicians. The carving on the portal to the banqueting hall in the Red

Portrait of Péter Perényi by Augustin Hirschvogel, c. 1548. (Austrian National Library, Vienna.)

Detail of carved stone corbel in the courtyard.

Staircase and gallery in the courtyard.

Tower, also contemporary, is extremely fine, and a richly ornamented festoon of fruits adorns the frieze of the entablature. One story with fine halls had been added to the eastern wing of the palace when the family first moved in, ramparts had been reconstructed, and guards doubled.

Sárospatak remained the family's home until Rákóczi was himself offered the Transylvanian throne on Bethlen's death in 1630. Thereafter he entrusted the estate with his other Hungarian lands to a warden who resided there. Although the castle still contained his archives and treasury, no new building work was undertaken and the palace wing remained uninhabited.

All this changed in the 1640s, when Rákóczi, feeling secure in his principality, ordered the remodeling and enlargement of his castle. A story was now added to the southern palace wing and a suite of magnificent halls was continued along the western side as well, forming the courtyard into a diamond shape. In 1644 the prince visited Sárospatak from his capital at Gyulafehérvár, the modern Alba Iulia, and inspected the new additions before marching on west. In 1645 his wife, Zsuzsanna, came and she gave orders for the external staircase of the Red Tower to be demolished. Instead an arcaded gallery with stairs leading to it was built between the keep and the eastern palace wing and another staircase was added between the southern and western wings. The new halls were richly decorated inside and splendidly furnished, yet their exteriors were

Staircase to the gallery of the courtyard.

Detail of carved columns in the courtyard.

architecturally undistinguished, illustrating the extent to which the local Renaissance style had ossified since contact with Western Europe had been lost. Zsuzsanna looked after the estate's farms and vineyards and most of all her beloved Gombos Garden in which rare flowers and fruit were grown. In these years the plague decimated the local population, and the town was twice besieged by the imperial troops. Nevertheless the castle survived unscathed, and when Rákóczi died in 1648 it became the property of his widow.

The Calvinist College at Sárospatak, as it had now become, was enjoying a golden age during these years. Rákóczi had been a passionate bibliophile, and with his support the library, which possessed 300 books in 1623, contained fifteen times as many only thirty years later. The famous Czech educator Jan Amos Comenius moved there in 1650 and produced a plan for reforming the college's educational system. He also founded a printing press during his four-year stay and wrote one of his major works, *Orbis Sensualium Pictus*. The textbooks he recommended remained in use for many years afterwards and were repeatedly reprinted. The town was similarly fortunate in that a colony of Anabaptist craftsmen, transplanted there from the Moravian border, fostered much local artistic development.

In 1651 Zsuzsanna's son Zsigmond married Henrietta, daughter of Frederick, the Elector Palatine and ill-fated king of Bohemia, and his English Stuart wife. The young couple died the following year so his formidable mother continued to act as chatelaine. In accordance with her late husband's wishes she added a story to the Red Tower on top of the great hall to serve as a gun emplacement, covering it with a tall pyramidical shingle roof with a small turret at each corner. At her death in 1660 she was succeeded by her grandson Ferenc Rákóczi I who, like his mother Zsófia Báthory, was a Catholic convert. Regarding Sárospatak as a Calvinist stronghold, they spent little time there themselves, instead inviting the Jesuits to do missionary work in the town and giving them quarters within the castle. There they set up a chapel for the household in the keep's great hall.

But the traditional sympathies of the Rákóczis were not so easily changed. In 1666 Ferenc married Ilona Zrínyi whose father, Péter, was one of the leading malcontents chafing under Habsburg rule, which seemed more concerned with appeasing the Porte than listening to the grievances of the Hungarian citizens. Zrínyi soon involved his son-in-law and discontent turned into conspiracy. Many of the secret deliberations were held at the castle in the bay of the northeastern corner bastion under the stucco rose in the ceiling of what was called the Sub-Rosa Room. Ribs coming down from the dome that surmounts the octagon define panels spangled with painted flowers, which are set between windows. These ribs resembled six lances, serving as a warning to the conspirators to keep silent (as in the French pronunciation of "six lances" = *silence*). This did not manage to ensure their success as well.

Sárospatak saw the launching of the uprising when, on April 9, 1670, the local imperial commander, Prince Stahremberg, was taken prisoner during a visit. The conspirators proved sadly incompetent, failing to reduce the nearby garrisons, and on June 24 the castle was captured by Habsburg troops. All the leaders of the plot were executed with the exception of Rákóczi, whose mother obtained for him a pardon on payment of an enormous fine. Nonetheless there was a strict occupation. Stahremberg walled up the town gates, closed the Calvinist church, and forced the college into exile in Transylvania. The castle was looted and the Gombos Garden entirely destroyed. Coincidentally two years later a severe fire gutted most of the inner town.

In 1676 Ferenc died a broken man, leaving behind a son and a daughter. His widow promptly married Imre Thököly who headed another

Portait of Zsigmund II Rákóczi, c. 1600.

Ceiling of the Sub-Rosa Room.

more successful uprising. In 1683 his rebel troops recaptured Sárospatak, and Thököly, by this time the prince of Transylvania, marched in to the cheers of the inhabitants. The Jesuits fled and the Calvinists regained control of their church and college. But this newly-won freedom only lasted two years. Following the repulse of the Turks at the siege of Vienna, the Habsburg armies again went on the offensive. In autumn 1685 the town was besieged and, after a heroic defence lasting several weeks, stormed. Once more the Protestants were expelled and the Rákóczi children were removed with their mother to Vienna to be given a suitable Catholic education.

It took nine years before Ferenc II was allowed to return to his home after his marriage to Princess Charlotte Amalie of Hesse. The castle, badly damaged by years of occupation, was repaired to form a worthy residence. A peaceful period ensued, but a peasant uprising that had taken place in his absence continued to cause problems. After a century of sporadic warfare the countryside had been badly damaged and the lives of the peasants who lived on it had grown especially wretched. Enraged and frustrated, they had captured the town, but the army quickly recaptured it, executing thirty rebels on the spot. Despite his being in no way involved, Rákóczi was still treated by the government with suspicion and in 1701 he was arrested. Escaping from prison, he fled to Poland while the Habsburgs decreed the destruction of all his fortresses. Some walls and bastions were indeed blown up the following spring and the roof of the Red Tower was demolished, but the church at least was spared thanks to the entreaties of the Jesuits.

Finally this gentle soul was goaded into revolt. The prince was widely loved in the locality and Louis XIV's emissary described him as "virtuous, hard-working, charming, and mild-mannered"—quite a tribute to a man who had been taken away from his home at the age of twelve and later imprisoned by the Austrians in the cell his grandfather had once occupied. Ferenc returned from exile in 1703 and raised a volunteer army known as the Kurucs, which occupied Sárospatak that summer. Terrible destruction was again caused by a fire, however, which spread to both the inner town and the castle, destroying much furniture and the wooden interiors and rendering the buildings uninhabitable. So distressed was Rákóczi by this disaster that he did not revisit his property for several years. By then the roofs had been replaced but the rooms were still in ruins. Since he now controlled eastern Hungary, he decided nevertheless to convoke a diet at Sárospatak, which was duly done in the autumn of 1708. It met in the shell of the great hall on the fourth floor of the Red Tower. Yet Rákóczi's cause was already in decline and over the next two years the imperial troops drove back the slowly disintegrating Kuruc forces step by step. In 1710 Ferenc paid his last visit to Sárospatak, thence setting out for the Balkan exile where he was to end his days. On November 10, Habsburg soldiers entered the castle without meeting further resistance. The death in 1735 of the "homeless prince," as he was called, marked the extinction of the Rákóczis, a name now best remembered thanks to Berlioz's famous march derived from a Kuruc marching tune.

Emperor Joseph I awarded the confiscated property to Prince Trautsohn. The castle was repaired in its previous style, with undistinguished interior decoration, for use by the estate officials. Granaries were installed in the upper floor rooms of the eastern wing and on the lower levels of the roofless tower. Both Calvinists and Jesuits now coexisted in the town, the latter controlling the church while the former were permitted to stay in their college. During the eighteenth century no new building work was undertaken, but at least Sárospatak enjoyed a long era of peace. The town became a busy commercial center especially concerned with the wine trade. Greek and Jewish merchants arrived, and Swabian craftsmen were settled in the surrounding depopulated villages. Yet when another bad fire

Portrait of Ilona Rákóczi, mid-seventeenth century.

Portrait of Ferenc II Rákóczi by Ádám Mányoki, c. 1700.

Overleaf, general view of the library at the Calvinist College.

occurred in 1737 the church tower and all the castle's roofs were again burned. The Trautsohn family, absentee landlords, died out in 1776, so the estate reverted to the management of the imperial chamber. With the expulsion of the Jesuits from the Habsburg dominions in 1773, their building became the parish church. While only minimal maintenance was carried out on the castle, the church vaults were reconstructed, but in the process the Perényi and Dobó tombs were desecrated.

In 1806 Emperor Francis I of Austria sold the property to Prince Karl August Bretzenheim, scion of a bastard line of the Bavarian Wittelsbach dynasty. Unlike the Trautsohns, who left behind no family portraits or souvenirs, the new owners left their mark. The estates were well managed and a porcelain manufactory called Regéc was established, which introduced the baroque styles of Austrian and Bohemian ceramics factories, particularly Ellenbogen. The manufactory found only a tiny market, however, and survived only thirty years from its foundation in the 1820s. The castle itself was thoroughly restored beginning with the eastern wing, while the Renaissance carvings were removed from their original positions and built into the wall at various places. The end of the southern wing, joined to the Red Tower, was demolished, and the closed-in courtyard was opened up to a new terrace by filling in the bastion yard that encircled the keep.

Karl August died in 1823 and was succeeded by his son Ferdinand, who married Caroline Schwarzenberg, sister of the celebrated field marshal, Karl Philipp zu Schwarzenberg. He too continued to reconstruct the

castle. A first floor neo-Gothic gallery was built on the side facing the Bodrog River. The other wings were given vaulted galleries overlooking the courtyard, although their clear yellow stucco facings made for an unexciting ensemble. The outer facades were rebuilt in an eclectic style, and around 1845 the eastern wing was remodeled in neo-Renaissance style following the designs of Jean Romano. The Bretzenheims had no children so when Ferdinand died in 1875 his widow gave the estate to her favorite nephew, Ludwig Windischgrätz, whose mother had been killed by a stray bullet while standing at her palace window during the fighting in Prague in 1848. At that time Ludwig was fighting with the Austrian armies in Hungary, where he became betrothed to a Countess Desewffy, whose father had enlisted with Lajos Kossuth. Luckily this provided no obstacle to their engagement.

These were years of prosperity for the Calvinist College after a slow recovery in the eighteenth century. Under the aegis of a dynamic principal, János Szombathy, the library's holdings reached 15,000 volumes by 1823. A southern wing was built to the designs of Mihály Pollack with an immense hall twenty meters long by ten broad and fine ceiling paintings executed by József Lintzbauer. Finished in 1828, it is a fine example of a neoclassical library, with an apse at one end and a gallery supported by wooden columns. The college turned out an increased number of students and played an important part in the revival of the Hungarian language. Its collections continued to grow, quadrupling to 60,000 books by 1920,

Gold tankard and candlestick from the collection of the Calvinist College.

Portrait of Prince Ferdinand Bretzenheim by Friedrich von Amerling, c. 1830–40. (Prince Vincenz Windischgrätz.)

Wedding procession at the marriage of Count István Károlyi and Princess Magdalena Windischgrätz, July 1930. (Princess Natalie Windischgrätz.)

105,000 in 1945, and, miraculously unlooted in both world wars, to almost 300,000 today. In modern times the state has taken over the college, which has lost both its independence and its Protestant character.

Ludwig Windischgrätz, a corps commander and then inspector-general of the army, remained an active soldier until his death in 1904, and he spent only his leaves and the summer at Sárospatak. It was now very much a family home, although it didn't always appear so congenial to foreign visitors. An English traveler, Margaret Fletcher, noted in her diaries in 1892, "the ruined castle is joined to a modern chateau by a piece of Italian architecture . . . the whole belongs to a German duke and is stocked with German servants. As we passed through the old vaulted banqueting hall, a cloud of doves flew away through the gaping windows, and two colossal wooden figures of mediaeval workmanship gave a grotesque touch to the desolation."

Ludwig's second son, another Ludwig, inherited the estate. Married to Mary Széchényi, who descended from the founder of the National Széchényi Library in Budapest, he was also a soldier as well as an engineer by training. He served against the Russians in Transylvania and in 1917 became agriculture minister in the last prerevolutionary Hungarian cabinet. In the 1920s he became a deputy, but his ventures into politics were not very successful. As for the estate he inherited, Sárospatak by this point was quite small—about 12,000 jochs (one joch equals roughly one acre)—and some of this fell into postwar Czechoslovakia. By 1939 after sales and mortgages it had shrunk to a mere 1,500 jochs, mostly tenanted. Although little more was done to the castle, it was well maintained and the Windischgrätz family lived there for most of the year. They were destined to be the last generation of their family to own Sárospatak, which was confiscated by the state in 1945.

Today it serves as a museum mainly devoted to the Rákóczis and the struggle for national independence, although some of the rooms are decorated and furnished in nineteenth-century style. The castle has undergone extensive restoration indeed work is still in progress on the Red Tower and the outer fortifications. Probably the massive, five-storied Red Tower is best seen from across the Bodrog River, set among a jumble of buildings and fortifications—medieval, Renaissance, and nineteenth century—which attest to the castle's continuing importance through five centuries of history.

PÉCEL

The main route southeast from Budapest leads across the Alföld plain through the city of Debrecen and on into Romania. Soon after leaving the city a small road branches off to the left, and a short distance along it lies the village of Pécel. Little more than ten miles from the capital, it has been almost, but not quite, engulfed by Budapest's urban sprawl. Pécel is a pleasant enough place but the traveler must be alert when passing through it if the chateau hidden behind a screen of trees and a wall is likely to be noticed. For there is little about it today to proclaim that it had once been the home of one of Hungary's foremost families of Protestant intellectuals.

As a settlement Pécel is believed to have its origins in the Dark Ages, since burial grounds with funerary urns from that period have been uncovered there. The name may derive from a councillor to the Árpád kings named Pezil, but is more likely to come from Pecz, a common medieval place name. At all events the village was of some interest before the Turkish occupation, a Protestant church being recorded there before 1649. By the late seventeenth century the land in the area belonged to a family called Fay. Their daughter married an ambitious county notary named Pál Kajali, who had as apprentice in his office another able young lawyer called Pál Ráday. The Rádays, members of the gentry from Nógrád County, had originally been called Ratold in the fourteenth century when one of them, Balázs, is mentioned in the records. Since they had lost their estates during the Ottoman occupation Pál was keen to restore the family fortunes, and after completing his studies he became engaged to his employer's daughter Klara, heiress through her mother to the Pécel property. But at that precise moment in 1703, Ferenc Rákóczi raised the standard of revolt against the Habsburgs, and after a brief moment of indecision both Kajali and his future son-in-law joined the cause. Being highly literate and Protestant, they were doubly welcome and both were appointed secretaries to Rákóczi. Ráday soon proved himself the ablest diplomat in the entourage; indeed so busy was he negotiating with the government on the rebels' behalf that he did not find time to marry his fiancée until 1705.

After the revolt's collapse, Pál Ráday, still a man in his mid-thirties, settled down to a quiet life on his estates, and a son named Gedeon was born in 1713. Far from having been punished by the government, he became a deputy for Nógrád County and spent much time attending the sessions of the diet at Pressburg. Pál was also engaged in editing a newspaper and in laying the foundations of what was to become a famous book collection. Between 1722 and 1727 he also built a curia at Pécel, a one-story U-shaped house with two wings and reception rooms at the front. He supervised its construction by transmitting instructions from Pressburg via his wife. He also possessed a more distant home at Ludány, but when that building was gutted by fire Pécel became the family's principal residence, and another story was added between 1727 and 1730.

In his new house Pál received the great Hungarian artist Ádám Mányoki. Formerly Rákóczi's court painter and German-trained, Mányoki had returned to his native country after a stint at the Saxon court of Augustus

Main facade of Pécel, east of Budapest.

the Strong. At Pécel he was commissioned to paint portraits of the whole family. Ráday also persuaded him to act as escort to his young son, Gedeon, who was going to Germany to continue his studies. In 1733 Pál died, however, and at his mother's instigation Gedeon abandoned his studies at the University of Prussia to return and run the family estates. Now head of the family, he quickly married a local girl named Katalina Szentpétery. Ignoring his father's advice to avoid politics, he was elected as a deputy for Pest County and soon won himself a reputation as a true Hungarian patriot, avoiding all ties with the government and refusing the offer of an official post. As a result he was viewed with disfavor and was even unfairly suspected of plotting rebellion. But Gedeon was also active in Protestant causes, and thus was noted early for his interest in literature and the arts.

When Gedeon's mother died in 1742 she left Pécel, rather unjustly, to his younger brother. However, at the latter's death a mere five years later Ráday inherited everything. He had already decided to build himself a much grander residence, and he turned for advice to the leading Hungarian architect, András Mayerhoffer. In the relatively settled conditions of the mid-eighteenth century, chateaux were being built based on baroque models from western Europe, and more especially on the house built at nearby Ráckeve for Prince Eugene of Savoy by Johann Lukas von Hildebrandt. Mayerhoffer had already perfected his style at neighboring Gödöllő for the Grassalkovich family, and was to repeat the pattern again

Portrait of Pál Ráday by Ádám Mányoki, early eighteenth century. (Ráday Library, Budapest.)

at Hatvan. His designs featured a two-story building with a U-shaped ground plan in a distinctively Hungarian baroque style. More compressed proportions made for a narrow cour d'honneur and a much lighter shape than could be found in its German counterparts. Other characteristics included a large reception hall in the middle of the first floor, which otherwise might contain family and guest bedrooms; servants were housed on the ground floor near the service areas and most of the other reception rooms. The facades showed a protruding central block, often with an impressive wrought-iron balcony in its center, and side wings recessed under massive pediments.

At Pécel, Mayerhoffer was under instructions to incorporate the old curia into a larger building and to make use of the existing foundations. He delegated to his son János the supervision of the work on site, which was to prove no easy task. Work at Pécel began in earnest in 1756 and was to last intermittently for almost twenty years. The Rádays continued to live in the building during all phases of construction, moving from one section to another as circumstances permitted. Gedeon got on well with his architect, frequently presenting him with cases of wine, while Mayerhoffer permitted items ordered especially from Vienna to be stored in his house in the city before transit to the site. This congenial relationship was fortunate, for Ráday meddled incessantly with the work and interfered in the most trivial matters: he worried greatly, for example, that the earth moved in front of the kitchen might leave a ditch that would then need

Portrait of Klára Ráday (née Kajali) by Ádám Mányoki, early eighteenth century. (Ráday Library, Budapest.)

covering over, or that the walls might need shoring up to prevent a collapse, even demanding a double thickness of brick as a facing on the external walls.

Fifteen different craftsmen were at times working on the complex. Ráday paid them generously on a weekly basis: 3/4 of a forint per day for the plasterers, 1/2 a forint per day for the stonemasons, and 15 kreutzer for the unskilled laborers. The master stone dresser András Conti Lipót was brought in from Pest to complete the most difficult parts of the job. Although the bricks were baked and the stones cut in the vicinity, much else had to be imported. The income from the estates fell far short of covering the costs: 40,000 forints represented the accrued interest on monies borrowed for the project. Gedeon's detractors alleged that he was facing bankruptcy, to which he retorted, "Yes, I have debts. Who does not in Hungary? At least I am spending the money on something worthwhile and lasting."

Despite the problems, work at Pécel progressed steadily. The eastern wing housing the library was finished first, then the central block, and lastly the western wing, which abuts onto the church. A beautiful balcony was executed in 1763 by János Hepfner, who was also responsible for the splendid window grilles. The decoration of the interior went on through-

Wrought-iron grilles on the windows at Pécel,
executed by János Hepfner.

Front door of the house with monumental urn.

Overleaf, the former library with domed ceiling.

out the decade. By 1770 the house was virtually ready and the construction of the outbuildings had begun. Gedeon was relieved. Not only had he incurred enormous expenditure but his political career had suffered too. So preoccupied was he with the work at Pécel that it seems to have affected his normally sound judgment, for in 1764 he made a rashly anti-government speech in the Diet—quite different from his normally cautious stance.

The chateau itself was a triumph. An imposing wrought-iron balcony opened out over its entrance. At the ground level a corridor to the left connected with the kitchens and from there to the wine store and granary, the latter of which were older buildings from the early eighteenth century attached to the west wing. To the right lay the large library, the domed ceiling of which was supported by four marble columns. In the corner was placed a magnificent stove, on top of which was seated a biblical figure, usually assumed to be Moses. Adjoining this room was the small library. Gedeon was a passionate bibliophile who collected books from all over Europe, especially any connected with old Hungary. Altogether six rooms in the house contained books, a collection that amounted to some 12,000 volumes.

The ceiling of the large library was divided into nine frescoes depicting the nine muses, with one of Pallas Athena, goddess of widsom, at the center. They did not strictly adhere to the classical definitions but were free representations: of poetry with a harp, of eloquence with a caduceus, of grammar holding a book, of theology with a torch, of justice with scales, of medicine holding a knotted staff encircled by a serpent, of history as an old man, of philosophy and mathematics as two companions standing together. Ráday had personally chosen the artist for the work—one Mátyás Schervitz, who accepted the commission for fifty gold pieces, a not unreasonable sum. It must also be assumed that Schervitz did the frescoes in the small library, which depict the various adventures of Orpheus in the underworld and, on the ceiling, Arion riding on a dolphin.

Detail of frescoed ceiling in the former library, by Mátyás Schervitz.

Arion riding a dolphin, detail of frescoes in the former library by Mátyás Schervitz.

Near the back of the building an elliptical staircase leads up to a vaulted and pillared landing. There, double doors lead into the main reception hall, a large high room in the center of the chateau with French windows opening out on to the balcony. The grisaille frescoes painted on the ceiling here depicted Phaeton in his chariot—now, alas, destroyed—while around the walls appear a number of scenes from classical mythology: Phaeton's death, Bacchus's drunken servant Silenus, the Titans' siege of Olympus, Mercury and Jupiter in disguise being welcomed to earth by Philemon and Baucis, who convert their house into a temple in their honor. The frescoes have a delightfully naive quality about them and some are particularly charming: Tantalus reaching for the unattainable fruit; the Golden Age of Man with Deucalion and Pyrrha, ancestors of all mankind; the Flood, with people trying vainly to hang on to the branches of trees. In one, Ulysses sails away, ignoring the Sirens' blandishments; in another, Icarus begins to feel the wax that holds his wings together being melted by the sun; in a third, vain Narcissus peers at his own reflection in the water. The artist's identity is unknown and the frescoes offer no clue. It was recorded that Ráday met the painter at Pressburg in 1766 when he was attending the Diet and invited him to Pécel. The work was completed only one year later, but that is all we know. Under each of the frescoes Gedeon wrote two-line poems of his own composition, the themes of which were later explained in the journal *Orpheus*, edited by Ferenc Kazinczy. "He who loves himself too much," he wrote sagely for the Narcissus fresco, "never observes himself correctly."

On the upper floor of Pécel the corridor to the right leads to two guest rooms, each once containing three beds. One had frescoes depicting the Labors of Hercules, but these were later overpainted and have yet to be restored. Next comes the dining room and, at the end of the wing, a music room from which a passage led into the gallery of the church. To the left of the floor lies what were the family's quarters. Two rooms had fine frescoes: in one a frieze contained medallions with the heads of Roman emperors, while in the corner room, then the billiard room, only uniden-tifiable vestiges remain, perhaps of Hercules with female groups. The underlying sketches may be the work of Schervitz or Johann Nepomuk Schöpf. These two further were known as the "picture rooms," for they contained fine paintings. In the first, thirty portraits in gilt frames de-picted various Habsburgs—quite an irony from the descendant of Rákó-czi's lieutenant, who now wished to prove his loyalty to the dynasty. Fur-ther on still were the quarters of Gedeon's daughter-in-law. Apparently he frequently argued with her over her spendthrift ways, enquiring, "Why do you need all these trinkets?" to which she replied, "Why do you need all those books?"

Ráday lived on into old age and became a very well-known patron of Hungarian art and literature, one whom young men like Ferenc Kazinczy and János Bátthyany considered to be their spiritual mentor. He also fi-nanced two of the period's leading periodicals. He continued to live at Pécel with his son Gedeon II and his family. The latter, although still a Protestant, was far more of a courtier, and held important posts in Vi-enna. In recognition of this the Rádays were created barons in 1782 and counts in 1792. In that year old Gedeon died, still hard at work; his son followed him to the grave in 1801 and thereafter both house and family entered upon a slow decline. This was especially sad for the chateau was of such recent creation. The decoration of the church was only finished in 1800 and the fine baroque gardens, to which a fountain and pavilion were added in 1780, were just coming to maturity. A particularly beautiful view of the gardens, with their exotic fauna and fine trees, could be had from a large picture gallery attached to the east wing, which contained some no-table works of art.

Tragedy struck in 1825 when a terrible fire gutted the picture gallery and did great damage to the chateau. The dome fell in through the roof and many of the frescoes were ruined. Already burdened by debt and less interested in the property than old Gedeon had been, the Rádays were

Urns on the gate piers at Pécel.

Reception hall with grisaille frescoes depicting scenes from classical mythology.

Grisaille depiction of the legend of Tantalus in the reception hall.

A Fösvényeknek nem övék, még a' mi övékis.

appalled to learn that the damage was estimated at 60,000 forints. Only limited restoration was undertaken, at a cost of 18,500 forints. The frescoes were repaired by one Antal Mihályi, who did a poor job—having, it would seem, a sadly limited knowledge of human anatomy. The property continued to deteriorate. Although Gedeon had enjoined his heirs not to sell the book collection, they were about to do so anyway in 1861 when the Calvinist church stepped in and bought it, along with some family portraits, for 40,000 forints. The Ráday Library was established in Budapest near the National Museum, where it still flourishes today.

At length in 1872 Pécel and its contents were put up for auction. A family called Kelecsényi acquired the property but, since they lived some distance away, seldom visited it. By 1939 the buildings were in a nearly ruined state and World War II caused further problems. After 1945 Pécel was perhaps fortunate to be acquired by the Hungarian State Railways, which initiated a drastic restoration. Under the aegis of Dr. László Farkas, the work undertaken between 1953 and 1956 began to restore the chateau to its former glory. Subsequently its fate was less fortunate, for it was converted into a hospital—a purpose it still serves today, although there is talk of turning it into a museum if the money can be found. The remaining family portraits belong to the library and little trace of the now-extinct Rádays can be discerned. Yet it would be wonderful if Pécel again became what it originally was—not just a fine piece of architecture but a memorial to a remarkable Hungarian family.

ESZTERHÁZA

The Neusiedler See is the shallow, marshy lake situated on the border between Hungary and Austria that today forms part of the frontier between the two countries. Most of its shores are bounded by the Burgenland, Austrian territory since the map of Europe was redrawn in 1919 but historically Hungarian—as cultural and emotional ties still prove. The greatest family in this area, symbolic of the dualism of the old Habsburg Empire with its divided Austrian and Hungarian loyalties, was unquestionably the Esterházys; indeed on the Austrian side that is true to this day. And it was they who built the most grandiose of the nation's country houses in the late eighteenth century, near the southeastern corner of the lake. As Prince Rohan, French ambassador to the court at Vienna, wrote: "I discovered a Versailles at Eszterháza."

Any understanding of this great house and of its short-lived splendor is inextricably bound up with the colorful history of its former owners and with the character of the surrounding region. The Burgenland has been a border zone since prehistoric times, for here the hills form a natural frontier to the Hungarian plain. The shifting lines of the border meant that often landowners found themselves in the difficult position of having their estates divided on both sides of the frontier. The strongest influence in the area since the end of the Middle Ages has been Vienna, whose government has usually enjoyed first call on the loyalties of the local magnates.

In theory the Esterházys trace their lineage back to the biblical Solomon, later dividing into two branches, the Illéshaazys and the Esterházys. This sort of common claim to descent from one of Árpád's original clans can be disregarded—in fact the family was first mentioned in the late twelfth century, and its name probably derives from the villages of Zerházy and Eztherhas. The first recorded figure was Ferenc (1533–1604), a deputy governor of Pozsony, or Pressburg, who styled himself "de Galantha," from the name of his estates in upper Hungary. His son Miklós, however, was the real founder of the family fortunes. Born a Protestant, after a Jesuit education he converted to Catholicism at nineteen and remained a fervent believer all his life. Miklós combined loyalty to the Habsburg dynasty with a keen eye to the main chance. Two advantageous marriages enormously increased the size of his estates and his daughter's marriage to the great Ferenc Nádasdy further enhanced his importance in his native land.

A brave soldier, Miklós Esterházy quickly forged a distinguished military career. Besieged by the troops of the Prince of Transylvania Gábor Bethlen in 1620, he managed to break away and, although heavily outnumbered, to defeat the enemy general, Tarrody. The vanquished general was then buried alive with his horse and armor, a fate he had reserved for Esterházy. Chosen as palatine of Hungary in 1625, an office he was to retain until his death, Miklós was made a knight of the Golden Fleece three years later. The two Imperial castles of Frakno (Forchtenstein) and Kismarton (Eisenstadt) had already been pledged to him by Ferdinand II in compensation for lands lost in upper Hungary. His son Lajos fell in

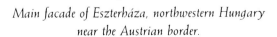

Main facade of Eszterháza, northwestern Hungary near the Austrian border.

battle against the Turks at Vezekeny in 1652, along with three of his cousins, but before his death he paid the Emperor the necessary sum to make both castles hereditary possessions of the Esterházys.

Pál, the younger son of Miklós, was born at Kismarton in 1635 and became the first major builder among the Esterházys. A talented musician whose favorite instrument was the cembalo, he also composed much sacred vocal music as well as poems of a spiritual nature under the guidance of the ill-fated Miklós Zrínyi, who would lead Hungary's first unsuccessful attempt to expel the Turks. As an art lover Pál struggled to transform his uncomfortable medieval fortress into a baroque chateau, and commissioned an architect from the Italian town of Como, Carlo Martino Carlone, to do so in 1663. The resulting alterations retained the original square ground plan with four projecting corner towers but enlarged the building by an extension one room thick all around the outer facades. The towers were covered with copper sheeting, given cellar stories beneath, and topped with double onion domes. All four facades were harmonized and painted blue, red, and white, although the front displayed on the mezzanine level a row of sixteen sandstone busts of Hungarian warrior heroes. In 1680 the castle was surrounded by a moat, with a balustrade facing in, while the provisional wooden roof was replaced by a brick one. Over the drawbridge that provided the sole entrance to the courtyard, Pál had a vaunting inscription placed recording his forebears' glorious deeds. The courtyard itself had Tuscan columns reaching to the upper story and richly ornamented by Italian stuccodores who, legend goes, carved the grotesque heads to represent the swindling court officials who had tried to withhold their proper emoluments. The interior included a huge ballroom decorated by Carpoforo Tencalla's splendid murals, and a chapel with a magnificent organ.

Like his father, Pál became the palatine of Hungary and a knight of the Golden Fleece. When the Ottomans attacked Vienna in 1683 he remained loyal to the emperor, following him to Linz and joining the relieving army. In gratitude Leopold elevated him to the rank of *Fürst*, or reigning prince, which allowed all his sons to designate themselves as princes. As a special honor they were allowed to add the letter *L* (for Leopold) to the family coat of arms. The Esterházy land was now comprised of some thirty estates totaling half a million hectares, for Pál too had made a couple of useful marriages. During the 1690s the emperor furthermore enabled the Esterházys to form their properties into an entail or "majorat," which could pass tax-free and in entirety to the eldest sons. This was to last until 1945, unlike the comparably grand landholdings of the Thökölys and Rákóczis, which were to vanish in the eighteenth century.

After Pál's death in 1713 the Esterházy fortunes ceased to advance in quite such a spectacular fashion. His two sons only survived him by eight years, and it was the younger of the two, József, whose children were to be his eventual successors. One of them, Pál Anton, succeeded to everything at only ten years of age in 1721; although Count Erdődy, a family friend, acted as regent, the child's mother wielded considerable influence. It was she who took on Gregor Josef Wiener as kapellmeister, in which capacity he notably raised the standards of the princely orchestra. As his deputy a young musician named Josef Haydn was engaged in 1761. Although the family undertook little new building during this period, they did continue working on a twenty-room hunting lodge at Süttör, which József Esterházy had commissioned Anton Erhard Martinelli to build in 1720. Only a central block connected to the two side wings by a stone wall was completed, thirty-eight meters long by twelve meters broad, when Gottfried Wolf was paid to paint the main rooms in 1754; work on the park and outbuildings began two years later.

When Pál Anton died childless in 1762 and his brother Miklós, then

Portrait of Palatine Pál Esterházy by Benjamin Block, 1655. (Hungarian National Museum, Budapest.)

forty-eight years old, succeeded to all the estates, the scene was now set for the grandest of all the Esterházys' achievements. Miklós already owned the property at Süttör, although little else, and had made a successful career as a soldier and diplomat. Having finally come into his enormous inheritance, and having fathered the children to ensure the survival of his name, he resolved to establish his fame for posterity. Many years before he had visited and admired Versailles; now he aspired to emulate it. As the proud possessor of 570,000 hectares the means were not lacking, and he soon adopted the maxim, "Whatever the Empress can do, I can do too." Not for nothing was he to acquire the soubriquet of *Der Prachtliebender*— literally, "the splendor-loving."

In January 1763 Miklós convened all his stewards and bailiffs to determine what everyone's role would be in what he termed "the forthcoming and completely new building at Süttör." Within two years he had rechristened the property Eszterháza as sign of his identification with it. Preparations lasted nearly twelve months before the work could begin in earnest—tenants had to be moved, materials assembled, and new roads built. Popular rumor put the work force at 20,000. The first task in the reconstruction of the palace, as it was soon to become, was to join up the main block to the two smaller pavilions and to build single-story colon-

Portrait of Miklós Esterházy by József Dorfmeister, late eighteenth century. (Museum of Fine Arts, Budapest.)

Overleaf, the music room with ceiling frescoes by Grundemann, a Viennese painter, mid-eighteenth century.

naded wings out on each side to form a horseshoe-shaped ceremonial courtyard.

The identity of this remarkable building's architect remains a mystery to this day. Traditionally art historians ascribed the design to Karl Jacoby von Eckholm, director of the provincial building office at Brno. But this assumption had largely rested on inscriptions saying *Jacoby del. et aedif.*; modern scholarship, however, has established that it refers to an architect named Miklós Jacoby, who was working in the prince's service and had produced plans for the Eisenstadt Hospital, a hunting lodge, and the so-called Red House in Vienna. Jacoby, however, cannot realistically be considered the principal architect because the difference in quality between his known works and the main facade at Eszterháza is so great. Similarly his colleague Johann Ferdinand Mödlhammer, a very competent renovator at Kismarton and Frakno and the architect who built Eszterháza's one-story wings, would be an equally unlikely choice.

Discounting the theory that Miklós himself initiated the plans for his grand design, a possible candidate is Girolamo Bon, whose drawings for the vanished opera house at Eszterháza bear some resemblance to the main building. Bon was more of a stage designer than an architect, which may explain the disregard of certain practical considerations such as the internal connection between various parts of the new palace. But there is yet one more probable candidate. Menyhert Hefele, a former student of Balthasar Neumann's at Würzburg, had worked as drawing master to the Hungarian Noble Guard at Vienna. In that capacity he became acquainted with the prince, who, recognizing an outstanding talent, might have entrusted him with the overall designs, while the site work would have been supervised by Jacoby and Mödlhammer.

The major changes made to the old core of the building included converting the former attic into a third story, constructing a double ceremonial staircase in two flights up to the second story, and further emphasizing the central axis of the house by creating a belvedere that projects steeply upwards above the portico and balustrade. The unusual eleven-bay facade is characterized by a ground floor that is not visually bound to the upper two stories, which are connected by pilasters. At the first-floor level in the middle of each side wing a balcony is supported by four Tuscan columns. Underneath each are strikingly carved wall fountains featuring a mythological figure killing a sea monster with the help of tiny putti. To avoid monotony the central axes as well as the backs of the connecting wings were enhanced with sculptural decorations. On the park facade the main block is flanked by two five-bay wings, and the Esterházy coat of arms is visible on the tympanum resting on the main ledge. The palace balustrades are adorned with elaborate partially gilded statues and vases, some of which have survived.

On the *piano nobile* the banquet hall and the adjoining music room formed the center of the building, rising through two stories. Beneath them was the entrance hall with a vaulted *sala terrena* or basement-level hall leading off it. All of Eszterháza's 126 rooms were richly decorated in the rococo style and a mediocre court painter named Johann Basilius Grundemann painted most of the frescoes. In the banquet hall *Apollo on the Chariot of the Sun* fills the ceiling while allegorical statues of the seasons occupy the four corner niches. The family chapel with its gray marble walls was especially magnificent. An artist called J. I. Milldorfer painted the dome frescoes here and in the *sala terrena*. Eighteenth-century visitors particularly noted the prince's collection of clocks and the library with its 22,000 volumes. His rooms and those of his wife were situated on the ground floor. In the eastern wing the famous Esterházy picture gallery with more than three hundred paintings was placed, the greatest treasure being a Raphael *Madonna*. Opposite was the winter garden, a veritable botanical treasure house, which led through to the kitchens.

The gardens were primarily designed in the formal French style by Mátyás Pölt. An artificial waterfall formed their boundary and beyond stretched a huge park where a variety of buildings were gradually erected. The two-story opera house with its mansard roof was completed in 1768. Boasting a wide, deep stage, it could seat four hundred people at performances that were staged free of charge for everyone who applied for tickets. The princely family and their guests watched from the second-floor boxes and the galleries. In symmetrical juxtaposition to the opera house stood the puppet theater, "perhaps the only one of its kind," according to a contemporary account. There, splendidly carved and dressed puppets performed operas as well as comedies in a spacious auditorium that resembled a cave, for its walls were covered with rocaille decorations, stones, and snails.

Largest of the pavilions in the park was the "Bagatelle" or Chinese house. A one-story building with five bays divided by slender pilasters, it had a high roof painted green and red with a seated Oriental figure holding an umbrella on top. When the wind blew, bells tinkled on each corner of the house. The interior was decorated and furnished in chinoiserie style, and intimate balls for just a few guests were held there. Four temples dedicated to Diana, Fortune, Venus, and the Sun, all roughly equal in size, also stood in the park, as did the hermitage, built in direct imitation of one at Versailles and finished in 1775. Lastly, by the road on the edge of the French garden stood the music house, where the singers, most of the court musicians, and intermittently for over twenty years, Josef Haydn lived.

In 1766 Haydn had succeeded Wiener as court kapellmeister, a post he was to occupy for the next twenty-four years. His duties were manifold: to manage and conduct a chorus and an orchestra of twenty-eight musicians, look after the instruments, copy the scores, and produce an unending stream of compositions. During the high season he staged a new opera every month on top of the mass of orchestral and chamber works for the daily concerts, normally starting at 6 p.m., that his patron demanded. Miklós himself liked to play the baryton, a stringed instrument somewhat like the viola da gamba, which he did with only moderate skill. Both men grew fond of each other and, despite his appalling work load, Haydn seems never to have complained.

While musical performances had been given for four seasons, life at Eszterháza only came into full swing in 1770. That year the main palace buildings were completed, and in September a three-day round of festivities took place with plays and operas, peasant dances, a military parade, and a ball for four hundred guests at which the fountains were illuminated by twenty thousand Chinese lanterns. A stream of visitors came and went, filling up the stables, which could accommodate 110 horses, and admiring the wonderful gardens, in which the alleys were lined with chestnut and linden trees and new flowers were planted every month. In September 1773 Empress Maria Theresa herself came to stay for two days, a visit marked by an especially spectacular firework display. The first picture visible in the night sky was of the Hungarian royal arms in a sky-blue field with winged angels on either side and three letters above: V. M. T. (vivat Maria Theresa). The finale illuminated the distant palace in a deluge of fireworks simulating waterfalls, while concealed mortars and exploding bombs created the illusion of a mock battle.

Thus life continued at Eszterháza until 1790, with an unceasing round of splendiferous entertainment and musical performances of as high a standard as anywhere in Europe. So enthused had the Empress been by the quality of the music she had heard there that after a performance of Haydn's L' Infideltà Delusa she had commented, "If I want to see a good opera, I shall come here." The prince, apparently unaffected by the decidedly damp climate and north winds that so bothered Haydn, spent ever

The sala terrena *with ceiling frescoes by Milldorfer, a Viennese painter, mid-eighteenth century.*

Portrait of Josef Haydn, kapellmeister at Eszterháza from 1766 to 1790, copy after Ludwig Guttenbrunn (incidentally the lover of Haydn's wife), c. 1770. (Private collection.)

Garden façade of Eszterháza, seen from along the avenue of yews.

Old view of the Esterházy villa of Eistenstadt by C. Rorick and L. Rohbock. (Princess Melinda Esterházy.)

more of the year at his beloved palace, returning briefly to Kismarton only in the autumn and going on to Vienna for the winter. His annual reappearance in the spring was heralded by a swarm of court officials and by his personal guard of 150 grenadiers dressed in a dark blue uniform with red flaps and lapels, white tie, shirt, and trousers.

In 1790 the world at Eszterháza abruptly changed, for in September Miklós died. His son, Anton, a man already in late middle age, was a very different character. Parsimonious and no music lover, he quickly disbanded the orchestra, closed the theater, and paid Haydn a retainer of only 400 forints per annum in addition to the 1,000 florin pension that had been left by the will of his old patron. The composer was actually not unhappy at this change in his circumstances. Whereas in 1778 he had written in his correspondence, "I am Kapellmeister to His Highness Prince Esterházy, in whose service I hope to live and die," by 1790 he was lamenting, "While I am doomed to stay at home, what I lose hereby Your Grace should certainly realise. It is indeed sad always to be a slave. Yet Providence deems it so; I am but a poor creature." Now he was free to move on to the wider stage of Vienna and London. Nor can Anton be blamed for making some necessary economies. After all, Eszterháza had reputedly cost his family thirteen million gold forints. Furthermore by 1790 Maria Theresa had been in her grave for a decade, her son Joseph's reforms had brought on a crisis in the Empire, and the first breath of the French Revolution was wafting across Europe. The dream-world of the rococo seemed remote and out of date. Only one festival in the old style was held at Eszterháza, this one in August 1791 to celebrate the family's hereditary post of *Főispán* or lord-lieutenant of Sopron.

Anton himself died in 1794 and was succeeded by Miklós, a figure more in the mold of his grandfather. The princely court was finally moved back to Kismarton, on a much reduced scale. There the property had been neglected for thirty years. Its new owner found its formal French baroque gardens outmoded and hankered for a garden in the English style. Soon he decided to remodel the entire castle and gardens in neoclassical taste. Most of the ambitious plans he commissioned were never executed, although limited alterations were made to the house and the park was relandscaped. A palm house and obelisques were added later and a steam pump to drive the waterfall was imported from London.

Meanwhile, little more than twenty miles away, Eszterháza stood abandoned. The family valuables with the picture collection had now been moved away and decay soon set in: the pavilions burned down or rotted, and sheep were kept in the *sala terrena*. A traveler named John Paget remarked in his book *Hungary and Transylvania* (1839), "The whole interior is in such a state that it might be rendered habitable tomorrow, but the gardens are already overgrown with weeds and have almost lost their original form . . . while the beautiful theater, in which an Italian company was formerly maintained, is now stripped of its splendid mirrors and serves only as a dwelling for the dormant bats, which hang in festoons from its gilded cornices." The stables, which had just received twelve thoroughbreds from England, were the only part of the palace still in use. Paget also noted the huge size of the family's estates, said to contain 40 towns, 130 villages, and 34 castles, and remarked that while it only produced £150,000 per annum, "it is capable of considerable increase."

The truth was that even the Esterházys' enormous wealth had been dented by years of prodigality. Miklós III was as complete an autocrat as his grandfather, although as Haydn ruefully noted he lacked the latter's charm and understanding of music. He was also almost as great a spendthrift. He bought the adjoining estate of Pottendorf in 1803 and then the Abbey of Edelstätten in Bavaria, thus ensuring his elevation to the rank of prince of the Empire. An insubstantiated story suggests that Napoleon offered him the crown of Hungary in 1807, but if it were true he would have refused it out of pride, as well as from ancestral loyalty to the Habsburgs, for Miklós felt he was a grand seigneur already. As one English visitor to Eisenstadt, Richard Bright, noted in 1818 in *Travels from Vienna Through Lower Hungary*, "The possessions of this nobleman are far more extensive than those of any other in Hungary, and his mode of life corresponds with the idea of outward state, which we naturally attach to his high rank." One famous story relates how the prince told a Scottish landowner who had boasted of his pedigree flock of 2,000 sheep that he employed 2,500 shepherds, one for every one hundred of his Merino flock.

Upon Miklós's death in 1833 the properties passed to his son Pál, who had been a distinguished diplomat—an ambassador in Dresden, Rome, and London who briefly emerged from retirement to act as foreign minister for six months in 1848. Major financial retrenchment began in 1866 when his son, another Miklós, succeeded and rapidly sold the bulk of the family's huge picture collection to the newly formed Hungarian National

Portrait of Prince Pál Esterházy and family, c. 1820. (Museum of Fine Arts, Budapest.)

Wall fountain in the courtyard at Eszterháza.

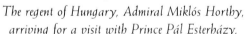

*The regent of Hungary, Admiral Miklós Horthy,
arriving for a visit with Prince Pál Esterházy,
c. 1935. (Wendel Farkas.)*

*The domestic staff at Eszterháza in the 1930s.
(Wendel Farkas.)*

Gallery—637 paintings, over 3,500 etchings, and 51,000 prints. He also presented it with an additional six Old Masters including a Rembrandt. The urgent need for economy still persisted, however, for bad management and inflation had plunged the Esterházy estates further into debt. A family agreement whereby Miklós's son should be sole heir to all the properties eased the financial problems, but his son was only to survive him by four years.

Saddlecloths in the tack room at Forchtenstein, another of the Esterházy family estates now in Austria.

Matters had sufficiently improved by the turn of the century for the new prince, Miklós IV, to decide to move his residence back to Eszterháza, although the family's central administration remained at Kismarton. A major restoration of the main palace was undertaken, some of the work being in questionable taste, and the park was brought back to life, although it came nowhere near its former beauty. After 1918 much land was lost in the partition of the Habsburg dominions; indeed the two chief properties now fell on opposite sides of the new frontier and had to be separately administered. But Prince Pál, who had inherited the estates in 1920, managed them skillfully. While he basically lived in Budapest, he used the palace periodically for parties and shoots, even entertaining the regent, Admiral Horthy, there.

From 1944 to 1945 Eszterháza suffered heavy damage, and at the end of the war extensive looting took place. Pál was imprisoned for years by the Communist regime until he managed to escape to the West during the revolt of 1956. Reconstruction of the palace finally began in the late 1950s, but although the facades and major rooms were put back in order, much remains to be done. Little in the way of decent pictures and furniture has been installed, and the French garden, the park, and the surviving smaller buildings await attention. Yet Eszterháza is still the grandest country house in Hungary, a fitting memorial to a remarkable family who still, thanks to the accidents of history, remain the owners of Kismarton, Frakno, and one of the largest estates in Austria. The legacy of Miklós, the splendor-loving prince, has not vanished in the mists of time.

N O S Z V A J

Behind the charming baroque town of Eger the hills rise steadily up to and across the border with Slovakia. In the vicinity of the town lie the vineyards that produce the most celebrated of all Hungarian red wines, Egri Bikavér, popularly known throughout the world as Bull's Blood. Northeast from Eger through the rolling foothills, a large village called Noszvaj is situated some twelve kilometers along the road. Nothing immediately evident here suggests that this village happens to contain one of the jewels of the country-house architecture of eighteenth-century Hungary.

A settlement then spelled Nozvey is first mentioned in a document of 1248; only later in the Middle Ages did the name assume its modern form. Up until 1457 Noszvaj remained a possession of the bishops of Eger, although the name was also mentioned in another context as that of an estate further east belonging to an eponymous family. In 1457 the bishop exchanged Noszvaj with the Cistercians for another property, and the order retained it until the Ottoman conquest. In 1552, however, Eger and the surrounding lands were besieged by Turkish troops who, failing to capture the town, caused great damage to the estate and chased away the resident monks. Lying as it did on the border between the Habsburg and Ottoman dominions where the hills begin to level out into the Alföld plain, Noszvaj's position was of necessity insecure in these troubled years.

In 1615 a family called Figedy is recorded as the proprietors of the estate, but they soon became extinct and the lands reverted to the crown. The Turkish zone of occupation never extended quite this far north and Eger remained continuously in Habsburg hands, so despite occasional raids the area was able to develop agriculture and vineyards. In 1648 Noszvaj was granted to one Ferenc Hanvay—fairly briefly, however, for he died in 1667 and left all his property to his wife. Her subsequent fate is unknown but she seems to have died without issue. At the end of the seventeenth century, when the Turks were finally evicted from almost all of royal Hungary, the estate was resold to a rich wine merchant from Eger, who himself adopted the name of Noszvaj. During the eighteenth century it again changed hands several times before becoming the property of Baron Sámuel Szepessy around 1770.

Szepessy was one of the new class of Hungarians who had grown rich from quite humble origins during the peaceful decades of economic growth following the end of the Ottoman occupation. If they were prepared to conform in matters of religion like Szepessy's father, who was a Catholic convert from the Calvinist faith, many of those families were often commensurately rewarded. In any case Sámuel decided to build himself a fitting residence, and work began on the site in 1774. The architect of the house has yet to be identified for certain but it was probably a talented local man, János Povolni, who also possibly designed the Lyceum at Eger. This too has decorations that may be described as of French inspiration, and the whole style of the building may loosely be termed rococo Louis XVI. In its excellent proportions, however, a more distinguished hand may be detected—that of Jakab Fellner of Tata, apostle of "braid architecture" and architect of the Calvinist church at Debrecen as well as of numerous castles. An Austrian by birth, he ended his days living, and then dying, at Eger. When he built the splendid late-eighteenth-century facade of Povolni's Lyceum, today the town's high school, he was the teacher and sometimes the collaborator of the younger designer, although the extent of his participation in Noszvaj remains obscure.

Work continued at Noszvaj at a brisk pace until 1778. The following year saw the first mention in official documents of a new noble residence in the village forming part of Szepessy's estates, although two contiguous residential houses were then still unfinished. The Miskolc Judicalia, the official property register, described it as beautiful, comfortable, and solidly built, with fine fruit and flower gardens. Unfortunately the costs of construction had proved considerably higher than anticipated. Despite his wealth, Szepessy had to take out loans of 60,000 forints to complete the project. Building now went on only intermittently, as money became available. By 1782 the main house was more or less finished but the financial embarrassment of its owner was considerable. His father's death afforded him a convenient pretext to move into his old home and to leave his new creation unoccupied. Having decided to sell, he quickly found a purchaser, Baroness Anna Vécsey. She bought it on March 5, 1783, for only 11,000 forints, an absurdly low price at a time when the average farmhouse fetched between 4,000 and 6,000 forints. Convinced that he was almost confronted by bankruptcy, however, Szepessy agreed to all her demands over the protests of his three sisters, who charged that he had acted rashly and had no clear title to sell without first consulting them.

The Baroness, who often used her maiden name, was in fact the widow of Count Antal Almássy. The Almássys came from Heves County in the environs of Eger, although family tradition maintained that they were originally Transylvanian. Up until 1677, when they were awarded their

Park facade of Noszvaj.

own coat of arms, their antecedents remain obscure, but by 1701 they were created counts. Antal had died young, leaving several children behind him, and in 1775 his widow had married Count Antal de la Motte. De la Motte's origins, by contrast, were entirely French. His father had entered the Austrian service in the suite of Francis of Lorraine, the consort of Empress Maria Theresa. As a military engineer he had played such an important role at the siege of Freiburg during the Seven Years' War that he had been ennobled by a grateful monarch. His son had followed him into the army where he likewise rose to be a colonel and then commander of the Eger garrison. Doubtless that was where he had met, wooed, and married the eligible widow.

As was expressly stated in their marriage contract, the baroness's five Almássy children would become her reversionary heirs at her death, a bone of much future contention since she produced de la Motte progeny as well. For the moment, however, there were no problems; the happy couple moved into Noszvaj and continued with the building program. Two side wings for storage and servants' quarters were completed, connected to but at right angles from the main house. The cour d'honneur was then formed and the grounds laid out, with the garden facade at the level of the *piano nobile*, on which the main reception rooms were situated. Not only was the chateau splendidly furnished, it was also extensively frescoed.

Povolni was at hand to recommend suitable artists who were available in Eger: János Lukács Kracker, his collaborator József Zach, and their pupils György Szikora and Antal Lieb. Thanks to Eger's ambitious and art-loving archbishop, Károly Esterházy, who planned to found a university there, the town had received several first-class, impressive baroque buildings, especially the Minorite church ascribed to Kilián Ignác Dientzenhofer. Its altarpiece was painted by his fellow Bohemian artist Kracker, who also frescoed the library in the Lyceum. The ceiling, full of life and movement, depicts the Council of Trent and contains 132 figures including Emperor Charles V. Interestingly the interior of the Lyceum depicts an imaginary late Gothic building, and was finished after 1782 by Kracker's faithful partner, Zach. The same team had worked on the neoclassical cathedral at Eger and the former provost's palace, where they again produced some fine frescoes. And it is unquestionably the frescoes that form the chief glory of Noszvaj. Moreover they appear to have been completed with astonishing speed. When these painters finished their job they had frescoed an unbroken enfilade of apartments at the first-floor level: the staircase hall, to which a double flight of stairs leads from the lower story, the central stateroom, and two further rooms on each side of it, one of them a small corner chamber. Their subject matter was largely mythological. In the staircase hall Zach painted six life-size deities stand-

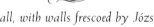

Staircase hall, with walls frescoed by József Zach and the ceiling by János Lukács Kracker in the late eighteenth century.

József Zach's curious frescoes of Apollo and Mars in the staircase hall.

ing on plinths in trompe-l'oeil niches: Venus, Apollo, and Mars to the left of the central doorway with Jupiter, Hermes, and Diana to the right, all curiously attired. On the ceiling Kracker painted a bravura view of Apollo in his sun chariot. The ceiling of the state room, frescoed by Szikora, is delightfully bucolic—putti frolic in a sylvan landscape, dragging a goat along, while opposite a drunken yokel, perhaps a symbolic pagan equivalent of the biblical depiction of the drunken Noah, sleeps off his excesses.

The frescoes in both rooms to the right were destroyed in the 1920s and no record of their subject matter exists any longer, but the rest have been beautifully restored in the postwar years. To the left of the state room is what is known as the Roman Room, the ceiling of which has a fresco depicting Jupiter, Juno, and Pan by Lieb. The walls of both these rooms painted by Zach display elegantly arranged panels with a variety of motifs next to enormous trompe-l'oeil urns adorned with flowers. Most delightful of all is the small corner chamber with panels of birds on the walls and ceiling along with several enchanting imaginary landscapes. The artist was possibly Lieb but exact attribution is difficult in a house where all four painters frequently assisted each other. To make matters trickier, when Kracker died halfway through the commission his colleagues combined to finish the task.

The subsequent history of Noszvaj is far less harmonious than the wonderful frescoes it contains. Soon after the baronness's premature death, the Almássy children initiated a court case in 1785 alleging that their stepfather was endeavouring to circumvent the provisions of their mother's will. De la Motte fought back with counter-allegations but he could not deny that the Almássys had been given the reversion of the property at its purchase by the baroness. Nonetheless he remained in occupation of the chateau, and after several years of litigation a settlement was reached entitling him to live at Noszvaj for the remainder of his life provided that he agree to the exclusion of his children from the succession. Actually his periods of residence until his death in 1800 grew increasingly brief and he had little to do with the management of the estate.

Detail of frescoes in the Roman Room, with walls
painted by József Zach and ceiling by Antal Lieb.

General view of the Roman Room, originally
decorated in the late eighteenth century.

János Almássy, the eldest son, moved in with his family in 1800 and proceeded to make further alterations to Noszvaj. The side wings were reconstructed and improved, while a fine pair of gates was constructed bearing the family cipher on two stone piers surmounted by unicorns. He also built a family chapel leading out from the ground floor at the side of the house, superseded by a larger one in 1830, which was subsequently demolished. Unfortunately debts and a lack of direct male heirs meant that the estate changed hands repeatedly during the nineteenth century, at first through marriage and eventually including one brief ownership by the Telekis. The last Almássy proprietor sold out in 1852 to a rich merchant from Eger, István Steinhauser. His daughter Bertha married one Gyula Gallassy in 1878 and thenceforward Noszvaj remained in that family's possession until World War II. They must have been well-to-do, for Bertha gave her name to another castle, Berthamajor, which was christened in her honor and built in 1900. The village of Noszvaj retained its prosperity too during the nineteenth century; it is recorded as having no less than two curias or small, single-story manor houses within its boundaries.

Today Noszvaj stands on its hillside, an undiscovered jewel. Luckily the chateau was scarcely damaged during World War II. It was comprehensively looted in the anarchy of 1945, however, and there is now hardly one piece of furniture in it that has any connection with the house. Similarly it has proved impossible to locate any old paintings or prints of

Fresco of birds possibly by Antal Lieb, from the corner chamber.

General view of the corner chamber with frescoes possibly by Antal Lieb, late eighteenth century.

Imaginary landscape possibly by Antal Lieb, from the corner chamber at Noszvaj.

Noszvaj or any portraits of the family who built and occupied it. The building itself, painted that inimitable Schönbrunn yellow so beloved in Central Europe, is in excellent condition and the gardens are well-tended. It is a pity that Heves County council, which now administers the property, has chosen to build a hideous modern addition to the side of the chateau to contain the halls and offices of an educational institution. But this cannot be seen directly from in front of either of the two main facades and the house itself is used solely as a museum, as well it should, for Noszvaj is one of the most charming and distinguished memorials to eighteenth-century taste in the whole of Hungary.

F Ó T

The village of Fót lies only about a dozen miles from the capital, and today it almost constitutes one of its suburbs. It still has a peaceful approach, although it lies between the two major roads running north and east from Budapest. One leads to Miskolc and on through Slovakia into the Ukraine, while the other follows the path of the Danube northward until the river makes its wide loop to the west and carries on over the mountains. While at first glance Fót appears unremarkable, it contains an imposing neoclassical mansion that must rank as one of Hungary's great houses, as well as a church that is one of the country's most important examples of Gothic revival architecture.

Fót is first mentioned in 1383 by the name of Folth, and in 1405 King Sigismund granted the property to Benedek Kálnay. By the sixteenth century it had passed into the hands of the Catholic Church and remained inhabited throughout the Turkish occupation. At the end of the seventeenth century, with the Habsburg reconquest, the estate was bought by the Fekete family, the head of which, György, was a distinguished judge. Sometime during the eighteenth century an unknown architect built what was later described as "a small chateau" for the family. It was sited on the gentle hill that may originally have been an earthworks and was surrounded on three sides by a marsh. To this day the whole place slightly resembles a fortified village. In Ottoman times the old Romanesque church had been taken over by its largely Protestant congregation, so the Feketes decided to commission a new Catholic church, the foundation stone of which was laid in 1779. They had become an important family in Hungary: Count János was a poet and writer in four languages, a correspondent of Voltaire, and a distinguished representative of the Enlightenment whose works attacked reactionary nobles and prelates. Every time he sent Voltaire another of his poems, he added a hundred bottles of Tokaj wine as a present; not surprisingly, they were always returned with an encouraging note.

Around 1803, following János's death, the Feketes decided to sell their property, although with the Napoleonic Wars in progress it took some time to find a buyer. When they eventually did, it was to a widow with a small son—Countess Erzsébet Károlyi, née Waldstein-Wartenberg. Her husband József had died as a result of wounds received from a duel and she was looking for an estate near Budapest. The Károlyis were a very old Hungarian family, originally called Kaplony, which dated back to the thirteenth century and took their name from a property of theirs called Nagykároly, located east of Debrecen. Created barons in 1609, they had long been leading figures in the country. One ancestor, Sándor, had been the general of Rákóczi's Kuruc army, but after the Peace of Szatmár in 1711, which he had signed as plenipotentiary, he had made his peace with the Habsburgs, for which he was created count and his estates confirmed. Although much criticized for this, Károlyi's actions can be justified, for with 410,000 people dead from the plague and a further 85,000 war casualties, he may have wanted to avoid further devastation and suffering in what had become a hopeless cause.

Main facade of Fót, northeast of Budapest.

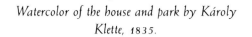

Watercolor of the house and park by Károly Klette, 1835.

Portrait of Count József Károlyi as a child, late eighteenth century. (Hungarian National Museum, Budapest.)

The church at Fót, designed by Miklós Ybl for Count István Károlyi, mid-nineteenth century.

Overleaf, general view of the church crypt where members of both the Fekete and Károlyi families are buried.

Thinking the house too small, the countess commissioned plans to add another floor and a chapel, but she died in 1813 before they were complete. Her son István, then a boy of sixteen, loved the place and was keen to live there. He married the beautiful Countess Georgine Dillon, daughter of the celebrated courtier "Le Beau Dillon" who had reputedly been allowed the honor of loosening the fainting Marie Antoinette's stays at a Versailles ball. In 1821 Georgine bore him a son Edouard, known as Ede, and István resurrected the project. Heinrich Koch, Sr., already the family architect since he had worked for them in Budapest, produced the designs, but Mihály Pollack and József Hofrichter were engaged as the construction supervisors on site. Work started in the early 1820s. A watercolor painted by Károly Klette in 1825 already shows some changes although the chateau still retained its high, old-fashioned roof.

The major alterations were made from 1830 onward. An imposing hexastyle portico was added with six Ionic columns that rose the height of both stories. On the upper floor the windows were square-headed with hood molds, and on the lower level they were round-headed. Well-proportioned pedimented wings of five bays extended on either side. Many fine furnishings and pictures were purchased for the house at this time. Klette's second watercolor, painted in 1835, also shows extensive landscape gardens à l'Anglaise, which had just been designed by Ignác Erményi. The huge park, almost a mile wide and well over two miles long, had two artificial lakes dug in its sandy soil.

Despite these achievements and a great public position, István's life was blighted by a string of tragedies. His wife Georgine died tragically young in 1827 and two of the daughters she had borne him perished in infancy. As a memorial Károlyi built on a tower to the church. He soon married again, this time to a twenty-year-old bride, Franciska Esterházy, who quickly bore him a son named Sandor in 1831. Yet then his beloved daughter Erzsébet died in Rome in 1840 at scarcely eighteen years of age. He had barely recovered from this dreadful shock when Franciska herself died at Fót in 1844. Despite these blows, István's religious faith was strengthened by the adversity and he determined to build a new church in remembrance of his loved ones, a church that would provide a fitting resting place for their bones.

He acted quickly. Having obtained the permission of the bishop, he engaged the youthful and famous Miklós Ybl as his architect. Initially a student of Pollack's, Ybl propounded the gospel of Romanticism, although the influence of Gottfried Semper had recently inclined him towards a

neo-Renaissance style. He submitted his plans, they were accepted, and work began immediately on demolishing the building erected by the Feketes. A number of springs that had to be diverted were discovered among the foundations, and this delayed progress. Essentially the design, broadly Romanesque but with Romantic and Moorish additions, was conceived as two churches built one upon the other—the upper, resembling an ancient Christian basilica with three naves, would be the parish church, the lower would be the mausoleum of the Károlyi family. There were to be four towers, one at each corner of the edifice, while the two framing the front facade would be significantly taller.

Before this work had even started, Ybl was already busy redesigning the chateau. István wanted his house adapted to the taste of the age for grandiose entertaining, and for that he needed more space for kitchen quarters and guest accommodation. Thus the wings were remodeled and enlarged into two protruding pavilions, each with three long bay windows and a balcony under the upper story. The old steep roof was replaced by a much more gently sloping one framed by a baluster railing along the attic story. The effect was imposing, for the facade now appeared immensely long, if rather impersonal. The mixture of styles, however, had spoiled the consistency of the clean neoclassical lines. Nevertheless Fót had assumed the final shape it still has today.

This spate of building activity was interrupted by the Revolution of 1848, during which Károlyi was closely identified with the nationalist cause. Indeed his brother-in-law Lajos Batthyány was appointed to head the new Liberal party ministry. When open hostilities with Austria ensued, István raised a Hussar regiment christened the Red Caps at his own expense to help the rebels. Both his sons fought in the ranks of Kossuth's army. But when the Habsburgs finally triumphed, retribution was bound to follow. Batthyány was condemned to death and shot, while Károlyi was taken away to imprisonment abroad where he spent two years in confinement until pardoned by the emperor. Tradition has it that he was also excused his fine of 150,000 forints, which he vowed to consecrate to the completion of the church at Fót. Both sons who had fled the country returned to Hungary after a general amnesty had been declared in 1854 on the occasion of Emperor Francis Joseph's wedding.

After so much excitement, work was resumed on the church in 1851. During the four years it took to finish the structure and decorate the interior, Ybl also designed a tiny convent and priest's house as two matching buildings on either side of the steps up to the church. Behind at the lower level lay a big churchyard with fourteen little chapels around its perimeter representing the Stations of the Cross. Inside it was sumptuously decorated with a magnificent wooden pulpit carved by Roman craftsmen, a polychromatic marble floor, and a splendid organ in the choir. All the frescoes and altarpieces had been painted by Károly Blaas, a Tyrolean-born art professor from Venice's Accademia. The picture on the left aisle shows Saint George slaying the Dragon and that on the right supposedly portrays István with members of his family.

The staircase leading down to the crypt has a blue and gold ceiling; halfway down an entrance forms a triumphal arch bearing the Károlyi escutcheon, and below a marble slab appears with the inscription "Non habemus hic manentem civitatem, sed futuram inquirimus" ("Here we have no eternal city but we look for one to come"). The crypt is of exactly the same dimensions as the upper church. Beneath the sanctuary lies the chapel, with a black marble altar and a white Carrara marble statue of the risen Christ seated above it. Under the naves run rows of recessed shelves containing all the family tombs as well as two Fekete ones. The several fine statues, one representing young Erzsébet as a New Testament wise virgin, were the work of the distinguished Roman sculptor Pietro Tenerani, a pupil of both Antonio Canova and Bertil Thorwaldsen, who had created

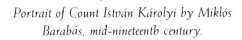

*Portrait of Count István Károlyi by Miklós
Barabás, mid-nineteenth century.*

*Painting of the Empress Elizabeth hunting at Fót
by Willibald Richter, mid-nineteenth century.
(Private collection, Vienna.)*

Statue of Erzsébet Károlyi depicted as the Wise Virgin by Pietro Tenerani, mid-nineteenth century.

Overleaf, steps leading up to the entrance of the church at Fót.

Pope Pius VIII's tomb in the Vatican. Although not all the work was finished, the church was consecrated amid much pomp in 1855.

Only a short excursion from Budapest, Fót came to life again during the 1850s as a center for intellectuals and politicians. Sport there was not neglected either. István had started a small hunt in the 1830s, which was now revived in 1856. Thirty-one couple of foxhounds were kept, an English huntsman called Thatcher resided, and some fine kennels were built. The family's friends were invited to participate and one of them, Baron Béla Wenckheim, waxed lyrical about what he described as the Hungarian equivalent of the Elysium of English hunting, Melton Mowbray. "I can only describe Count István Károlyi as a gentleman sportsman in the English tradition," he insisted. "As this means nothing to my readers I will elaborate—a gentleman of wealth residing most of the year on his estates and looking after the people who live on them in a friendly, thoughtful, and paternalistic manner. He does much for local charities, and for all sports too, without in any way damaging the environment. He invites many of his friends, acquaintances, and neighbours who share his love of riding and hunting." An expert observer, Major George Whyte-Melville described a typical day's hunting at Fót in 1859 and praised the professionalism and dedication of the hunt servants.

Unfortunately the hunt proved so expensive to run that it came to an abrupt end in 1859 until a solution was found by amalgamating with the nearby Csako pack of hounds. The next year it started again and continued to flourish for seven more seasons with a core of regular supporters, hunting over a large area. Twenty couple of harriers were imported from England to provide the additional sport of hunting hares, while foxes, of which there was a shortage at Fót, had to be brought in from elsewhere. But once more the money ran out and in 1866 the pack was disbanded. Revived in 1871, it continued thereafter for several decades and became the best hunt in Hungary. Indeed "the company of the fox hunters of Budapest," as it was called, fell under royal patronage, for the emperor took a personal interest in it. Other packs were less successful or long-lived: the Esterházys had one at Kismarton, the Festetics had several at both Keszthely and Berzence, and Empress Elizabeth kept her private pack at Gödöllő, making several hunting trips to England during the 1870s. The empress hunted regularly around Fót and in the park itself, where the biggest ditch on the property was actually named after her. She even had a changing room in the stables there at her disposal. She is believed never to have entered the house itself, however, for the Károlyis's proclivities were still viewed from Vienna as dangerously nationalistic.

This view did indeed contain a kernel of truth. Ede particularly was passionately patriotic, and when a Hungarian rising was being plotted in 1866 on the eve of the Austro-Prussian War he filled the cellars at Fót with arms. He was arrested at the frontier carrying gold from Italy to the revolutionaries in Budapest, and gave the compromising packet to an unknown fellow-traveler. This turned out to be the banker Nathaniel Rothschild, who returned it to him safely on the Schwarzenbergplatz in Vienna. The rising never took place, and after the Compromise had been reached in 1867 the Károlyis became friendlier to the government. István was appointed *Főispan* or lord-lieutenant of Pest County. He had married for the third time, to Baroness Maria Orczy, but there was no further issue.

István died in 1881 at the age of eighty-three, having outlived his elder son by two years. His young son Sandor then succeeded to Fót. He married his brother's widow, Clarisse Korniss, to whom he too had proposed as a young man, and started to put into effect the ideas he had learned while living in exile in France in the aftermath of 1848. Sandor became a leader of agrarian reform, founding cooperatives and insurance and credit organizations for smallholders. The couple was much loved in the countryside as great philanthropists. Fortunately they could afford to be so, for

the Károlyi properties were considerable: six thousand jochs of land at Fót, the industrial suburb of Ujpest, a palace in the city, and a large estate called Felgyö in the Alföld plain—at least 60,000 acres altogether. His nephew Lászlo had inherited Nagykároly and another property called Radvány, off to the northeast toward Slovakia, which had been in the family since the seventeenth century.

When Sándor died childless in 1906, Lászlo and his young children succeeded to all the Károlyi estates. According to a description of Fót from this period, the house was entered between two spacious courtyards under a porch capable of sheltering a coach and four. The hall, where an old Hussar was always standing on guard, opened onto a billiard room and to the right a small anteroom led into a yellow salon. The reception rooms along the south front made a fine enfilade, moving from the dining room with Louis Philippe–style murals on the east, to the billiard room with green silk wall hangings and leather-covered Empire furniture, and to the salon with two enormous triangular chandeliers (one of which had come from Malmaison). Next came the library, with another smaller library leading off it, and last the count's study at the end of the house. In the summer the weather was frequently hot and low-lying Fót suffered from a plague of mosquitoes, so the family tended to decamp to Radvány up in the mountains. In the autumn they returned for pheasant and partridge shooting. Although a shortage of foxes had meant that fox hunting had almost ceased, there was a flourishing drag hunt in the locality.

In the spring of 1914 a tornado destroyed many of the trees in the park, especially the chestnuts and poplars. But the outbreak of World War I caused few problems until the collapse of the Central Powers. Then, Budapest was occupied by the Allies and on their orders the German Field Marshal August von Mackensen and his staff were interned at Fót. When the People's Republic was proclaimed in March 1919, Lászlo Károlyi fled the country with his sons, although the women stayed behind in the chateau. They survived unscathed despite a visit to the village by Kun's bloodthirsty commissar Samuely, who had the parish priest publicly executed.

Under Miklós Horthy's regime, life returned to normal. Even if some of the estate's land lay across the Transylvanian border, now ceded to Romania, plenty remained in Hungary. Foreign travel was curtailed but there was entertainment enough at home. Every year between 1920 and 1925 a large ball was given at Fót, usually in May. Each had a new theme: once colored lights shone in the park trees so that they resembled Christmas trees; another time Shetland ponies drew carts full of Easter roses into the ballroom. Equestrian life loomed large at Fót, featuring a round of gymkhanas and horse shows, and for some years the drag hunt was revived, albeit on a limited scale. The staff was still enormous—one family of five sisters and two brothers all worked on the estate, and twelve people worked in the laundry alone. When the family was in residence there were up to eighty mouths to feed every day, although the numbers fell dramatically when they were not, for many of the servants were taken along on the move to other properties.

Economies became necessary by 1930, however, so the Károlyis moved from the big house into the pretty baroque pavilions in the park that had survived from the eighteenth century. The countess's was comprised of only a drawing and dining room with a kitchen. Her son István occupied the former gardener's cottage, consisting of two big rooms and a cellar, while his sister's apartment on the courtyard was frequently visited by the head groom's goats. The stud had been relocated at Felgyő after its manager had smuggled 300 horses out of Transylvania under the noses of the border guards, by liberally supplying them with brandy. When Lászlo died in 1936 his heir tried to rationalize the estates, planting fruit trees by the thousands at Radvány and turning the castle there into a hotel. During World War II Fót was requisitioned as a hospital and then an orphan's

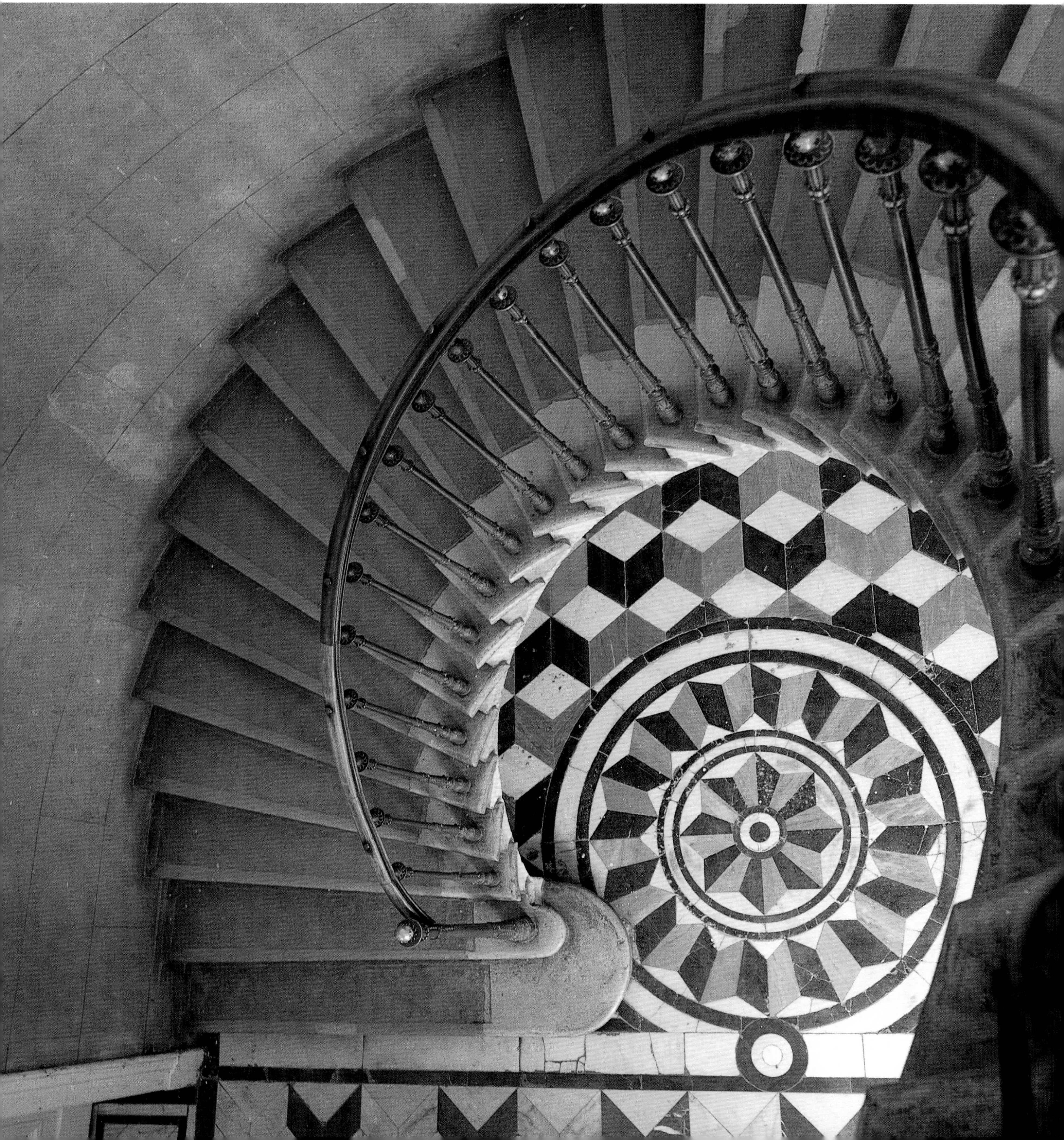

View of the stairwell at Fót.

*Portrait of Countess Clarisse Károlyi
(née Korniss), late nineteenth century.
(Count László Károlyi.)*

home, although the Károlyis were allowed to go on using two bedrooms and the small library.

Nemesis arrived with the Russians in 1945. Evicted from Radvány, then from Fót, the family fled to the west. Fót was confiscated, its contents were looted, and the trees in the park felled for firewood. Today it is a children's school, and modern buildings plus an extension to the chateau have been constructed adjoining the main block. The garden front, well painted and maintained, looks exactly as it must have in 1860, even if the landscape has changed for the worse. The inside is a sadder story: of the 107 rooms in the old house, only one survives in anything like its former condition. This is the former dining room, which has retained its decor and its fine nineteenth-century frescoes. The church, however, has also survived intact. Services are held by the resident priest and down below in the crypt the Károlyi tombs are as impressive and evocative as ever. If István, its builder, were still alive today, he might feel that not all of his family's great heritage has vanished into history.

SEREGÉLYES

The ancient city of Székesfehérvár lies across the main roads that run from Lake Balaton and southwestern Hungary to Budapest. Since the city is only thirty-five miles or so from the capital, it is no surprise that a number of large houses and estates flourished in the fertile surrounding countryside. Indeed a short distance away to the southeast on a road leading down to the Danube lies the small village of Seregélyes, which contains one of the best examples of Hungarian neoclassical domestic architecture—albeit one little known outside the area.

No mention of a settlement at Seregélyes exists before the sixteenth-century Turkish Conquest. The first recorded grant of a property there was to István Zichy and his wife Maria Baranyai in 1650 by Emperor Ferdinand III—a somewhat premature one, it would seem, for the area was then still under Ottoman occupation. Zichy's forebears are known to have owned land south of Lake Balaton in the thirteenth century, when they went by the name of Szajki Gál, but as a noted soldier and loyal servant of the Habsburgs, Zichy was granted the title of count and became the first member of his family to come into prominence. It seems unlikely, however, that István would have built on his new estate, for he died in 1693, only seven years after the Turks were finally driven from Budapest.

Exactly when the house at Seregélyes was begun is unclear—no written records of a mansion-house exist in the eighteenth-century land registry, which mentions only a small village. Possibly this is because the documents have been lost, or it may corroborate an amusing story about the reason Seregélyes was built. Reputedly Emperor Francis I enquired in 1821 of Count Ferenc Zichy, his finance minister and owner of the estate, if it was not true that he possessed a fine castle there—in which case, His Imperial Majesty continued, he would be delighted to be the count's guest at Seregélyes the next year when military manoeuvers were scheduled to be held nearby in Fejér County. Actually Zichy had no habitable house on the property, but as an experienced courtier he immediately saw the need for one. Since business did not allow him to leave Vienna for any length of time, he sent his steward off to Hungary with instructions to have a chateau in the midst of an apparently mature park built from scratch within about a year. Such was the steward's zeal, according to legend, that the whole project was completed within a record eight months. Needless to add, firm historical evidence to support this tale is conspicuously lacking.

Whatever its origins, either as an entirely new construction or as the replacement of an earlier house on the site, Seregélyes's U-shaped design and neoclassical style is typical of its period. Its unknown architect has afforded posterity no clue as to his identity. Nevertheless, with its fine attention to detail and good proportions the chateau is unquestionably the work of a builder well versed in his profession. A regular two-story, center block overlooking the park is adorned by a portico with four columns surmounted by a triangular pediment that bears the Zichy coat of arms. Five windows appear on each side of the portico and a pilastered

235

bay projects from either end of the house. On the entrance front facing east two wings, one story high and over thirty meters in length, project at right angles from the main block to form a courtyard of over 1,750 square meters. A uniform style characterizes the whole building, both externally and internally.

One of the most striking features of the house can be found in the enormous great hall in the middle of the house. There, fine grisaille frescoes by Ferenc Pich depict battles in which Zichy had taken part. There are traces of mural decoration in the other reception rooms, too, although sadly these have not been restored. Seregélyes's other notable element is the park, which, if not large, is still delightful. Directly in front of it is a small lake crossed by a Chinese bridge and around it are several small follies—today painted, it must be admitted, in rather questionable taste.

The chateau never housed contents of the first rank, for it was only one of several family seats. Ferenc Zichy's own wealth had been greatly increased by his marriage to Countess Maria Ferraris, an heiress of such stature herself that a special royal dispensation was given to allow their children to bear both names. The family's building activities continued, and Franz Beer was commissioned to construct a castle for them in the fashionable mid-nineteenth-century Gothic revival style at Orosvár, now in modern Slovakia. So extensive had the Zichy properties become late in the century that the female children were given estates for their dowries, not at all the common practice. Thus it came about that the twenty-year-old Alexandra Zichy received Seregélyes on her marriage in 1893 to Count János Hadik, scion of a remarkable dynasty.

The first distinguished Hadik was an early and fiery Protestant convert during the mid-sixteenth century. Perhaps of Bohemian origin, this Balthasar Hadik (also called Hadikius) was condemned to death for heresy. After defending himself in an impassioned public address, he then man-

Main facade of Seregélyes by night.

Zichy coat of arms on the portico.

aged to escape the executioner's axe and fled to the cities of the Hanseatic League. A university professor, he passed on his literary talents to his son, János, the author of several books who lived near the Slovakian town of Trenčín. János's son, another János, chose to return to Hungary, however, where he spent a lifetime fighting the Turks. The real founders of the Hadik family fortunes were two famous eighteenth-century soldiers, Andras and his younger son Karl-Josef, who served the Habsburgs with distinction and who both rose to the rank of field marshal. After serving as one of Empress Maria Theresa's most successful generals against the Prussians in the Seven Years' War, Andras was appointed to govern the provinces of southern Poland, newly annexed by Austria in the 1770s. Karl-Josef followed his father into the army, and also rose to high command, this time in the 1790s against the forces of Revolutionary France. A brave if unlucky warrior, he died aged only forty-four in 1800 of wounds received at the Battle of Marengo in Italy. By this time the Hadik Hussars, a light cavalry regiment originally raised by the family, had become one of the most celebrated of all regiments in the Imperial Army.

During the nineteenth century the Hadik family continued the tradition of pursuing distinguished careers in the public service. Béla, the grandson of Karl-Josef, was the aide-de-camp and close friend of Austria's Archduke Maximilian. He was a captive of the Venetians for a year in 1848 and served as an observer in the Crimean War, where he was wounded and suffered from blood poisoning. Béla was also in China during the Taiping Rebellion and the Anglo-French intervention. A keen advocate of Austrian naval expansion, he became part of the archduke's headquarters based at Trieste and commanded one of the first Habsburg warships. Sensibly he did not follow Maximilian on the doomed expedition to claim control of the Mexican throne, although he remained on close terms with his former royal patron. Indeed, after the latter's execution at Querétaro, Hadik was sent most of the archduke's personal effects.

Ballroom at Seregélyes.

Detail of plasterwork in the ballroom.

Main facade.

Portrait of Count Ferenc Zichy, early nineteenth century. (Hungarian National Museum, Budapest.)

Yet Béla's wife's family, the Barkóczys, were scarcely less interesting. In the late sixteenth century one had been military adviser to Stefan Báthory, king of Poland, while another had been prominent in the recapture of Buda from the Turks, commanding a division of 7,000 men. In the mid-eighteenth century another had become the *Főispán* or lord-lieutenant of Pest County, and his cousin was the primate of Hungary. Ferenc III resided for some time in France during the Revolution, thus incurring the suspicion of the imperial government, and his son, János, proved a financial genius on the London Stock Exchange. With János the male line of the Barkóczys, counts since 1668, died out, and it was his only daughter Ilona who married Rear-Admiral Béla Hadik in 1860.

Despite such distinguished antecedents their son János preferred a more private life, and for the next forty years until his death at the age of seventy he lived quietly at Seregélyes in the bosom of a large family. Himself one of seven siblings, he produced four children of whom two were sons, László and Béla János. The estate remained intact: no alterations were made to the house and the park was preserved in the English style in which it had been laid out during the preceding century. On János's death the younger son moved into the house. Trained in agricultural management, he ran the farming operations efficiently until he joined the Hungarian Army during World War II. A bomb unfortunately demolished the right wing of the house in 1944 and the revolution in 1945 forced most of the family to flee to the West. Only the old Countess Alexandra stayed on in Budapest, and at her death in 1949 had her ashes interred on the grounds of her former home.

Although the Hungarian ministry of health took over Seregélyes, for many years it remained unoccupied and in a ruined condition. In 1985, however, it was thoroughly restored by the Taurus Rubber Company as a conference center and hotel able to accommodate up to one hundred guests. The restoration has been done to a high standard, so that the external appearance of the old chateau has been exactly re-created and some of the interiors, especially the great hall, provide some impression of what Seregélyes may have looked like in prewar times, although any contents of artistic merit are lacking. Nevertheless, considering the fate that has befallen all too many of the great houses of Hungary, Seregélyes as seen today presents a far from depressing prospect.

KESZTHELY

L ake Balaton is both the playground and the pride of Hungary. Some fifty-four miles in length and on average about seven miles across, its shores are littered with holiday villas and resorts catering to the tourist. From the slopes of the hills to the north come the country's finest dry white wine and at the southwestern corner of the lake lies Keszthely, originally a Roman settlement, the area's largest town, and the center for touring the region. But the town also contains the Georgikon, a still famous academy, as well as one of Hungary's largest, most impressive, and most ostentatious castles.

The estate, only mentioned relatively recently in history, is recorded in the late seventeenth century as belonging to the Pethö family. In 1739 they sold it to Kristóf Festetics, a man who had risen rapidly in eighteenth-century Hungary. Of Croatian origins, his first known ancestor, whose name was recorded as Pétur Ferstetics, was an early fifteenth-century Dalmatian pirate from near Dubrovnik. A century or so later the family was given knightly status by the bishop of Zagreb, but their real rise to riches began with a literate descendant who became administrator to the Batthyánys, one of the great noble families, which he turned into a very profitable post. Kristóf then decided he needed a residence worthy of his status and commenced work in 1745. The existing fortified house on the site, dating from the preceding century, was enlarged, improved, and encased in a baroque shell, while a special room was added to house his book collection of over 2,000 volumes. He employed an Austrian architect named Kristof Hofstädter to advise him, and the work lasted on and off for ten years. Most of the furniture he commissioned locally, although the more important pieces were bought in Vienna or Pressburg. As if to crown his achievement his son Pál, a confidant of the Empress Maria Theresa whom she made president of the Hungarian royal chamber, was raised to the dignity of count in 1766. He took the title Festetics de Tolna from the county in southern Hungary where the family owned another property, in order to differentiate his immediate family from the two other branches. After he succeeded his father in 1768, Pál, who had further increased the family fortunes with various lucrative sinecures, added to the house, beautified the gardens, and bought more good furniture and paintings.

It was his son, György, however, who really established the Festetics' reputation. Beginning his career as a soldier, he rose to the rank of colonel in the Graeven Hussars by the age of thirty-five. Then in 1790 in company with his brother-officers he submitted a petition to the crown asking that Hungarian regiments have native-born officers and that the Hungarian language be used in the army. The government rejected it as another symptom of aristocratic disaffection and he was court-martialled and deprived of his commission. Despairing of further concessions from the emperor, he determined to renounce all further political activity. Instead Festetics devoted himself to the care of his estates, having succeeded to them some eight years earlier. He also began to patronize aspiring writers and thinkers such as János Nagyváthy and Sámuel Tessedik,

Main facade of Keszthely on Lake Balaton.

one an outstanding economist, the other an Evangelical pastor with a reputation as an agrarian reformer.

Thanks to their encouragment, György then founded the Georgikon at Keszthely as the first purely agricultural institution in all Europe. A true son of the Enlightenment, he longed to impart his knowledge to others less fortunate than himself. Having helped draw up the plans for the college, named in György's honor, Nagyváthy became its first principal after Tessedik had declined the post, feeling himself too busy already with the Experimental Economic Institute in his own parish of Szarvas, which focused primarily on peasant youths. By contrast the Georgikon was established to draw recruits from the impoverished gentry and the middle classes, training them as bailiffs to manage the aristocracy's estates. The college proved an immediate success and quickly gained a reputation far beyond the country's borders. Not content with this achievement, Festetics contributed to help found a gymnasium for higher education at Keszthely as well as a primary school at nearby Csurgó.

Until his death in 1819 György remained a veritable Maecenas, patronizing a variety of causes. The library was greatly extended and housed in a wing especially built in 1799–1801 by Andreas Fischer. Scientists were encouraged to use its facilities, although some of his more frivolous relations were deliberately excluded. After the Napoleonic Wars he began to organize the annual Helicon festival. Held each February and named after the legendary mountain home of the Muses, the festival brought together leading intellectuals from all over Hungary. Keszthely became the center for many of these writers and poets, to whom the count awarded prizes for outstanding new works.

One English traveler named Richard Bright, in his book *Travels from Vienna Through Lower Hungary* (1818) stayed with Festetics and recorded both his hospitality and his scholarship. "Never was politeness more marked than in the Graf [count]," he observed. "He welcomed me heartily and after touching on a few topics, sent to request that the Professor of Botany and the Professor of Veterinary Medicine would join us, and finally, recommending me to their care and that of the Prefect, left us for a time." Bright praised "the fine library of nearly 15,000 volumes. From this source of amusement and and instruction he has drawn deeply and successfully." He also described the school, divided into three principal departments, each directed by two professors. Ten scholars supported by him directly could study for three years, although other students could take one- or two-year courses during an academic year lasting from August to November.

A farm was attached to the Georgikon, as was a riding academy and a girls' school to teach such appropriate female subjects as dressmaking and household management. Bright also admired the fine stud, the buffalo herd kept at another property called Keresztur, and the warm-water mineral baths at Hévíz. He also made several excursions from Keszthely. "From the farm we drove past a Roman encampment on our way to the lake, where we found a boat with six rowers in Venetian costume, waiting to convey us on board the vessel, which the Graf calls his frigate, being by far the largest if not the only vessel with sails upon this fresh water sea."

For the next seventy years the Festetics star was not to burn quite so brightly. György's son Lászlo tried to carry on his father's cultural interests, although he was not really concerned with them and soon allowed the festival to lapse. He also discouraged all public access to the castle library, even excluding his father's official biographers. His great passion was the family's stud at Fenékpuszta, where several Arabian stallions were standing and a host of brood mares kept. Although popular enough locally, he supported the Georgikon on a much reduced scale, as another English visitor, John Paget, noted in his book *Hungary and Transylvania* (1839). "'Though no longer in so flourishing a state as formerly, the

Pietra dura portrait of Pál Festetics, late eighteenth century.

Bust of Mary Festetics (née Douglas-Hamilton) as Winter, from a series of the Four Seasons by J. Kopf and L. McDonald, late nineteenth century.

Tassilo I Festetics at a horse auction in Vienna, mid-nineteenth century.

Georgikon has still several professors and practical teachers maintained at the Count's expense," he wrote. "There are few countries in which more philanthropic endeavours to better the condition of the people have been made than in Hungary; but, unfortunately these have wanted a character of permanency, and have in consequence almost always declined on the death of their first founder."

Little was done to the castle in this period although the collections remained intact. László was succeeded by his son Tassilo in 1846. A dedicated soldier, he seems to have had little affection for Keszthely and made only infrequent visits there, preferring society in Budapest or Vienna. Indeed money to maintain the building was not always forthcoming, and by the time of his death in 1883 the castle had assumed an air of neglect if not decay. A new, dynamic proprietor was needed to breathe fresh life into house and estate; fortunately at that moment one appeared on the scene.

Tassilo II was a very different man from his uncle and predecessor. Aged a mere thirty-three, he was determined to assert his position as one of Hungary's foremost landowners and to create a residence worthy of his family. He was already married to Lady Mary Douglas-Hamilton, offspring of a Scottish ducal house and formerly the wife of Prince Albert of Monaco, whom she had abandoned, marrying Festetics some years later. Work began in 1883 and lasted four years. The castle was greatly enlarged, a new wing being added as well as a tower and an immense portico, all of which made the building asymmetrical. So long was the facade now that any artist depicting it used the "fisheye" technique to make it fit a normal format. Both exterior and interior were thoroughly renovated and redecorated.

In charge of this major project was a Viennese architect named Viktor Rumpelmayer, who was accustomed to refurbishing his clients' homes in the grandiose taste of the late nineteenth century. When he died halfway through the work an Austrian firm, Haas & Pashky, took over the assignment. The result could best be described as a blending of neobaroque and eclectic styles. Many new chattels were bought for the castle, one special

Overleaf, general view of the library at Keszthely.

245

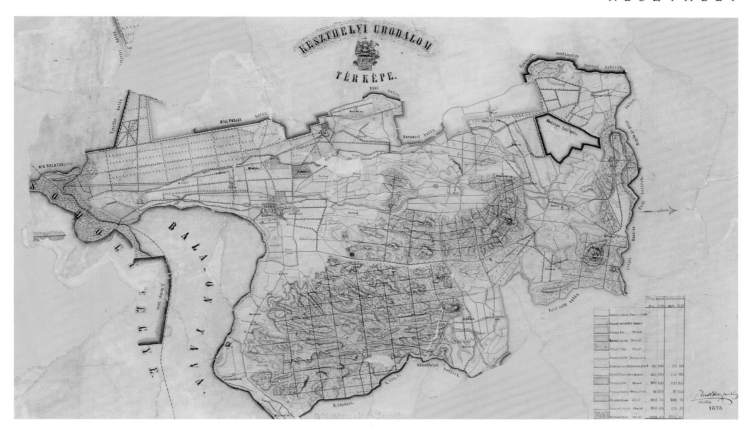

General view of the Blue Salon at Keszthely.

Map of the Keszthely estate in 1878.

train load of furniture came from London, a large number of pieces were ordered from the famous Vienna establishment of Portois & Fix, and magnificent chandeliers were commissioned from Lobmeyer. The collections were supplemented by items from all over Europe, in particular some splendid French eighteenth-century furniture, which today forms the core of the exhibits in the Budapest Museum for Applied Arts. Massive stables were erected at the northern end of the park and the grounds were laid out amidst a wealth of statuary by an English landscape designer named Milner. Water was piped five kilometers to feed the canals and fountains, and thirty-five cottages plus a small chapel and cemetery were demolished to give an uninterrupted view over Lake Balaton.

By the autumn of 1887 all was nearly finished. Tassilo wanted to re-inaugurate Keszthely with a flourish so he invited the Prince of Wales to visit the castle the following year. The royal visit generated much publicity. As reported in *Vasárnapi Ujság*, a newspaper concerned with the doings of high society, "At Keszthely the Prince of Wales was the guest of Count Tassilo Festetics, where he stayed five days, arriving from Gödöllő on September 16th, and hunting stags and partridges. . . . this is the first time the castle has been reopened since work began in 1883. The work cost two million kroner, while the bricks have all been made on the estate. Every modern comfort includes gas lighting and a hot water system for the house. . . . the cast-iron gates are Hungarian made, leading into the English-style gardens extending over 100 *bölds*. . . . the blocks of stone from which the statues were made each weighed twenty tons, and were brought fifteen kilometres from the quarries by carts with eighteen span of oxen. . . . the interior of the castle shows a mixture of luxurious decoration and pleasant simplicity. Wonderful wooden staircases lead to the second floor, with portraits of the family covering the walls. The floors are made of mahogany and other rare woods. The two storey—high library and the Count's study contain 35,000 volumes, showing the proprietor's deep interest in literature."

*Old view of Keszthely by Rudolf von Alt, 1887.
(Prince György Festetics.)*

*Portrait of Prince Tassilo II Festetics by Gyula
Benczur, late nineteenth century.*

The future Edward VII paid further visits to Keszthely, although reputedly on one occasion the invitation was withdrawn because the prince insisted on bringing with him his Jewish crony Baron Hirsch, an instance of blatant anti-Semitism. Much of European society came as well. The shooting in the forests behind the house and in the family's lodge at Berzence was famous, attracting such keen sportsmen as Archduke Francis Ferdinand. The emperor bestowed the title of prince upon the family in 1913 in official recognition of their prominent rank in society. Life continued in the grand manner and stories of Tassilo's behaviour abounded. He was supposed, for instance, to have ordered the flowers in the garden's beds changed overnight to reflect colors particularly related to guests staying at the castle. He was even reputed to have added a thin strip of red to the Festetics blue and yellow flag, although only sovereign countries were entitled to tricolor flags.

Some disruption came with World War I. The family survived Béla Kun's regime safely in exile in their Vienna palace, while a guard of British sailors was placed around the castle to protect it from revolutionaries or looters. During the 1920s life went on much as before but the number of royal guests declined sharply. When the regent Miklós Horthy arrived on a visit he was barred from entering the castle through the main gate, a privilege reserved for the monarch only and one that reflected the Festetics motto, "Deum time, Regem honora" ("Fear God, honor the king"). With border changes after the war, some of Keszthely's former 100,000 hectares now lay in Slavonia (the newly independent Yugoslavia) and Tassilo complained that he had to feed eighty-six mouths every day. Yet he was still the second largest landowner in Hungary.

No more changes were made to the castle, but even if no further important additions were made to the library it continued to grow, amounting to some 52,000 books in 1939. An excellent catalog had already been made by the librarian Jószef Parkanyi in 1891. Everything at Keszthely was kept in perfect order—the house and grounds, the farms and stud, the property in the town (for the Festetics owned most of it). Although not especially interested in the Georgikon, Tassilo went on supporting it generously. His year had settled into a pattern: he resided at Keszthely from October until January, from thence moving to the Riviera and Saint-Moritz, and returning in the spring. Part of the summer was spent in Austria or racing in England, going on to Berzence once the shooting had begun. One of the last magnates to have a private train, one in which he usually traveled, Tassilo refused to stay at hotels in "the Republic" when he visited Vienna and slept instead in his private salon car on the tracks at the Südbahnhof.

By then a widower for eleven years, Tassilo lived until 1933, an active octogenarian and increasingly eccentric in his ways. He permitted his fleet of cars to be driven only every other day, for example, since he believed that like horses they ought to rest. His son György succeeded him. Already a middle-aged man, he slowly brought the estate into the modern world. Access to the library, recently tightly restricted, was improved, and another room was added to house the new books. Without a chatelaine to organize the social whirl, life at Keszthely was somewhat quieter in the 1930s, although it retained considerable style, as Margaret Bourke-White's article for *Life* magazine showed. The prince finally married Countess Mia Haugwitz in 1938, but he died in 1941 soon after Hungary's entry into World War II, leaving behind his widow and a baby son. The castle survived unscathed until 1945 when it was looted by German and then Russian troops. Fortunately a civilized Soviet officer had the doors leading into the library walled up and the collection escaped without loss. In 1948 it became a part of the National Széchényi Library and was opened completely to the public.

Keszthely has certainly been fortunate, for today it is probably the best maintained country house in Hungary. The Georgikon, too, still flourishes in the town both as an institute and an agricultural museum; in fact, it is now spread over three different campuses. Realizing that the over-300-year-old castle was showing signs of wear and tear, the authorities began a major restoration of the structure in 1969, which lasted five years and brought many of the rooms back to their former splendor. Only a few of the contents survive from the Festetics collections, mainly the pictures,

The Prince of Wales, the future Edward VII, visiting the Festetics at the family's hunting lodge of Berzensce. (Prince György Festetics.)

Prince and Princess Festetics photographed at Keszthely by Margaret Bourke-White for Life *magazine, 1939.*

but they have been supplemented by objects from other sources, including some fine furniture—indeed one or two of the rooms are virtually exact copies of what they were early in this century. The enormous ballroom provides the setting for concerts and conferences and the central wing now houses an extensive collection of African big game trophies, all shot by a Windischgrätz cousin in the post-war years. The fact that over half a million visitors saw the museum in the castle during 1988 is surely proof of its renown and popularity.

Any book seeking only to describe the architectural masterpieces of Hungary could not include Keszthely. Its proportions are asymmetrical, its style hybrid, its sheer size overwhelming, if not frankly vulgar. This does not, however, detract from its odd and compelling charm. For it stands as a splendid monument to a vanished age when the riches and self-confidence of a noble family could create almost overnight one of the grandest residences in all the old Habsburg Empire.

P O L A N D

Introduction

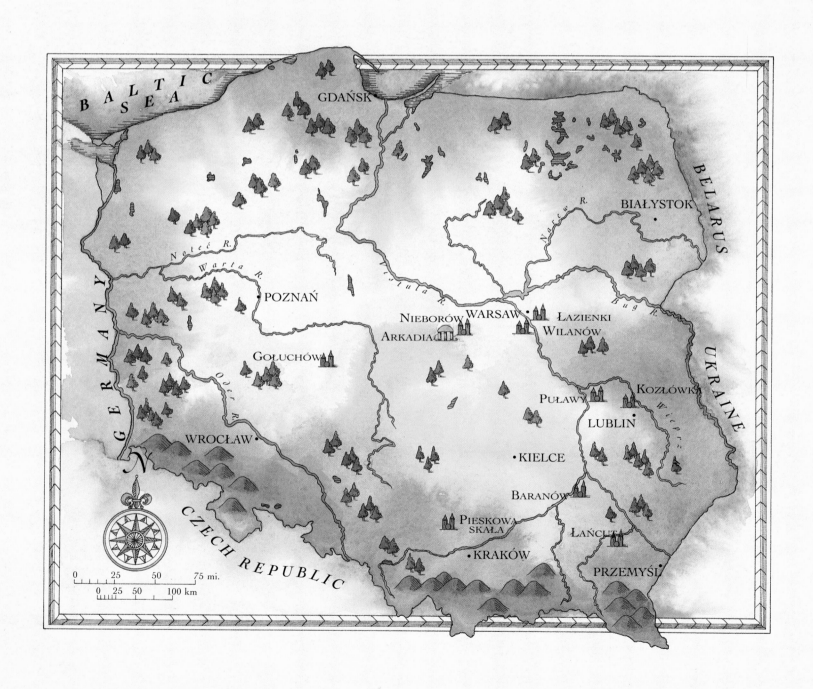

*B*etween the Hammer and the Anvil is the title of a fairly recent history of Poland, an aptly chosen one indeed, for the country has been ground between the German hammer and the Russian anvil for the past millennium. The Poles at one time ruled the largest state in Europe, but their nation lacked natural frontiers; later on it was erased from the map for over a century. Theirs has been a past both heroic and tragic.

Both of these traits were exemplified by the *szlachta*, as the gentry and the nobility were called. For centuries they constituted the political nation in Poland, a phenomenon unique in Europe, and were largely responsible both for their country's rise to greatness and for its decline into partition and foreign occupation. Thanks to the repeated devastation that Poland has undergone, the houses and castles of the *szlachta* are in quite variable condition and some no longer even stand on Polish soil, yet they provide an eloquent memorial to a remarkable class.

If an arbitrary starting date is necessary, Poland's history can be said to have begun in the mid-tenth century. Before that the country existed in relative isolation, for a ring of Slavic tribes shut it off from the outside world—indeed the Roman Empire had never penetrated anywhere near its boundaries. The Poles were an agrarian people living in self-sufficient village communities, yet sharing a common language, religion, and way of life. By the tenth century, however, the Piast dynasty had established its rule over a relatively wide area and had developed a fiscal system and a small standing army. When the Holy Roman emperor Otto I encountered it on his eastern campaign in 955, Poland's ruler, Prince Mieszko I, realized that isolation was no longer possible. Aware of the benefits that his neighbors the Bohemians had derived from Christianity—principally that it would remove the emperor's pretext of conversion for subjugating his people—he decided that his people, too, should be converted. After his own baptism and with Otto's approval he married a Christian Bohemian princess, and in 966 the Duchy of Polonia became a part of Christendom. Nevertheless Mieszko continued his independent policies most successfully, fighting the Germans again several times, adding Silesia and Pomerania to his dominions (and thereby control of the Baltic seaboard), and repulsing a Russian invasion by Vladimir the Great. At about that time Russia was converted by missionaries from the Eastern Orthodox Church, and its consequent alignment with Byzantium, in contrast to Poland's with Rome, foreshadowed a good number of future conflicts between the two nations.

Mieszko's son Bolesław the Brave succeeded in 992. A brilliant soldier and politician, he persuaded the pope to make Gniezno into an archiepiscopal see and create three other Polish bishoprics, thus underlining the Polish Church's independence. The Empire was alternately friendly and hostile, but Bolesław contained the military threat and had himself crowned king of Poland in 1025, shortly before his death. Unfortunately his achievement did not endure. The two weak rulers who followed and the regional factionalism that resulted from the country's rapid enlargement led to a period of decline. One king lost his throne by quarrelling with the papacy and his successor was forced by the nobility to carve up his kingdom into five duchies of equal status for his five sons. But a national consciousness had begun to evolve, and the country's economy had started to develop. By 1100 over eighty castle towns existed, while cities like Kraków, the capital, Sandomierz, Wrocław, and Poznań, were solidly established. Nevertheless, rival claims between the larger towns and the regional lords meant that Poland continued to fragment, for having evolved from clanlike structures, its society was not feudal in the western sense.

At the bottom of twelfth-century Poland's economic and social hierarchy stood the peasantry, still mostly free and not tied to the land. During the next century, however, an agrarian boom meant that peasants who

owned land thrived, but the landless peasants, who had nothing but their labor to offer, increasingly became tied to the land in a form of economic vassalage. At the top of the social scale the gentry or *szlachta* inherited both their status and the lands over which they acted as independent magistrates, although they were obliged to perform military service for their ruler and submit to his courts.

The nascent middle class was represented by the settlers in the towns, who were largely foreigners. The towns had evolved as separate entities, distinct from the surrounding countryside thanks to their royal charters and governed by German rather than Polish customary law. These developments tended to weaken royal power, still exercised by directly appointed officials called castellans. However these officials were increasingly superseded by the *voyevods* or palatines, who administered the various duchies.

The Mongol invasion of 1241 devastated Poland and further exacerbated the difficulty of achieving national unity. Fortunately it was of short duration, but the Mongols returned twice more in the course of the century, depopulating the south and east. The vulnerability of the divided country was exposed, just as it was by the growing power of the Teutonic Knights, whom Duke Konrad of Mazovia had foolishly invited in 1226 to subdue the heathen Prussians. The Order's ruthless warfare and skillful diplomacy enabled them to conquer all of Prussia and Polish Pomerania by 1300. Together with the newly emergent Margravate of Brandenburg to the west, they threatened Polish access to the Baltic. Meanwhile German settlers were pouring into the country to replace the population lost by the Mongol invasions, and the resulting anti-Teutonic feelings fueled the drive for reunification. Duke Władysław the Short of Kraków forged an alliance with Angevin Hungary, and with papal approval embarked on the

Szlachta *from various regions of Poland in national dress, late sixteenth century.* (Łańcut *collection.*)

reconquest of the country, but it was his son Kazimierz the Great who completed the task. During the latter fourteenth century, even as Western Europe was ravaged by the Hundred Years' War and the Black Death, the Poles enjoyed an era of relative peace and prosperity.

With the spread of Christianity throughout the country, the Romanesque style pervaded Poland with churches built mostly in stone. The first traces of Polish Romanesque were timid enough, small rotundas erected near the major castles in the late tenth century, but within a hundred years, towered two-aisled basilicas were being constructed, already showing Rhenish influence. By the twelfth century religious artifacts of a high standard were being produced, and monasteries were being established. Along with the cathedral schools, the latter became the main educational force in the land, even if their pious zeal was notably lacking. In the realm of secular as opposed to ecclesiastical architecture, the short supply of good quality building stone meant that residences were almost entirely wooden, sometimes reinforced by clay and stone—although Bolesław the Brave appears to have had a stone palace as early as 1000. Fortresses multiplied both as administrative centers and to satisfy military needs in the endless feuds between the Piast duchies.

In Wielkopolska or Greater Poland (the western region around Gniezno and Poznań) much Romanesque building took place, more commonly in stone than in Małopolska or Lesser Poland (the southern area around Kraków). In the early thirteenth century, however, the introduction of brick enormously stimulated construction, especially in the triangle formed by Kraków, Kielce, and Sandomierz, the core of the late-medieval Polish kingdom. Further north in Pomerania and along the Baltic coast, brick was used almost exclusively for both churches and castles, stone being employed only for door and window casings and for decorative details. The Gothic style had already arrived before 1300, thanks mainly to the Cistercians, but was properly established by the ambitious building program of Kazimierz the Great. Gniezno and Kraków cathedrals, along with a mass of other churches and castles constructed during these years, were fitting monuments to his reign, which also saw the fortification of old towns and the foundation of new. In these urban areas the architecture reflected the inhabitants' growing opulence and elegance. On the Wawel Hill in Kraków the king created his own stronghold by replacing the upper castle and its adjoining rampart protected by a moat and earthworks with walls of dressed stone and a central gate. Laid out around a large courtyard, the Gothic design remained until the great fire of 1499 and the subsequent alterations.

Kazimierz was indeed aptly named "the Great." In 1333 he had succeeded to a weak, poor, and backward realm only recently reunited by his father. He proceeded to overhaul the fiscal and monetary systems, create a central chancellery, codify the whole corpus of existing laws, and establish guilds in the towns. Favorable climatic conditions encouraged an agrarian boom, and industry—especially mining, which uncovered new deposits—expanded dramatically. An influx of refugees from Western Europe brought in artisans and merchants while the Church's promotion of studies abroad meant that Polish scholars and poets became known throughout the continent. In 1364 Kraków University was founded, the second of its kind in Central Europe after that in Prague.

A good central government and fair justice were complemented by skillful diplomacy, on which the king relied more than on warfare. He never surrendered his claims to Silesia and Pomerania, lost earlier to Bohemia and the Teutonic Knights respectively, but he did reincorporate Mazovia (the region round Płock and Warsaw) into his dominions, which he almost redoubled by conquering Podolia and Volhynia to the southeast. Here the population was Orthodox rather than Roman Catholic and Ruthene rather than ethnic Polish. Yet even as Kazimierz supported the spread of Catholicism, he allowed wide religious freedom. The Polish Commonwealth, which was to stretch from the Baltic to the Black Sea, had been inaugurated. Fittingly toward the end of his reign the king played host to a glittering summit of his fellow monarchs discussing the possibility of a new crusade.

On his death in 1370, Kazimierz left no legitimate male heir, instead bequeathing his throne to his nephew Louis of Hungary. When he too died twelve years later, the "Kraków lords," who effectively ran the country, chose Louis's ten-year-old younger daughter, Jadwiga, for their queen. Disregarding the child's protests that she was already betrothed to William of Habsburg, they married her off to the pagan grand duke of Lithuania, twenty-six years her senior. After Władysław (as he had been renamed) had been baptized, the couple married in the Wawel's cathedral in 1386 and simultaneously the two kingdoms merged. Poland's destiny for the next four centuries was to be linked to Lithuania, its backward eastern neighbor and three times its size. The union may have been of dubious benefit in the long term, but in the short run it bolstered national security and brought in a vigorous new dynasty, the Jagellon, to rule the country. Also of significance was the fact that the nobility had willingly chosen a foreign king, a development that in effect ensured a constitutional monarchy in the future.

Although Jadwiga's marriage was childless and she died young, Władysław reigned on until 1434. A joint Polish-Lithuanian army routed the Teutonic Knights at Grunwald in 1410 and they were defeated again several times during the next decades. Nevertheless the Polish king avoided crushing the order, for it had powerful friends in the papacy and the Empire whom he hesitated to alienate. Besides, his government, which advocated religious tolerance, was branded schismatic at the Council of Constance in 1415 and he had no wish to have a crusade launched against him. Moreover the union of Lithuania, a nation of pagan Balts and Orthodox Slavs, with the far more developed Poland remained uneasy. Nevertheless by 1500, after the Jagellon rulers had gained the thrones of Bohemia and Hungary as well, the dynasty ruled over a third of the European mainland. After the young King Ludwik fell fighting the Turks at Mohács in 1526, both realms passed to the Habsburgs.

Under the Jagellons and free from foreign invasions, Poland enjoyed its golden age. Its political institutions assumed a definite shape and the principle of government by consensus between the crown and the seyms or assemblies was now firmly established. Each province had its own seym composed of representatives of the *szlachta*, although the crown did not summon them too frequently. The castellans and palatines were granted seats on the Grand Council during the fifteenth century but it was the Privy Council, dominated by a caucus of palatines and bishops, that wielded the real power and dictated the succession. Not surprisingly the *szlachta* objected to the concentration of power in the hands of this oligarchy, so when Kazimierz IV sought their support in the 1450s they demanded in return that no troops or taxes could be raised by the crown without the consent of the eighteen provincial seyms. Thus the principle of no taxation without representation ensured the *szlachta* a voice. The National Seym, which by the sixteenth century represented Mazovia as well as Wielkopolska and Małopolska, was now split between the Senate, containing the bishops and administrative office holders, and the Lower Chamber, consisting of deputies from the *szlachta* and the larger cities.

By the sixteenth century the crown's power was so circumscribed that it could not be used arbitrarily. The Seym closely vetted each new king before electing him, even if he was the only son of his predecessor. The new county courts, with their centrally appointed sheriffs or starostas and judges, were constantly challenged by the seyms, by the manorial courts, and above all by the ecclesiastical tribunals, all of which had overlapping areas of jurisdiction. Legislative functions were taken over by the Seym, which spoke for the enfranchised ten percent of the population and could plausibly claim to be more representative than any other comparable contemporary body.

The system, however, had an inherent weakness, for it had developed exclusively in the interests of one class, which was restricted both in its vision and composition. The *szlachta*'s privileged status was enshrined by the neminem captivabimus statute, a forerunner of habeas corpus that guaranteed their freedom from arrest or punishment except under due process of law, and by the nihil novi statute, which required that the crown take no action without endorsement by both chambers of the Seym. With their bitter internecine rivalries and fierce class solidarity, the *szlachta* had little in common with the feudal nobilities of Western Europe. Even their coats of arms were never personal to the bearer and were borne by all members of a family impartially, often by families of different names that may have shared a common origin. Perhaps their closest parallel was to the Scottish clan system. Father Stanisław Orzechowski remarked on the *szlachta*'s remarkable status in the mid-sixteenth century. "Consider the Pole's position in the world"—and by Poles he meant the *szlachta*—"proud in his freedom, resplendent in his liberties, dressed in the glorious robe of rights equal with those of the King. That is why the

Distant view of Pieskowa Skała, near Kraków.

Pole wears the fine gold ring of nobility, which makes equals of the highest and the lowest in the land."

By the sixteenth century Poland had become the granary of Europe, and during this period the *szlachta* grew rich. The labor days tenants worked in lieu of rent were increased from twelve to fifty-two per annum, thereby imposing a form of economic serfdom since most could not afford to move away. Hitherto estates had remained small by Western European standards but now the magnates in particular became large landowners—the Tarnowski family, for example, doubled the size of their properties. Taken by itself the yield from land could still not produce a high enough income for the ambitions of many members of this class, so lucrative public office and business ventures, especially mining, became necessary supplements. Thus many families like the Szafraniec based themselves near the larger cities where some of their newfound wealth was soon to be channeled into artistic patronage.

The growth of prosperity in fifteenth-century Poland combined with the increase in the local population and in immigration from the West fostered much building activity. In the north the Teutonic Knights brought in Flemish architects, whose massive city walls and ecclesiastical and civic buildings can still be seen; in central Poland, on the other hand, in Mazovia and Wielkopolska, a modified local style predominated that harked back to a lighter German-Burgundian Gothic most akin to Bohemian architecture. Churches like Saint Mary's in Kraków were continually modified: the wonderful stellar vaulting there and the charming steeples were later additions. Ornamentation was normally plain in comparison with the rich work found in France or Flanders, but in eastern Poland a surprising result of the union with Lithuania was the fine frescoes of Russo-Byzantine provenance executed in some churches such as the chapel at Lublin Castle.

Secular architecture now began to assume the same importance as ecclesiastical. Innumerable fine town halls and burghers' houses were built all over Poland displaying the same range of foreign influences. Castles became larger and more elaborate, although they were still usually constructed in brick in the north and in stone elsewhere. The majority were lacking in the basic amenities, however, although there were exceptions like the magnificent Malbork, the former seat of the Grand Master of the Teutonic Order. Perhaps the finest example of Polish late Gothic is the Collegium Maius at Kraków University. Dating from 1494 with a quadrangle created from earlier buildings, it is a model of elegance and fine proportions. Yet it represents a style that was gradually losing ground by the turn of the century to that of the Renaissance. The Gothic was to linger on for some time, nevertheless, producing more fine monuments in Pomerania and Lithuania during the early sixteenth century and many others in the more remote country districts for decades after that.

By 1500, Poland—although not Lithuania, which was still largely untouched by civilization—formed an integral part of Europe. Indeed printing had arrived in Kraków before London. The city's university had become the focal point for the dissemination of the humanist ideals of the Renaissance as well as the finishing school for the Polish upper classes, who also traveled to Italy and returned imbued with its culture. One of its professors, the Tuscan scholar Filippo Buonaccorsi, tutored the children of Kazimierz IV, and his political and philosophical writings under the pen name of Callimachus were immensely influential. Mikołaj Kopernik or Copernicus was a student of astronomy at the University in the 1490s whose research, published fifty years later, shook the world by showing that not the earth but the sun was the center of the planetary system.

The Lithuanian Jagellons had absorbed Polish culture remarkably well, even if Kazimierz IV did not fully inherit his father Władysław's native intelligence. The enlarged Poland of well over five hundred thousand square miles was the biggest country in Europe, but its inept foreign policy drove its two principal foes, the rising powers of Muscovy and Ottoman Turkey, into an alliance that posed a serious threat. Meanwhile the ambitious Habsburgs watched and waited. Yet Kazimierz's youngest son, Zygmunt I, and his grandson, Zygmunt II August, reigned between them from 1506 to 1572 and managed to preserve a peaceful continuity in their dominions. This in turn encouraged every kind of cultural activity and allowed the Poles a freedom of religious conscience, enabling them to escape the excesses of the Reformation and of the Counter-Reformation. For if religion had always mattered in Poland, it was as a very tolerant kind of Christianity. Considering the variety of creeds the country contained, this was hardly surprising. The union with Lithuania had brought in large numbers of Orthodox Ruthenes; Armenian communities were scattered throughout the major cities; Jews, governed by their own laws although lacking any political rights, had settled in Poland in substantial numbers; even some Muslims, descendants of the Tatars, were now loyal citizens. Much of Lithuania, supposedly converted to Christianity in toto after the union, was widely regarded as pagan two centuries later. Even the Polish Catholic Church enjoyed an unusual degree of independence, for its bishops were appointed by the crown, not by Rome, although the candidates were submitted for papal approval. When the pope evinced violent disapproval, however, as he did of Archbishop Jan Łaski in the 1530s, nothing whatever was done.

The church hierarchy wielded considerable influence, some of its bishops being drawn from the magnate families while others were trusted royal nominees of plebeian origins. Moreover the Church was the largest landowner in the country, far larger than the crown—possessing, for instance, five times as much property in Mazovia. Yet the Polish clergy was no more corrupt and often more tolerant than their counterparts in Western Europe. Thus when the Reformation came it caused fewer tremors in Poland than elsewhere. Lutheranism rapidly penetrated the north and west, gaining many converts among the German populations of the towns and few elsewhere. In an astonishing about-face, Grand Master Albrecht von Hohenzollern converted to Lutheranism and secularized the Teutonic Order in 1625, being granted the duchy of Prussia by a formal act of homage to Zygmunt I. The arrival of Calvinism was more significant; with its democratic organization and its eschewal of pomp and ceremony it swept the country, appealing especially to the *szlachta*, who were traditionally suspicious of the power of the Catholic Church. Extremer sects were also tolerated, including Anabaptists, Mennonites, and even the Arians, who rejected the Trinity and the divinity of Christ. By the 1550s a majority of deputies to the Seym were Protestants, as were members of the Senate by the 1570s. Many magnate families like the Leszczyńskis and Radziwiłłs had converted to Calvinism, and even some prelates remained open-minded: Andrzej Zebrzydowski, bishop of Kraków, told his congregation they could worship a goat if they went on paying their tithes. King Zygmunt I made it clear that the religious debate was none of his business, while many of the most staunchly Catholic among the *szlachta* sided with the Calvinists if they felt that liberty was imperiled by persecutions. In 1555 a majority of the delegates to the Seym demanded the establishment of a Polish church independent of Rome.

The indecisive Zygmunt August faced a dilemma: to do nothing was obviously impossible, but he feared to do too much. Therefore he referred the Seym's demands to Rome, where the pope promptly condemned them as heretical and left it at that. The Protestants, divided by internal squabbles and lacking a strong leader, had missed their chance. Yet the Reformation in Poland was really less of a spiritual movement than a vehicle for the intellectual and political emancipation of the upper classes, embodied in the executionist movement, which demanded an end to the Catholic Church's immunity from taxation and the diocesan courts. Slowly the Counter-Reformation gained momentum. Its tactics were moderate for its spokesman, Cardinal Hosius, was an articulate and decent man. It was he who introduced the Jesuits to Poland, and one of their luminaries, Piotr Skarga, wielded enormous influence as confessor to the king and chaplain to the Seym. Gradually reconversions occurred; Mikołaj Radziwiłł abjured his father's Protestantism, setting a pattern for many of his peers. Persecutions were substantially avoided and where mixed marriages still occurred they worked eventually to the Catholics' advantage, since the children were brought up in the Church. Freedom of religion was enshrined in the constitution in 1573 with the Confederation of Warsaw and remained an element of Polish policy even after the majority of Protestants had peacefully returned to the Roman fold.

The Reformation was not the only problem worrying the Poles in the late sixteenth century, however—the end to the dynasty was also in sight. King Zygmunt August was a sad figure, the only son of Zygmunt I and the sinister Milanese, Bona Sforza. His first wife, Elizabeth of Habsburg, had died after two years of marriage, while his great love, the beautiful Barbara Radziwiłł, also perished four years after their elopement; both were reputedly poisoned by his mother. He refused to touch his third wife, the epileptic Katherine of Habsburg, and so remained childless. Some of the *szlachta* were concerned. With the Union of Lublin in 1569, the Polish and Lithuanian Seyms had merged. Although they retained separate laws, treasuries, and armies, they formally shared one monarch and one combined Seym, which met in the small Mazovian city of Warsaw, the future capital. The dearest wish of most of the *szlachta* for a "royal republic," which was what the Most Serene Commonwealth of the two nations of Poland and Lithuania actually was, had been granted. But there was no question of managing without a king. Unfortunately nothing had been agreed about the succession by the time Zygmunt August died in 1572.

During the sixteenth century the development of Polish architecture

Detail of fortifications at Pieskowa Skała.

had been spectacular and had led to the creation of some of the finest Renaissance monuments in Europe. The Renaissance style had reached Poland in two ways. From Hungary—where it had been in evidence since 1450 and with which there was a dynastic link—the Renaissance arrived via highly accomplished Tuscan craftsmen who brought Italian sculpture and architecture to Kraków; from there it spread to other areas of the Jagellonian realm. From centers in Western Europe the new trends gradually infiltrated the Gothic tradition in every field of the arts, and the two currents merged at Kraków.

On his accession in 1506, Zygmunt I had determined to rebuild Kraków's fire-damaged Wawel, and he commissioned the recently established Italian atelier of his protégé Francis the Florentine for this purpose. Work began immediately on the Queen's House, as the Wawel's west facade was known, and for three decades a steady stream of prepared lime- and sandstone was sent up the hill. The splendid inner courtyard, three stories high with arcades around the two lower levels, conformed to the precepts laid down by Vitruvius—although by Polish custom the state apartments were located on the top floor, not on the *piano nobile* as in Italy. The steeply pitched roof, another local refinement, was supported by a series of columns rising through the whole of the upper story, their height tempered only by the rings binding the shafts, while their capitals directly supported the eaves.

Francis died in 1516, to be succeeded by his compatriot Bartolomeo Berrecci, likewise a sculptor as well as an architect. From 1517 to 1533 Berrecci with his entire atelier labored on the burial chapel for King Zygmunt, located near the courtyard and resting against the south aisle of the Wawel's cathedral. The result, with its fairly plain exterior and its sumptuously decorated interior, is a sophisticated Renaissance building, perhaps the finest Italian exemplar of its date north of the Alps. The Berrecci

263

atelier also executed other commissions such as the oratory and pres-
bytery of Saint Mary's Church in Kraków, which housed a superb late-
Gothic carved altarpiece by Wit Stwosz, and two grandiose tombs, of
Bishop Piotr Tomicki at the Wawel, and of Barbara Tarnowska at Tarnów
Cathedral.

As well as Italian architects, Polish, Slovak, and German craftsmen
were involved in pioneering a transitional style from the Gothic to the
Renaissance. In these early years the work of this local school, which was
responsible for buildings like the castle at Drzewica, was more widespread
than that of the Italians. Their main representative was a royal architect
simply known as Benedykt of Sandomierz, who was given the responsibil-
ity for designing several dozen portals and window frames in the Wawel
since there were not enough Italian craftsmen to do everything. Here
late-Gothic patterns mingle with Renaissance ornament without any attempt at integration. Other elements in the Wawel's decoration also combined both styles.

At Berrecci's death in 1537, his place was taken by Giovanni Maria
Padovano. But rival ateliers had now sprung up such as that founded a few
years earlier by Bernardino de Gianotis and Giovanni Cini. These two architects built the new cathedral at Płock for Bishop Tomicki's nephew and
the castle of Ogrodzieniec in Małopolska for the banking dynasty of
Boner. The latter is a good example of the Renaissance fortress as was
Ostróg in Volhynia, seat of the Princes Ostrogski, where huge buttresses
reached down to the river. By the 1520s other Italian craftsmen from
Ticino and Como had arrived too. Of more modest aspirations, they represented a less purely Italianate style, unattached to the Gothic but more
sensitive to local traditions.

By the mid-sixteenth century the Renaissance style in Poland had assumed an independent standing—at least in architecture and sculpture,
for painting played a far less important role. (Indeed no Italian painter is
known to have visited the country before 1540.) The geographical spread

*Domed tower at Krasiczyn with Renaissance
sgraffiti, southeastern Poland.*

of the style was ensured since it was widely disseminated throughout the urban patricians and the more prosperous of the *szlachta*, who were building country houses of their own. For in the towns Renaissance architecture had blossomed as town halls and Gothic mansions were modernized or reconstructed; in Tarnów or Sandomierz, relatively small stylistically pure civic buildings were produced with simple, nearly cubic forms and facades closed horizontally by the attic parapets. Best of them all was the Poznań Town Hall (entirely rebuilt between 1550 and 1560 by Giovanni Battista Quadro), which was plastered with sgraffiti. Its loggia and staircase were similar to those that embellished the Cloth Hall in Kraków reconstructed by Padovano during the 1550s.

The Italian high and late Renaissance still decided the general character of the period's architecture. Treatises like Sebastiano Serlio's were influential, as were copies of the northern European mannerist engravings. Kraków remained the artistic center, full of ateliers engaged in decorative and figurative sculpture as well as in architecture. A few Dutch and German craftsmen arrived but most of the new practitioners were Polish. The Italians formed a closed circle no longer, blending ever more closely with their adopted country.

Despite the general supremacy of Italian Renaissance traditions, the style did not completely dominate developments in Poland. Penetrating Pomerania spasmodically, it secured only a tiny foothold in Gdańsk, where the Gothic continued to flourish. The emergence of local schools of architecture meant furthermore that Kraków's ability to create a uniform style diminished—in western and eastern Poland, for instance, numerous craftsmen propagated a decorative vernacular northern Italian version of the Renaissance. Continuity was also hampered by the fact that most buildings were not new but had been converted from the Gothic.

A distinctive feature of the national style first used in urban architecture was the Polish "attic." Designed as a decorative parapet wall to mask the roof, it was given specific constructional and functional tasks and became very imposing and ornate. Normally running around the entire building, it isolated terrace roofs from one another and prevented the spread of fire. The visible parts were richly decorated with ornament varying from late Gothic crenellations to Venetian pinnacled crests. Often attics were extended upward and given a lower tier divided by pilasters, columns, or blind arcading, and a crowning ridge indented with spheres, volutes, pinnacles, or socles. Almost their first recorded appearance was in mid-century, on Kraków's Cloth Hall, but the fashion quickly spread throughout the country.

The other characteristic feature that developed in Polish architecture during this period was the arcaded loggia. Although the Wawel provided the celebrated original example, the element became commonly used in country houses, the number of which, whether new projects or conversions, markedly increased in the second half of the sixteenth century. Of the new projects the royal hunting lodge built by the Polish architect Tomasz Grzymała for Zygmunt August at Niepołomice (1550–71) was a landmark of purely residential rather than defensive design. The best of the conversions included the enlargements of the castles at Wilno and Tęczyn. An outstanding new Florentine architect named Santi Gucci arrived in Kraków during the 1550s and worked in the Kielce region, where he converted the castles of Pińczów and Janowiec.

Sepulchral architecture was probably the most important decorative art of the time and the greatest native craftsman was Jan Michałowicz, whose superb tombs include Bishop Zebrzydowski's in Kraków (1560–65). He represented an anticlassical trend that treated architectural elements as decorative motifs. The compositional schemes were freely embellished and the niches crowned with decoration. Michałowicz was also an architect who designed the Padniewski and Zebrzydowski family chapels in

*Old view of Krasiczyn by Napoleon Orda,
nineteenth century. (Łańcut collection.)*

the Wawel's cathedral, examples that show how inseparably architecture and sculpture were connected in Renaissance Poland.

Painting remained the poor relation. In the Middle Ages there had been several regional schools, admittedly mostly dominated by foreigners, but throughout the sixteenth century Poland had failed to produce any outstanding painters, with the exception of the miniaturist Stanisław Samostrzelnik. Royal patronage of painting was minimal although Zygmunt August did have enthusiasms for goldsmithery and weaving. His tapestry collection, the famous *Wawel Arrases*, was rated among the best in Europe. Few of the magnates and fewer of the *szlachta* exhibited a comparable zeal for collecting; instead their taste was for objects—weapons, clothes, jewels, saddlery—that could be used for opulent public display.

Enormous disparities of wealth existed, indeed grew, in sixteenth-century Poland, and as a class the *szlachta* generally became much richer. During the century the price of the agricultural produce from their lands more than tripled and their buying power increased commensurately. At the apex, a few score of great landowning families, usually with estates in the eastern provinces, became vastly rich. The Ostrogskis possessed a hundred towns and castles, over twelve hundred villages, and an income reputed to exceed the state's revenue. This wealth was not necessarily inherited: Jan Zamoyski started with a small estate in 1571 and within thirty years controlled over eleven thousand square miles, a large amount of which he owned outright.

During this period more of the *szlachta*, both Catholic and Protestant, began to study abroad, especially in Italy—indeed Poles regularly made up a quarter of the student body at Padua University. Travel was often mixed with studies, and many returned home with foreign objects and foreign tastes. The Renaissance rediscovery of ancient Rome, which provided apparent analogies to their own nation, made a strong impression on them. So later did the myth of Sarmatism, which claimed that they alone had descended from a mysterious warrior caste that sprang from the steppes near the Black Sea—an origin that neatly distinguished them from the rest of the native population.

With these sorts of convictions, and this sort of wealth, it is hardly surprising that the *szlachta* held the real levers of power and dominated Poland. When the nation was left without a monarch after Zygmunt August's death in 1572, they moved to further extend their political power. The Seym of 1573 drew up two documents, the Pacta Conventa and the Acta Henriciana, to which all kings would have to swear. Although only a repetition of extant privileges, they severely limited royal power, making the monarch into the commonwealth's chief executive. The ambitious young deputy Zamoyski then forced a measure through the Seym that gave an equal vote to every member of the *szlachta* in the selection of a king, who might only be chosen from among their ranks or from a foreign ruling house. Thereafter the session proceeded remarkably smoothly and Henri de Valois, younger brother of Charles IX of France, was elected by an overwhelming majority. Reluctantly he swore to observe all the articles of the Acta Henriciana, including those regarding religious toleration, despite having just enthusiastically participated in the Saint Bartholomew's Day Massacre of the Huguenots in Paris. He arrived in Poland in midwinter, but in May 1574 his brother died and he became king of France. Within days he had absconded from the Wawel and refused all pleas to return—although, anxious to retain both crowns, he offered his younger brother as viceroy.

The throne was declared vacant and, after a hotly contested election in which the Habsburgs made a determined bid for it, Stefan Báthory, duke of Transylvania, was chosen in December 1575. Within four months he was installed, married to Zygmunt August's sister Anna Jagiellonka, and crowned. He proved a vigorous king and an able soldier, fending off threats from the Empire and Muscovy, but he reigned for only ten years and his death left the throne empty once again. After the Habsburgs had failed to assert their claims by force, the Seym elected Zygmunt Vasa, son of King John III of Sweden and a Jagellon princess. Their choice turned out to be less than satisfactory. A fanatical Catholic with a Habsburg wife, Zygmunt signed an "eternal" peace with Vienna while his Jesuit camarilla excluded all other influences and plotted to reconvert Poland. Succeeding to the Swedish crown on his father's death, he soon made himself so unpopular there that he abandoned Stockholm and was formally deposed by the Swedish parliament. As king of Poland for forty-five years, he dragged the country intermittently into war with Sweden, a policy for which the Seym felt no enthusiasm. Thus when in 1605 he presented proposals including a larger standing army plus the abolition of the Seym's lower chamber and the guarantees of religious freedom, discontent came to a head. A rival assembly of the *szlachta*, meeting at Sandomierz and led by Janusz Radziwiłł and Mikołaj Zebrzydowski, palatine of Kraków, voted his dethronement. While the royal troops stayed loyal and rapidly dispersed the rebels, no one was punished. But Poland was clearly no longer the peaceful and stable society it had been during the previous century.

The weaknesses of the Polish constitution, unwritten like that of England, were now plainly apparent. The elective monarchy only functioned when the king—the sole source of executive power and responsible for appointing the castellans, palatines, and bishops who constituted the Senate—acted in harmony with the political nation. Zygmunt III did the opposite. Likewise the Seym acted exclusively in the interests of the *szlachta*. During the sixteenth century the towns, always underrepresented, were steadily excluded from the legislative process, while the *szlachta* were barred from engaging in trade. The right of legal rebellion, unique to Poland, came into effect if the king broke his coronation oath to observe traditional rights and privileges. This was theoretically a healthy brake on tyranny, but it could all too easily become a prescription for anarchy. Similarly the *liberum veto*, the principle that no legislation could be enacted without unanimity, held the potential to paralyze the country's government in years to come.

Despite the uncertainties of the age, architecture continued to flourish. After 1575, however, the cultural picture became more diverse. By the seventeenth century the Renaissance style, even with its mannerist variations, no longer occupied the entire stage, for the baroque was already in evidence. Stefan Báthory and his queen as well as the magnates continued to convert and construct palaces and castles in the towns and the countryside, as well as numerous sepulchral chapels. Poland was now split into two artistic areas, one centering on Gdańsk and the other on Kraków, the importance of which had dwindled with the rise of rivals like Lublin or Lwów. In the former city, where the Renaissance had only appeared in mid-century, the style was enriched by mannerist influences from the Netherlands ably expounded by such architects and sculptors as Anton van Opbergen, Willem van der Blocke, and his son Abraham. They designed splendid municipal buildings as well as decoration and sculpture. Van Opbergen's Arsenal at Gdańsk (1602–05) is a masterpiece, its exterior adorned with rich decoration and shaped like burghers' gabled houses. Gates and town mansions were the hallmark of their work, usually including orderless elevations, foreporches, big mullioned windows, and stone features contrasting with the deep red brick background of the walls and gables. The Netherlandish influence was felt in Silesia, too, but only to a modified extent.

The architect Santi Gucci was the major figure in southern Poland. At Ksiąź Wielki near Kielce he built a palatial residence for Bishop Piotr Myszkowski (1585–95). This *palazzo in fortezza* (an undefended palace within defensive walls) is mannerist in its forms, with a compact central block and rusticated walls counterbalanced by light, airy pavilions on either side connected to the main building by openwork arcades. For the first time the traditional inner courtyard was dispensed with in favor of a compact plan and regular interior layout. A vanished country house, Łobzów near Kraków, was also built by Gucci for the king, and he was probably the architect of Baranów for the Leszczyńskis. Working as a sculptor he designed many tombs in an idiosyncratic style: the completed monuments were often ferried down the Vistula to Mazovia, especially around Płock.

Eastern Poland also witnessed a burst of architectural activity. The Lublin ateliers were full of craftsmen from Como producing fine churches, particularly in the city and at Kazimierz Dolny; their decorative rib vaulting and stucco work gained national renown. They also designed delightful arcaded town houses, the surfaces of which are filled with bas-relief decoration, presented with the charm of naive popular art in which the elements are combined indiscriminately. Large castles were also built, the grandest of which was Krasiczyn near Przemyśl, constructed over twenty years for Marcin Krasicki. In 1597 Galeazzo Appiano planned a Renaissance building around a square interior courtyard with irregular galleries and arcades plus a tiny second-story loggia off the staircase. The attics were of special magnificence and the four massive towers were christened "Papal," "Royal," "Gentry," and "Divine" (the latter contained the domed chapel). Most interesting of all were the magnificent sgraffiti on the external walls depicting themes connected with Sarmatism and the Counter-Reformation. This particular element was one of the few here that reflected the influence of the baroque, although it must be remembered that the remodeling of the Royal Castle in Warsaw in pure baroque style was exactly contemporary.

The most remarkable building project of the age was undoubtedly Jan Zamoyski's creation of an entire Renaissance town, Zamość. The eminent Venetian architect Bernardo Morando was commissioned to create the ideal town in 1579, one designed to house several thousand people as a craft center and commercial entrepot close to important trade routes. Work began the next year. A walled and turreted pentagon enclosed two rectangles, one containing the main and subsidiary marketplaces, the other the residential quarter. The longitudinal axis ran from Zamoyski's palace to the central eastern tower through the marketplace and there intersected the latitudinal axis on which stood two smaller squares. On a second transverse axis stood the collegiate church and the academy. A synagogue, library, arsenal, public baths, churches for other denominations,

Main square in the town of Zamość, eastern Poland.

and a sophisticated sewage system were all envisaged in the original plans. By the early seventeenth century Zamość was thriving and the main public buildings were completed, although work continued until around 1640. Other magnates tried to copy the idea but never with such success. The town survives as a unique monument to the belief the Polish upper classes still held—that it was possible to create a utopia on earth.

That concept receded steadily as the seventeenth century progressed. The vacillations of the government and the intrigues of overmighty magnates, several of whom interfered in the succession struggles in Russia, led Poland into a full-scale war. Polish troops occupied Moscow and Zygmunt's son Władysław was elected tsar by the boyars. His reign was brief, for a rival tsar, Mikhail Romanov, was elected in 1613. Nevertheless the situation remained confused, with spasmodic fighting until 1633 when Władysław formally abdicated all claims to the Muscovite throne. Thereafter, with the rest of Europe absorbed in the Thirty Years' War, Poland presented a peaceful picture, albeit an illusory one. The strains implicit in the Commonwealth had begun to show, particularly in the vast, fertile, and underpopulated Ukraine, where the heterogeneous inhabitants chafed under Polish rule. The papacy's folly in trying to win Orthodox converts into the Uniate Church, which acknowledged the supremacy of Rome, by allowing them to retain the Slavonic liturgy, the institution of married

priests, and communion in both kinds, enraged the bulk of the population. Only a few Ruthene nobles, keen to embrace Western culture, converted directly to Rome.

The Cossacks, communities of freebooting soldiers living on the Dnieper River, were also alienated by the government. In 1648 they rose in open revolt, defeated the royal troops, and, aided by their Tatar allies, ravaged the country. At that moment Władysław died, to be succeeded by his uninspiring younger brother, Jan Kazimierz, who was dominated by the Jesuits and his termagant wife, Marie-Louise de Gonzague. The Russians invaded in support of the Cossacks, then the Swedes attacked from the Baltic, and Lithuania seceded. By 1655 the Commonwealth appeared to have fallen apart, although a few cities held out. At last the king launched a counteroffensive. After years of warfare, peace heralded a return to the status quo except in the Ukraine, which was divided between Poland and the tsar. But Poland was left lastingly impoverished, exhausted, and in a much weaker position vis-a-vis Russia and Turkey.

The society had also become less tolerant. The advance of the Counter-Reformation meant that by the late seventeenth century admission to the ranks of the *szlachta* was restricted to Catholics. While freedom of personal religion remained, sects like the Arians and Quakers were banned and the Protestant population dwindled. The number of monasteries soared, however, and new ascetic orders were founded. The dynamic Jesuits, in the vanguard of reconversion here and across Europe, opened colleges throughout the Commonwealth and slowly forced the closure of such rival institutions as the Arian Academy of Leszno founded by the Leszczyński family. Although their artistic patronage was notable, especially in the fields of painting and architecture, the Jesuits contributed to the ossification of thought by rejecting any ideas that did not conform with their dogma. In their propaganda they skillfully portrayed Poland as the defender of Christendom against Turks and Tatars. The religious fervor they instilled made for fine soldiers, particularly among the Husaria, the famous winged cavalry. In Polish armies the latter outnumbered the infantry by three to one.

Disparities in wealth among the *szlachta* increased as grain prices dropped, exports diminished, and an agrarian recession began. In Wielkopolska many managed to hang on to their fairly small estates but elsewhere bankruptcy loomed and often they took service with one of the great magnates. A new oligarchy emerged as magnates like the Potockis, Lubomirskis, and Zamoyskis grew ever richer and more powerful, monopolizing the offices of state. In Lithuania, where the *szlachta* had always been politically immature, the situation was still worse. Frequently the newly impoverished became introspective, disinterested in advances in the outside world and convinced of the superiority of a bucolic country life close to God and nature. With many of the *szlachta* bothering less about national politics than petty local issues, the Seym lost all coherence. During the seventeenth century the Poles came to resemble their historic adversaries, the Turks, in many of their habits, costumes, and hairstyles; they even came to appreciate Islamic art. In their love of extravagance and ceremony, which they derived from their imaginary Sarmatian origins, they resembled the Ottomans. All surplus money was put into moveable property, pictures, tapestry, and statuary, which could and did suffer terribly from looting during wartime. The magnates maintained small courts, moved about the country with enormous retinues, and ignored the government's decrees when they chose. More and more the Commonwealth's exotic east/west synthesis seemed alien to the mercantilist world of Western Europe.

Poland's economic situation worsened steadily during the seventeenth century. With its economy dependent on agriculture and the export of raw materials, it was vulnerable to any slump in demand from overseas,

Portrait of Stanisław Herakliusz Lubomirski, probably by Ádám Mányoki, late seventeenth century. (Łazienki collection.)

although its import of "colonial" or finished goods was rising. The wars in mid-century had taken a heavy toll on the population, which was markedly lower in 1660 than in 1600. Larger cities had lost up to two-thirds of their inhabitants and much arable land was lying fallow. The Vasa kings only bothered intermittently with economic development. Minimal taxation meant that the most productive areas escaped proper assessment altogether and the national revenues amounted to barely one-tenth those of France. Economic retrenchment was impossible, however, for it presupposed political reform, which the ruling class rejected out of hand. Without the normal dynastic continuity the crown lacked a real power base to force through change, had the desire for it even existed.

Against this sorry slide toward decline, the Poles managed a last fine flourish. The ailing Jan Kazimierz, his queen deceased, abdicated in 1667 and retired to France. An aristocratic nonentity was elected in his place and the Turks mounted two huge invasions, conquering all of Podolia and the Ukraine. The crisis of the hour produced the man. After the Seym had voted enough money for fifty thousand soldiers, their commander-in-chief or hetman Jan Sobieski led them into battle at Chocim in 1673 and annihilated the Ottoman armies. The next year he was elected king and Poland had a vigorous ruler again. Publicly honest and pious, he was also cynical, greedy, and ambitious, yet a brilliant soldier and a capable politician. A true Sarmatian noble, he loved all things Oriental despite a lifetime spent fighting the infidel. At the same time he was a man of cosmopolitan tastes, living in an Italianate palace and marrying a French wife. Sobieski realized that a successful foreign policy would restore national prestige. Although he failed to thwart Prussian expansion, he gained European renown by raising the Turkish siege of Vienna in 1683 and routing their army. But the jealousy of his fellow-magnates undermined his

Statue of King Jan Sobieski trampling the Turks, late seventeenth century. (Wilanów collection.)

position and frustrated his aims. Ill and apathetic, he died in 1696 and the Polish ship of state was left drifting dangerously rudderless.

It is frequently remarked that a country's artistic health has little to do with its political well-being, an observation that certainly holds for Poland, both in the seventeenth century and thereafter. True enough, the country's golden age had passed, but it was succeeded, the optimists contended, by a silver age. This was the era of baroque architecture, the final traces of which were only to fade two centuries later. Three trends had coalesced to produce the Polish baroque: the Italianate art of the Counter-Reformation, imported by the Jesuit and Carmelite orders and patronized by the court and the magnates; the humanism of the Netherlands, which fostered an interest in man and his environment and mainly influenced urban building; and the new artistic forms and motifs developed by the provincial guilds of craftsmen.

The first baroque building in Poland was the church at Nieśwież, which the Radziwiłłs commissioned from Giovanni Maria Bernardoni in 1584 with many similarities to Vignola's Gesù in Rome. It was quickly followed by others in Lublin, Lwów, Kraków, and Warsaw. Their striking use of space emphasized the simple interiors under a vast cupola with a strongly-lit apse, which gave wonderful visibility as well as excellent acoustics to the nave. Royal patronage was soon forthcoming: when the north residential wing of the Wawel burned down in 1595, Zygmunt III ordered it to be rebuilt in the baroque style, entrusting the work to the court architect, Giovanni Trevano, from Lugano. At the king's request the portals, window frames, and fireplaces were all constructed of brown marble, the staple material used during his reign. Trevano eschewed all ornament, relying for effect on his stark powerful architecture.

When the king decided to move the capital from Kraków to Warsaw in 1597, he wanted a new residence built on the site of a small medieval fortress. The resulting Royal Castle by the chief court architect, Matteo Castelli, took twenty years to complete. A notably austere edifice with a total absence of decoration and elevations interrupted only by discreet moldings, the irregular five-winged structure was designed around a dominant clock-tower with an exuberant baroque spire, which, with its corner turrets, recalled medieval Polish traditions. A glamorous court life evolved there by degrees; indeed touring companies of English actors regularly visited to present the plays of Shakespeare and Marlowe. In the 1620s Castelli designed an equally massive summer palace for Zygmunt at nearby Ujazdów, which, with octagonal turrets at each corner, harked back to Gothic precedents. It did contain some innovations, however, including the triple arcaded loggia overlooking the Vistula River as well as a tall sloping roof unconcealed by an attic.

It did not take long for the magnates to adopt the prevailing style. For Stanisław Lubomirski, palatine of Kraków and prince of the Holy Roman Empire whose father had made the family's fortune as commissioner for the salt mines, Matteo Trapola built the castle of Łańcut and from 1615 onward reconstructed that of Nowy Wiśnicz in Małopolska. The latter, strategically placed on a hill, was extended to a massive three-story rectangle surrounded by a bastioned pentagonal wall and approached through a showy main gate ornamented with scrolls and banded masonry. The interior housed a court of up to two hundred, a large staff, and a permanent garrison. An elegant arcaded loggia was added to the courtyard and the chapel was redesigned to be tall and narrow with an ornate gallery. Some of the period's buildings were less harmonious; the bishop of Kraków's new summer palace at Kielce appears curiously heavy with its twin towers theatrically joined to the main block and the enormous castle of Podhorce in Podolia, built for the Koniecpolskis in the 1630s, was more a fortress than a residence. Counter-Reformation piety inspired other kinds of building, too, such as the pilgrimage site at Kalwaria west of Kraków, begun

Distant view of Nowy Wiśnicz, southern Poland.

after 1600 by the Zebrzydowskis. There, an entire hillside was covered with chapels and monuments.

By mid-century Poland had a reasonably uniform baroque, both in architecture and in painting, where the Venetian school, which produced monumental canvases, fused with that of the Flemish portrait painters' followers to produce a stream of pictures in the Sarmatian style, often more iconography than art. As Warsaw gained artistic supremacy the standardization that resulted led to a decline in the importance of the provincial centers. Refined linear construction employing concave panels and flat pilasters epitomized the period's buildings. The monumental castle of Krzyżtopór was typical. Built for Krzysztof Ossoliński, it consisted of a number of courtyards set on sprawling star-shaped fortifications and radiating from a central cour d'honneur. Fashionable black Dębnik marble was used for plaques over the windows, which carried Latin inscriptions, and for the magnificent baroque rebus over the main gate depicting a crucifix and an axe, the family coat of arms. It took thirteen years to complete this gigantic stage set but its life was sadly brief: Krzyżtopór was gutted by the Swedes in 1655 and never rebuilt.

Fortunately baroque architecture was to be reinvigorated by a man of remarkable talents, Tylman van Gameren. Born in Utrecht in 1632, he arrived in Poland at the age of thirty-four at the invitation of Stanisław Herakliusz Lubomirski, a young man married to an intellectual wife who fancied himself a writer-philosopher. Tylman was to take Polish citizenship and the name Gamerski. After the havoc caused by the Swedish invasions in the mid-seventeenth century, Warsaw had to be substantially rebuilt, and Tylman, with his patron, largely dictated artistic taste in the transformed capital. Emphasizing contour, simplicity, and restraint as elements of "harmonious" art, he soon became the most sought-after architect. For Lubomirski he designed a garden pavilion in the Ujazdów Park with a bathhouse that one day would be turned into the Łazienki Palace. He also created two less successful bigger houses, Puławy and the grandest of all, Łubnice, since totally destroyed. Beside the Vistula he may also have built the delightful Otwock Stary for the Bielińskis, a house with exquisite red stucco reliefs, urns and trophies, broken pediments over the windows, and a garlanded Bacchanal on the central tympanum, influenced more perhaps by French than Dutch taste. Grabki Duże, an especially charming house built under his influence in Małopolska, was designed for a diplomat who had returned from Turkey, with four miniature pavilions linked by a hall under a swirling octagon.

As king, Jan Sobieski favored the baroque as well, commissioning a summer palace for himself in 1677 on land he had bought at Wilanów just outside the capital. More and more aristocratic residences rose in Warsaw, the majority constructed by Tylman. Although the Morsztyn and Ossoliński palaces have been lost, the small Ostrogski and the splendid Krasiński palaces still survive, the latter's elevation adorned with an order of colossal pilasters. Not all of the seventy-five secular and ecclesiastical buildings attributed to Tylman were of an equally high standard. And the quality of work produced by the so-called Wilno and Kraków Schools, with their emotive and restless aesthetic, which appealed primarily to the spectator's feelings, was extremely uneven. It was reassuring, however, that the embattled Commonwealth could go on begetting such a profusion of fine buildings despite the succession of political disasters it endured.

The Seym of 1697 was a dismal affair, aptly illustrating the nation's decay. Although a French candidate had been chosen to succeed Sobieski, who had died the year before, the rival candidate Friedrich Augustus, elector of Saxony, seized the throne and was crowned as Augustus II,

View from across the garden of Otwock Stary, near Warsaw.

nicknamed the Strong. The epithet applied more to his physique and virility than to his intellect. He dreamed of turning Poland into an absolutist monarchy and in alliance with Peter the Great promptly embroiled his new subjects in war with Sweden. When the Russians were routed at the Battle of Narva, Augustus tried to sue for peace, but the Swedes were not so easily pacified. First invading Saxony and demanding the king's dethronement, they then arranged another "election" with an assembly of compliant *szlachta* and proclaimed the Palatine of Poznań, Stanisław Leszczyński, king of Poland in 1704. His rule was short-lived, however, for when the Swedes were defeated at Poltava five years later Augustus reascended the Polish throne. He had been immeasurably weakened in the process and was now practically a Russian puppet. When the king reached an impasse with the Seym, for instance, the tsar's envoy arrived in Warsaw in 1715 with eighteen thousand troops to maintain order. The rising power of Prussia displayed a similar disregard for Poland's pretensions—the elector of Brandenburg now styled himself "king in Prussia," although the duchy was still notionally a vassal of the Commonwealth.

Augustus's death from alcohol poisoning in 1733 was accompanied by the immortal words, "My whole life has been one uninterrupted sin. God have mercy on me." The thirteen thousand electors gathered in Warsaw unanimously voted for Leszczyński, but Russia, Austria, and Prussia thought otherwise. They had decided that the king's son, another Augustus, should succeed, and with a small assembly of overawed *szlachta* they arranged matters accordingly. Their presumption did not go uncontested, for Louis XV of France was Stanisław's son-in-law, and forthwith began the War of the Polish Succession. Two years of sporadic fighting accomplished nothing and Leszczyński was compensated with the duchy of Lorraine. Augustus III soon proved himself an indolent disaster. His reign was to last three decades, only a fraction of which he spent in Poland. Since he did nothing to curtail their privileges he was not unpopular with the *szlachta*. Indeed Polish constitutional liberties, especially the *liberum veto*, which could be used to thwart the passage of any legislation through the Seym, were zealously protected by the neighboring governments who well knew they were the safest way to perpetuate anarchy. The country was run by a handful of magnate families whose good offices were courted by half of Europe.

Disparities of wealth had grown further by the mid-eighteenth century. The war against Sweden had done immense damage. Agricultural prices continued to fall while yields increased a negligible amount in marked contrast to Western Europe. Most of the peasantry and the lesser *szlachta* experienced a decline in their standard of living; indeed a large proportion of the latter now owned no land at all. Poorly educated and chiefly preoccupied with the chase, military service, the sale of agrarian produce, and lawsuits with their neighbors, they bore little resemblance to the image of the cultivated Polish gentleman of two centuries before. Although serfdom in the Russian sense was unknown in the Commonwealth, the peasants, except for a significant number of small freeholders, were tied to the land by economic necessity. And because the landowning class controlled the courts, they could exercise the power of life and death over their tenantry. Significantly, in an era of mercantile stagnation the Jewish community was the most pauperized of all.

But the magnates undeniably prospered. In eastern Poland, the proportion of land in estates of over seventy-five hundred hectares had tripled to over half of the total since the sixteenth century. In Lithuania and the Ukraine, some properties were larger than many German principalities. Luxury had become ostentatious, and frequently in questionable taste. Nieśwież, an immense ensemble of buildings constructed around a hexagonal courtyard and enclosed by a moat, had been continuously added to by the Radziwiłłs since the 1580s. Yet with its twelve great halls, seven

gilt domes, and a peristyle of gilt columns, the prevailing impression was
one of vulgarity. Neither was Nieśwież alone—four towers at Żółkiew
Castle were covered in gilt copper and Podhorce was wrecked by clumsy
eighteenth-century alterations, which coarsened the original silhouette.
(Nevertheless its architectural hanging gardens on three terraces still excited admiration.) Białystok, a house designed by Tylman van Gameren
for the Branickis, was enlarged by Sigismund Deybel in the 1730s into an
overpowering mass, occasioning Princess Marthe Bibesco's famous jibe,
"C'était Versailles sans la Révolution française, mais aussi Versailles sans génie." Indeed it is recorded that while the stables held two hundred horses and the
theatre could seat four hundred, the library only contained 170 books.

Whatever their shortcomings, both Saxon kings genuinely loved the
arts, for it was they who turned their capital at Dresden into one of the
jewels of Europe. Their sole major contribution in Poland, however, was
to add a new wing to the Royal Castle in Warsaw and to refurbish it
throughout. Yet thanks to their patronage, the influence of Italy in Polish
architecture was superseded by that of France and the Dresden rococo. Its
most distinguished exponents were Józef and Jakub Fontana, members of a
Polandized dynasty of craftsmen from the Swiss canton of Ticino who had
settled in the country a century before. They designed one of the most
distinguished of Mazovian country houses at Radzyń Podlaski, where reconstruction for the Potockis started in 1750. Three wings framed a square
courtyard: the main two-story house with a slightly higher central block
and two end bays pushed subtly forward. Both of the low side wings had
central gateways surmounted by towers with pilastered concave recesses
topped by obelisks. The orangery was similarly muted, with nine big windows and pairs of plain Ionic columns between pilasters at either end.
Radzyń Podlaski was all very French and formal, a brilliantly conceived
scheme showing that the Poles were still capable of great creativity.

General view through the gates at Radzyń
Podlaski, eastern Poland.

The chaos notwithstanding, rays of hope shone on the horizon. In 1747 the Załuski brothers' book collections were opened as the first public reference library in Europe, which grew to over a half-million volumes in fifty years. A few of the higher aristocracy advocated reform, led by the "Familia," the name given to the relations and supporters of the Czartoryski family, consisting of the five children of Prince Kazimierz Czartoryski's marriage to the heiress Izabela Morsztyn. One son, August, produced a boy, Adam Kazimierz, for whom royal hopes were nurtured, since the family descended from the Jagellons. A daughter married a man of humble *szlachta* origins, Stanisław Poniatowski, who became an accomplished soldier and diplomat. They too produced a son named Stanisław. Carefully brought up and widely traveled, he settled in Saint Petersburg in 1755 and there became the new lover of Grand Duchess Catherine. It was a friendship that was to stand him in good stead. Her seizure of the Russian throne seven years later just preceded the death of Augustus III. When the Seym met to choose a new king the tsarina let it be known that she would have no objections to the election of her former paramour, who happened to be the Familia's candidate anyway. He was duly chosen in 1764, taking the name of Stanisław II August.

Reforms were initiated immediately. Among measures placed before the Confederated Seym (so-called because it could now pass legislation by majority vote) were the establishment of fiscal and military commissions, a national customs tariff, and a state academy for training public servants. Majority voting was made mandatory for the provincial seyms as well. When the abolition of the *liberum veto* was proposed, however, the reaction from Russia and Prussia was explosive. Not only did they demand the invariable observation of Poland's traditional constitutional liberties, which negated any prospect of reforms, but they also called for full civic rights for their particular religious minorities, the Eastern Orthodox and the Lutherans. While the king and the Seym bowed to such irresistible pressure, others did not. An organization called the Confederation of Bar, a strange mixture of reactionary magnates and liberal idealists, declared the dethronement of Stanisław August and started a civil war. But the Russians quickly crushed the rebels, five thousand of whom were deported to Siberia.

Using the insurrection as an excuse, Frederick the Great persuaded Russia and Austria to join with Prussia in the First Partition of Poland in 1772. The three powers took about 30 percent of Polish territory and 35 percent of the population. Alarmed by the public outcry this evoked, they forced the Seym to rubber-stamp this fait accompli and the country subsided in outraged impotence. Yet curiously it engendered an amazing renewal in the political life of the nation. For the next sixteen years the remaining Poles were governed by the Permanent Council, effectively the first modern administration they had ever had. The dissolution of the Jesuit Order in 1771 handed over fifty colleges, twenty thousand pupils, and substantial properties to the state, which proceeded to set up a commission for national education to supervise the schools and overhaul the universities. Extensive legal changes were proposed, although not adopted in the end.

Acknowledging that political reform was unattainable, Stanisław August played an enormous role in encouraging the intellectual revival. He founded the *Monitor*, a weekly journal modeled on England's *Spectator*, set up a national theatre, promoted writers and poets, brought foreign composers like Giovanni Paesiello and Domenico Cimarosa to Warsaw, thereby resuscitating a musical tradition vibrant in Poland since the fourteenth century, and patronized art and architecture on a grand scale. Sadly his dream of founding academies of science and of fine arts as well as the Museum Polonicum were never realized. But he spent a fortune on his scheme for he sincerely believed that his cultural legacy was to inspire future generations with a vision of an enlightened nation. Nor were his efforts in vain. By 1780 a Polish intelligentsia could definitely be said to exist and various enlightened magnates followed his lead, including Stanisław Lubomirski, Ignacy Potocki, and Andrzej Zamoyski. A few began to set up factories, dig canals, foster industrialization, even found banks. Trade slowly revived and the urban population grew, even as the law forbidding the *szlachta* to engage in commerce was repealed.

But the Familia, joined by members of the Potocki and Lubomirski clans, had turned against the king. Without personal wealth, he relied on his natural charm and intelligence plus the advantages of his position. Cultured, cosmopolitan, and patriotic, he was nevertheless no hero and, in need of support, turned once more to the Russians. Unfortunately his meeting with Catherine in 1787 was not a success, for she disdainfully rejected his proffered help in her Turkish war. The following year the "Great Seym" met and, with Stanisław August's stature so reduced, took matters into its own hands. An increase in the size of the army was voted, funded for the first time by a land tax of 10 percent for the *szlachta* and 20 percent for the Church. The Permanent Council was abolished and a commission was appointed to draft a written constitution. The radicals pressed for more drastic reforms and, against the background of the French Revolution, introduced proposals to make the Seym into the chief legislative and executive power to whom the king and ministers would be answerable. The veto was abolished and far-reaching economic changes discussed.

Catherine did not hesitate. Alarmed by this evidence of revolutionary fervor, she lined up Austrian and Prussian support and in 1792 a large Russian army invaded. Resistance was obviously futile and Stanisław August hastened to submit. But it was to no avail: the next year the powers signed a Second Partition of Poland under which three-fifths of the country was annexed, leaving the non-viable rump of a buffer state with a population of four million. Although the Seym was browbeaten into ratification, revolt was inevitable. In 1794 it broke out in Kraków, where the heroic Tadeusz Kościuszko defeated the Russian troops. Warsaw rose as well, and the garrison retreated from the city. But the insurrection could only have one outcome. Within six months all resistance had been crushed, the king was removed to Saint Petersburg, and in 1795 the Third Partition wiped Poland off the map.

Architectural evolution in the later eighteenth century was almost as dramatic as the political. The neoclassical style arrived in the country around 1760, mainly through French influence, although England also contributed much to a movement that included architecture, decorative art, painting, sculpture, and garden design. At the start neoclassicism co-existed with the decaying baroque and rococo, and later with the romanticizing strains of the neo-Gothic. For its proponents, Greek art was considered the ideal reflection of the philosophy of the Enlightenment. The style was meant to follow designated rules and instructions, to be linear rather than freely inventive, simple in form and restrained in decoration. Magnates like the Czartoryskis and Branickis had already brought back textiles and objets d'art from Paris in the new fashion, and interest in classical architecture such as that depicted in Piranesi's engravings was growing—at least ten Poles were studying it on the spot in Italy. But it was Stanisław August's active patronage that established neoclassicism in Poland.

By the time Augustus III died, the Royal Castle in Warsaw was half ruined and its reconstruction became one of the new regime's most urgent tasks. Under the supervision of Jakub Fontana, work began on the creation of a series of official halls with an impressive facade facing the old town, and of such cultural focal points as a theatre, library, and picture gallery. Plans were commissioned from the French architect Victor Louis

Portrait of Marie Walewska by François Gérard, early nineteenth century. (Polish National Portrait Collection, Wilanów.)

Pompeian-style decoration at Mała Wieś, central Poland.

in Paris, but were substantially abandoned on grounds of expense. With a shortage of materials and craftsmen in Poland, it was said to cost as much to build a brick palace in Warsaw as a marble one in Rome. Work was delayed by a bad fire in 1767, although it soon recommenced under the direction of the official court architect, Domenico Merlini, a pupil of the Fontanas, in partnership with the talented interior designer Jan Chrystian Kamsetzer. Improvements and extensions to the original plans continued until 1786 when the king decided to concentrate his severely reduced funds and aspirations entirely on the Ujazdów estate, which he had bought from the Lubomirskis on his accession.

Stanisław August's patronage also extended to painting. He invited many foreign artists to Warsaw: Marcello Bacciarelli, who set up his studio in the Royal Castle; Canaletto's nephew, Bernardo Bellotto, who became the official court painter for twelve years until his death in 1780 and produced a stream of city and architectural views. His example was to be followed by Zygmunt Vogel, and in the nineteenth century by Marcin Zaleski. Both the king and magnates patronized such portraitists as Giovanni Battista Lampi, Angelica Kauffmann, and Marie-Louise-Elizabeth Vigée-Lebrun, and Polish artists were sponsored to study abroad. Franciszek, Smuglewicz became a successful painter of historical and genre subjects; Aleksander Kucharski developed into a fashionable portrait painter. So the foundations were laid for the solid achievements of the Romantic School in Poland during the next century.

The major changes in Poland's economic and intellectual life began to be reflected by the mid-1770s in new architectural concepts. A house designed by Efraim Szreger for the banker Piotr Fergusson Tepper was intended to be both an office and a home divided into apartments, the first of several similar urban dwellings. Both Szreger and Szymon Bogumił Zug created buildings for a variety of purposes in their own neoclassical idioms. Zug built a number of town halls, a hotel, and even a well-head in Warsaw. Stanisław Zawadzki specialized in military construction, especially of barracks. A typically Polish mansion reflecting national taste evolved by this time, particularly in the countryside—a one- or two-storied building set into the surrounding landscape. Good examples of this were Walewice (future home of Napoleon's inamorata, Marie Walewska) and Mała Wieś, both designed with rectangular layouts by Hilary Szpilowski in the 1780s. The latter also had excellent stucco work and very fine murals.

Italian influences on patrons and architects remained important, particularly the influence of Palladio. The work of Chrystian Piotr Aigner best represented this trend although Merlini's villa of Królikarnia and Zawadzki's of Lubostroń were both broadly modeled on the Villa Rotonda. Many Polish houses had their *corps de logis* linked to wings by a variety of galleries: semicircular, elliptical, refracted at right angles, or even straight. While Palladio's galleries were open rows of pillars, the majority here were closed and arcaded. So popular did this style become that forty such buildings were constructed from 1775 to 1800. Their monumental appearance concealed utilitarian advantages in the siting of bedroom and service quadrangles. In the later works of Zug and Szreger, an avant-garde trend was discernible based on juxtaposing geometric solids, and using minimal decoration, rusticated surfaces, and the Doric order; but at first this was confined to church design.

Architectural developments in Wielkopolska during the eighteenth century well illustrate the course of events in all of Poland. Except for the Leszczyńskis (until King Stanisław's exile in France) and the Sułkowskis, favorites of the Saxon kings, there were no magnate familes of wealth equivalent to their peers elsewhere. But the *szlachta's* estates were the best run in Poland, with more intensive agriculture and higher yields, better sheep breeding, and a certain amount of nascent industry. Since Sobieski's reign there had been much building activity—these years produced Pompeo Ferrari's Rydzyna, a grand aristocratic residence integrated into the town, which he designed for the Leszczyńskis. The local style predominated: a great room placed on the house's main axis across its entire breadth with a simply built staircase parallel to the facade. The marked influence of Austrian baroque was shown in the rich, high cornices.

Evidence of the shift of taste in mid-century may be found in Rogalin. Initially conceived in Viennese taste around 1770, a severer style prevailed with only six plain Ionic pilasters on the front facade. The curved orderless wings of 1782 joining up the flanking pavilions are definitely of English inspiration, but Kamsetzer's internal work from six years later was mainstream neoclassical. The final touch was provided by the picturesque Roman-style chapel built beside the road in 1820 and based on the *Maison Carrée* at Nîmes. The Silesian architect Karl Gothard Langhans was the first to introduce the English style to Wielkopolska; his best country-house was Pawłowice (1779–83), which he designed with big Ionic columns under a straight architrave crowned by statues and a flat mansard roof. Pilastered quarter-circle galleries connected to elegant side-pavilions. Internally Kamsetzer enlarged the circular salon in 1789, adding two rectangular bays and twenty-four freestanding Corinthian columns to create a room as grandiose as any in Warsaw's Royal Castle. Other houses, however, were more in the French taste, such as Lewków, its elevations charmingly overornamented with painted and sculpted plasterwork, or the more splendid Czerniejewo, which boasted a massive portico and two circular halls one above the other. Merlini's Racot was simple in design while Zawadzki's Śmiełów from the 1790s was more elaborate. The main facade of the latter was enriched by an Ionic columned portico combined with pilasters of the same order and trophies on the end bays, while the pavilions had entrances framed by sunken Doric pillars, triglyph friezes, and ingenious two-stage roofs.

After 1780, as the ideals of Romanticism succeeded the baroque, smaller country houses, more like villas or *maisons de plaisance,* came into vogue,

Neoclassical chapel at Rogalin, western Poland.

Rogalin seen from across the garden.

epitomizing the wish for a more intimate and family-oriented lifestyle. Delicate white stucco decor blending with pale marbled walls were contrasted with Pompeian red, the favourite color, while gold disappeared completely. Zug's first commission from Izabela Lubomirska was Natolin near Warsaw, begun in 1780 and known as the "Bażantarnia" (Pheasantry). No portico crowned the entrance and the oval salon opened onto the garden. The courtyard lay between two long projecting wings. Natolin mixed French and English ideas; the oval peristyle, an element propounded by Sir William Chambers, blended with the form and proportions of the windows drawn from Neufforge's *Receuil elementaire d'architecture*. Merlini's Jabłonna, built for the king's brother, Michał Poniatowski, the primate of Poland, was even simpler: a circular ballroom within square walls projects onto the terrace. The house was roofed by a cupola concealed in a belvedere and the octagonal drum thus formed was surmounted by a baroque spire bearing a globe.

From the start neoclassicism was accompanied by ideas of landscape emanating from England and partially derived from China. These arrived in Poland around 1770 via Chambers's writings and the designs Capability Brown made for Catherine the Great. According to landscape theorists the park should imitate nature in all its asymmetrical irregularities. With serene landscapes to represent beautiful nature, melancholy ones to evoke wild nature, and surprising ones to attract the spectator's attention, the aim was to create the picturesque. The park should contain inscriptions on patriotic or humanist themes and ideally should be separated from its surroundings by a ditch rather than a wall. In this private domain freedom, not reason, ruled. In 1774, however, the first Polish treatise on landscape design appeared. Written by August Moszyński, it was intended to influence the king's projects but it sensibly described the Warsaw area as largely unsuitable for such schemes, being too flat and monotonous except for the Vistula escarpment.

Architects like Zug were already converted to these theories and soon began to put them into practice. The first Polish landscape park was designed at Powązki by its owner Izabella Czartoryska, who would later lay out the most famous park of them all at Puławy. With the help of the French painter Jean-Pierre Norblin, she created an escapist paradise. It was quickly copied at Siedlce, where Zawadzki was commissioned by the Ogińskis to remodel the house and park. Zug was simultaneously embarking on the landscape at Mokotów in the suburbs of Warsaw for Izabela Lubomirska. In 1778 he started work at Arkadia for Helena Radziwiłł, the park that would survive as his masterpiece. The fashion later spread to Volhynia and the Ukraine where an Irishman known as Dionizy McClaire laid out many landscapes, the best known being on the Potockis' estate at Zofiówka. Great ingenuity was shown in using all features of the terrain, in establishing surprising vistas, and in producing unusual combinations of vegetation and architecture. The decorative and architectural motifs employed were extremely varied: temples, ruins, triumphal arches, aqueducts, obelisks, altars, urns, and sarcophagi. From the classical world, amphitheatres were borrowed; from the Chinese, pagodas and bridges; from the Turkish, kiosks and minarets. Neo-Gothic follies, hermitages, sham castles, and grottoes were mixed together with orangeries and aviaries, and a rustic touch was provided by shepherds' cottages, mills, and cow-barns. Monuments of all kind became a feature of Polish landscape architecture, dedicated to the patriotic cult.

Patriotism was a virtue of which the Poles stood much in need at the close of the eighteenth century. However, many had no intention of submitting tamely to their nation's extinction. Under French auspices a regular army commanded by Jan Henryk Dąbrowski was formed in 1797, bearing the proud motto "Poland is not yet lost so long as we are alive." Despite its apparent support, France consistently failed the Polish cause, which it abandoned whenever convenient at successive peace treaties. Yet Napoleon captured the imagination of a people forced by circumstance to desire the overthrow of the established European order. In 1806 Bonaparte's troops entered Poznań and Dąbrowski was allowed to issue a call to insurrection. A triumphal entry into Warsaw ensued with patriots donating their plate and jewelry to the national cause. After Napoleon and Tsar Alexander I met at Tilsit, it was agreed the duchy of Warsaw should be formed from the territory seized by Prussia. Eminent Poles served in its government, including Józef Poniatowski, the last king's nephew, who became commander-in-chief and war minister. The French blatantly exploited the duchy, which actually went bankrupt, but they did not forfeit the country's affections. In 1812, on the eve of Napoleon's invasion of Russia, ninety-eight thousand men, the largest foreign contingent, joined the Grande Armée and performed prodigies of valor during the campaign; three-quarters of them never returned.

The victorious allies showed clemency. Urged by Adam Jerzy Czartoryski, his intimate friend and adviser, Tsar Alexander I suggested the formation of a Polish state under the Russian sceptre. What emerged from the Congress of Vienna was a country of almost eighty thousand square miles carved out of all three partitions—the so-called Congress Kingdom. Although the tsar's brother Grand Duke Constantine was installed at Warsaw to command the army, Czartoryski's constitution was the most liberal in Central Europe. In this congenial cultural climate, education flourished: the University of Wilno became a center of academic life, the Zamoyski and Czartoryski libraries were opened to the public, and the late-eighteenth-century revival continued. However Alexander soon tired of his liberal experiment. The Seym was dissolved in 1820 and over the

Marshal Prince Józef Poniatowski by Frantisek Paderewski, early nineteenth century. (Polish National Portrait Collection, Wilanów.)

*View from across the park of Pawłowice,
western Poland.*

next decade the Congress Kingdom's theoretical liberties were steadily eroded.

His successor, Nicholas I, hated all dissent, so when the Poles rose in 1830 in the wake of the revolution in France he demanded unconditional surrender. The Seym voted his dethronement and Czartoryski headed an independent government. But it did not last long. Polish military incompetence, Czartoryski's fatal indecision, and the lack of any material support from the western powers facilitated the task of the huge invading Russian army. Warsaw was stormed, the remaining rebels seeking refuge in Austrian or Prussian territory. Retribution was brutal—the constitution was abolished, many families had their estates confiscated, ten thousand officers were deported to Russia, and the universities were closed. Even the fiction of an independent Poland vanished once more for nearly a century.

It is a tribute to Polish resilience that the three partitions of the country affected its art and architecture relatively little. Naturally the loss of royal patronage was felt, especially in the territories annexed by the Austrians and Prussians where the infiltration of government-sponsored artists was resented. But Stanisław August's achievement had been to create a large group of artists, Polish by origin or naturalization, who now formed part of the urban intelligentsia and who were involved in the struggle to maintain the national identity. Neoclassical painting and architecture continued to flourish until 1830, although the neo-Gothic had appeared in the preceding decade. Admittedly until 1815 there were few construction projects in the big cities, but this was balanced by a growth in rural building, including smaller country houses. After the creation of the Congress Kingdom, the foundation of an industrial dimension to the economy brought a need for new approaches to planning and architecture—medieval town ramparts, for instance, needed to be destroyed to make way for wide thoroughfares. And with the reestablishment of a national capital adding to the revival of state patronage, an enormous boost was given to the development of Polish architecture.

In Wielkopolska, which stayed in Prussian hands throughout this period, the country houses of Lubostroń and Pawłowice were both completed after the final partition. By degrees some magnates even turned to Berlin for ideas. In 1822 Karl Friedrich Schinkel designed the hunting lodge at Antonin for the Radziwiłłs. There, four three-story wings under steep gables radiated from an octagon; inside, a central hall rising the height of the house and centered on an enormous stove was surrounded by galleries, off which led smaller rooms. In 1834, Tytus Działyński remodeled his moated house at Kórnik following Schinkel's gothicizing plans, which were very different from his usual neoclassical edifices. Gradually he turned it into an arcaded, machicolated, and turreted Gothic castle. The entrance hall was star-vaulted while another hall had three-dimensional rib vaulting with elaborate capitals. Other buildings were still in pure neoclassical style, such as Białaczów in Małopolska, begun in 1800 on the grand scale by the prolific architect Jakub Kubicki. The main block has an imposing portico on its southern facade and a projecting octagonal salon on its northern. Natolin, too, was remodeled by Chrystian Piotr Aigner in the early 1800s at the behest of its owners, Aleksander and Anna Potocki, who also had a large landscape in the English style laid out there. Jabłonna, too, the property of Anna Potocka, was similarly remodeled and a monument was later erected to the heroic Józef Poniatowski, drowned while covering Napoleon's retreat at the Battle of Leipzig. At Puławy, Izabella Czartoryska was busy transforming the park into a shrine to Polish patriotism.

With the birth of the Congress Kingdom, older architects like Aigner,

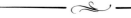

Main facade of Śmiełów, western Poland.

in his seventies, and Kubicki, nearly sixty, recommenced work. Possibly according to Aigner's plans, the Krasińskis had a delightful neo-Gothic house built at Opinogóra in which a suite of rib-vaulted rooms lead to an octagonal corner tower. The older architects were soon joined by two young Italians, Antonio Corazzi and Enrico Marconi. The former was to spend twenty-seven years in Poland working mainly in the towns and for the government; the latter was to play a major role in country-house building, marrying a Scotswoman and producing two sons who, after his death in 1863, continued his practice until 1914. Corazzi contributed four monumental buildings to Warsaw, which breathed a romantic element into the neoclassical movement.

One symbol of continuity was provided by the painter Marcello Bacciarelli, who had become a sort of director-general of fine arts for Stanisław August and outlived his patron by almost two decades. Until his death in 1817, his atelier in the Royal Castle continued to function as something of a private business. The theme of history painting was taken up by Franciszek Smuglewicz's numerous pupils, who often alluded to current events with their classical subjects and stressed the attributes of a virtuous life: simplicity, sacrifice, and patriotism.

These were qualities needed by the Poles in the nineteenth century. Tsar Nicholas, who decreed Russian to be the official language, ruled Poland as a defeated enemy country. Not surprisingly the people regularly rebelled, in 1846 and again in 1848, "The Year of Revolutions," when the desperate Prussians and Austrians did make initial concessions. They proved merely ephemeral. Risings in Poznań, Lwów, and Kraków were crushed and the rebels bombarded into submission. As if to vent their frustrations, many Poles fought in the revolutions abroad: three thousand under General Józef Bem joined Lajos Kossuth's Hungarian army and some even served under the Turkish banner in the Crimea. Nicholas's death made little difference, for his successor, Alexander II, was only ostensibly liberal, admonishing one deputation of his Polish subjects, *"Pas de rêveries, Messieurs!"* Some reforms were nevertheless instituted. Practical aristocrats like Aleksander Wielopolski, who despised romantic revolutionaries, persuaded the Russians by 1860 to concede a measure of administrative reform, allow the creation of consultative bodies, and ease the educational clampdown. His rival, Andrzej Zamoyski, advocated land reform and the possibility of commuting labor rents to money rents with permanent tenancies convertible into freeholds. Yet national discontent boiled over again. In 1863 an insurrection was proclaimed. Peasants and *szlachta* united and, aided by risings in Lithuania, for eighteen months defied Europe's largest army. But the struggle was to no avail—the insurgents were defeated, their leaders hanged, and intensive oppression resumed.

Only about eight thousand Poles had escaped to the west in 1831, but their importance was disproportionate to their numbers and their departure was christened "the Great Emigration." Most settled in Paris, where the conservative emigrés led by Adam Jerzy Czartoryski worked for Poland's independence through international diplomatic channels. They were encouraged by the outbreak of the Crimean War, for Napoleon III's half-Polish foreign minister was Count Alexandre Florian Walewski, the bastard son of his uncle Napoleon I by Marie Walewska. In the end, however, France and Britain bought Austrian and Prussian neutrality by burying the issue. A plethora of other emigré groups also existed, united only by their agreement on the need for national regeneration. Although its attempts were continually foiled, the most effective of these was the Democratic Society, an organization committed to fomenting mass revolution. The nearest the Poles came to having a universal spokesman was the poet Adam Mickiewicz, who for the last twenty years of his life abandoned literature to devote himself to the national cause.

*View from across the garden at Natolin,
near Warsaw.*

View of Jabłonna, near Warsaw.

Hope was not quite extinguished by mid-century. The tsar's promise, made under the pressure of revolution, to emancipate the peasants by granting them the land they tilled was subsequently honored, leaving many Poles far better off than their Russian counterparts. Yet Saint Petersburg's attack on the Catholic Church caused widespread resentment, for Catholicism and nationalism were by now inseparable. Even the traditionally reactionary minor *szlachta* were turned into fierce extremists. Those opinions were fully shared by most magnates, although some still believed in the necessity of limited cooperation with the occupying power to keep the state functioning. But gradually the nineteenth-century positivist belief in self-help and material progress mitigated the most uncompromising nationalism and fostered the notion that qualified loyalty would lead to qualified concessions. Russian protectionist policies engendered an economic boom from the 1870s and a Polish industrial revolution belatedly occurred. The agricultural picture was less rosy, for the emancipation of the peasants in 1864 had ruined many of the minor *szlachta*, forcing them to sell up and drift off into the towns. The big estates, on the other hand, were minimally affected.

The drive to Russify the Poles was paralleled by Otto von Bismarck's endeavours to Germanize them in the Prussian zone of Wielkopolska. This was perhaps the best-governed region, for if its administration was heavy-handed at least it avoided overt persecution. Attempts to buy out Polish landowners and forbid the language failed, and in industry the Poles started to take over from the Germans. Agriculture in Wielkopolska became more competitive and conditions in the villages were eased thanks to wholesale emigration to the Americas. As fellow Catholics, the Austrians should have been the most sympathetic rulers of partitioned Poland, but their bureaucratic rigidity made them averse to compromise, while they viewed their heavily-taxed province of Galicia primarily as a source of manpower and raw materials for the Empire. Indeed Galicia remained backward. Its industrial development was hampered by competition from Bohemia and its great landholdings were still operated along traditional lines. Successive military defeats made Vienna more conciliatory, however. De facto local autonomy was granted; the Poles were given their own Seym as well as an indigenous viceroy, while deputies

Park facade of Kórnik, western Poland.

Emperor Francis Joseph with Count and Countess Lancoroński on army maneuvers in Galicia, 1903. (Prince Stanisław Lubomirski.)

were elected to the Imperial Parliament. Their independent education system boasted two universities, at Lwów and Kraków.

In the Russian zone of Poland it became apparent as the twentieth century dawned that tsarist policies alternating between partial autonomy and outright incorporation had failed. The irreconcilable differences were compounded by the new tsar's disinterest in any significant changes in Poland's status, which in turn led to the revival of revolutionary activity. The Socialists (the PPS), led by Józef Piłsudski, were adept at dodging the police and conducting a terrorist campaign. With tacit Austrian approval they used Galicia as a base for their activities. They were opposed by Roman Dmowski's middle-class, anti-Semitic National Democrats, who regarded Germany rather than Russia as the chief enemy and who even participated in the tsarist Duma or parliament. The Catholic Church cleverly identified itself with no specific party and thus came to symbolize the nation. Poland's chance came with World War I. Although Piłsudski's Polish legions fought with the Austrians against the Russians, he astutely refused to become the pawn of anyone, since all three occupying powers seemed to be considering the idea of an independent Poland. The western powers were slowly persuaded to endorse this idea, too. Facilitated by the German collapse and the Russian revolution, at length it became a reality in 1918.

It is hardly surprising that Polish architecture suffered from so prolonged a loss of nationhood. At first after the final partition the neoclassical style carried on. Marconi continued to convert and design country houses in the 1830s and '40s, as well as embellish such parks as Natolin, where he constructed a Doric temple based on that at Paestum. Excellent sculptors like Paweł Maliński, Ludwik Kaufman, and Jakub Tatarkiewicz (a pupil of Bertel Thorvaldsen) continued to produce a stream of work. New architects like J. Gay and Franciszek Maria Lanci introduced the use of ironwork into their buildings in the form of columns, cornice supports, and even staircases, while the delicate elevations were ornamented with elegantly thin pilasters. But the occupying powers were not interested in promoting Polish culture, so as the generation of craftsmen trained in Stanisław August's reign died off they were not replaced.

As for the magnates, some like the Radziwiłłs had connections at both the Russian and Prussian courts and led their lives principally in Saint Petersburg or Berlin. In late-nineteenth-century Galicia some aristocrats chose to make political careers in Vienna; indeed members of the Potocki, Gołuchowski, and Badeni families rose to be prime ministers. Both magnates and *szlachta* retained their estates unless forfeited for rebellion or lost through economic disaster—after the rising of 1830–31, for instance, some patriotic magnates had their estates confiscated. But the incentive to build or even rebuild on the grand scale was lacking, although there were naturally exceptions—minor alterations as at Rogalin, or an occasional major remodeling as at Gołuchów. Such building as there was, mainly urban, consciously harked back to the past, even searching for models in the remote villages of the Tatra Mountains (the so-called Zakopane style). Later, in fairness, some of the period's new styles were employed— Kraków, but not Warsaw, has a little good art-nouveau architecture. But Warsaw's Royal Castle, symbol of the country's heritage, was neglected by the Russians, who installed civil and military offices and removed part of its collections.

Instead Polish cultural talents were channeled into other fields such as literature, music, or painting. The diaspora produced some outstanding figures, who rejected eighteenth-century rationalism, yearned for free expression, and longed for an earlier idealized Poland. Adam Mickiewicz, a cosmopolitan and brilliant linguist, translator, and classicist, the friend of Pushkin, wrote great poetry in Paris, culminating in *Pan Tadeusz* (1834); Juliusz Słowacki was the nationalist movement's bard, producing beautiful lyric poetry; Zygmunt Krasiński's play *Undivine Comedy* was a masterpiece. Later in the nineteenth century poets were increasingly replaced by novelists as the nation's spokesmen, cool positivist analysts like Bolesław Prus. In music the immortal genius of Fryderyk Chopin was succeeded by fine composers like Henryk Wieniawski and Karol Szymanowski who, unlike Chopin, did not languish in exile. History painting as practiced by Jan Matejko evoked the myths of a heroic past, providing some panacea for the dreariness of foreign occupation. Fortunately by the early twentieth century representatives of other more modern styles such as Impressionism, the Viennese Secession, and even symbolism had established their reputations, evidence of Poland's determination to stay within the mainstream of European culture rather than wallow in indulgent nostalgia.

In 1918 the Poles could certainly not afford to wallow, for they faced enormous problems. Piłsudski, offspring of the Lithuanian *szlachta*, dreamed of reconstituting the Jagellonian commonwealth of Poland, Lithuania, and the Ukraine, while Dmowski demanded the pre-partition frontiers plus Upper Silesia and and East Prussia as a bulwark against Germany. The Allies, however, wished to set up a relatively small Polish state in which the Poles constituted a majority. This they did, giving it a minute Baltic coastline and making ethnically German Gdańsk a free city. An accord with Bolshevik Russia could only be reached by force of arms, but Piłsudski's invasion rebounded and by August 1920 the Soviet armies stood at the gates of Warsaw. In the so-called "eighteenth decisive battle of the world," Piłsudski routed them with a flank attack and peace was finally signed the next year.

The independent Poland's new constitution was modeled on that of the French Third Republic and its inherent defects led to weak governments that lasted on average five months. So Piłsudski, who had retired from politics, reemerged in 1926, mounted a coup d'état, and ruled as quasi-dictator until his death nine years later. Despite his immense achievements, he had destroyed parliamentary democracy without providing a substitute, and his successors were men of lesser stature. Their foreign policy was ill-conceived, for while they failed to create an alliance of Central European states they did encourage Nazi aggression against the former Czechoslovakia, seemingly without realizing they might become victims of it themselves.

During these interwar years, Polish architecture generally lacked distinction. The official style could be described as functional-classical, or more rudely Piłsudski populist—indeed it bore some resemblance to contemporary fascist buildings. At least Warsaw's Royal Castle, which became the official residence of the president of the republic, was properly restored and all its collections reunited under one roof. Innovative designs in the 1920s produced such projects as a garden city in the Żolibórz suburb of Warsaw and a few pleasant villas. The Brukalski and Syrkus families, for instance, commissioned schemes from such inventive architects as Romuald Gutt. Yet although life in most country houses continued uninterrupted by political convulsions, no more were built. With Warsaw a capital city once more, cultural and social life there revived, attracting both intellectuals and aristocrats—those from Galicia who had previously gathered in Kraków or Lwów, and others from Wielkopolska who had never regarded Poznań as a real cultural center.

The nobility's town palaces were opened up in early winter after the end of the shooting season. Although they were usually better furnished than their country seats, they were no longer run along prewar lines. In a difficult economic climate many estates were encumbered with debts, up to twice their notional value in some cases. Thus the Zamoyskis were forced to sell off a third of their property to right the family finances, requiring a special act of Parliament because with a "majorat" or entail it was forbidden to sell or mortgage land. The crash of 1929 disastrously affected some indebted landowners when the banks foreclosed on them. Additionally there were worries over land reform, which beginning in 1925 annually redistributed some two hundred thousand hectares, mainly from the larger estates. Landowners' protests on the subject were ignored, for their voice was not among the truly influential in the new Poland—even if Zamoyskis, Sapiehas, and Potockis held important political and diplomatic posts and much of the officer class was drawn from the ranks of the *szlachta*. Big estates survived nevertheless, especially in the eastern provinces. At Nieśwież the Radziwiłłs still possessed 104,000 hectares, although half of it was unproductive. And countless smaller properties existed, averaging around one thousand hectares with their dwory or small manor houses, of which there were reckoned to be over twenty thousand throughout the country in 1939 and around six hundred a decade later.

Count Maurice Zamoyski with his sisters in front of Klemensów, c. 1910. (Count Jan Zamoyski.)

Prince Stanisław Lubomirski in Polish national dress, 1920s. (Prince Stanisław Lubomirski.)

Few if any nations suffered catastrophe on the scale of the Poles in World War II. Once the Germans had invaded in September 1939, to be followed soon afterwards by the Russians in unholy alliance, economically and militarily weak Poland never stood a chance. All resistance ceased within a month and the victors divided the spoils. Germany annexed some provinces outright and ruled the rest from Kraków. In both zones of occupation Poles were deported *en masse* for slave labor or because they were viewed as social undesirables, and the Nazis began their systematic extermination of the sizeable Jewish community. A Polish government-in-exile was duly formed in London. By 1945 nearly 250 thousand Polish soldiers were fighting under British command and a further 400 thousand were active in the resistance known as the Home Army, which undertook extensive sabotage operations. As the Soviet forces pushed back the Germans, Warsaw rose against its occupiers in August 1944. But while the Russians sat on the opposite bank of the Vistula, the Wehrmacht totally destroyed the city, which had held out for two months. Stalin then proceeded to occupy the whole of ruined Poland, his theoretical ally, installing his handpicked Communist administration and excluding the government in London. At Yalta he gained agreement to redraw the Polish frontiers so that nearly half of the prewar state, including the two historic centers of Wilno and Lwów, was swallowed by Russia. In return it gave up half of East Prussia and territories up to the Oder-Neisse line containing seven million ethnic Germans. By ruthless manipulation of the political system, the Communists gained power in the "free" general election of 1947; thereafter the Sovietization of Poland began, turning it rapidly into a Russian satellite.

Amid all this devastation, a substantial part of the nation's cultural heritage had been destroyed. Warsaw had been obliterated, its Royal Castle razed on Hitler's express orders, and almost every town and city had been extensively damaged except Kraków, which miraculously emerged virtually unscathed. The Polish castles and country houses had undergone a similar fate: shelled, burned, and looted, the majority of their contents vanished. Yet forty-five years later most have arisen, like Warsaw and its Royal Castle, lovingly reconstructed stone by stone like a phoenix from the ashes. The fate of their former owners has been less fortunate. Every property over fifty hectares, and many under, were expropriated after the war, the buildings and contents included. In the conditions then prevailing, few were prepared to question the legality of this. Although in the postwar world their owners were regarded as members of an outcast, parasitic class, the vast majority chose to go on living in very reduced circumstances in their native country, perhaps feeling that their roots were of more importance than their comforts.

Polish history over the last millennium has been as dramatic, tragic, and intermittently uplifting as that of any European nation. Its triumphs and its all-too-frequent failures encapsulate the achievements and the shortcomings of humanity. But while only a handful of the monuments left deserve to rank among the architectural masterpieces of the continent, it would indeed take a foolish man to ignore the merits of Poland's castles and country houses, for they form an integral part of the cultural legacy of a remarkable people.

P I E S K O W A
S   K   A   Ł   A

*I*t would be a misconception to characterize the Polish countryside as flat and featureless, for there are occasional enchanting surprises. One such may be found a mere twelve miles or so northwest of Kraków, off one of the main roads leading toward the great pilgrimage center of Częstochowa. There lies the Ojców valley, thickly wooded with steep cliffs and so full of geological curiosities as to merit that overworked word "picturesque." A favorite spot for eighteenth- and nineteenth-century artists as it is for countless tourists today, the valley also contains one of the grandest and best-preserved of Poland's medieval castles: Pieskowa Skała.

Little mention is made of the structure in early chronicles, although a document of 1315 from the reign of King Władysław I "the Short" (the monarch who reunited the country) refers to a modest wooden castle housing the royal garrison, which guarded the vital trade route from Kraków to Silesia. In his *Liber Beneficiorum* the fifteenth-century historian Jan Długosz, a cleric and tutor to the royal family, recorded that in the mid-fourteenth century Kazimierz the Great had erected a stone castle on the site, a high rocky bluff standing 120 feet above the Prądnik River. But its days as a royal fortress soon came to an end, for in 1377 Pieskowa Skała was presented to Piotr Szafraniec of Łuczyce in Małopolska, high steward of Kraków, in whose family's hands it was to remain for the next two centuries and more. Like many aristocratic families around this time, the Szafraniecs became rich by using their capital and influence at court to gain entry into various business enterprises, especially mining. Although the crown owned all mineral concessions, fortunes could certainly be made by developing the most lucrative of those deposits, including gold, as well as by closely supervising the mines and by keeping them drained and aerated. Thanks to its members' financial acumen the family was to retain its wealth, producing a string of notable courtiers and patrons of the Jagellon University (previously the Kraków University), one of whom, Jan, became rector in the 1420s; later on the Szafraniecs counted humanists and Protestant converts among their ranks.

During the fifteenth century the Szafraniecs transformed Pieskowa Skała into a castle with suitable grandeur. The original fortress had been built along a rock that occupied the northern edge of the site, but its outlines have been concealed by subsequent reconstruction. It was divided into an upper and a lower castle, joined and protected by curtain walls, although the disparity of height between the two parts of the castle was not considerable. The original Gothic architecture has now been largely obscured by subsequent reconstruction, but vestiges of it remain in the round tower with a ground-floor passage leading to it hewn out of the limestone rock of the northern range, or in the circular interior of the gateway to the courtyard, which shows the shape of the earlier gate-tower. A

Pieskowa Skała seen from the Ojców Valley,
southern Poland near Kraków.

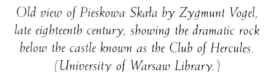

Old view of Pieskowa Skała by Zygmunt Vogel, late eighteenth century, showing the dramatic rock below the castle known as the Club of Hercules. (University of Warsaw Library.)

Tombstone of Stanisław Szafraniec, now on view inside the house.

Portrait of Mikołaj Zebrzydowski, c. 1600. (Catholic Hospice of St. John, Kraków.)

Castle with its Renaissance loggias.

wall oven and a late-Gothic portal from this period also still exist, and many fragments of fifteenth-century walls stand, for the most part only reaching to the second floor.

A more fundamental reconstruction was undertaken in the sixteenth century. The Szafraniecs had remained a wealthy and important family: one of them, Hieronim, starosta or sheriff of Chęciny, had been one of the principal commanders during the 1530s in the army of Hetman Jan Amor Tarnowski, the founder of Polish military tactics; another, Stanisław, was a leading Protestant intellectual and humanist and founded a house of prayer for the Arians, an extreme sect otherwise known as the Socinians, who rejected the Trinity and the divine nature of Christ. Stanisław's tomb still lies in the castle chapel, and it was he who decided to remodel Pieskowa Skała in Renaissance style, work that was completed in 1578, according to an inscription over the gateway. The building's fundamental character was changed from that of functional fortress to magnate's residence. The main part of the lower castle was rebuilt around a rectangular courtyard lined by two-story arcaded galleries off of which led light spacious rooms. A slim loggia on two stories was built out next to the gate tower to afford views of the surrounding landscape. Attics crowned the roofs and rich sculptural decoration of realistically rendered human masks appeared on portals, window frames, fireplaces, and arcades. The splendid architecture was matched by the terraces, ponds, and gardens around the foot of the castle rock. Comparisons with the Wawel in nearby Kraków, so recently reconstructed and beautified by the Jagellon kings, were inescapable.

Early in the seventeenth century following Stanisław's death the Szafraniec family became extinct. Pieskowa Skała was then bought by another great noble dynasty from Małopolska, the Zebrzydowskis, who had already produced Andrzej, the redoubtable bishop of Kraków. The head of the family was the Palatine Mikołaj, a comrade-in-arms of Jan Zamoyski, and a man of many good works especially noted for his endowment of hospices and hospitals. Between 1605 and 1609 he also created only a short distance south of Kraków Poland's first Kalwaria, or Calvary, a popular place of pilgrimage. Here his Dutch architect, Paul Baudarth, laid out an open-air Way of the Cross along a hillside, with each of the fourteen stations possessing a chapel in a different style. Mikołaj had already sent a secretary to the Holy Land to establish the layout of all places relating to the Stations of the Cross and to measure the exact distances between them.

Not all of Zebrzydowski's actions were of an equally charitable nature.

He was the moving spirit in 1605 behind the convocation of a rival seym at Sandomierz, which voted to dethrone the Vasa king, Zygmunt III, for allowing his Jesuit advisers to propose abolishing established religious toleration. Mikołaj was no intellectual, but he personified the antiabsolutist and anticlerical discontent of many of the *szlachta*. Together with the other leaders of the bloodlessly suppressed abortive revolt, he was not penalized, and led a quiet life until his death in 1620. His son Michał also rose to high public office, becoming palatine of Kraków in his turn. He fortified Pieskowa Skała in the fashionable Italian style, endowing it with high bastions and a new entrance gate some way to the east, and enclosing the big outer forecourt within curtain walls. The castle chapel was refurbished and dedicated to his patron saint, Saint Michael, while the galleries around the courtyard were remodeled. Nevertheless none of this saved the castle from being sacked by Swedish troops in the course of their devastating invasion of 1655. For the remaining twelve years of his life, Michał was the proprietor of a semi-ruin, and after his death Pieskowa Skała was sold once more.

The new owners, the Wielopolskis, were also an ancient family from the region around Kraków, who traced their origins back to the eleventh century and had close blood ties to the fabulously rich Ossolińskis. Jan Wielopolski was a confidante of King Jan Kazimierz, who sent him to beg for the Habsburg emperor's help against the Swedes in 1656. Starosta and

later palatine of Kraków, he was then created count of Pieskowa Skała by the grateful sovereign. He restored the damaged buildings in baroque taste, walling in the open galleries and loggia while giving the outside elevations geometrical painted decoration. The interiors were furnished according to the latest fashions—during the eighteenth century this meant rooms with Dutch, Turkish, and Chinoiserie decor—and these interiors, together with the Wielopolskis' celebrated collections of treasures, earned for the castle the epithet "The Museum of Poland." Jan was married three times, the last time to the French-born Marie Anne d'Arquien de la Grange, sister of Jan Sobieski's queen. Daughter of a commander of a guards regiment at the French court who later became a cardinal, she had arrived to visit Poland in 1675 after her brother-in-law's election to the throne and had wed Wielopolski soon afterwards.

The family continued to prosper in the eighteenth century as father succeeded son for five generations. The Wielopolskis founded convents, made advantageous marriages, and played an intermittent role in national politics, several times as palatines of Kraków. In mid-century they inherited the rich entail and estate of Pińczów and assumed the additional surname of Myszkowski. But they made few changes at Pieskowa Skała, although it remained the principal of the family's several residences.

After the Napoleonic Wars Jan Wielopolski, the third Jan in the family line, was appointed a senator in the Congress Kingdom set up by the Russians and his title of count was officially recognized by the tsar. A tireless campaigner for justice and legal reform, he was also keen to promote his

Portrait of Maria Anna Wielopolska (née d'Arquien de la Grange) by Claude Callot, late seventeenth century.

Arcades in the courtyard.

General view of the library.

country's industrial regeneration and established iron foundries with his own capital. His son Aleksander was equally remarkable, an intelligent, urbane aristocrat devoid of the romantic delusions so common among his contemporaries. He was sent to London in 1831 by the insurgent government to negotiate loans; there he realized the severe practical limits of the western powers' willingness to help the Poles, and he subsequently determined to find an accommodation with the Russian occupying power. Immensely capable, in particular with figures and statistics, Aleksander was placed in charge of the finances at Warsaw in the 1850s and propounded limited administrative, educational, and land-tenure reforms in return for the maintenance of order and the curbing of nationalist agitation. Unfortunately his scheme for selective conscription into the Russian army provided the direct spark for the insurrection of 1863 by excluding land-owners and settled peasants and so ensuring that the burden fell principally on discontented town-dwellers and intellectuals. The result was only further repression, the shelving of his ideas, and the end to the political career of an unlucky yet courageous and patriotic man.

Corner turret in the lower garden.

Not surprisingly the Wielopolskis, so engrossed in affairs of state in Warsaw, had begun to spend increasingly less time at Pieskowa Skała, which then lay in the Austrian-occupied part of Poland anyway. In 1842 the decision was taken to sell the property and it was bought by the Mieroszewski family. Unfortunately eight years later a severe fire destroyed the library plus many other interiors; the oldest buildings were also severely damaged and had to be demolished. Sobiesław Mieroszewski promptly began reconstruction, although it was still unfinished at the outbreak of the rising of 1863. On March 14 of that year Russian troops shelled and seized the burning castle, although a group of insurgents put up a stout defence. The next day Russians and Poles fought a stubborn battle at the village of Skała, just down the Ojców valley, from which the latter ultimately emerged victorious.

Undaunted by the disaster of the war, the Mieroszewskis started once more to restore Pieskowa Skała between 1864 and 1887. Although the money was lacking to return the interiors to their previous splendor, parts of the castle were again given a Gothic or rather neo-Gothic appearance, with small towers or turrets added here and there. The formal Italianate parterre was recreated, having originally been laid out in place of the former stables and coach house along the southern boundary of the forecourt and at a level some feet lower. Yet the expense proved too great for the family, which did not enjoy resources similar to their predecessors, the Wielopolskis, and in 1902 the whole property was put up for auction.

At first no prospective purchaser came forward and the future looked grim. But at the prospect of losing Pieskowa Skała an outcry ensued. By the twentieth century its status as a national monument had been assured, for almost all other medieval fortresses were in a state of total ruin; its magnificent setting and striking landscape had also been frequently mentioned in nineteenth-century literature and memoirs, even in the correspondence of Fryderyk Chopin. In response to the prospect of its loss a group of benefactors formed a joint-stock company called "The Castle of Pieskowa Skała," based in Warsaw. They raised the required price and converted the complex into a guesthouse. As such it survived both world wars, albeit in increasingly poor condition, until in 1950 Poland's State Monuments Commission undertook a thorough restoration.

Today Pieskowa Skała is again a remarkable castle, part medieval and part Renaissance. Under the aegis of the Wawel Museum administration it has acquired a variety of exhibits arranged in twelve rooms on the second and third floors. Additionally a collection of English pictures is housed together with the library from the Sapiehas family seat at Krasiczyn. In the most recent restoration, completed in 1963, the walled-in galleries and loggia were again uncovered, beamed ceilings were put back in the rooms, and stone door and window frames were reinstated.

For all its charm, the long-unlived-in castle lacks the personal warmth of a private home. Yet Pieskowa Skała should not be overlooked for that reason. Gaunt and austere as it appears, standing high above its river and silhouetted against the sky, its fine architecture is the product of three great Polish magnate families who lived there in succession, and their work has made it a national monument. In its many vicissitudes of fortune, in its periods of prosperity and of decay, Pieskowa Skała mirrors the history of its native land.

ŁAŃCUT

The notion that Poland is the gateway to Russia, even to the vast, empty steppes of Central Asia, becomes more vivid traveling east along the main road from Kraków. The landscape, although undulating, becomes barer and the towns, with their modern boxlike buildings, more charmless. But there are unexpected compensations. On the way to the border fortress of Przemyśl and the historic Polish city of Lwów, now incorporated into the Soviet Union, the large dusty village of Łańcut lies off a sharp bend of the road. In the middle of it, surrounded by extensive grounds and largely hidden from the world by discreet park railings, stands one of the grandest of Poland's country houses, more akin to a royal palace than a private residence.

A settlement has existed at Łańcut for over 650 years, as we know from that indefatigable chronicler Jan Długosz, later bishop of Lwów, who mentioned a property here in 1333 given by King Kazimierz the Great to his cousin Princess Elżbieta. It later passed to the family of Otto Pilecki, who built a wooden castle on a gentle slope, of which few traces remain. The Pileckis were of importance in the kingdom: Otto was a palatine and a close confidante of the king, while his wife, Jadwiga, stood sponsor to the pagan grand duke of Lithuania, Jagiełło, when he was Christianized and christened Władysław in the Wawel in 1386. The duke became a good friend of the Pileckis, frequently visiting Łańcut, and in 1417 as a long-time widower he secretly married their daughter Elżbieta, a move strongly opposed by his courtiers.

Although the castle of Łańcut remained in the hands of the Pileckis, little was done to it for the next two centuries. In 1580 it became the property of Stanisław Stadnicki, starosta or sheriff of Zygwold, whose hot temper and violent unruly behavior earned him the title of "the Łańcut Devil"—indeed it is still claimed that his ghost haunts the house. Between 1610 and 1620, Stadnicki's three sons constructed a new castle on the site. Its three wings formed a horseshoe-shaped courtyard facing south, their corners reinforced by projecting pentagonal turrets that marked a transition from the medieval fortress to a defence system based on outer bastions. The Stadnickis' tenure was short-lived, however, for two of the brothers were killed and in 1629 the third sold it to Stanisław Lubomirski.

As palatine of Kraków and a prince of the Holy Roman Empire, the new proprietor's talents as soldier and statesman were already established. Since 1615 the architect Matteo Trapola had been laboring to make the castle of Nowy Wiśnicz, one of his several enormous estates, into a worthy residence; now a similar transformation was to be undertaken at Łańcut. Until his death in 1637, Trapola was the man chiefly responsible for supervising the expansion and renovation of Łańcut. Lubomirski wanted it as thoroughly fortified as possible, according to the concepts expounded in the *Architectura Militaris* of Adam Freytag, a leading military theoretician of the time. Five bastions connected by curtain walls formed a pentagonal star, while the raised ramparts were provided with earthworks on which eighty cannon were placed. A deep dry moat enclosed in turn by another rampart surrounded the whole edifice. In the middle of

Garden façade of Łańcut, southeastern Poland.

300

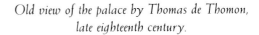

Old view of the palace by Thomas de Thomon, late eighteenth century.

The sculpture gallery, with walls painted by Vincenzo Brenna in the late eighteenth century.

these fortifications the rectangular castle had been reoriented from a north–south to an east–west axis. Henceforth the entrance would be from the west, the village side, over a drawbridge across the moat and through a massive gateway; the village, also encircled by walls, would be connected to the castle too, an important strategic consideration.

Although the exterior was austere, for the elevations lacked any architectural features except for the baroque portal in the middle of the front facade, the interiors were sumptuous if not indeed palatial. Extra rooms had been gained by converting the corner turrets into habitable towers and replacing the loopholes with windows. From 1633 the royal stuccodor, Giovanni Battista Falconi, worked at Łańcut with his assistants. The dome of the Zodiac Room on the first floor of the northwestern tower, so-called because the signs of the zodiac were painted on the ceiling, was certainly decorated by him; there, lavish baroque stucco work surrounded the painted allegories symbolizing the four seasons of the year. Falconi was also responsible for the ceiling of a room called the Great Antechamber as well as other interiors since destroyed. Major work at Łańcut lasted twelve years until 1641, although polychromed beams dated 1642 have recently been uncovered.

Stanisław died in 1649 and was succeeded by his son Jerzy Sebastian, who, as marshal of the crown and field hetman, occupied half the great offices of the Polish state. He loyally supported King Jan Kazimierz, and it was at Łańcut that representatives of the Polish nobility signed a pact binding them to repel the invading Swedes. Nevertheless the latter's ally György Rákóczi captured the area with his Transylvanian army in 1657 and burned the village, although fortunately the castle was spared. Jerzy was one of the most energetic Polish generals, but he suffered badly in the war when the Swedes pillaged his seat at Nowy Wiśnicz, carrying off 152 wagonloads of plunder. In retaliation he led a daring raid into Transylvania, forcing Rákóczi's troops to withdraw precipitately. Łańcut was not left in good repair, of course, so when Stanisław Herakliusz Lubomirski took over from his father, he decided to have it restored by his protégé, the architect Tylman van Gameren. The need became more imperative after a bad fire in 1688, but since the plans have been lost it is impossible to know all that Tylman did. He certainly remodeled the towers in late baroque taste, modernized the fortifications, repositioned various windows, widened the main staircase, and divided the Great Antechamber into an entrance hall and another smaller room.

302

The last of the Lubomirskis to own Łańcut, another Stanisław, inherited it as a young man in 1745. Eight years thereafter he was to marry Izabela Czartoryska, an energetic, highly educated, and immensely rich figure in her own right who had once been considered as a possible bride for her cousin King Stanisław August. Under their aegis Łańcut was transformed from a heavily fortified castle of an essentially severe character into a true palace, a worthy residence for the grandest magnate. Work started in the 1770s and, despite Stanisław's death in 1783, continued with short intervals until Izabela herself died at the age of eighty in 1816.

On the north and east fronts, all twin windows were eliminated and regularly spaced replacements were put in. The castle itself was extended by elongating the west wing at its southern end, so creating the Great Dining Room, as it was called, and a pavilion was added behind the northwestern tower to house the library. Most of the ramparts were leveled and a landscape park with neoclassical buildings was laid out by degrees. Initially the family's architect, Hieronim Jędrzejowski, was used, but some of the most distinguished exponents of neoclassicism in Poland were later employed too.

The decoration of the interiors began in earnest in the 1780s. Vincenzo Brenna, a Florentine painter who subsequently worked at Pavlovsk for Tsar Paul, produced a variety of antique, arabesque, and grotesque painted motifs, which adorned the walls of what was known as the Chinese Chamber on the second floor and a guest apartment with a study and bedroom on the ground floor. In the Views Room his work was supplemented

The Hall of Columns with Antonio Canova's statue of Izabela Lubomirska's adopted son Henryk as Cupid.

The court theatre at Łańcut, inaugurated in 1792.

Lions forming the base of a fountain in the garden.

by two oval murals depicting Łańcut, while in the sculpture gallery he created the illusion of an ancient sunlit ruin overgrown with vines. Other artists were commissioned as well—many of the doors, for instance, were decorated from drawings done by Franciszek Smuglewicz. The magnificent rococo paneling in the Mirrored Study, with wonderfully delicate gilt frames, was probably imported from South Germany.

Szymon Bogumił Zug, who had already worked for Izabela at Natolin and Wilanów, and had helped her design the landscape park at Mokotów, was soon brought to Łańcut and was joined in 1796 by his collaborator Jan Chrystian Kamsetzer. Together they designed Izabela's bedroom and the adjoining salon in Louis XIV style, along with the Hall of Columns at one end of the sculpture gallery, where a circle of Ionic pillars framed a statue from 1787 by Antonio Canova depicting the princess's adopted son, Henryk Lubomirski, as Cupid. Yet it was Chrystian Piotr Aigner, imported during the 1790s, who made the most significant contribution. In company with his accomplished stuccodor Fryderyk Bauman, he created the interiors of the state rooms in the west wing: the vast ballroom, the Great Dining Room, the theatre, and the chapel. In the first two the arrangement of the wall panels was carefully and logically planned and the restrained decoration was harmonized with the architecture. Equally elegant were the small chapel in the southwestern tower of the west wing, with its coffered, rose-encrusted dome, and the lovely theatre, which could seat an audience of ninety in its stalls and gallery.

Izabela greatly enjoyed entertaining in a style suitable to the grand palace she had brought into being. Music and drama flourished at Łańcut as she hired a court composer, Marcello di Capua, and a Haydn pupil named Peter Hänsel as kapellmeister. The princess herself played the clavichord in the palace's small orchestra, and commissioned numerous musical pieces, mainly operatic, which have been preserved in the archives. In 1792 the theatre was inaugurated with a performance of *Parady*, five humorous one-act plays written by her son-in-law Jan Potocki. In her widowhood, Izabela traveled all over Europe, bringing back most of Łańcut's antique sculpture collection from a buying trip to Rome in 1786. She purchased paintings and furniture extensively in Paris, too, where she became a close friend of Queen Marie Antoinette. Loathing the French Revolution and its Napoleonic aftermath, she welcomed to Łańcut such Bourbon princes as the future kings Louis XVIII and Charles X as well as their sister Queen Maria Carolina of Naples and Madame Anne Louise Germaine de Stäel.

Despite her eighteen other residences, the princess regularly visited Łańcut, which was kept fully staffed with around two hundred servants, inside and out. Improvements continued after 1800 as Aigner remodelled the main facade and, in association with Bauman, designed a variety of buildings for the gardens. Chief among these was the well-proportioned neoclassical orangery finished in 1802, its roof concealed by an attic and an Ionic-columned portico under a triangular pediment. Several years later a neoclassical house by the northern gates to the park, which had originally been erected by Kamsetzer's pupil Jan Griesmeyer, was rebuilt by Aigner into a little romantic castle in a neo-Gothic style, with Bauman's stucco work inside; there the family could escape from the formal life of the palace. In 1810 the pair constructed a gloriette, or folly, in the form of a semicircular Corinthian colonnade on the northwest bastion. Inside redecoration went on. The walls of the Chinese Chamber and the adjacent parlor, decorated in Pompeian taste, were covered by tiny, brightly-colored textile fragments glued to a linen base to simulate oriental wall-paper, although they concealed Brenna's painting.

When Izabela Lubomirska died in 1816, her enormous estates were divided among her heirs. Łańcut was inherited by her grandson Alfred Potocki, whose mother, Julia, had died over twenty years before. His father, Jan, a genuine polymath (writer, archaeologist, and traveler), had never cared to share the house with its redoubtable owner, preferring instead to live on his own property of Uładówka in Podolia. There the previous year, in a fit of depression over the treatment of Polish aspirations at the Congress of Vienna, he had committed suicide. Alfred was a good patriot too as well as a Francophile, and with his brother he fought under Marshal Józef Poniatowski in Napoleon's Russian campaign of 1812. Held prisoner for two years, he then returned and married his cousin Józefina Czartoryska. Yet compared with his father he was no fiery nationalist, choosing instead to stay on good terms with the Austrian government and opposing the several rebellions in Galicia against its rule. He also took advantage of the Austrian legal structure in 1821 to turn Łańcut into an entail, requiring that the huge property be passed down intact—although part of Izabela's collections had already been left to her adopted son, Henryk Lubomirski, who lived at neighboring Przeworsk.

Alfred also continued to improve Łańcut by removing the remaining interior ramparts, leveling the ground in front of the palace, and demolishing the entrance gates and drawbridge. These were replaced by a neo-Gothic gateway and a railed stone bridge across the moat. Various small buildings in the park were renovated—a hermitage, an Orthodox church, and a cottage orné (all now vanished)—while a neoclassical *manège* or riding school was constructed in 1828–30 to the plans of Ludwik Bogochwalski. A landscape architect, Jan Zulauf, was put in charge of the gardens, and greenhouses for oranges and peaches were erected. Aigner and Bauman, who still paid intermittent visits to Łańcut, were involved with the partial Gothicization of the north and east facades. And during the 1830s fine parquet floors, locally made to designs by Karol Chodziński, were laid in various rooms in the palace.

At his death in 1862, Alfred was succeeded by his son. Unlike his father, Alfred II pursued an active political career, mainly at Vienna where

The ballroom designed by Chrystian Piotr Aigner,
c. 1800.

he became minister of agriculture, briefly prime minister, and a close confidante of Emperor Francis Joseph. But he also served for eight years as governor of Galicia, and helped found the Academy of Kraków. His wife, Maria, was the daughter of Prince Roman Sanguszko, who had walked to Siberia in chains after the Poles rose against their Russian masters in 1830, and became the eponymous hero of Joseph Conrad's short story. She also brought an immense dowry with her to add to the Potockis' possessions. But with so busy a public life her husband had little time to visit Łańcut, where no new projects were undertaken, inside or out, and which suffered from a lack of maintenance.

Their elder son, Roman, inherited Łańcut in 1889 and for the next two-and-a-half decades was responsible for the third major reconstruction of the palace. In this he was ably assisted by his second wife, Elżbieta Radziwiłł, known as "Betka." Two architects, Armand Bauqué and Alberto Pio, were employed with a variety of craftsmen from Paris and Vienna. They extended the library pavilion at one end of the west wing and built out the Great Dining Room so that it could now seat over a hundred guests. A short south wing was added just near the dining room, thus forming a second small courtyard. Roman and Betka also began to modernize Łańcut, installing a new water supply through sixteen miles of piping as well as sewerage, central heating, electricity, and even telephones. The best interiors were retained but many others were redecorated in historicizing nineteenth-century style. At the neglected theatre, refurbished by the Austrian architects Hermann Helmer and Ferdinand Fellner, performances recommenced and new scenery changes were made.

Exterior changes were equally extensive, and during these years the landscape park assumed its present shape. Within the area enclosed by the dry moat a seventeenth-century powder magazine was demolished, an Italian parterre laid out in front of the eastern wing, and a rose garden created to the south of the orangery, all under the aegis of a gardener called Maxwald, who had formerly worked for the Rothschilds. The English garden was also reestablished and a diversity of flowers cultivated, especially orchids, pinks, and roses. Bauqué built a large complex of stables and a coach house, for Roman loved horses and carriages and collected the variety of equipages that form the nucleus of the exhibition now on display at Łańcut. Lastly all the facades of the palace were again remodeled in French neobaroque style, although the distinctive twin onion domes flanking the entrance front were kept.

With the outbreak of World War I, Galicia was on the frontline of hostilities, although both tsar and kaiser instructed their commanders not to damage Łańcut. During six months in 1914–15 it changed hands four times between the Russian and the Austro–German armies. The Potockis returned in the summer of 1915 to find the palace virtually undamaged, although the farms and forests indeed suffered terribly. But Roman, whose health was weak anyway, died a few weeks later and was succeeded by his elder son, yet another Alfred. The end of the war brought a further host of problems. Polish independence and the Russian revolution meant that some of the Potockis' eastern properties, like Antoniny where Roman's younger brother had lived, were lost to the Soviet Union. The family's entire entailed esate amounted to some forty thousand acres, the income from which was insufficient to cover the vast upkeep costs at Łańcut. In fact the estate's non-entailed lands were larger and more productive, but the war had drastically reduced both the labor force and the family's revenue. The already-evident fact was that only industrial development rather than agriculture could support the Potockis' way of life, and between the wars Alfred sold land and invested with varying success in a variety of enterprises: banks, oil companies, distilleries, coal mines, or brickworks. Despite a fairly healthy financial situation, however, he found it necessary periodically to raise capital.

Portrait of Jan Potocki by Giovanni Battista Lampi, late eighteenth century.

Frieze of horses' heads on the riding school.

Carriages in the coach house.

Nevertheless life carried on at Łańcut with all the old splendor: a private orchestra still performed, hunting and shoots continued, and enormous house parties were held attended by European royalty, aristocrats, and members of cafe society. Entertaining was mostly done during August and September, intermittently in the winter shooting season, and again from late spring to early summer. Łańcut's huge staff ensured that everything ran smoothly, including the wooden shooting lodge a few miles away at Julin, the Arabian and thoroughbred stud at Albigowa, and the immaculate hunt kennels. As Alfred wrote in his memoirs: "Year by year the number of guests increased. . . . in entertaining them and keeping open Łańcut as a meeting place for diplomats and distinguished foreign visitors, I believed that I was serving my country." A golf course was built, Turkish baths were installed, and on a less significant level, minor alterations were made inside the palace. The collections were much enhanced in the 1920s, especially in the field of painting, by a magnificent bequest from Alfred's cousin Mikołaj Potocki.

In 1925 Łańcut was designated a national monument and major conservation work was scheduled for 1939 before World War II intervened. On the outbreak of war, the Polish army immediately requisitioned three-fifths of the estate's horses. But within a week German troops arrived, occupying the Orangery and the second floor of the palace—although they did not damage the palace. When Hitler and Stalin partitioned Poland, Łańcut remained in the German sphere, but the border ran not far away along the San River. Alfred was arrested and interrogated several times by the Gestapo, although never held for long. It appears, in fact, that he held aloof from all the Underground activities, despite his later claims of having assisted them. By early 1944 Alfred recognized that a Russian victory was inevitable, so before his own departure in July he organized the systematic packing of some six hundred cases containing the cream of the

Early twentieth-century bathroom in the tower.

Portrait of Betka Potocka (née Radziwiłł) by Czederowski, early twentieth century.

Meet of the Potocki hunt outside the stables at Antoniny, now in the Ukraine, pre-1914.

Alfred Potocki driving the Duke and Duchess of Kent, 1937.

palace's contents. With German cooperation they were sent to Vienna by train. After various problems they reached his cousins in Liechtenstein, and eventually he took them into exile in France. After his octogenarian mother's death, Alfred married a Polish-American, published his memoirs, and died childless in 1958. Tragically, his possessions never returned to Poland, for the Communist régime refused to negotiate with a man they insisted on regarding as a traitor.

Fortunately the Soviet army that reached Łańcut in August 1944 did not occupy the palace—indeed orders were issued for its protection. That November the palace was officially opened to the public as a museum, although repairs and conservation work continued throughout the 1950s. Today the buildings are in excellent condition, and possess a slightly less lifeless feel than is usually the case with the great houses in former Iron Curtain countries. Quite a large number of the palace's 308 rooms are open to visitors. Yet even if Łańcut appears well furnished, only a quarter of the paintings and a bare third of the sculpture originate from its prewar contents, just as the tapestry, furniture, plate, and porcelain collections have also been grievously depleted.

Despite the loss of much of its original furnishings, Łańcut ranks as one of the grandest private residences in Poland—indeed in all of Europe. Over the past four-and-a-half centuries its fate has been closely bound up with that of two of the greatest Polish magnate families, the Lubomirskis and the Potockis, and it has reflected their wealth and glory even as it has suffered in their tribulations. Any visitor to it will appreciate what a showcase of the nation's cultural and aesthetic achievements it affords, for Łańcut remains a palace of legendary splendor.

BARANÓW

*I*f a river can be said to embody the soul of a country, we can see Poland most clearly in the path of the Vistula, just as Czechoslovakia is revealed by the Vltava and Hungary by the Danube. In its long course from its source in the Tatra Mountains to its estuary emptying into the Baltic Sea near Gdańsk, the Vistula flows almost the whole length of the country through some of its most historic regions. Wending its way through the heart of Małopolska, a short distance upstream from the ancient town of Sandomierz it passes by Baranów, one of the finest of all Polish Renaissance castles.

According to Anton Schneider, a mid-nineteenth-century historian, a wooden fortress existed on the site of Baranów by the early twelfth century. Built by Bogusław Jaksyc, a lieutenant of King Bolesław the Wrymouth who later rose to be governor of Pomerania, the fort was established to control this stretch of the Vistula. Nearby an important ford crossed the river to the high left bank, along which ran the trade route from Kraków to Sandomierz. By the thirteenth century the fort had become the property of the Gozdawa family, who kept it in good condition and afforded the local inhabitants a degree of protection against the numerous Tatar invasions. Paweł, the last of the Gozdawas, supposedly entertained King Kazimierz the Great there before accompanying his sovereign on a campaign into Ruthenia where he was killed.

The king then presented Baranów to a knight of outstanding prowess known as Pietrasz, who had reputedly saved his royal master's life in the Ruthenian war. From him descended the Baranowski family, who took their name from Baranów. But both names derive from "Baran," which means ram in Polish, for this was great sheep-breeding country. Here cloth weaving flourished too, and the local guild of clothworkers remained active until the nineteenth century. Especially from 1500 onward the grain trade was of commercial importance; silos were constructed along the river banks to store grain brought from the interior before it was floated on barges down the Vistula to Gdańsk and later exported. Positioned between the Vistula and its tributary the Babulowka and surrounded by ponds and water meadows that regularly flooded, the virtually impregnable Baranów was well able to dominate and guard the surrounding countryside.

By the sixteenth century the castle had again changed hands, twice in fact, and was now owned by the Górka family from Wielkopolska. They extended and modernized the existing fortress, although it was still a building entirely designed for military purposes. In 1569 Stanisław Górka sold the property to Rafał Leszczyński, starosta or sheriff of Radziejów, member of a rising noble dynasty, and also a native of Wielkopolska. Rafał was notable both for his ability to make money and for his advocacy of the reform program advocated by the executionist movement. When presiding over the Seym he had continually called for a reorganization of the army, and for equal rights for religious dissenters; indeed he had a personal interest at stake, for he was a member of the Czech Brethren in Poland, also known as the Arians, a strict Calvinist sect for whom he

*Corner view of main facade at Baranów,
southeastern Poland.*

had built a college and church at Leszno and a chapel on his estate at Gołuchów.

Although he lived on until 1592, a mere ten years after his purchase of Baranów, Rafał passed on the property to his eldest son, Andrzej. The latter was a famous warrior who participated in all the wars waged by Poland in the mid-sixteenth century, but he was also a widely traveled patron of art and learning, who corresponded with scholars all over Europe. Realizing Baranów's favorable position for defence, commerce, and communications, he made it his principal residence and entertained King Stefan Báthory there on several occasions. But the cramped medieval fortress was not to his taste and within a few years he had decided to rebuild.

The architect he commissioned was perhaps the most famous then working in Poland. A native Florentine of about sixty who had spent almost two-thirds of his life in his adopted country, Santi Gucci had developed an idiosyncratic and capricious style of his own, which relied strongly on such decorative elements as Ionic volutes, concentric bosses, low wide bands of acanthus leaves, and flamboyant vases. His connections with the royal court, for which he had undertaken many projects, was very close, and he now had a large atelier to assist him. Although conclusive documentary proof that Gucci was the main architect is lacking, much of the work at Baranów—the richly decorated portals along the upper galleries, for example—can be closely linked on stylistic grounds to his funerary monuments in the Wawel's cathedral, to the Firlej family tombs at Janowiec, and to the castle of Mirów. Baranów was a happy symbiosis of Italian theory and Polish practice.

Work began at Baranów in 1591 and lasted until 1606—in the last few years under his pupils' supervision, for Gucci had died. The result was a rectangular building some eighty by forty-three yards in roughly a two-to-one ratio. The blocks appeared massive, but the quite slender round

Front door with sundial above it.

314

Ceiling in the Tower Room, with plasterwork by Giovanni Battista Falconi, early seventeenth century.

towers at each of the four corners, with helmets underset on their longer sides by decorative gables, imposed a compositional discipline on the whole. An attic-crowned block containing the entrance gate projected from the center of the front facade, and attics were later added on to both of the sides.

With an interior courtyard surrounded by arcaded galleries, Baranów received a fairly traditional Renaissance layout, yet its design was highly polished. The front facade was formed merely of a curtain wall, which joined onto the remaining three wings on a rectangular ground plan. Gucci raised the level of the courtyard three meters to prevent any flooding from the Vistula, so internally the building had one less story than it appeared to from the outside. Closed by an iron gate, which had been given an artfully carved grille, the arched entrance doorway with square stone surrounds led up a flight of steps into the courtyard. Directly ahead a vaulted, two-branched staircase, facing out onto the courtyard and supported on the arcade, led to the upper level, its lower part open between arches resting on columns and joined by a balustrade. The arcaded galleries, rising through two stories, surrounded the other three sides of the courtyard, with the reception rooms and bedrooms leading off them. The gallery columns had Ionic capitals on both levels, although the lower ones rested on socles, the bases of which were decorated by grotesquely carved faces, or mascarons. The rosettes in the spandrels of the archivolts were equally typical features. Colored friezes, recently unveiled during restoration, adorned the outer facades and ran along the courtyard walls. The polychromatic heraldic devices simultaneously uncovered under the arcades and on the staircase's vaulted ceiling were from the same period.

The Leszczyńskis' new castle soon became a cultural center filled with numerous works of art and a notable library. Under the influence of Andrzej, a staunch Calvinist, the Baranów parish church ceased to be Catholic and a printing press was established in the village to disseminate the

Vaulted ceiling of the courtyard staircase.

The external staircase and arcades in the courtyard.

Row of grotesque heads in the courtyard.

works of famous Protestant theologians. Andrzej's death in 1606 coincided with the completion of the main reconstruction. His son Rafał, palatine of Bełz and another enlightened statesman, succeeded him and further added to the library. During the thirty years of his ownership further work was carried out on the attics of the two long facades—the front curtain wall and the back—and on the outer fortifications that surrounded the castle— the latter a typical attribute of a *palazzo in fortezza*. Today solely the underground foundations of these elements are visible, for the portions remaining aboveground were demolished during the nineteenth century to allow the erection of protecting walls along the Vistula escarpment.

Rafał was a great landowner with many other residences, although he spent much of his time at Baranów. Evidence of the scale on which he lived is provided by the fact that when his wife died in 1635 he supplied over two thousand mourning costumes for his servants, a number that excluded the kitchen staff, since they were never seen. This proved to be a sensible measure, for he himself followed her the next year. His successors were first his son, another Andrzej, and then his grandson Samuel, but the latter could no longer finance the accumulated debts on the estate and sold it to his paternal uncle, Bogusław, chancellor of the Kingdom. Only one more generation of Leszczyńskis was to live at Baranów, for Bogusław's son Rafał III, the royal treasurer and ambassador to Constantinople who played a notable part in lifting the Turkish siege of Vienna in 1683, sold the property in 1677. The Leszczyńskis did not fade away altogether after that—Rafał's son Stanisław was to be twice elected king of Poland, although he enjoyed a very short reign, was twice dethroned, and retired to France as duke of Lorraine, where he created one of Europe's most perfect eighteenth-century cities at Nancy. His daughter Marie would also become the faithful, long-suffering wife of the notoriously dissolute King Louis XV of France.

The purchaser of Baranów was Prince Dmitry Wiśniowiecki, scion of one of the great Ruthenian aristocratic houses. But he only survived for six more years, and after a brief interval his widow, Teofila, married Prince Karol Józef Lubomirski, a union of two major fortunes. By this date

*The picture gallery built by Tylman van Gameren
in the late seventeenth century.*

*Portrait of Queen Marie of France, daughter of
Rafał Leszczyński, by Jean-Marc Nattier,
mid-eighteenth century.*

*Old view of Baranów by Napoleon Orda,
nineteenth century. (Łańcut collection.)*

the Lubomirskis' estates stretched much of the way from Kraków to Lwów, and Baranów became just one of the family's many residences. However, substantial sums of money were available for the upkeep or renovation of the castle. From the Lubomirskis' point of view one drawback to Baranów was that none of the rooms were large enough to permit entertaining on a really grandiose scale. They decided to rectify that and accordingly commissioned Tylman van Gameren to refurbish the interiors. He introduced baroque plasterwork into many of the rooms, while in the west wing he created a long picture gallery with two adjoining antechambers to make an appropriate enfilade of rooms. The rich heavy stucco decoration is as magnificent now as in the late seventeenth century, but sadly the main feature, the specially carved frames with enormous canvases of landscape scenes that lined the new picture gallery, has been replaced by insipid modern copies.

Karol Józef Lubomirski's son and then his granddaughter inherited Baranów. In the course of the next seventy years it continued to change hands through sale or marriage several times, until in 1771 Józef Potocki bought it. His daughter Anna received the estate as her dowry when she wed Jan Krasicki and their descendants were to keep Baranów until the late nineteenth century, filling it with valuable contents, furniture, objets d'art, and a fine picture collection as well as building up the library once more with many precious books and manuscripts. There were also many mementoes of a cousin, Bishop Ignacy Krasicki; a true child of the Enlightenment, he was a poet, playwright, essayist, biographer, and author of a delightful book entitled *Fables*.

Tragically everything was lost in a terrible fire that broke out in September 1849 and devastated Baranów. After this catastrophe the Krasickis lacked both the money and the will to restore the castle to its former splendor. They also seemed to lack any interest in their few remaining art treasures, and no repairs were undertaken to make good the damage. At

length the property was put up for auction, and in 1867 it was bought by Feliks Dolański, who immediately set about the restoration. This proved an enormous task, but before it was finished another fire in 1898 set back the work again by several more years. Yet the Dolańskis—Feliks and his son Stanisław Karol—remained undaunted, ably supported by their supervising architect, Tadeusz Stryjeński from Kraków. One of the main rooms at courtyard level, for example, was successfully converted into a chapel, with fine art-nouveau stained-glass windows designed by Józef Mehoffer and an altar triptych by Jacek Malczewski.

During World War II the Dolańskis yet again experienced the sadness of seeing their work destroyed as the castle endured fierce fighting. In the autumn of 1944 the Russians crossed the Vistula near Baranów to establish a bridgehead, which held out against repeated German attacks until the big Soviet offensive begun in January 1945 swept the fighting westward. The castle was not obliterated by the shellfire, but did suffer extensive structural damage, while all the contents not previously removed were smashed or stolen. Nevertheless the Dolańskis continued to retain Baranów until it was expropriated in the wake of the Communist takeover in 1945.

Despite the castle's desperate condition, in 1956 the Ministry of Culture started a major restoration program and two years later its efforts were joined by the Ministry for Chemical Industry. The discovery of large sulfur deposits in the neighborhood had revolutionized Baranów's prospects, for a renovated castle could obviously be used as a center for conferences and for business entertaining. Executed at a very high standard, the work was supervised by Professor Alfred Majewski, whose team had been responsible for repairs to the Wawel. New exhibits were loaned by museums, and the rooms on the upper two stories again resembled castle interiors, albeit somewhat sparsely furnished; an archaeological and geographical exhibition concerning the sulfur industry was also arranged on the ground floor.

Baranów is not the best known or most accessible of Poland's surviving great houses. Yet in purer form than almost anywhere else it encapsulates the finest flowering of Renaissance architecture, unencumbered by the legacy of the Middle Ages, for only vestigial traces of the medieval fortress are still visible. Quite apart from its historical interest, which is compelling enough on its own merits, Baranów is one of Poland's most satisfying and beautiful monuments.

WILANÓW

Main facade of Wilanów, near Warsaw.

Monumental doorway in one of the side wings.

Many of the major cities of Europe have a great summer palace on their outskirts built during the seventeenth or eighteenth century: Versailles, Schönbrunn, Sans Souci, Nymphenburg, and Caserta, to name but a few. Warsaw is not lacking in this respect either, for on its southeastern edge and beyond the suburbs stands the palace of Wilanów. This magnificent baroque residence belonged to a succession of the nation's most remarkable families both royal and noble, and its history provides any visitor with a fascinating glimpse into the history of Poland itself.

In the mid-seventeenth century the first foundations of a building at the Wilanów estate were laid. Bogusław Leszczyński, the owner, planned a rectangular block with small alcove towers at the corners and two larger octagonal towers farther away linked to the main building by screen walls. Work had not progressed very far when the property was sold to King Jan Sobieski in 1677. Ever since his accession to the throne three years before, the king, essentially a countryman, had hankered for a rural retreat near the capital, for his own family residences were far away to the east and he found Warsaw's Royal Castle uncomfortable. At Wilanów he had discovered precisely what he wanted.

Since funds were limited, Sobieski instructed his court architect, Augustyn Locci, to utilize the existing foundations with various adjustments. Without delay work began in May 1677, and within two years the first phase in the building was completed. On the site of Leszczyński's center block a modest one-story manor house had been constructed under a high hipped roof with four corner alcoves, each with its own little roof. No wings or towers were constructed, but two outbuildings faced each other to form a small courtyard in the front. Behind, a modest garden containing several ponds gave an idyllic, rustic character to the place.

In 1681–82 a second phase of construction began that transformed Wilanów into a much grander residence. Both the main block and the alcoves were raised half a story, while open galleries instead of the screen walls Leszczyński had envisaged linked this structure to imposing square towers erected on the octagonal foundations. The galleries were given monumental portals shaped like triumphant Roman arches, and all the facades were covered with stucco sculpture executed by Italian and Polish craftsmen. The front elevation was divided by monumental pilasters supporting an elaborately sculpted pediment, which depicted a solar orb surrounded by allegorical figures of fame blowing trumpets; cherubs holding up the Sobieski coat of arms and a statue of Minerva crowned the whole. Balustraded attics also crowned the end towers, with stone statues of the Muses imported from Holland standing at each corner.

A final phase of building started in 1684 and continued intermittently until Sobieski's death in 1696. During these years an entire additional story was constructed over the central part of the main block, the sculptural decoration from the dismantled pediment was transferred to its facade, and the statues of the Muses were moved to adorn the roof line. The front elevations of the corner alcoves facing the courtyard were given an attic level covered with statues of ancient goddesses and with bas-reliefs glorifying Sobieski's military victories. The sculptor Stefan Szwaner from Gdańsk was responsible for these and for the compositions filling the archivolts of the galleries.

The grounds were also laid out by the royal engineer, Adolf Boy, in a style hitherto virtually unseen in Poland. The large courtyard in front of the palace—for this is what Wilanów had now become—was divided into two sections. The front area was framed by the coach house and storehouse and was entered through a handsome stone gateway crowned by martial trophies, while the rear part, surrounded by the principal buildings, was separated from the front by a low, ornamentally carved wall. Behind the palace a geometric Italian garden on two levels sloped down to the lake. The upper parterre contained box trees, stone urns, and mythological gilt figures cast in the Gdańsk bell foundry, as well as red marble fountains and wooden summerhouses with green and gilt roofs. A double flight of steps led down to the lower parterre, which contained two rectangular ponds. To one side of the garden the orchard was planted with a range of fruit trees behind the stables and granaries. The entire landscape was designed along a symmetrical central axis from the entrance gate through to the lake, beyond which a straight canal extended, prolonging the line. A vegetable garden and a farmyard situated to the south formed the only other deviations from this geometric layout.

The interior of Wilanów was equally symmetrical although by contrast to Italian custom the main rooms were situated on the ground floor and not on the piano nobile. The cavernous entrance hall rising through two stories led onto the drawing room behind and formed a definite axis dividing the king's apartments from the queen's. Each of their suites had a large antechamber leading directly off the hall and a bedchamber of similar proportions, along with several other smaller rooms. On the mezzanine floor the rooms had relatively low ceilings, but in the belvedere created by adding a level to the central part a magnificent banqueting hall was installed.

To decorate his new palace Sobieski set up an atelier, which was to grow into the first academy of painting in Poland. The French painters Claude Callot and Abraham Paris were joined by the Polish artists Jerzy Szymonowicz-Siemigonowski and Jan Reisner. A team of sculptors and stuccodores also collaborated with them, and many other skilled craftsmen were employed as well. The Italo-French influence was paramount:

Family group with King Jan Sobieski and Queen Marie-Casimire, c. 1693.

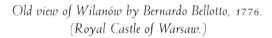

*Old view of Wilanów by Bernardo Bellotto, 1776.
(Royal Castle of Warsaw.)*

Central tower seen from the garden.

the royal bedchambers were modeled on Pietro da Cortona's designs for the Pitti Palace, for instance, while Szymonowicz-Siemigonowski's ceiling paintings owe much to Carlo Maratta and Nicholas Poussin. Yet the polychrome decoration of the ceiling beams was typically Polish, and Dutch taste was also apparent in the choice of some of the furniture and pictures. Much was intended to extol Sobieski's glory, like the enormous equestrian statue placed in the entrance hall of the king trampling down the Turks, or the self-aggrandizing portraits of himself and his family in a variety of poses. Yet his sincere interest in incorporating Poland's art into the classical European mainstream was unquestionable and the work he commissioned was often very fine.

By the end of the seventeenth century the modest manor house had been turned into an Italianate baroque palace. Locci had certainly looked to Rome for his inspiration, but he also cleverly adapted many motifs to match Polish styles and his master's Sarmatian tastes. If Sobieski had not died in 1696 perhaps Wilanów might almost have become a rival to Versailles, for the King's personal and dynastic ambitions were boundless as were those of his French queen, Marie-Casimire. Within days of his death, however, all valuables were moved to safekeeping in Warsaw, and the best furniture and pictures were locked away in the palace treasuries. Two of his three sons, Aleksander and Konstanty, inherited Wilanów. The former continued to extend the palace wings until, utterly disappointed in his hopes for the throne, he retired to Rome where he was ordained as a Capuchin monk. Now the sole owner, Konstanty took scant interest in the property, and his straitened financial circumstances precluded any further improvements. Largely emptied of their contents, the buildings began to decay. In 1720 Konstanty sold Wilanów to the daughter of Stanisław Herakliusz Lubomirski, Elżbieta Sieniawska, whose husband was both grand hetman and palatine of Kraków.

For the remainder of the eighteenth century Wilanów was owned by three rich, powerful, and determined women in succession, grandmother, mother and daughter. Elżbieta, the first, already possessed several other properties including Puławy. She was an art connoisseur with definite tastes who regularly bought German silver and porcelain along with fine fabrics, clocks, and chandeliers from a variety of dealers. Upon purchasing Wilanów she decided to begin maintenance work immediately, so between 1723 and 1729, side wings of the palace were constructed in place

of the open galleries, harmonizing with the main block and vastly increasing the building's size. When her original architect, Giovanni Spazzio, died in 1726, his place was taken by Sigismund Deybel; the work itself was supervised by Józef Fontana. The new facades they created were adorned with stucco depictions of battles, allegorical figures, and scenes from Ovid's *Metamorphoses*. An orangery was built to Spazzio's plans and the gardens were extended northward. Inside the palace a number of frescoes were executed by a painter, Józef Rossi, and other walls were covered with huge mirrors and velvet tapestries.

Elżbieta's daughter Zofia, who became Princess Czartoryska on her

General view of Queen Marie-Casimire's bedroom.

Ceiling fresco in Queen Marie-Casimire's bedroom portraying her as Aurora, late seventeenth century.

marriage in 1731, inherited Wilanów on her mother's death in 1729. With a mass of other commitments, she agreed to lease the palace to King Augustus II the Strong, who had repeatedly requested the arrangement, on the stipulation that nothing should be altered. Nevertheless the king had the south wing further extended, adding a large single-story dining room commissioned from Deybel. He moved in during 1731 and held court there with appropriate splendor for several weeks that summer. But his death two years later halted any other "improvements" he might have contemplated, and Zofia did not renew the lease to Augustus III. Instead, Wilanów was kept up with little done by way of alterations. Only the orangery was remodeled in mid-century and a late baroque stone parish church was erected in place of the old wooden one.

Zofia's daughter Izabela Lubomirska succeeded to Wilanów in 1771. For the preceding eighteen years she had been the chatelaine of Łańcut, and she had long before evinced her iron determination to get what she wanted. In 1775, then, she began her improvements by commissioning Szymon Bogumił Zug, who was also soon to begin building a villa for her at nearby Natolin. Zug first designed a bathhouse in neoclassical style to be added to Deybel's extension to the south wing. Here she created her own apartment, with an antechamber, salon, bedchamber, and bathroom, all luxuriously appointed. A new palace kitchen and guardhouse in the same style were constructed a little to the west. Inside the main house the walls of the entrance hall were marbled and decorated by Fryderyk Bauman. Izabela once more increased the size of the gardens, in 1784 instructing Zug to lay out an irregular garden in Anglo-Chinese taste with luxuriant vegetation, winding paths, and waterfalls. A team of gardeners was drafted, some of whom had been working on the landscape at Izabela Lubomirska's Mokotów garden near Warsaw, and under the supervision of the brothers Krystian and Godfryd Symon, the vegetable garden was reshaped in a rococo design, with linden trees and clipped hornbeams forming arbors with fountains, statues, and stone benches. Three alleys radiating from the palace's front gate were planted with lime trees.

When Izabela returned to Poland in 1789 after a long stay in France, she decided to settle as far away as possible from impending war or revolution. Since Łańcut seemed to offer the safest refuge, she decided to concentrate her collections there, emptying Wilanów and her residences in Warsaw of their contents, which were dispatched down the Vistula by barge. Her intuition of impending trouble was correct. In 1794 Tadeusz Kościuszko led an insurrection against the foreign powers occupying Poland during which Wilanów was stripped of its copper roofs and requisitioned for military purposes. Russian troops were later billeted there, and badly damaged both the palace and the gardens. Unwilling to return to her devastated property, Izabela handed it over in 1799 to her daughter Aleksandra, wife of Stanisław Kostka Potocki, a versatile scholar and a passionate collector.

For almost the next hundred years the Potockis were to own Wilanów, and they were to transform it lastingly. Stanisław Kostka's great aim was to reassemble as many Sobieski mementoes as possible, and while on countless trips to Western Europe he notably added to the palace's collections—in particular Chinese artifacts and antique vases (as a practicing archaeologist he also directed excavations himself) as well as paintings, all of which were to form the nucleus of the Wilanów gallery. Helped by his brother Ignacy, he also founded a magnificent library, which he installed within the superstructure of the belvedere. Wishing to open his treasures to the public, in 1805 Potocki established one of Poland's first museums in a neo-Gothic gallery especially designed by Chrystian Piotr Aigner as an extension of the north wing.

Stanisław Kostka's energies extended to the exterior too. Although the baroque parterres on the eastern side were left alone, he converted the rococo and Chinoiserie gardens created by his mother-in-law into an English-style landscape park. Follies and pavilions were added in the northern part of the garden: a Chinese summerhouse, a Roman bridge, and an ancient tomb with a mock triumphal arch. Potocki's multifarious interests also embraced cottage architecture and he was keen to improve the peasants' living conditions. He therefore designed new and more hygienic cottages, which gradually replaced the unhealthy old thatched hovels around the park. A hospital and village school were built as well to cater to the needs of the estate staff.

When Potocki died in 1821 his projects were faithfully continued by his widow and then by his son Aleksander. In 1836 the latter erected a neo-Gothic mausoleum to the memory of his parents in front of the palace gates, employing the sculptor Jakub Tatarkiewicz and the architect Enrico Marconi. The result was striking, even if it did not entirely blend in with its surroundings, but other refurbishment was less felicitous. From 1845 Franciszek Maria Lanci began reconstructing Aigner's neo-Gothic gallery, giving it a neo-Renaissance elevation with neorococo interiors. Izabela Lubomirska's bathhouse was substantially modified, and extra outbuildings were erected following Lanci's plans as well as a large stone pergola in the garden. Marconi then took over from Lanci, extending the hospital, building a chapel, and installing an ugly pump house down by the lake to supply water to the fountains.

Aleksander Potocki only lived until 1845, at which point Wilanów passed to his son August. He married his cousin Aleksandra, yet another Potocki, and she lived at Wilanów until 1892—for the last twenty-five of those years as a widow. Aleksandra became very much the controlling force on the property, adding new works of art to the collections and carrying on with the reconstruction of the palace. In this she was helped by Marconi's sons Władysław and Leandro, who had taken over his practice. During the 1870s a chamber for the family's antiquities was created in

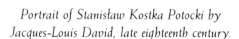

Portrait of Stanisław Kostka Potocki by Jacques-Louis David, late eighteenth century.

Interior of Izabela Lubomirska's bathroom.

the south gallery and another for their Etruscan artifacts in the north tower and the big library within the superstructure of the belvedere was redecorated. Yet again the parish church was altered as it acquired a lofty neobaroque dome.

With Aleksandra's death in 1892 the direct line of the family died out, so Wilanów was bequeathed to her nephew Ksawery Branicki. His ancestors had sprung to prominence in the Ukraine during the fifteenth century and had produced a leading Catholic bishop, a few grand hetmans, and a string of distinguished soldiers. One member had married Catherine the Great's illegitimate daughter and had fought a celebrated duel with Casanova; on capturing a notorious brigand named Ivan Gonda, this same Branicki had granted his prisoner's request to have his portrait painted before his execution and afterwards for it to hang in every subsequent Branicki's bedroom. Ksawery's grandfather had been part of the "Great Emigration" after the rising of 1831, departing to France where he had bought the chateau of Montrésor on the Loire; his father was a painter who regularly exhibited in the Paris Salon and lived there collecting pictures. After he had inherited Wilanów, Ksawery moved to Poland where he led a retiring life, augmenting the magnificent library and running his estates. Like his father and grandfather he financed scientific expeditions, in his case to Africa, Asia, and particularly the Caucasus; he also became a

The painting gallery arranged by Count August Potocki in the mid-nineteenth century.

Painting of King Jan Sobieski's former banqueting hall, converted into a library in the early nineteenth century, by Willibald Richter, mid-nineteenth century.

Count Adam Branicki in Polish national dress at a wedding, c. 1930. (Anna Branicka-Wolska.)

noted ornithologist. While he established a museum of national history in his Warsaw palace he eschewed politics, and although a chamberlain to the tsar, avoided going to the Saint Petersburg court.

Władysław Marconi was kept on as the consulting architect at Wilanów, and from 1893 embarked on another thirteen-year stint of reconstruction, primarily focused on the palace outbuildings this time, and with largely unfortunate results. By the early twentieth century the fabric of the building was starting to decay and there were various losses in the sculptural decorations. After World War I, when Adam Branicki had succeeded his father Ksawery, a restoration program was undertaken, but limited funds and mediocre workmanship meant that the underlying problems were not solved.

An amateur historian, Adam was also a devotee of Poland's national culture and a great supporter of the museum the family had established at Wilanów. The Potockis only lived in the south wing of the palace, leaving the north wing and central block as a museum, which, with the gardens, were regularly opened to the public. Like his father, Adam was essentially a private man who established a traditional, tranquil, and family-oriented life. His daughter Anna, in her recently published memoir, *Unposted Letters*, described Easters at Wilanów during her childhood in the 1930s. On the preceding Thursday the family would organize expeditions to the woods to gather violets, to the greenhouses for flowers, and to the kitchens to sample the food; on Good Friday, with no butter on their bread or sugar in their coffee, they went to church up to seven times to pray for redemption, and visited other churches in Warsaw in their Hispano Suiza to inspect the Easter crèches; and on Saturday huge tables laden with food were set up to be blessed by the priest—turkeys, glazed hams, and colored eggs alongside cakes bearing the word "Hallelujah" on their icing. Finally on Easter Day, after an early morning mass to celebrate the Resurrection, the household settled down to an enormous breakfast and to several days of merrymaking, entertaining innumerable friends and neighbors.

These happy days were rudely terminated by World War II. Germany's occupation of Poland led to the requisitioning of the palace, the removal of most of its contents, and the destruction of the gardens and many of their monuments. At length in 1943 the Branickis were evicted from Wilanów altogether and plans were made, luckily never realized, to turn it into an officers' club. After the Soviet takeover things were no better; Adam, who had already been imprisoned three times, was deported to Russia with his family in 1945 and returned three years later so worn out and emaciated that he died at a mere 55. His daughters were forbidden to live anywhere near their former home, or even to visit it.

Wilanów today seems to have banished these sad memories. After the contents looted by the Germans had been restored, in 1955 the Communist government at last began a thorough restoration, a process that took nine years and has brought the palace and its grounds back to their old splendor. In addition to the museums that Wilanów housed before the wars, a Polish portrait gallery has also been installed in one part of the palace. Clever restoration has removed most of the excrescences added in the nineteenth and twentieth centuries while allowing the best of the Lubomirski and Potocki alterations to remain. Externally and internally, Wilanów has been revealed again as the grand baroque residence of one of Poland's greatest kings.

NIEBORÓW
& ARKADIA

The landscape of Mazovia in central Poland is fairly flat and somewhat featureless, punctuated only by thick swathes of woodland. Nevertheless the area holds some unexpected and fascinating attractions, among them Fryderyk Chopin's delightful birthplace at Żelazowa Wola, west of Warsaw. Nearby and close to the pleasant town of Łowicz stands the small village of Nieborów. There, clearly visible through elegant railings and down a broad alley, rises an imposing chateau, the former residence of one of Poland's greatest noble families. And a mile or so further lies the entrance to its delightful pendant, the landscape garden of Arkadia.

The origins of Nieborów date from the late Middle Ages, when a group of yeoman farms first developed in the area. Embracing six neighboring villages and located near the old trade route from Warsaw to Poznań, used since the time of the Piast kings, the farms were gradually consolidated into one property, named like the main village after its founder, Niebor. By the early sixteenth century a family calling itself Nieborowski owned this property, and there just south of the road they built a two-story brick manor house decorated with many Gothic elements. To the north of the house stood the parish church, already in existence for over two centuries. No records of the house survive, although recent restoration work has shown that its large vaulted hall must have been positioned asymmetrically. There the Nieborowskis lived in respectable obscurity until they sold the estate in the early 1690s.

The purchaser was a far more significant figure, Cardinal Michał Stefan Radziejowski, archbishop of Gniezno and primate of Poland, who resided in nearby Łowicz. By 1695 he decided to build himself a magnificent chateau on the site and commissioned Tylman van Gameren, the royal architect, accordingly. The contrast with some of the more flamboyant buildings he designed in Warsaw was marked. Laying out his building on a rectangular plan, Tylman used the walls of the existing manor house but extended them at both ends, creating a long low edifice with twelve bays under a high copper roof. Two square alcove towers containing rooms, surmounted by finial-capped cupolas and protruding slightly, were added to flank the facade, a device often employed in Polish baroque architecture. The central four bays were framed by a pediment resting on unobtrusive pilasters. Internally the hall was realigned along the symmetrical axis of the new chateau, and a grand staircase led up to the state rooms on the upper floor. The garden, which stretched southward, derived from the formal French gardens then in fashion, with a canal, flat parterres, elaborate hedges, and thickets.

Before his new creation was even ready, the cardinal apparently tired of it, for in 1697 he presented Nieborów to his protégé, Jerzy Towiański,

Main facade of Nieborów, central Poland.

Old view of Arkadia by Zygmunt Vogel, c. 1800.

Seventeenth-century bench in the garden at Nieborów with the inscription Non sedeas sed eas *(Do not sit down but go on).*

Portrait of Helena Radziwiłł by Ernst Gebauer, c. 1800.

Garden façade of Nieborów.

castellan of Łęczyca. The latter did not keep it for long, however—indeed over the ensuing seventy years the estate changed hands twice more. At length it was bought in 1766 by Michał Kazimierz Ogiński, grand hetman of Lithuania and palatine of Wilno. The new proprietor embarked forthwith on a major refurbishment of the neglected interiors. The main staircase was widened and its walls inlaid with Dutch tiles, while the Red Drawing Room, as it was called, and the adjoining bedchamber were redecorated in rococo taste. Much valuable furniture was brought in as well, and some splendid chimneypieces installed. In 1768 the pediment over the front door was filled with stucco carvings of war emblems, and in the middle a cartouche was created with the heraldic devices of Ogiński and his Czartoryski wife. A brick inn was also built just outside the front gates to improve the amenities of the village.

Despite his many talents as musician, poet, art patron, and entrepreneur (he was a backer of the Polesie Canal), Michał Kazimierz was not fated to enjoy his new property for long. In 1770 he joined with other malcontents and declared the deposition of King Stanisław August. Russian troops quickly crushed the rebels and, like many other magnates similarly placed, Ogiński fled into exile in Paris. Since he was unable to live at Nieborów any longer, he sold it in 1774 for four hundred thousand gold zlotys to his niece Helena Przeździecka and her husband, Michał Hieronim Radziwiłł.

After rising to prominence in Lithuania during the fifteenth century, the Radziwiłłs had played a major part in Polish history. Descended from the two cousins Mikołaj the Black and Mikołaj the Red—so-called in both cases for the respective color of their beards—they had regularly held many of the highest offices of state and had occasionally toyed with the idea of an independent Lithuanian state. The family owned the freehold of the enormous estates of Nieśwież and Ołyka, both of which were entailed and which conferred upon their holder the title of duke. The Radziwiłłs were also princes of the Holy Roman Empire and regarded themselves as quasi-independent, far better than the motley procession of Poland's kings. Their family pride, however, was tempered with hardheaded economic realism.

Michał Hieronim, then aged thirty and soon appointed palatine of Wilno, was a fairly typical Radziwiłł. Not overburdened with political scruples, he was one of the members of the Seym who duly recognized the First Partition of Poland in 1772, and as a member of the Confederation of Targowica in 1792, invited in the Russians again to suppress the

liberal reforms that had just been introduced. His chief concern was in making money, at which he succeeded brilliantly—for thirteen years in a row his annual income exceeded five million zlotys, much of it gained by administering the estates of Nieśwież and Ołyka for his young cousin Dominik Radziwiłł. Since the young head of the family was killed fighting with the Polish Legion in 1813 and left no heirs, Michał Hieronim was able to establish his own children's claim to the huge inheritance.

Helena, his wife, was equally ambitious in the social sphere, permanently engaged in friendly rivalry with Izabella Czartoryska over who should be the arbiter of taste and fashion in Warsaw. If her rival was to indulge in the new mania for landscape gardening, first at Powązki and then at Puławy, Helena was not to be left behind. Thus in 1778 the Radziwiłłs summoned Szymon Bogumił Zug to Nieborów. His brief was to extend the baroque garden, creating a promenade with alleys leading off it that would afford vistas of the new deer park established on the far side of the formal canal, the latter of which was now L-shaped with three pools and terraced slopes. Hothouses were erected, principally to shelter the large collection of orange trees brought from Dresden in the 1790s, and an earthen amphitheatre was also made. In addition Zug designed a complex of buildings near the chateau, including a coach house, stables, a brewery, estate offices, and a pavilion housing the main kitchen. On the other side of the public road a farmyard with a big central granary was also built.

But Helena aspired to more than just modernizing and improving the surroundings of Nieborów. She wanted to create an ideal rustic paradise, a place to escape from the frequently depressing realities of the age in Poland. The theories of Jean-Jacques Rousseau and the cult of the classical

and medieval worlds strongly informed the development of Arkadia, a romantic English-style landscape park she built only a mile or so from Nieborów. The name Arkadia derived from the pastoral region of ancient Greece, and had subsequently been used to describe a mythical isle where could be found the carefree bliss of an imaginary past. As she wrote, "You may call Arkadia an ancient monument to beautiful Greece. The traces of mythological worship, once preserved in art, are to be found here. The soul is overcome by a strong desire to express the feelings experienced, or those awakened in tender hearts by the mysterious charm of sacred groves."

In order to realize Helena's dream, Zug first dug an artificial lake christened the Big Pond. From there, steps led up to a Temple of Diana finished in 1783, a well-proportioned edifice with a portico of four columns and a semirotunda at the back surrounded by six Ionic pillars. Along the frieze ran a quote from Petrarch: *"Dove pace trovai d'ogni mia guerra"* ("Here I found peace after each struggle of mine"), while at the back appeared another inscription, this time from Horace: "I escape the others to find myself." Inside the temple, the walls of the central room were decorated with white stucco glazed to simulate marble, which contrasted effectively with the yellow Corinthian columns. The ceiling was painted by the French artist Jean-Pierre Norblin with a dramatic rendering of Aurora, goddess of the dawn, leading the horses of the sun god, Apollo. Next door in the so-called Etruscan study, depictions of utensils and

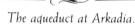

The aqueduct at Arkadia.

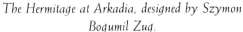

The Hermitage at Arkadia, designed by Szymon Bogumil Zug.

lamps were made in distemper on the plaster, while a ceiling fresco depicted a charmingly naive scene of Eros and Psyche. Guarded by a lion and a sphinx, the terrace provided views across the Big Pond to what was called the Isle of Feelings, where flowers were regularly placed on altars dedicated to love, friendship, gratitude, and memories. The grounds beyond were known as the Elysian Fields.

At one end of the Big Pond, Zug constructed a two-tiered, four-arched Roman Aqueduct. In a very different style he built a building called the High Priest's Sanctuary from brick and local ironstone. It contained fragments of friezes, moldings, frames, tablets, and armorial cartouches from the archbishop's castle at Łowicz and from tombs in the collegiate church there. To one side a columned terrace extended above an arched open vault. From 1795 to 1798 Zug constructed the Margrave's House, with its square battlemented tower approached through a wide brick and stone arch. Two herm heads and a lion mask were built into its walls and rosettes decorated the inside of one of the small doorways, all the work of the eminent Renaissance sculptor Jan Michałowicz.

By the dawn of the nineteenth century, neoclassical conventions were increasingly being discarded at Arkadia in favor of an eclectic Romantic style. About 1780 Zug built one of the first neo-Gothic edifices in Poland, a medieval-style house with twin spires designed by Aleksander Orłowski, a pupil of Norblin. Next to it the Sibyl's Grotto was created, its entrance framed by huge stones and a ruined altar picturesquely draped with bindweed and jasmine. Helena's tastes were growing ever more fanciful. Next she employed a young architect named Henryk Ittar who used marble, porphyry, and granite for his Tomb of Illusions, sited on the Poplar Isle in a stream, rechristened the River of Forgetfulness, which flowed out of the Big Pond. He also designed a circus for chariot racing and an amphitheatre, and although both were widely praised at the time, nothing of them has survived except for three obelisks in the circus.

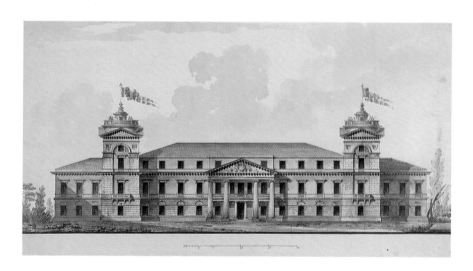

General view of the library.

Project for the reconstruction of Nieborów
by Giacomo Quarenghi, c. 1800.
(National Museum, Warsaw.)

During these years Nieborów was not neglected either. In the 1780s Zug redecorated the rooms at the eastern end of the second floor in early neoclassical style. The chateau was filled with good furniture—English, French, and local—and with an impressive picture collection of both Old Masters and Polish portraits. The library contained twelve thousand books and two superlative globes from Venice, one terrestrial and one celestial, carved by Vincenzo Coronelli. Wishing to embellish the severe external appearance of the building, Helena commissioned Giacomo Quarenghi, later famous for his work at Saint Petersburg, although his grandiose new plans were never executed. The gardens were further remodeled *à l'anglaise*, with a wide variety of tree species being planted and more alleys cut through the lime woods, one of which terminated in a haha, the name given to the hidden, semicircular projection over the ditch. Sculpture of all kinds from Europe and Asia, including figures, bas-reliefs, columns with inscriptions in Greek and Arabic, and sarcophagi, were scattered around the gardens as if to emphasize their owners' cosmopolitan identity.

The Radziwiłłs adapted very skillfully to the extinction of the Polish state under the partition. Their eldest son, Ludwik, was sent to Saint Petersburg where he obtained a commission in the Russian army, while his son Leon was later appointed aide-de-camp to the tsar. Helena contrived to marry off her second son, Antoni, to Princess Louise of Prussia, niece of Frederick the Great, and from this union, a genuine love-match, the future senior line of the family would spring. Her father, King Frederick William II, intimated that a generous wedding settlement would be welcome, so Antoni's famously parsimonious father bought him a magnificent residence in Berlin and an estate in the Prussian zone of occupied Poland where an unusual wooden house, named after him and designed by Karl Friedrich Schinkel, would one day be built. A Maecenas of music and the arts, Antoni wrote the first musical score for Goethe's *Faust* and

Empire chair in the study at Nieborów.

337

became the friend and patron of Chopin. His appointment in 1818 as viceroy of the Grand Duchy of Poznań, which the Prussians had created from the Polish territory they had annexed, suggests how greatly respected he was by the Russian government, a status further enhanced by being granted Nieśwież and Ołyka by the tsar.

The Radziwiłłs' third son, Michał Gedeon, was a complete contrast. A liberal who fought in Kościuszko's uprising, he subsequently accompanied Helena to Paris where he became an enthusiastic supporter of Napoleon. When the French created the duchy of Warsaw, he was given command of one of its infantry regiments, and he later served with distinction as a brigadier in the War of 1812. After 1815 he married and was made a senator in the Congress Kingdom. When the remarkable Helena died in 1821, ten years before her long-lived husband, Michał Gedeon inherited the properties of Nieborów and Szpanów. But ten years later he was forced to flee abroad and his estates were confiscated after his having accepted the post of commander-in-chief of the Polish forces during the suppressed revolt against Russia. Only through the family's intercession at Saint Petersburg were the properties offered to their Russified cousin Leon Radziwiłł, who generously gave them back again a few years afterward to Michał Gedeon's sons, still minors. Their father was eventually allowed to return

*Grotesque head with foliage painted by
Szymon Mankowski.*

Neo-rococo boudoir.

*Armorial stove produced in the Nieborów
workshops, c. 1885.*

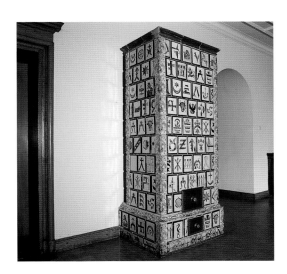

and lived in reduced state at Nieborów, for the property had been damaged in the fighting and there were numerous creditors demanding satisfaction. His masterful wife, Aleksandra, provided the real impetus to keep up the estate, and after her husband's death in 1850 she set about restoring the chateau and gardens, redecorating the White Salon in late neoclassical taste.

Trouble struck when her elder son, Zygmunt, took charge on her death in 1864. A hopeless spendthrift and entirely uninterested in the character of his inheritance, he removed the whole of the library to Paris where it was sold at auction. In constant need of money, he disposed of numerous works of art too, and even put the neglected Arkadia up for sale. He finally decided to settle in France, and in 1879 agreed to sell Nieborów to his brother's son Michał Piotr.

Luckily the new proprietor, an active philanthropist who endowed many orphanages and led a busy public life, was to prove a far worthier figure than his profligate uncle. Restoration recommenced, and in 1886 Leandro Marconi, son of the distinguished architect Enrico, was commissioned to alter the chateau both inside and out. The results were not wholly felicitous. The insertion over the front door of three tall closely spaced windows plus a balcony destroyed the external proportions of the building. The main vaulted hall was given heavy oak, pseudo-Renaissance wainscoting and an overly ornate fireplace, while several of the state rooms at the western end of the second floor were refurbished in elaborate neo-rococo taste. The medieval parish church was demolished and replaced with the neo-Gothic edifice that still stands today. But Michał Piotr also set up joinery workshops at Nieborów and Szpanów, which produced badly needed furniture for the chateau. Moreover in 1881 he established a majolica works, which intermittently over the next twenty-five years produced a stream of tiled stoves, plates, candlesticks, jugs, vases, lamps, and wall tiles; in its final phase under the direction of the outstanding potter Stanisław Jagmin, it also turned out decorative pieces in an art nouveau style.

Since Michał Piotr was childless, he decided before his death in 1906 to bequeath Nieborów to his cousin's son Janusz, the great-grandson of Antoni. Having just acquired a bride, Anna Lubomirska, Janusz wished to make a comfortable home, but he did not find Nieborów large enough for the needs of the age, with its enormous staffs and elaborate house parties. Two schemes to add wings to the front of the chateau were under consideration when World War I intervened. In 1915 Józef Piłsudski's Polish Legion skirmished against the Russians in the neighborhood, and Arkadia, with several of the pavilions, was damaged in the fighting. Fortunately Nieborów itself escaped unscathed, although both sides did a limited amount of plundering. Curiously, all of the eighteenth-century carriages were requisitioned during the war and, of course, never returned.

In the newly-independent postwar Poland, Janusz Radziwiłł found himself one of the nation's largest landowners. His properties included Szpanów and Nieborów, with nearly twenty-five thousand acres, along with Ołyka, an immense and beautiful castle located to the east in Volhynia, with a courtyard larger than the Piazza San Marco, over two hundred rooms, and a landholding still amounting to nearly eighty thousand acres. His eldest son was furthermore to marry his distant cousin Izabela, daughter of the line that owned the still larger Nieśwież estates. All lay within the post-1919 frontiers.

Despite being such a large landowner, Janusz was an active politician and close associate of Piłsudski's who preferred to spend most of his time in his Warsaw palace or within easy reach of the capital. Since Nieborów was relatively near, plans to enlarge it were pursued. In 1922 the architect Romuald Gutt created a third floor by converting the spacious attic into guest bedrooms, covering the roof with tiles instead of copper plate, which permitted the insertion of windows in it. The ground floor, too, was reconstructed in 1929–30: at one end a smoking room and a dining room were created, while at the other Janusz made his offices. The chateau's furnishings were completed, to a great extent with eighteenth-century copies, and more paintings were brought in. They, along with the rest of the Radziwiłłs' collections, were readily made available to scholars. The front drive was also changed to enable a large lawn to be made along the main facade, and baroque lion statues now guarded it.

Within a fortnight of the outbreak of World War II, in mid-September 1939, the area round Nieborów became the scene of heavy German-Polish fighting, although once more the buildings were not damaged. Janusz happened to be at Ołyka at the time and after the Russian invasion was deported to the Soviet Union with his family. Thanks to high-level intervention, he was released that December and returned to Poland, where he immersed himself in welfare work for his compatriots. With large forests and strategic railway lines in the vicinity, Nieborów was a center for Resistance activity, in which his elder son and daughter-in-law participated. In consequence the population suffered from German reprisals—indeed some of the estate staff were shot or sent to concentration camps. Later the chateau was turned into a German headquarters and a committee of Nazi art historians confiscated nineteen crates of the best contents, although these were mostly recovered after the war.

Portrait of Duke Janusz Radziwiłł by Waclawa Radwana, 1920.

Radziwiłł family reunion for Princess Mary
Radziwiłł's eightieth birthday, 1980s.
(Princess Mary Radziwiłł.)

Although he had refused all offers to cooperate with the Nazis, Janusz was nevertheless rearrested by the Soviets in 1945, and in company with other aristocrats who had sought refuge at his home—sundry Branickis, Krasińskis, and Zamoyskis—he was taken off to captivity in Russia. Just before his return almost three years later, his wife died in prison, but he survived until 1967, living in a tiny flat in Warsaw. Nieborów and Arkadia had meanwhile been declared a branch of the National Museum in February 1945 and opened to the public, later becoming a conference center and retreat for intellectuals. Major restoration work on the chateau from 1966 to 1970 has left the interiors in good condition, while the outbuildings, gardens, and park have been well maintained. At Arkadia the garden layout with its large pond and streams has been recreated, but some of the buildings are still in urgent need of renovation.

The appeal of Nieborów and Arkadia does not lie solely in the fine architecture and decoration found at the former, nor in the status of the latter as perhaps the most completely preserved Romantic landscape in Poland. It is also their connection for nearly two centuries with one of the country's greatest noble dynasties, and with one exceptional woman in particular, who substantially brought into being what we see today. As Helena Radziwiłł's inscription by the entrance gate puts it, "Oh you sweet land of Arkadia, more sweet to me than any other. I touch you with my feet and with my thoughts I welcome you."

PUŁAWY & GOŁUCHÓW

ollowing the interesting minor road that runs southeast from Warsaw toward Lublin and parallel to the Vistula River, after a hundred kilometers or so the small town of Puławy appears. This enjoys an historic fame out of all proportion either to its size or to the massive and undistinguished chateau it contains. For here lived the Czartoryskis, one of the most important families in Poland and the creators at Puławy of a patriotic shrine and a wonderful landscape garden. Some seventy years after the family fled from Puławy a daughter of this same aristocratic dynasty was responsible for transforming another chateau called Gołuchów, far to the west in Wielkopolska, into a museum with the similar purpose of preserving Polish culture.

In the seventeenth century Puławy was a fishing village on the Vistula, which Zofia Opalińska, the first bride of Stanisław Herakliusz Lubomirski, brought with her as her dowry. On this site Lubomirski commissioned his favorite architect, Tylman van Gameren, to build a baroque villa in 1671, a residence of considerable charm, as the surviving drawings show. In 1702 the property passed to his daughter Elżbieta, who had married Adam Sieniawski, future grand hetman of the crown. Unfortunately the villa was burned down by the Swedish troops of King Charles XII only four years later, and it was not until 1722 that Elżbieta Sieniawska began its reconstruction, a task continued by her daughter Zofia, who inherited Puławy before her marriage to Prince August Czartoryski in 1731. For over fifty years the couple spent most of their summers at the property, and during that time transformed it into one of the principal artistic monuments of Poland.

When most of the work was complete by 1736, the villa had grown into an imposing baroque chateau whose wings surrounded a large cour d'honneur and a fountain. The two eminent architects involved were Giovanni Spazzio and, after his death, Sigismund Deybel. Yet the end product was not inspired, for the chateau, although large, was heavy and undistinguished, unrelieved by any flashes of originality. The best facade, which overlooked the river, displayed Doric pilasters above a rusticated basement and entered onto a fine rococo pillared entrance hall. Italian stuccodores were employed, and the Frenchman Juste-Aurèle Meissonier was instructed to design the interior of the polygonal Golden Salon on the second floor. The fittings of this rococo room were made in Paris during the 1730s and later shipped to Poland; tradition also claimed that François Boucher painted the ceiling. A large park with geometric alleys in the French style was also laid out, and a succession of skillful gardeners proceeded to fill it in. Several pavilions were built on the grounds. By the mid-eighteenth century Puławy had become a center of artistic activity, home to the studios of the painter Sebastian Zeisel and the Hoffman family of sculptors.

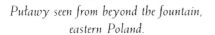

Puławy seen from beyond the fountain, eastern Poland.

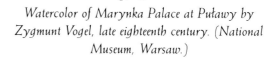

Watercolor of Marynka Palace at Puławy by Zygmunt Vogel, late eighteenth century. (National Museum, Warsaw.)

Portrait of Izabella Czartoryska by Kazimierz Wojniakowski, c. 1796. (Czartoryski Museum, Kraków.)

Portrait of Adam Kazimierz Czartoryski in the costume of the general of Podolia, by Louis Mathieu, c. 1790. (Czartoryski Museum, Kraków.)

A seminal date in Puławy's evolution was 1782, the year Prince August died and was succeeded by his son Adam Kazimierz Czartoryski. A man of nearly fifty, highly educated with wide historical, literary, and classical interests, he avoided a public career of his own, preferring instead to mediate between the Familia, as the Czartoryskis' cabal of friends and relations was known, and other groups of aristocratic politicians who wielded power in eighteenth-century Poland. Although he now disagreed politically with his cousin the king, he supported all Stanisław August's cultural iniatives. Furthermore he was blessed with a remarkable wife. Rich and intelligent, Izabella was the daughter of Jerzy Flemming, the treasurer of Lithuania. She had married Adam Kazimierz, who was her mother's cousin, aged a mere fifteen, and originally her marriage was not happy. She traveled widely, enjoying the frivolous, cosmopolitan life of the Ancien Régime, but she was always interested in the arts, and by 1785 was commissioning further work at Puławy. Her architect, Chrystian Piotr Aigner, first designed an orangery in a Doric Greek style, soon followed by the little neoclassical Marynka Palace intended for her daughter.

Izabella enthusiastically espoused the nationalist cause, as did her husband in characteristically restrained fashion, so when Kościuszko's rising had been crushed, the Czartoryskis faced the full force of Russian vengeance. Their estates were declared forfeit, although this was subsequently reversed, and her two sons were packed off to Saint Petersburg to ensure the family's good behavior. Puławy had been thoroughly pillaged by Catherine the Great's troops both inside and in the park. Izabella's emotional energetic nature reacted violently: henceforward she would dedicate her life and energies to the nationalist cause, and it was in this spirit that she began renovating Puławy in 1796. Her intention was not just to renovate, but rather to create a patriotic museum. As she wrote, "It was when Poland ceased to exist that the idea came to me to gather together all manner of Polish mementoes and bequeath them to posterity. A person who loses a mother or child holds dear those objects they have left behind, and although these mementoes evoke sorrow, their sight also brings relief."

Aigner was instructed to build a model of the Roman Temple of the Sibyl at Tivoli on a site overlooking the Vistula. Each of its two stories consisted of a circular hall; the lower level was so set back into the hillside as to be accessible only from the river front, while viewed from the chateau the upper floor resembled a single-story domed peripteral rotunda. The upper hall's stuccoed white walls formed a smooth cylindrical surface

beneath a frieze of griffins and a coffered dome, which was encircled by 18 columns with composite capitals. Over the high double doors of its portal was inscribed, *"Przeszłość-Przyszłości"* ("The Past to the Future"). The lower hall had vaulting supported by thick buttresses, and nine pillars formed a central aisle. Originally entitled the Temple of Memory, the building was soon rechristened the Temple of Sibyl and combined pagan architecture with such Christian motifs as the apse being turned east. When completed it was crammed with a variety of military trophies, souvenirs, or relics of national heroes ranging from King Bolesław the Brave to Copernicus the astronomer.

From 1800 to 1803 Aigner was also busy constructing a church modeled on the Pantheon in Rome, in which Ionic columns carried an airy gallery in the charming interior. And his patron Izabella was dreaming of another museum pavilion as a depository for curiosities she had acquired on her foreign travels. So Aigner created a building called the Gothic House, based on an existing structure and with walls of brick and stone. These were inset with over three hundred tablets and inscriptions, while the six rooms inside contained a diversity of exhibits emphasizing chivalry, heroism, and the struggle for liberty. Izabella then transformed the formal French gardens into a landscape park *à l'anglaise* spread along both sides of the Vistula. Grottoes were built above the river bank, picturesquely-sited clumps of trees were planted, and vistas were created between the chateau and pavilions. Her widely acclaimed *Treatise on Gardening* showed her deep love for and knowledge of the subject. Although her husband was relatively uninvolved with the extraordinary revival of Puławy after 1794, Adam Kazimierz did reestablish the splendid library that the Czartoryskis had assembled, and installed a printing press and a lithographic workshop on the estate.

As a middle-aged man, Adam Jerzy inherited Puławy on his father's death in 1823. He had been the chief progenitor of the Congress Kingdom, but his growing alienation from Tsar Alexander I persuaded him to withdraw substantially from politics in order to concentrate on writing and his new family, for he had married late in life. Although many years before he had bought important pictures including a Raphael, a Leonardo, and a Rembrandt for the family collection, he had never found the time to devote to patronage of the arts. Now he began a collection of scientific books for the library and settled down to running his estates, although his octogenarian mother was still extremely active.

Nemesis arrived in 1830. After the collapse of the uprising of 1830–31 during which Adam Jerzy had headed the provisional government, the vengeful Russians again attacked Puławy. The family had already closed the museum and library and hidden their exhibits. Now a full evacuation was ordered, and, supervised by the indomitable Izabella, the contents were removed for safety to neighboring churches, monasteries, and the Zamoyski residences of Klemensów and Kozłówka. Russian troops captured part of the library while the rest was brought down the Vistula in boats under heavy fire. Izabella and her daughter fled to the Czartoryski estate at Sieniawa in Austrian-occupied Galicia, taking the choicest articles from the Temple of Sibyl with them. When tsarist officials arrived to sequestrate the property, they found both chateau and museum empty. This time, however, the decree was not to be rescinded. A school called the Alexandrian Institute for the Education of Young Women was transferred to Puławy, to be succeeded by an agricultural institute. The chateau underwent some immediate rebuilding, and more in the 1840s after a fire had damaged it badly. The interior was inevitably destroyed by degrees, but the park landscape and pavilions of the grandiloquently renamed "New Alexandria" remained intact.

Although their connection with Puławy had been severed forever, this was not the end of the Czartoryskis or of their collections. The family still owned large estates in Galicia, the part of Poland annexed by Austria, and Adam Jerzy had escaped to western Europe. Condemned to death in absentia, he settled in Paris where he became head of a government in exile, "an uncrowned king," as he was reckoned, although his policies and diplomacy were condemned as useless by the radical emigrés. In 1843 he managed to buy the dilapidated Hotel Lambert, a grand seventeenth-century building by Louis Le Vau on the Île Saint-Louis, which became his headquarters. He financed journals, a Polish library, and various charitable institutions for his compatriots, and every year a ball plus a fair was held for the emigré community in the tented-over courtyard. On the facade was carved the optimistic inscription: *Le Jour viendra.*

Adam Jerzy's children, in particular his younger son Władysław and daughter Izabela, took on the mantle of his leadership in the Polish emigré community; they had also inherited their grandmother's mania for collecting. Władysław, born in 1828 and married to a distant relation of the Spanish royal house, displaced his sickly elder brother as heir to the family traditions, especially after his father died aged 91 in 1861. An art connoisseur, he assembled a fine collection of Flemish and Italian primitive paintings, objects d'art, oriental pieces, silverwork, glass, porcelain, textiles, and miniatures, as well as a range of classical objects. In 1865 a portion of these treasures were exhibited in a major French exhibition and received high praise from the critics. Nevertheless, he still dreamed of reassembling the Czartoryski collections on Polish soil. Finally in 1876 Władysław reached an agreement with the Kraków city council, which offered him several buildings, principally the former arsenal, for a museum. He accepted the offer, commissioning Maurice-Auguste Ouradou to redesign the interiors, but since his library took up most of the available space, it became necessary to buy an old monastery as well, which was similarly adapted. The result was a triumph. Many of the Puławy treasures, like the commanders' shields from the Temple of Sibyl, were reassembled, while the splendid collection of paintings, including the Raphael, Leonardo, and Rembrandt, excited universal admiration. The Emperor Francis Joseph even paid a visit, and the Austrian government, which had now conceded substantial autonomy to Galicia, where the Czartoryskis' Sieniawa estates were located, allowed them to form an entail with provision made for the maintenance of the museum and library. The Kraków collections stayed as a private foundation until 1945, when they were taken under state control, but since they were never actually nationalized, their legal status has remained equivocal.

Portrait of Adam Jerzy Czartoryski by Leon Kaplinski, 1860. (Kórnik collection.)

View of Sieniawa, southeastern Poland, the third of the Czartoryskis' houses. (Prince Adam Czartoryski.)

Temple of Sibyl at Puławy.

Watercolor of the Temple of Sibyl, by Zygmunt Vogel, late eighteenth century. (Kórnik collection.)

His sister Izabela married Jan Działyński in 1857, whose father, Tytus, had been instrumental in getting out some of the family's treasures, large numbers of which found their way from Poland to France. Tytus was himself no minor collector, and his son Jan followed in his footsteps, turning their neo-Gothic castle of Kórnik, near Poznań, into an important library and museum collection. In 1853 Tytus had bought the ruined castle of Gołuchów, also in Wielkopolska northeast of Kalisz, which four years later he presented to his son on his marriage. But the young couple scarcely lived there to begin with, and after 1863, when Jan was condemned to death for his part in the revolt against Russian rule, they were forced to flee abroad.

Gołuchów's history was already several centuries old, the earliest parts of the castle having been built around 1560 for Rafał Leszczyński. A leading Protestant, chancellor of Poland, and spokeman for the executionist movement, he had commissioned a square, three-story fortified keep with four octagonal corner towers. His son Wacław became chancellor too, and after inheriting the castle in 1592, proceeded to convert it into a splendid magnate's residence. A one-story dwelling house plus a loggia and a hexagonal tower were built south of the courtyard and connected to the main block by two short wings. But the Leszczyńskis' star waned during the seventeenth century, at the end of which they sold the property. For 150 years Gołuchów stood empty, for none of the many succeeding owners ever lived in it, and by the mid-nineteenth century it was almost totally derelict.

When the confiscation decree on Jan Działyński's estates was revoked, he gave the castle to his wife Izabela in 1872 in consideration of various debts he owed her. Originally she had not liked Gołuchów but slowly she came to love it, christening it "her paradise on earth." It was her restoration that gave Gołuchów its present-day appearance. With her French education, she had at first consulted the celebrated architect Eugène

Prince Władysław Czartoryski and his son Adam, c. 1880. (Czartoryski Museum, Kraków.)

Watercolor of Gołuchów by Jan Kopczynski, l nineteenth century. (Kórnik collection.)

Gołuchów seen from the park.

348

Viollet-le-Duc, who recommended Ouradou, his own son-in-law and pupil. The latter chose not to reconstruct the Renaissance castle; rather, he transformed it in the fashionable style of the sixteenth century, modeled on the Loire chateaux—hence the slate roofs, the narrow chimneys, and the sculptural decoration so typical of the period. Most of the courtyard's sculptures have a genuine French or Italian provenance, even though other features are straight copies, such as the staircase, which is copied from the Bargello in Florence. The restoration, lasting from 1875 to 1885, preserved some of the original parts of the castle. The north terrace of the courtyard lay above the sixteenth-century cellars, while three of the towers and the foundations of the belvedere also survived from the earlier structure.

Izabela's purpose in all this was entirely deliberate. She wanted to re-create a sixteenth-century Polish royal residence, and not merely because of the Czartoryskis' past connections with the throne. In an era of enforced Germanization, she intended to challenge Prussian authority by establishing a museum collection of international importance emphasizing her country's cultural heritage. Like her grandmother at Puławy, she required that everything about Gołuchów, both architecture and contents, must be worthy of this goal. The inscription above the main entrance encapsulated her aims: *"Vito dei cadunt, surgunt, resurgunt aedesque regnaque"* ("By God's will kingdoms and buildings rise, fall and rise again"). The Leszczyński device and the royal crown can be found throughout the house. The Polish and Museum Halls along with the Spanish and Italian Rooms, a drawing room, a dining room, and a state bedroom comprised a magnificent ensemble, which displayed Izabela's treasures in a spirit of eclectic historicism.

Jan Działyński died in 1880. Although he had been responsible for laying out the fine landscape park at Gołuchów, he lived his last years at Kórnik. His widow survived him by nineteen years, building unsightly

Chapel in the park at Gołuchów.

Interior of the library at Gołuchów.

Izabela Działyńska (née Czartoryska), late nineteenth century.

Wedding of August Czartoryski and Princess Marie Dolores of Bourbon-Orleans at Sieniawa, 1937. (Prince Adam Czartoryski.)

residential quarters elsewhere in the park to enable the castle to function purely as a museum; a nearby chapel was also erected to her memory shortly after her death. Her nephew and great-nephew, Władysław Czartoryski's younger son and grandson, successively inherited Gołuchów during the next four decades. It continued uninterrupted as a museum until September 1939, when, after the German occupation, the exhibits were seized. Many were lost, stolen, or exported, although the wonderful collection of antique vases was returned after World War II. Izabela had created an entail that guaranteed the indivisibility of the property and public access to the collections, but now the state expropriated Gołuchów and the administration was given to the Poznań National Museum.

Both Puławy and Gołuchów are of great interest to any student of Poland's political and cultural heritage. The visual charms of both are somewhat limited—one, although a fine museum, is too much of a pastiche of a Loire chateau, while the other has served institutional purposes for more than a century and therefore lacks its original charm. Yet the beauty of Puławy's park and pavilions along with the extraordinary diversity of Gołuchów's exhibits combine to provide an imperishable memorial to one of Poland's greatest families.

Ł A Z I E N K I

South of the city center of Warsaw lies a large and beautiful park called Łazienki, a Polish equivalent of Hyde Park, Central Park, and the Bois de Boulogne. Although it was originally built as a country retreat, Warsaw has grown to the point that today the park is very much in the urban area. Little is visible from the roads that run along its perimeter aside from the imposing Belvedere Palace, now the residence of the country's president. Hidden within thick clumps of trees, however, stand a number of delightful pavilions and monuments, the chief of which, now known as the Palace-on-the-Water, must rank among the architectural jewels of Europe.

The history of Łazienki began simply enough during the Middle Ages when the dukes of Mazovia, rulers of one of the petty principalities into which Poland was then divided, built a castle they called Ujazdów on the escarpment of the Vistula River some two miles south of Warsaw. During the thirteenth century it was twice burned down—once during a Lithuanian invasion and once in the course of a civil war. By the sixteenth century a wooden house belonging to Queen Bona's daughter Anna Jagiellonka had been constructed down near the river and close to the site of the medieval castle. Here in 1578 the wedding of Chancellor Jan Zamoyski to Krystyna Radziwiłł took place, at which the first Polish drama, *Odprawa Posłów Greckich* (*The Dismissal of the Greek Envoys*) was performed. In 1624 the Vasa king Zygmunt III built a quadrangular, two-storied brick castle with corner towers and an arcaded loggia where the old fortress had stood. The architect, Matteo Castelli, followed the plans of Giovanni Trevano.

After the wooden house was decimated and the castle partially destroyed during "the Swedish Deluge," as the Swedish invasion of Poland in the mid-seventeenth century was known, the Ujazdów estate was bought in 1674 by Stanisław Herakliusz Lubomirski, grand marshal of the crown, patron of the arts, writer, and philosopher. Some time before 1690 he commissioned his protégé, the Dutch architect Tylman van Gameren, to build two pavilions for him on the wooded marshy land where a menagerie had previously been located. In one of them, called the Hermitage—a small, square, one-story building with a mansard roof—Lubomirski was wont to retire from the travails of public life. The other structure, the Bathhouse (or Łaźnia in Polish), stood on a rectangular islet surrounded on three sides by canals and on the fourth by a symmetrical pond. This luxurious and spacious pavilion was built on a square plan with a pedimented and pilastered north elevation rising through two stories. Externally its severe lines were relieved by three cupolas, the larger central one forming a dome over an internal rotunda, which was illuminated through a lantern. Inside, the Bathhouse was richly decorated in what was described at the time as "the grotesque taste." The building's rotunda had a fountain in the middle and walls studded with shells and pebbles to create the illusion of a grotto. Off this chamber led a bathing apartment with a cascade, twin tin tubs, and a good number of rest chambers.

After Lubomirski's death King Augustus II the Strong leased the Ujazdów

General view of the Palace-on-the-Water at Łazienki, near Warsaw.

Old view of the Palace-on-the-Water, by Zygmunt Vogel, late eighteenth century. (National Museum, Warsaw.)

Portrait of King Stanisław II August, by Marcello Bacciarelli, late eighteenth century.

estate from the grand marshal's heirs in 1720 and built a large canal along what had been the axis of Castelli's castle. He envisaged a grandiose reconstruction of the building and had plans drawn up by Matthias Daniel Pöppelmann, architect of the Zwinger palace in Dresden. But the plans were never realized, and for the next forty years little was done to the property. In 1764, however, Ujazdów was bought by Stanisław August Poniatowski, who would be elected that same year as Poland's last king. The great age of the estate was about to begin.

Work began almost immediately. The king had an entrance avenue laid out some three miles in length, leading from the city to Ujazdów. Within the park a star-shaped grid was developed of straight alleys lined with linden trees, a concept derived from French models. Under Lubomirski the largely-ruined Ujazdów castle had undergone a limited restoration by Tylman van Gameren, who had created some baroque interiors, but from 1766 King Stanisław August began adding another story and refurbishing the interiors. His chief court architect, Domenico Merlini, provided the designs, while the artists Bernardo Bellotto and Franciszek Smuglewicz provided most of the interior painted decoration. A new facade was also erected as well as large side pavilions. Yet the king found the resulting architectural hotchpotch inharmonious. Additionally it was too small for the court, and by 1775 he had ceased to live there. Nine years later it was converted into a monumental classicist army barracks by Stanisław Zawadzki and remained in this service the rest of its life, even serving as a military hospital in this century before being burned out during World War II. The reconstructed castle is a twentieth-century copy of its seventeenth-century forebear.

After abandoning the castle, in the summer of 1775 the king moved into the partially-remodeled Łaźnia or Bathhouse, which was soon to become known as the Palace-on-the-Water in reference to its location on a small islet. Finding once more a lack of space, the king made a dining room out of his ground-floor bedroom and there held his Thursday dinners, gatherings noted for their conversational brilliance and attended by writers and scholars. His move to the second floor meant that further rooms had to be added there. On either side of the building small Chinese galleried bridges covered with green and gilt roofs were constructed to link the islet on which the little palace was situated to the mainland.

The end product was still unsatisfactory, however, so in 1784 a third rebuilding by Merlini replaced the south facade with a recessed portico framed by four composite columns. Four years later the other three fronts acquired classical facades too, the northern one being given thirteen bays of the same colossal order and a pedimented portico. Further work in 1792 produced two lateral pavilions on the mainland linked to the main block of the building by stone bridges with colonnaded galleries. At last the various parts of the structure were harmonized, the pilastered elevations crowned by a flat sculpture-lined attic. The belvedere rising from the middle section gave an elegant flourish to the whole ensemble and signaled the erstwhile bath pavilion's transformation into a miniature palace. Along the roofs, statuary by André Le Brun was installed representing the four elements, the four continents then known, and the four seasons, while the north portico's pediment was filled with the seated figures of Fame and Peace. The inscription on a baroque cartouche above the entrance read: *"Haec domus odit tristitias, amit pacem, fundat balnea, commendat rura et optat probos"* ("This house hates sadness, loves peace, offers baths, recommends rural life and welcomes the virtuous").

Inside, three rooms retained their baroque features: the vestibule, the tile-paneled Bacchus room, and the bathing apartment, where only the tin tubs and the cascade were removed. By contrast the purely neoclassical ballroom, designed by Jan Chrystian Kamsetzer on a simple rectangular plan, was decorated with painted panels of warm red-and-brown—toned

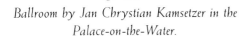

Ballroom by Jan Chrystian Kamsetzer in the Palace-on-the-Water.

grotesques by Jerzy Bogumił Plersch. The closely hung picture gallery and Merlini's Solomon Hall were added in the rebuilding of 1788. Although the latter is more exuberant, featuring Marcello Bacciarelli's huge paintings of biblical and allegorical subjects, it displays fine architectural proportions as well. The rotunda, which became the only chamber to survive the destruction of World War II virtually unscathed, was the object of Stanisław August's last alteration to the palace. This room he redecorated as a sort of national pantheon, with monumental statues of Poland's four greatest kings in niches, and busts of Roman emperors set above the doors. Interestingly, all of the rooms in the Palace-on-the-Water were of different heights; the dining room, for instance, was around ten feet high, while the gallery was perhaps two-and-a-half feet taller and the rotunda maybe five feet taller than that.

The residential rooms on the second floor had originally been constructed on a more intimate scale, and they remained that way. With the picture gallery and the portrait study on the ground level, they alone contained paintings on canvas. The fine royal collection contained many Dutch works including six Rembrandts, and such contemporary French masters as Pierre Fragonard and Hubert Robert. Many more were assembled for the king in London, but since after his abdication he was in no position to pay for them they remained in England and became the nucleus of the Dulwich Picture Gallery in London. Elsewhere in the palace, murals and stucco work carried symbolic representations of the virtues or of human fate and greatness, providing a decorative backdrop to the opulence of the marble, bronze, and gilding. At the beginning the furniture, clocks, and porcelain all came from Paris, but gradually Stanisław August commissioned pieces by Polish craftsmen.

Unable to accommodate his guests, the king at first had an inn built near the park entrance, followed in 1775 by a pyramidal guardhouse, which was demolished early in the following century. That same year a

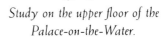

Study on the upper floor of the Palace-on-the-Water.

Detail of wall frescoes in the White House.

Bedroom in the White House furnished with King Stanisław August's bed; the paintings on the walls are by Jerzy Bogumił Plersch and Jan Scisko, late eighteenth century.

square villa called the White House was completed, built to Merlini's plans. The king may originally have intended it for himself, but he soon gave it to his mistress, Elżbieta Grabowska; his sisters later lived there too. Entirely regular externally with four identical elevations, an attic, and a small belvedere on the roof, the structure was designed in early neoclassical style, although the first-floor segmental window arches harked back to the rococo. In contrast to the building's regular exterior, all the rooms were of a different shape. Plersch, the principal decorator, covered the dining room with his grotesque compositions, while the drawing room contains big mural views of China, which, with the adjacent bedroom, are the sole remaining remnants of Chinoiserie taste so much in evidence at Łazienki in the days of Stanisław August. Arranged around a central staircase, all the rooms have survived virtually intact from the period.

In 1777 Stanisław August remodeled Lubomirski's Hermitage, which had been struck by lightning, and gave it as a residence to his confidante, the fortune-teller Madame Lhullier. From 1775–78 he also had Merlini occupied with constructing a new palace called the Myślewice. Initially planned as a square like the White House, it had two semicircular wings added even before completion to give it a horseshoe shape. Although it was intended to house the royal court, the king soon handed it over to his nephew Józef Poniatowski, future marshal and hero of the Napoleonic Wars, whose initials appear above the front door. A reservoir was also built, a cylindrical structure modeled on the tomb of Cecilia Metella near Rome, with no exterior openings but miniature rooms looking onto a tiny courtyard.

The king's work on Łazienki, as the entire complex was now called, continued through the 1770s and into the 1780s. Finished in 1780 and designed in the Chinese style, the Trou-Madame pavilion was named for a game akin to billiards, which consisted of throwing metal balls into numbered goals. Within two years it was transformed into a small theatre. By 1788, however, a far larger one seating two hundred spectators was available in the east wing of Merlini's Orangery, with nine boxes at second-floor level separated by female figures holding candelabra that stand between pairs of pilasters. A circular ceiling mural was created for the theatre by Plersch. Stanisław August's mania for theatricals led him to have a stage erected on the islet in the pond near the Palace-on-the-Water. On the bank opposite, an earth amphitheatre with a canvas roof was raised, but the king dreamed of a stone or brick structure where he could entertain large numbers of guests. This was designed by Kamsetzer in 1790, modeled on the theatre at Herculaneum, with a stage door derived from the Roman temples at Baalbek. Sixteen famous playwrights' statues by Le Brun decorated the amphitheatre's upper parapet. One thousand people could be accommodated to watch the ballets and pantomimes, and afterward guests were frequently entertained in a new little pavilion by Kamsetzer called the Turkish House, which was dismantled in the nineteenth century.

Around the grounds the pace of activity was no less frenetic. Both main ponds were given artificially informal shore lines and more waterfalls, while many different species of trees were planted. Bridges and statues were also added to the park, including in 1788 an equestrian statue of King Jan Sobieski by Franciszek Pinck.

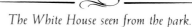

The White House seen from the park.

Copy of the tomb of Cecilia Metella in the park.

Jakub Kubicki's Egyptian Temple.

Stanisław August spent much of his time at Łazienki and seemed to be happiest there. He hosted an open-air festival with games in the park attended by around thirty thousand people; rowing on the canals also became one of his favorite occupations, and he had decorative steps constructed leading down to the water. Not all his plans were realized: the small mausoleum for his parents, in which he too wished to be buried, was never completed, nor was Kamsetzer's reconstruction of the baroque Belvedere Palace, or the vast church dedicated to Divine Providence, envisaged by Jakub Kubicki as a memorial to the constitution of 1791.

Retiring increasingly from the appalling problems confronting Poland, Stanisław August concentrated his energies on his private dream world at Łazienki. The court gathered there en masse in the summer, and the public was always admitted to the unfenced park if not the buildings. When forced to abdicate in 1795 he continued to send a flow of instructions concerning future improvements from his Russian exile until his death in 1798. The estate then passed to his heir and nephew, Józef Poniatowski. Four years after he perished at the Battle of Leipzig in 1813, Łazienki became the personal property of the Russian tsar. At his behest, Kubicki rebuilt the Belvedere Palace in a modest neoclassical style for the tsar's son Grand Duke Constantine in 1818; shortly afterward follies in the form of Diana and Egyptian temples were constructed, as well as a no-longer-extant neo-Gothic orangery, while the old Trou-Madame pavilion was transformed into a guardhouse. The grounds along the Vistula embankment were transformed into the estate's botanical gardens, and a large astronomical observatory developed by several architects replaced the king's extensive hothouses.

In 1846 an Orthodox church with a low dome in classical style was added to the west pavilion of the Palace-on-the-Water, although it was demolished a century later. Two new orangeries were also built to house the huge Radziwiłł collection of orange trees, brought from Nieborów.

The amphitheatre seen from across the lake.

Old view of the Palace-on-the-Water at night,
by Zygmunt Vogel, late eighteenth century.
(National Museum, Warsaw.)

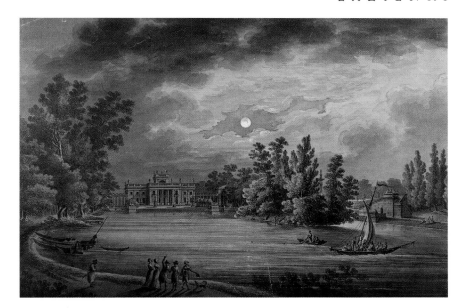

Although the palaces remained private, the park was maintained at a high standard as the city's principal public garden. As the trees matured, it was even expanded southward. Slight damage was caused in World War I, during which the contents of Łazienki were removed to Russia—although after independence they were returned safely. The new Polish government then removed the alterations done in tsarist times, and joined Łazienki's park with that of the Belvedere Palace (originally both parks had been one, but they had been divided in the nineteenth century). To symbolize its national importance, a monument to Fryderyk Chopin was erected there in 1926.

World War II brought far worse developments. Łazienki escaped the destruction that befell much of Warsaw in 1939, and the bulk of its contents were moved to the National Museum there for safekeeping. Under the German occupation, however, it was entirely closed to the public, and following the Warsaw Uprising in 1944, the rooms of the Palace-on-the-Water were burned when the Nazis poured petrol into them. Luckily German troops lacked the time to blow up the building too, as they had planned. Postwar reconstruction took twelve years, but at the end of that time the interiors of the Palace-on-the-Water, the White House, and the Old Orangery theatre had been painstakingly restored to their former glory, fitted with elegant furnishings both old and new and reopened to the public.

Today Łazienki, "Warsaw's Drawing Room" as it is sometimes nicknamed, stands again, a recreated model of eighteenth-century taste and a tribute to the vision and patronage of one man. With its lovely park, its rich variety of buildings, and the glorious Palace-on-the-Water, it would be hard to find a more delightful ensemble anywhere in the world. "A happy combination of Roman and French good taste," was how a visitor, the Abbé Renard, described the Old Orangery theatre in 1788, a remark that could be applied to the whole ensemble, with the coda, "and of Polish inspiration."

KOZŁÓWKA

T he landscape of eastern Poland stretches, flat and unvarying, toward the frontier with the Soviet Union and its endless plains. Yet there are compensations—numerous beautiful monuments stand in the old city of Lublin and several fine chateaux and country houses can be found in the area. Of these, none is more charming or interesting than Kozłówka, situated some twenty miles or so north of Lublin near the little town of Lubartów.

The origins of the small settlement at Kozłówka are obscure, but soon after 1700 the property was recorded to have been owned by Jadwiga Niemyska, who also possessed several other estates. In 1728 she left everything to her niece Tekla Pepłowska, who brought a substantial dowry with her seven years later when she married Michał Bieliński, starosta or sheriff of Sztum. That same year Michał had ended a colorful marriage to Maria Rutowska, daughter of Augustus the Strong by his Turkish mistress, Fatima, thus enabling himself to take Tekla as his new bride some months later. The Bielińskis were a family who had risen high in the favor of the Saxon kings, one sister, Marianna, being one of Augustus the Strong's countless mistresses. Michał's elder brother, Franciszek, was marshal of the crown, an enlightened patron of the arts, and proprietor of the magnificent chateau of Otwock Stary. On Franciszek's death without issue in 1757, Michał's son, another Franciszek, succeeded to all the family estates.

By 1742 the Bielińskis had decided to build themselves a residence at Kozłówka. In fact by the mid-eighteenth century many aristocrats were busy constructing or improving houses in the vicinity: the Czartoryskis at Puławy, the Lubomirskis at Opole, the Potockis at Radzyń Podlaski, and the Sanguszkos at Lubartów. Kozłówka was originally intended as a *maison de plaisance* in the French sense, used for short stays by its owners—in contrast to the typical Polish country house, which was meant to be the center of a working estate. Architecturally, however, the country seat built by the Bielińskis was typical of the period, consisting of a single two-story block covered by a mansard roof and situated on an axis between the courtyard and the garden. The reception rooms and the private apartments of the owners were placed on the second floor, the ground level being occupied by administrative and domestic offices along with their two sons' rooms. At Kozłówka the ground floor was divided by a corridor which ran across the entire breadth of the house behind the large entrance hall; rooms opened off either side, not in a long enfilade as in grander buildings. In one corner upstairs a small chapel led off Tekla's bedroom.

In the front the large lawn was framed by stables and the kitchen block on one side with the coach house on the other, although the effect was slightly marred by the lack of anything to balance off the kitchen. On the other side an avenue ran straight from the house toward a fairly small park, laid out traditionally with a parterre in the Renaissance style adjoining the chateau and a flower and vegetable garden along its southern edge. There were no terraces, fountains, or statuary, for the grounds of

View of the fountain and the garden facade of Kozłówka, eastern Poland near Lublin.

the house were designed on the same modest scale as the interior.

Precise information about the architect employed by the Bielińskis is unfortunately lacking, but it can most probably be ascribed to Jakub Fontana. Originally Italian, his family had been settled in Poland since the mid-seventeenth century and his father, Józef, had worked mainly in and around Warsaw up to his death in 1741. At that point Jakub, aged about thirty and trained in Italy and Paris, took over his practice. The elder Fontana had already worked for the Bielińskis at Otwock Stary, and Kozłówka certainly has stylistic similarities to other buildings designed by the Fontanas. The family's less well known cousin Paweł Antoni Fontana may also have been involved, however; he had already been commissioned by the Sanguszkos for a new parish church at nearby Lubartów and continued to work in the Lublin region.

Born in 1740, the young Franciszek Bieliński inherited his uncle's and father's properties, married Krystyna Sanguszko, his neighbor, and led an active public life during Stanisław August's reign. As a politician with a close interest in education, he was appointed by the king to his commission for national education. Franciszek advocated universal schooling as well as the foundation of special craft schools where Polish rather than Latin would be the language of instruction. A fervent patriot, he joined Tadeusz Kościuszko's uprising and offered the whole of the produce from his estates to alleviate the people's suffering. By contrast his younger brother Stanisław was a rake and a drunkard with an evil reputation, a man willing to preside over the puppet Seym convened by Catherine the Great in 1793 to ratify the partitions of Poland. Thus family relations were inevitably strained. In 1799 Franciszek, despairing of both his family's and his country's future, sold Kozłówka and all its contents to Aleksander Zamoyski for 1.6 million zlotys.

Zamoyski was the head of the noble dynasty that had risen to prominence in the late sixteenth century with Jan, the builder of Zamość. The

Kozłówka seen through the entrance gates.

Stanisław Kostka Zamoyski with his wife, Zofia (née Czartoryska), and their family, by Józef Grassi, 1810.

View of the Red Salon, decorated with family portraits.

youthful son of Chancellor Andrzej Zamoyski, who had endeavoured to introduce many liberal reforms under Stanisław August, Aleksander had seemed destined for a distinguished career himself, but unfortunately he died suddenly in 1800. Since he was childless, Kozłówka was inherited by his sister Anna Sapieha, although his widow, Anna Maria, retained a life interest in the house. This she kept through two later marriages and a move to Vienna, where she died in 1846, bequeathing the contents of the chateau to her ward, Maria Soltan. Meanwhile ten years earlier Anna Sapieha had sold the property to her cousin Jan Zamoyski. This awkward situation resulted in an impasse and the house stood empty and unfurnished.

Jan, the new owner, was the son of Stanisław Kostka Zamoyski, who had succeeded his brother as head of the family and had managed to produce seven sons with his wife Zofia, daughter of the formidable chatelaine of Puławy, Izabella Czartoryska. Not surprisingly with such ancestry, two of Jan's six brothers became outstanding patriots: Andrzej, a noted agronomist and moderate politician, and Władysław, who went into exile in Paris in the wake of the rising of 1830, became the indispensable lieutenant of his uncle Adam Jerzy Czartoryski, and never ceased to work for Polish independence. Jan, however, was a very different character. Well-educated at Geneva and Berlin, where he had been a pupil of Friedrich

Hegel, he was possessed of a kind heart and a lively imagination. But he was by no means a practical man and found life a constant disillusionment. He did become an attaché at the Russian embassies in Naples and then in London, but resigned after the Polish revolt had been crushed in 1831. Fundamentally apolitical, Jan retired into private life and in 1843 married Anna Mycielska, a union blessed with two sons and a daughter. He only visited Kozłówka occasionally, bringing a few pieces of furniture and pictures from Puławy to enliven the empty house and adding others that his wife had inherited. Finally in the 1850s he closed the chateau and moved altogether to France, settling at Auteuil. During the rising of 1863 partisans sought refuge in Kozłówka, but luckily no damage was done.

A dramatic change in Kozłówka's fortunes occurred in 1870. According to land registry records, in September of that year Jan made over the estate to his son Konstanty. The latter had been born in Warsaw in 1846, but his formative years had been spent in France. His mother had died of tuberculosis when he was only thirteen, so his father had strictly supervised his education. In the late 1860s Konstanty had returned to Poland and trained in estate management, and in 1870 he had married Aniela Potocka shortly before settling into his new home. At last the chateau had a resident proprietor again, one who would live there until his death fifty-three years later.

There was indeed much to be done. No improvements and limited maintenance had taken place during the whole of the nineteenth century, so the buildings were in a dilapidated condition. The architect whom Konstanty consulted for all the changes he envisaged is unknown but was probably Leandro Marconi, one of the two sons of Enrico, the well-known exponent of late neoclassicism. It had definitely been Leandro whom he commissioned to build a city residence in Warsaw in 1878. The remodeling of Kozłówka began shortly after that, lasting throughout the 1880s and 1890s and intermittently up to 1914. The style was essentially French baroque with various Polish touches. All the elevations were re-faced and two cupola-crowned towers were added at either end of the façade. The side elevations also acquired pillared arcades, above which terraces were created on the second-floor level with balustrades adorned by groups of sculpted putti.

Mantel in the Red Salon with Boulle clock and four Meissen figures.

Portraits of the four young sons of Stanisław Kostka Zamoyski by Firmina Massot, 1819.

A monumental portico rising the entire height of the building was added to the front elevation, giving it a much heavier appearance. At ground level the portico was made into a vaulted covered porch behind an open arcade, approached from the drive by a raised ramp for carriages. The massive pediment bore a shield with the Zamoyski coat of arms, a device of three spears known as a *jelita*. (The legend ran that Florian the Grey, a Zamoyski ancestor, had received three spear wounds in the abdomen from the Teutonic Knights at the Battle of Płowce. Asked by the king if he was in great pain, he replied theatrically, "It hurts less than the wounds inflicted on the Fatherland.") A new entrance sealed the drive in the form of a wrought-iron gate surmounted by the family crest, which hung between two gate piers topped by stone urns. A row of domestic offices now flanked the drive on either side for most of its length.

Less evident were the changes made inside the chateau. The rear of the ground-floor hall was partitioned into three sections, the outer two of which were transformed into two more bathrooms. The walls of the grand staircase, which led off the middle space, were lined in white marble while a splendid wrought-iron stair-rail was brought from Warsaw. The second floor reception rooms were all redecorated in a neobaroque or neorococo taste that could more properly be described as eclectic, with rich stucco ornamentation, marble fireplaces in a variety of colors, and mahogany doors with gilt details. Fine parquet floors of light and dark oak made by local workmen were also installed. Despite the sumptuous decor,

Portrait of Anna Zamoyska (née Mycielska) by Claude-Marie Dubufy, mid-nineteenth century.

Portrait of Jan Zamoyski by Claude-Marie Dubufy, mid-nineteenth century.

however, the rooms seemed rather uniform as well as ostentatious in a fin-de-siècle way.

As a typical product of his class and era, Konstanty was keen to stress the cultural role of the aristocracy, so the collections he established at Kozłówka were intended to inculcate a sense of history and of patriotism in visitors. Eventually the number of pictures grew to almost one thousand altogether, many of them copies, family portraits, or canvases depicting scenes from Polish history, although there were a few Old Masters and a quantity of splendidly-carved frames. With a house so denuded of contents, the Zamoyskis brought in furniture from everywhere, often French but in the main nineteenth-century reproductions. A large library with some ten thousand volumes in English-style bookcases was created and elsewhere a big display of Chinese porcelain was installed. In 1904 Konstanty began to construct a chapel based on the upper half of the chapel at Versailles, with French altar ornaments and fine plasterwork; the tomb of his grandmother Zofia was also copied from one in the Church of Santa Croce at Florence, yet the effect is curiously cold. During the early years of the century the tsar consented to form an entail out of the Kozłówka estate, then extending to nearly fifty thousand acres, thus safeguarding it against being broken up in the future. The property suffered no significant damage in World War I, although a few shells did land on the roof. Konstanty died in 1923, by then a lonely widower, although his intellect and sense of humor had remained unimpaired and he had kept up a multitude of good works until the end. His first cousin, Adam Zamoyski, then succeeded him. Adam had led a busy public life both before and after Polish independence, having earlier lived in Saint Petersburg and having

Statuary group of putti on the roof.

View of the Billiard Room.

Members of the Zamoyski and Branicki families on the terrace at Kozłówka, c. 1910.

been appointed aide-de-camp to Tsar Nicholas II in 1916. In the revolution of 1917 he had been with the imperial family at Tsarskoë Seloe and had strongly advised them to flee to Finland. Despite his Russian connections he was nevertheless a good patriot, holding a string of civic offices in the 1920s and erecting in Kozłówka's park a memorial to the Polish dead from the campaign of 1812. Otherwise he made no changes to the appearance of the chateau.

Adam died in 1940 and his son Aleksander succeeded. But as a cavalry officer he was immediately arrested by the Germans and imprisoned in a concentration camp. His wife, Jadwiga, remained at Kozłówka, which became a sanctuary for their relatives and other refugees including the future Cardinal Stefan Wyszyński; arms for the resistance were also hidden in the chateau's cellars. Jadwiga moved to Warsaw in 1944, unfortunately taking many of the best contents with her, some of which were stored in the National Museum's depots. Everything was completely destroyed when the residents of the capital rose against the German occupation that summer. Kozłówka itself remained undamaged, and the new Communist regime took over the property and the surviving collection in November 1944. The Zamoyskis emigrated to Canada after their home was declared to be a museum, but its contents and fabric continued to decay for over twenty years. Finally a major restoration was belatedly undertaken, after which the chateau, once more in proper condition, reopened to the public in 1976.

Kozłówka is not the most famous of Poland's great houses, nor can it claim the interesting historical associations of many of its peers. Moreover its position far to the east, albeit just off the main road north from Lublin, makes it less easily accessible. Yet it stands as a splendid monument to Konstanty Zamoyski, a great collector of wide-ranging tastes and a member of one of Poland's most distinguished families. Kozłówka is likely to delight those who appreciate fine things, opulent decor, and the opportunity to see an aristocrat's chateau much as it must have looked in its glory days before World War I.

SELECTED BIBLIOGRAPHY

CZECH REPUBLIC AND SLOVAKIA

Baumstark, Reinhold. *Liechtenstein, the Princely Collections* (Exhibition catalog.) New York, 1985.

──────. *Joseph Wenzel von Liechtenstein* (Exhibition catalog.) Vaduz, Liechtenstein, 1990.

Bradley, J.F.N. *Czechoslovakia: A Short History.* Edinburgh, 1971.

Clary-Aldringen, Prince Alfons. *A European Past.* London, 1978.

Herzogenberg, Baroness Johanna. *Prag.* Munich, 1966.

Hootz, R., and E. Poche. *Kunstdenkmäler in der Tschechoslowakei.* Leipzig, 1986.

Jelínek, J., and Jaroslav Wagner. *Czech Castles and Châteaux.* Prague, 1971.

Knox, Brian. *The Architecture of Bohemia and Moravia.* London, 1962.

Kusák, Dalibor. *Lednice and Valtice.* Prague, 1986.

Leisching, Julius. *Kunstgeschichte Mährens.* Vienna, 1932.

Mann, Golo. *Wallenstein.* Frankfurt, 1971.

Metternich, Princess Tatiana. *Tatiana.* London, 1976.

Nicolson, Nigel. *Great Houses of the Western World.* London, 1968.

Palacký, František. *Geschichte der Familie Šternberg.* Prague, 1828.

Palmer, Alan. *Metternich.* London, 1972.

Polisenský, J. *Gesellschaft und Kultur des barocken Böhmens.* Vienna, 1956.

Rokyta, Hugo. *Die Böhmischen Länder.* Salzburg, 1970.

Schacherl, Lilian. *Böhmen.* Munich, 1966.

──────. *Mähren.* Munich, 1968.

Schwarzenberg, Prince Karl. *Geschichte des Hauses Schwarzenberg.* Neustadt, Germany, 1963.

Seton-Watson, R.J.W. *A History of the Czechs and Slovaks.* London, 1943.

Silva-Tarrouca, Count Egbert. *Denkwürdigkeiten des Hauses Šternberg.* Vienna, 1953.

Stekl, Hannes. *Osterreichs Aristokratie im Vormärz.* Vienna, 1973.

Šternberg, Countess Cecilia. *The Journey.* London, 1977.

Tapié, V. L. *L'Europe de Marie-Thérèse du Baroque aux Lumières.* Paris, 1973.

Wirth, Z., and J. Benda. *Czech Castles and Mansions.* Prague, 1955.

HUNGARY

Bright, Richard. *Travels from Vienna Through Lower Hungary.* Edinburgh, 1818.

Browning, H. Ellen. *A Girl's Wanderings in Hungary.* London, 1896.

Evans, R.J.W. *The Making of the Habsburg Monarchy, 1550–1700.* London, 1979.

Feuer-Toth, Roza. *Renaissance Architecture in Hungary.* Budapest, 1977.

Gerö, László. *Hungarian Architecture.* Budapest, 1954.

Károlyi, Count Mihály. *Faith Without Illusion.* London, 1956.

Király, Béla K. *Hungary in the Late Eighteenth Century.* New York, 1969.

Kornis, Gyula. *Hungary and European Civilization.* Washington, D.C., 1947.

Libal, Wolfgang. *Ungarn.* Munich, 1985.

Macartney, C. A. *A Short History of Hungary.* Edinburgh, 1962.

Marczali, Henrik. *Hungary in the Eighteenth Century.* Cambridge, England, 1910.

Paget, John. *Hungary and Transylvania.* London, 1839.

Pantz, Baron Hubert von. *No Risk, No Fun.* New York, 1975.

Siegert, Hans, and F. Peer. *Das Bleibt vom alten Osterreich.* Vienna, 1978.

Spencer, E. *Travels in European Turkey.* London, 1850.

Stadtländer, Christina. *Joseph Haydn of Eisenstadt.* London, 1968.

Tábor, Gerevich. *Hungarian Castles.* Budapest, 1939.

Tissot, Victor. *La Hongrie Inconnue.* Paris, 1880.

Wenckheim, Baron Béla. *Hunting in Hungary.* Budapest, 1857.

Windischgrätz, Prince Lajos. *My Adventures and Misadventures.* Vienna, 1965.

Zador, Anna. *Revival Architecture in Hungary.* Budapest, 1977.

POLAND

Branicka Wolska, Anna. *Unposted Letters.* Warsaw, 1990.

Coxe, William. *Travels in Poland.* London, 1792.

De Ligne, Prince Antoine. *Memoirs.* London, 1899.

Evans, R.J.W. *The Making of the Habsburg Monarchy, 1550–1700.* London, 1979.

Fabre, J. *Stanislas Auguste Poniatowski et L'Europe des Lumieres.* Paris, 1952.

Fijałkowski, Wojciech. *The Residence-Museum at \Wilanów.* Warsaw, 1986.

Gieysztor, A., and A. Rottermund. *The Royal Castle in Warsaw.* Warsaw, 1982.

Jabłoński, K., and W. Piwkowski. *Nieborów and Arkadia.* Warsaw, 1988.

Knox, Brian. *The Architecture of Poland.* London, 1971.

Konarski, G. *La Noblesse Polonaise.* Paris, 1958.

Kozakiewicz, H. and S. *The Renaissance in Poland.* Warsaw, 1976.

Lednicki, Wacław. *The Life and Culture of Poland.* New York, 1944.

Majewska-Maszkowska, B. *The Château of Łańcut.* Warsaw, 1964.

Morton, V. B. *Sobieski, King of Poland.* Glasgow, 1944.

Ostrowska-Kebłowska, Zofia. *Palace Architecture in Greater Poland in the Later Eighteenth Century.* Poznań, Poland, 1969.

Perey, Lucien. *Histoire d'une grande dame.* Paris, 1888.

Potocki, Count Alfred. *Master of Łańcut.* London, 1959.

Radziwiłł, Prince Michael. *One of the Radziwiłłs.* London, 1971.

Reddaway, W. J. *The Cambridge History of Poland.* 2 vols. Cambridge, England, 1951.

Siegert, Hans, and F. Peer. *Das Bleibt vom alten Osterreich.* Vienna, 1978.

Sitwell, Sacheverell. *Great Houses of Europe.* London, 1961.

Sołtyński, Roman. *Glimpses of Polish Architecture.* Warsaw, 1958.

Syrop, Konrad. *Poland: Between the Hammer and the Anvil.* London, 1968.

Zamoyski, Count Adam. *The Polish Way.* London, 1987.

Żygulski, Zdzisław. *The Czartoryski Collection.* Warsaw, 1978.

PRONUNCIATION GUIDE

CZECH REPUBLIC AND SLOVAKIA

Betliar   (BET-LEE-are)
Buchlov   (BOOKH-loff)
Buchlovice   (BOOKH-LOW-VITZ-eh)
Český Krumlov   (CHESS-kee KROOM-loff)
Český Šternberk   (CHESS-kee SHTERN-berk)
Dobříš   (DOB-rzeesh)
Frýdlant   (FREED-lahnt)
Hluboká   (HLOO-BOH-kah)
Krásná Hŏrká   (KRAS-nah HOR-kah)
Lednice   (LED-NEETS-eh)
Opočno   (OH-POCH-noh)
Valtice   (VAL-TEETS-eh)
Veltrusy   (VEL-TRU-seh)

HUNGARY

Eszterháza   (ES-ter-haas-uh)
Fót   (FOTE)
Keszthely   (KEST-hey)
Noszvaj   (NOS-voy)
Pécel   (PAY-tzl)
Sárospatak   (SHAA-rosh-po-tok)
Sárvár   (SHAAR-vaar)
Seregélyes   (SHER-e-gay-esh)

POLAND

Arkadia   (Ar-KAH-dyah)
Baranów   (Bah-RAH-nooff)
Gołuchów   (Go-WOO-hooff)
Kozłówka   (Kuzz-WOOFF-kah)
Łańcut   (WAHN-tsoot)
Łazienki   (Wah-JYEN-kee)
Nieborów   (Neh-BOH-rooff)
Pieskowa Skała   (PYESS-koh-vah SCOW-ah)
Puławy   (Poo-WAH-vih)
Wilanow   (Vee-LAH-nooff)

Detail of the tower at Pieskowa Skała, Poland.

I N D E X

INDEX

*In fond memory of Josef and Gina Liechtenstein, who inspired me
to write this book, and Ian Moncreiffe, whose esoteric historical
scholarship I have sorely missed.*

Editor: Constance Herndon
Designer: Molly Shields
Production editor: Philip Reynolds
Production supervisor: Hope Koturo
Map illustrator: Sophie Kitttredge

A previous edition was cataloged as follows:
Library of Congress Catloging-in-Publication Data

Pratt, Michael, Lord
The great country houses of Central Europe : Czechoslovakia, Hungary,
Poland / by Michael Pratt ; photography by Gerhard Trumler.
p. cm.
Includes bibliographical references (p.   ) and index.
ISBN 0-7892-0848-2
1. Castles—Central Europe. 2.Manors—Central Europe.
3. Central Europe—History, Local. I. Trumler, Gerhard, 1937-
II Title.
DAW1012.P741991   91-14414
943-dc20   CIP

Second edition

10 9 8 7 6 5 4 3 2 1

Front cover: The garden façade of of Esterháza, Hungary.
Back cover: The sculpture gallery at Łańcut, Poland.
Back flap: The amphiteatre at Łazienski, Poland.
Frontispiece: The former library at Pécel, Hungary.
Page 6: Distant view of Frýdlant, Czech Republic.
Page 7: Detail of tower at Frýdlant

*Note: Unless otherwise indicated in the caption, all objects and pictures illustrated are
from the collections of the houses featured in the chapter.*

For bulk, and premium sales and for text adoption procedures, write to
Customer Service Manager, Abbeville Press, 137 Varick Street, New York,
NY 10013 or call 1-800 ARTBOOK